D1414862

STUDIES IN COMPARATIVE ECONOMICS 8

Studies in Comparative Economics

1. E. H. Phelps Brown, THE ECONOMICS OF LABOR
2. Charles P. Kindleberger, FOREIGN TRADE AND THE NATIONAL ECONOMY
3. Theodore W. Schultz, TRANSFORMING TRADITIONAL AGRICULTURE
4. Jan Tinbergen, CENTRAL PLANNING
5. Abram Bergson, THE ECONOMICS OF SOVIET PLANNING
6. Joe S. Bain, INTERNATIONAL DIFFERENCES IN INDUSTRIAL STRUCTURE
7. Simon Kuznets, MODERN ECONOMIC GROWTH

INSTABILITY AND ECONOMIC GROWTH

by Erik Lundberg

NEW HAVEN AND LONDON
YALE UNIVERSITY PRESS
1968

Set in Times Roman type,
and printed in the United States of America by
The Carl Purington Rollins Printing-Office of the
Yale University Press, New Haven, Connecticut.
Distributed in Canada by McGill University Press.

Library of Congress catalog card number: 68–13917

FOREWORD

Modern economics has been bred chiefly in Western Europe and the United States, and despite its aspiration toward generality it bears the stamp of institutions and issues characteristic of these areas.

But the economic world no longer revolves about London and New York. Dozens of new nations are struggling toward economic independence and industrial growth under institutional arrangements quite unlike those of the West. Economies of a novel type also extend eastward from central Europe to the Bering Strait and have been busily developing their own principles as a by-product of administrative experience. It is asserted that "Western economics" has only limited analytical value in these other countries.

The problem of the content and relevance of economics thus arises inescapably. Are the economic principles taught in the West really susceptible of general applications? Or are they culture-bound and relevant mainly to industrial capitalist countries? Is it possible to create a general economics which would be as useful in Poland or India as in Canada or France? Or must we be content with several species of economics which will remain distinct in intellectual content and applicability?

"Comparative economics" has been regarded as a separate area of the economics curriculum, consisting of a botanical classification of national economies into a few loosely labeled boxes. But surely any course in economics is potentially comparative. A concern with comparative experience can profitably be infused into any of the standard branches of economic study.

Foreword

This series is inspired by the hope that a rethinking of particular branches of economics in world perspective, combined with a bibliography of available material from many countries, may help teachers to give their courses a broader and more comparative orientation.

In pursuing this objective, we deliberately chose autonomy over standardization. Each author was left free to determine his own approach and method of treatment. The essays thus differ considerably in length, analytical as against descriptive emphasis, geographical coverage, and other respects. How far the original intent of the series has been accomplished is for the profession to judge.

We are grateful to the authors who have struggled with possibly insoluble problems, to the Ford Foundation for its support of the enterprise, and to the staff of the Yale University Press for their helpful cooperation.

The Inter-University Committee on Comparative Economics: Abram Bergson, Arthur R. Burns, Kermit Gordon, Richard Musgrave, William Nicholls, Lloyd Reynolds (Chairman)

ACKNOWLEDGMENTS

Work on this book has been interrupted several times—because of a variety of exogenous disturbances. One important consequence of the protracted process of writing has been the succession of new business cycles and policy experiences that I have had to cover. The several rewritings of parts of the text may have put certain "development marks" on the presentation of the material as well as on the analysis. To the extent that a process of changing emphasis may be noticeable, it might be accepted as an expression of a developing understanding of changing instability patterns referring especially to shifts from the 1950s to the 1960s.

This survey would not have been possible without the partnership of Franz Ettlin. He was already my research assistant in 1961 at the University of California, Berkeley, when the first very tentative steps for the study were taken. Over the following years he has—with some long interruptions for other duties—been assisting me in collecting statistical material, going over the sources of information, and giving the interpretations systematic form. Mr. Ettlin is responsible for the construction of the instability measures in Chapter 3 and the source material given in the Appendix. Generally it can be said that the book would have been much worse than it is without Franz Ettlin's keen eye for mistakes and his good judgment about the presentation of the issues.

The manuscript was reviewed critically by Robert A. Gordon of the University of California. I have profited greatly from his most useful criticism and good suggestions for improvements as well as from his pertinent question marks. Pieter de Wolff of the Central Bureau in The Hague and Toshihiko Yoshino of the Economic Research Bureau of the Bank of Japan have read the preliminary versions of the chapters on the Dutch and Japanese experience respectively, and I have made great use of their valuable comments. Marian Neal Ash at the Yale University Press has been extremely helpful in polishing my English and editing the manuscript.

Erik Lundberg

Stockholm, Sweden
March 1967

CONTENTS

FOREWORD v

ACKNOWLEDGMENTS vii

LIST OF TABLES AND FIGURES xii

1. PROBLEMS OF ECONOMIC INSTABILITY 3
   - Various Kinds of Instability 3
   - Demarcation of the Problem 9
   - Examples of Issues to Be Discussed 11
   - Application of Theory—Some Illustrations 13
   - The Statistical Revolution 16
   - Government Policies and Country Studies 18

2. INSTABILITY ISSUES OF THE INTERWAR PERIOD 22
   - Main Differences from the Postwar Period 22
   - Some Questions Concerning the Fundamental Behavior Within the Private Sector of the Economy 42
   - Changes in General Conditions 54
   - A General View of the Interwar Experiences 71

3. GENERAL SURVEY OF POSTWAR ECONOMIC INSTABILITY 85
   - Manifestations of Economic Instability 85
   - Deviations from Potential or Full-employment Output 96
   - Variation and Variability of the Growth Rate and Its Expenditure Components 114

Trends and Fluctuations 123
Conjunctures and Government Economic Policy 132
The Need for Country Studies 140

4. GROWTH INTERRUPTIONS AND BALANCE OF PAYMENTS RESTRICTIONS IN THE UNITED KINGDOM 148
General View on Interrelations Between Growth and Cycles 148
The Policy Cycles 166
Direct and Indirect Policy Effects 172
A Sketch of a Model with Policy Alternatives 187

5. STABILIZATION POLICY EXPERIENCES IN SWEDEN 192
The Policy Milieu 192
The Instability Problems 197
Methods of Forecasting 212
The Instruments of Stabilization Policy 219
Discussion of Direct Policy Effects 236
Indirect Effects of Stabilization Policy on the Functioning of the Credit and Labor Markets 247

6. ECONOMETRIC FORECASTING AND POLICY PLANNING IN THE NETHERLANDS 261
Some Background Conditions 261
On the Country's Short-term Reaction Mechanism 268
Policy Effects on Stability 279
Applications of the Econometric Model for Policy Planning 295
How Good Is the CPB Model in Describing Reality? 306

7. "EXPLOSIVE" GROWTH AND GROWTH INTERRUPTIONS IN JAPAN 313

The Statistical Picture 313
Factors Determining Instability 318
Some Features of the Japanese Business Cycle 328
The Financing of Investment and the Role of Monetary Policy 329
The Conjuncture Mechanism and Its Changes 340

8. POSTWAR STABILITY PROBLEMS IN THE UNITED STATES AND CANADA 348
Differences Between American and European Experiences 348
The Instability of the U.S. GNP During Recession and Recovery 352
Ex Ante Saving and Investment at Potential GNP 355
The Role of Policy 367
General Survey of Some Specific Canadian Problems 377
Policy Experiments in Canada 382
The Success and Failure of Flexible Exchange Rates 386
The Deficiency of Supporting Policies in Canada 390
The Ending of the Canadian Experiment 393

APPENDIX: Variation and Variability of the Growth of GNP and its Expenditure Components in Fourteen Countries, 1950–64 397

LIST OF REFERENCES 415
INDEX 423

LIST OF TABLES AND FIGURES

TABLES

2.1 Compound Annual Growth Rates of Gross National Product and Industrial Production 25

2.2 Cyclical Setbacks in Annual GNP and in Industrial Production 29

2.3 Average Unemployment Levels, 1921–60 32

2.4 Ratios of the Percentage Growth of the Import Volume to the Percentage Growth of GNP 54

2.5 Declines of Industrial Production, GNP, and Export Volume During Interwar Contractions 73

3.1 Annual Rates of Growth of Real GNP 86

3.2 The Variability of Growth of the Expenditure Components and the Variation of GNP Growth 118

3.3 Relative Contribution of Expenditure Components to the Growth of GNP 120

3.4 Variation of the Expenditure Components of GNP Growth 121

3.5 Relative Levels of Industrial Production after the Two World Wars 126

List of Tables and Figures

4.1 Growth Rates, Investment Ratios, and Incremental Capital to Output Ratios (ICOR) 154

4.2 Export Price Development and Share in World Trade 161

4.3 Fluctuations in the Savings Ratio and Changes in Consumer Debt 180

5.1 An Illustration of the Primary Effect of Built-in Fiscal Stabilization Features 239

5.2 Investments and Savings as Percentages of GNP 250

6.1 Consequences of a Tax Reduction of 500 Million Guilders 280

6.2 Estimated Consequences of a Wage Increase and a Rise of Investment 281

6.3 Some Short-term Effects of a 5 Per Cent Appreciation of the Guilder 283

6.4 Changes in Value from Previous Year 285

6.5 The Creation of Liquidity 290

6.6 Normal Rates of Change and Indicators of Forecasting Errors, 1953–63 298

6.7 Comparison Between Investment Survey and Model Forecast 303

7.1 Variations of Seasonally Adjusted Quarterly Real GNP 314

7.2 Long-term Growth Composition, 1950–64 315

7.3 Cyclical Percentage Composition of GNP Changes 315

7.4 Growth of Investment and GNP 323

FIGURES

3.1 Index of Industrial Production, Percentage Deviations from Trend of Seasonally Adjusted Data 89

3.2 Development Profiles: Growth of Actual and Potential GNP at Constant Prices 103

3.3 Average Annual Change of GNP Deflator Related to the Average GNP Gap, 1950–64 113

4.1 Average Annual Rates of Growth of Export Volume and of Real GNP, 1951–64 158

4.2 Development of Interest Rates in the United Kingdom, 1951–64 171

5.1 Annual Percentage Changes of Private Consumption and of Private Disposable Income, 1952–64 198

5.2 Annual Changes of Wages per Hour in Relation to the Percentage of Vacancies Filled (Manufacturing Industry), 1950–63 200

5.3 Annual Changes of the Volume of Exports and Imports; Surplus or Deficit of Current Account of Balance of Payments 206

5.4 Development of Wages, Productivity in Manufacturing, and Prices 209

5.5 Forecasts and Results with Regard to the Annual Changes in the Volume of Exports, 1950–64 214

5.6 Changes in Money Supply and Bank Lending, Actual and Recommended Liquidity of Commercial Banks, 1953–64 233

List of Tables and Figures

6.1 Labor Reserve and Unfilled Vacancies 292

6.2 Forecast and Realization 300

7.1 Industrial Production and Value of Imports 316

7.2 Quarterly Development of Private Fixed Investment and Inventory Investment, 1953–64 317

7.3 Postwar Growth of GNP and Extrapolation of Interwar Trend 320

8.1 Ratio of Actual to Potential GNP Related to the Ex Ante Savings Ratio and Investment Ratio 360

8.2 Quarterly Development of GNP at Constant Prices in the U.S. and Canada 377

8.3 Canadian Exchange Rates and Reserves, 1947–63 387

INSTABILITY AND ECONOMIC GROWTH

1 PROBLEMS OF ECONOMIC INSTABILITY

VARIOUS KINDS OF INSTABILITY

When we speak about economic instability, some kind of reference to stable or more stable conditions is always implied. The development of the real gross national product of a country does not follow a smooth path but shows irregularities that can be described as deviations from or fluctuations around such a smooth path. This is a kind of economic instability that can be observed and measured—for example with a trend, determined by statistical or economic criteria, serving as the base of reference. Similarly, production or employment in a certain line of activity may show irregular changes during a year (apart from seasonal variations) or over a period of years that are considered as a form of economic instability. The individual firm is exposed to changes in demand for its products or to changes in supply conditions, which the management of the firm considers as a form of economic instability to be dealt with by adjustments of orders to other firms, by adjustments of working hours, employment, production, and prices. Income and employment conditions may then appear as unstable also to the workers in this firm or branch of activity.

The development of incomes, prices, and so forth may appear unstable to the wage earner or the management of a firm because there are changes up and down around a constant level or because yearly changes deviate from some trend or average rate of change signifying stability. The same kind of outlook characterizes observations on the aggregate level for a national economy. Real income in the economy as well as the price level may move up and down, and the fluctuations may be regarded as a kind of instability of income formation; or the level of income and prices may at times deviate from a trend—the instability of income formation eventually taking the form of spells of inflation and deflation of varying duration.

Instability may refer to conditions of production, for example to variations in harvests, to supplies of fish in the ocean, to conditions in the labor markets (strikes). There may be technological changes causing substitutions of one raw material for another, machinery for labor, shifting demand from old commodities to new ones. Shifts in demand from one firm to another, from one group of goods to another, from one country to another will imply economic changes that may be considered as one form of instability in supply and demand conditions.

Looking at international trade statistics one will notice large changes, from year to year and over the years, of exports and imports of individual commodities as well as of total exports and imports of individual countries. The volumes and the prices of exports and imports belong to a group of variable factors that imply instability in the balance of payment conditions of individual countries.

Instabilities of this nature do not relate only to changes inside the private economy of individual countries. Government expenditures of various kinds, tax receipts and tax rates, and changes in central bank policy that affect interest rates belong to a group of phenomena often with high variability that may very well be included in a picture of overall economic instability.

A picture of economic instability might go into the utmost detail, covering the smallest units of economic flux from day to day or month to month. Or the observations might refer to the annual changes of broad aggregates. Interesting examples of economic change, implying instability in some way, occur continuously in the microcells of the national economy. New decisions as to production, prices, sales activities, investment, consumption, saving, as well as changes in government economic policy, are being made more or less continuously by individual consumers, firms, organizations and government agencies, successively creating new situations for any number of economic units of this kind and disturbing their positions or developments and causing reactions throughout the economic system.

As economists we have propensities to put change-phenomena in categories, considering them important and interesting if they fall into certain recognizable patterns. One such way is to group economic change into seasonal, cyclical, and trend patterns—the rest being put into a category of irregular, nonclassified, or uninteresting changes. In this book attention is concentrated on the group of change-phenomena called "cyclical" or "conjunctural," implying a kind of instability that has certain properties that, although rather easily recognized, are difficult to define clearly.

What we are looking for is a kind of systematic economic instability that affects large sectors of the economy, so large in fact that this kind of instability implies disturbance to the whole economy. This means that we exclude irregular changes in production, employment, and trade in individual firms or branches of activity that average out over the whole economy and therefore do not show up clearly in the series of total production, employment, and trade for the whole economy. We also disregard seasonal variation as a special phenomenon, and such irregular ups and downs in production, employment, and trade from one year to the following that are apparently caused by, for example, external factors such as bad harvests, big strikes, or major wars. Here we have to be careful, however. Changes of economic activity determined by wars or strikes do not interest us as such in this study, but these changes may be of great importance for the kind of cyclical instability that is our subject of analysis. To be more concrete: although we are not studying the development of production and prices during the two world wars, the actual experiences in the different countries during the years 1919–21 and 1945–49 cannot be understood without looking at the special economic conditions in 1918 and 1945 created as consequences of the wars. Or, to cite other examples, the British coal strike in 1926 and the Korean war in 1950–51 had direct effects on the movement of the production index. The irregularities are not our primary concern, but we are interested in finding out how these occurrences affected the patterns of change that we refer to as cyclical fluctuations.

We are arguing that there is a class of economic change-phenomena that can be put under the heading of conjunctural or cyclical instability and can be distinguished from other economic changes. However, this distinction is not quite clear if we look at experiences of economic change only from an empirical point of view. In order to demonstrate the kind of difficulty in defining the subject of our research, let us take a concrete example. The development of production and employment in the United States during the period 1954–58 may be taken as a clear case of cyclical fluctuation or instability. Even though there were many differing developments in the various time series of production and employment in individual branches of activity, there was sufficient conformity so that a general fluctuation of total production and employment can be observed, with overall expansion up to the summer of 1957 and general contraction to the beginning of the second quarter of 1958.

Nobody would doubt that this American development can be classified as a business cycle phenomenon, although some of the important series such as the general price level and public expenditures did not manifest any absolute declines. Similarly, we can without much hesitation classify the earlier and later fluctuations in United States production and employment during the postwar period in the same class of phenomena. The careful observations of the National Bureau of Economic Research give us confidence in identifying the postwar experiences with those during the interwar period. But as the National Bureau always tries to remind us, there are significant differences among these individual cyclical experiences as to amplitudes, timing of the series, and so forth.

History never repeats itself in exactly the same way. There are such important differences between the catastrophic United States depression of 1929–33 and the very mild recessions of 1926–27 and 1960–61 that from some points of view they can very well be classified in different categories. But if we assume there is empirical evidence to make it sensible to talk about United States experience with cyclical instability over the period 1919–64 as a tolerably homogenous set of phenomena, what about, for instance, British, Dutch, or Swedish economic developments during the same period? Or similar experiences in Japan, Australia, or South American countries? Do we have empirical evidence permitting us to classify the instability experiences of these countries in the same category? It seems plausible, for instance, to consider the Dutch and Japanese postwar instability experiences as different types of instability phenomena. The same may be true of the repeated balance of payments disturbances of countries like the United Kingdom, Denmark, and Finland, or corresponding balance of payments crises in a number of countries exporting mainly raw materials. During the interwar as well as the postwar period several countries had spells of relative economic stagnation manifested by slow or zero growth: for example the United Kingdom during the 1920s and again in 1956–58, the United States during the 1930s and again between 1953 and the beginning of the 1960s; France during a considerable part of the interwar period; and Denmark during the years 1954–56. Such periods of stagnation may be regarded as a form of instability in the rate of economic growth, but they may not fit very well into the popular conception of business cycles.

Is there any common denominator in these different kinds of

economic instability? They *should* have some common denominator, since this book deals with all of them, but the popular business cycle concept is too narrow to serve. We might say that the various types of economic instability exemplified above are short-term (embracing periods of a few years up to less than ten) and that they are important to the whole of the economy in question—so important that they actually or potentially affect total production, employment, the price level, or the foreign exchange situation.

The adjective "important" is to be interpreted in terms of the common policy aims during the postwar period—and in fact the word "potential" also has this bearing. It may be that the relatively even growth rate of the United Kingdom and the rather steady state of full employment in Norway and Sweden during the postwar period are to a large extent effects of government stabilization policies. Potentially these economies may tend to show fluctuations of production and employment like the American or Canadian economies, but government policy measures may have neutralized the tendencies. This hypothetical statement implies that empirical evidence of the degree of instability is not a sufficient criterion for classifying the instability phenomena we are after. We must also include a characterization of the reaction pattern or mechanism of the economic system we are observing. It may thus be possible to find more common features in the instability patterns of economic development in the Western economies than the direct statistical observations indicate. In fact, we are dealing with market economies containing relatively large private sectors, where business firms of various types and free consumers are behaving and reacting under continuous economic change. Public sectors of varying relative size interact with the private sectors, partly by means of conscious economic policy. At the same time the economies of the various countries interact with each other by way of international trade and capital movements.

Problems of Economic Instability

DEMARCATION OF THE PROBLEM

Instability of economic growth may thus refer to a very wide range of phenomena. The concept is in fact more embracing than the term "business cycles," although this expression might cover the main issues. In a way the old term "conjuncture" used on the European continent may better circumscribe the subject matter of this book than the term "business cycles." The latter term usually tends to suggest the association of more or less regular waves of fluctuating production, employment, prices, and so forth along the lines of the United States experience as presented by the National Bureau of Economic Research. Of course, we also speak of "conjuncture-waves" ("Konjunkturwellen"), but the main connotation of the term "conjuncture" refers to changing business situations that may take any variety of forms without implying any rhythmic regularity.

This very broad concept of the business cycle, or rather of the conjuncture, used in this book means that we need not bother much about the rather sterile problem sometimes raised as to whether the phenomenon of business cycles (in the pre-World War II sense) still exists, especially in the countries of Western Europe.[1] The wide definition used here implies that this type of phenomenon exists and is likely to continue to exist.

1. "The idea of the business cycle is not à la mode; it is considered a bit prewar as an analytical concept and not particularly applicable to the present-day problems of the European economy." Milton Gilbert, "The Postwar Business Cycle in Western Europe," *American Economic Review* (May 1962), p. 93.

"Konjunktur und Wachstum sind in Wirklichkeit keine getrennten Tatbestände, sondern verschiedene Aspekte der gleichen Wirklichkeit." Eugen Böhler, *Die alten und die neuen Herren der Konjunktur,* Sonderdruck aus *Industrielle Organisation* (1963), p. 4. The references are taken from Walter Jöhr, *Gegenwartsfragen der Konjunkturtheorie,* Sonderdruck aus *Jahrbücher für Nationalökonomie und Statistik, 1965.*

The essential questions are, instead, how serious these conjunctural instability problems are, or how seriously they are taken, how they are related to the growth issues, and to what extent the conjunctural problems change character over time and as between countries. These questions are the central topics of this book.

We may take for granted that not every "conjunctural change" as such is or need be a subject for detailed analysis. There are continuous changes going on in specific branches of industry involving current production, investments, and profits, as well as business prospects and investment plans. Such changes are of interest in the present context only insofar as they have a sufficient impact to modify the general pattern or conditions of growth in GNP. This means that our center of interest lies in the rate and pattern of growth in GNP, so that the phenomena of instability that will be discussed and analyzed are the various kinds of deviations from certain norms of balanced growth.

This is of course a typical way of transferring the vagueness of one concept—instability or conjuncture—to the vagueness of another concept—balanced growth. There is no escape from this kind of vagueness, except by introducing a theoretical model world, using exact definitions and equations connecting the variables. But then the vagueness is again shifted to the difficulties of translating the economic realities of our existing world into the concepts of the model. A flight into a model world will give no solution to our definitional problem.

In fact, the reader should not mind a certain degree of vagueness in the definition and demarcation of the phenomena to be discussed in this book. It is preferable to keep the unavoidable vagueness in mind, to accept it as a realistic expression of the nature of the problems to be treated rather than to put them into a straitjacket of false precision. Ultimately, our definition of the problems of instability is spelled out in the choice of issues discussed in the following chapters. But, of course, even if the boundary lines are vague there are certain very general criteria that influence our selection of problems. There are in fact three main criteria: the problems should refer in some ways to deviations from balanced growth; they should be sufficiently important; and they should be interesting from the point of view of stabilization policy.

EXAMPLES OF ISSUES TO BE DISCUSSED

As a concrete way of introducing the topics of this book, we shall now give some examples of problems that will be treated. This presentation will be complemented by an account of the reasons for the exclusion of some important subjects that very well could have been treated.

The issues of balanced economic growth are put in the center of observation and analysis not because economic growth—its patterns, conditions, and causes—is the subject matter of the book, but because instability, in its various forms, is defined and measured as deviation from some conception of balanced growth. It is necessary in various connections to discuss the conditions and factors determining the actual growth process in the selected countries during the periods in question. Notions of full capacity and balanced growth must therefore be discussed and related to conditions varying with periods and countries.

Instability in the growth process has taken a variety of forms. The simplest form, which underlies what we call GNP variation index in Chapter 3, is the irregularity of the yearly rate of growth of real GNP. It would have been desirable to take quarterly, instead of annual, data; but unfortunately such quarterly data are not available for a sufficient number of the countries that we are considering. Variations of a country's annual rate of growth between, for example, zero and 8 per cent are prima facie evidence of economic instability. This instability also implies variations in the rates of employment and unemployment. (Alternative methods can be applied for measuring this type of instability when comparing different periods and countries. This kind of instability can easily be given a cyclical connotation, since even if growth is continuous, that is without setbacks, the variations in the annual rates of growth usually convey the impression of cyclical swings. Cases of negative annual growth rates—actual contractions—have also occurred during the postwar period, but such events were certainly much more frequent and much more accentuated during the period between the world wars.

One special form of instability in the behavior of GNP that is of considerable interest and will be much discussed refers to the already mentioned periods of relative stagnation, when gaps appear between actual production and potential production as determined by full or normal use of labor and capital resources. Such "deflationary gaps" may of course be merely the result of recurring short-term retardations of actual growth (below capacity growth), and are thus just a consequence of the fluctuating growth rates. But considerable production gaps lasting over a period of several years are here taken as a special form of instability that should be given separate attention.

Fluctuating growth rates represent only one important type of the instability issues that are the concern of this book. We have also to look at the development of total demand, which is not always adequately pictured in the rate of growth of production. Total demand in nominal terms will in most cases show higher variability than real GNP, owing to variations in price and wage levels. Deflationary and inflationary development should of course be regarded as important deviations from balanced growth. Looking at the postwar period we find in all countries a persistent long-term trend of rising prices and hardly any declines in the general price level; this is in contrast to the interwar period, when there were distinct phases of rising and declining price levels. But during the postwar period there are variations in the speed of the general price rise between countries and subperiods. In general we may consider inflationary developments as deviations from the price stability targets of economic policy, and from this point of view they are part of the general problem of instability with which we are concerned.

Such observations of growth instability may not, as such, be very interesting—although comparative measures will give a stimulating introduction to the experiences during different periods and in various countries. Our main objective is to put these and other forms of instability experience into an analytic framework in order to obtain some causal interpretations. We should like to know how varying rates of growth are determined and influenced by changes within and outside particular economies. This means that we need to study the fluctuations or changing rates of development of a number of variables besides real and nominal GNP. In pursuing this problem we may, for instance, as is done in Chapter 3, investigate the expenditure composition of GNP in order to determine the arithmetical contribution of the main expenditure categories (consumption, fixed private investment, inventory investment, government expenditures, exports, and imports). Doing so will provide us with a useful account of the composition of "GNP instability," possibly indicating the sources of the disturbances and in any case giving characteristic differences in the instability patterns between countries and periods.

APPLICATION OF THEORY—SOME ILLUSTRATIONS

As economists we have an honorable propensity to put our statistical observations into the framework of more or less accepted theory. One of the main purposes of this book is to illustrate the application of our usual analytical tools for an interpretation of the instability experiences as they are recorded in current statistics.

The most general (and common) approach to an explanation of the phenomena of instability is to formulate a disequilibrium hypothesis. We may, for instance, try to understand a too-rapid rise in wage rates (from the point of view of balanced growth) as caused by excess demand for labor, that is, a general disequilibrium in the labor market; the analysis has then to proceed by trying to identify supply and demand in the available labor market statistics. We try to use similar notions with regard to the total demand for goods and services in order to derive, for example, a concept of total excess demand (as the difference between ex ante total demand and total supply under conditions of full employment) which underlies the concept of demand inflation. When breaking up the aggregates into the main components, we have to apply consumption and investment functions of various kinds in order to interpret the changes in the corresponding variables. The issues of balance of payments disequilibria that so often appear as disturbances to growth have to be treated as results of disequilibrating developments of exports and imports as well as of capital movements.

In the application of analytical tools of the type mentioned above, no effort is made to be unnecessarily sophisticated. The simplest possible theories are used in order both to illustrate their usefulness and to discuss their limitations for explaining instability. General knowledge of the usual consumption and investment theories is taken for granted; there is no systematic presentation of these and other theories in this book. There are, in fact, many excellent books that perform that task, and the main purpose of this book is, instead, to confront commonly accepted theories with some central issues of growth instability as they appear in our rapidly changing economies. This means that the theories to be applied should be the humble servants, helping us to clarify the often very complicated issues that are raised. We seem already to have a quite sufficient supply of literature in which the theoretical models live a complicated life of their own, rather undisturbed by economic reality.

In this book the actual phenomenon of unstable growth, as it has appeared during the years since the First World War, is the starting point for description and analysis. The aim of the study is to give the student a rather rich and varied range of instability experiences and issues, extracted from a number of countries over a rather long period of time. One of our intentions is to show how variable the conjuncture situations have been and to describe the great variation in the underlying conditions. This variation will imply tests with available analytical tools and models of interpretation. The development of our theories and research methods is to a certain extent determined by the "needs" of current problems and the concomitant policy issues. However, there is certainly no very close correlation. On the one hand, theory formation to a large extent follows its own laws of development; new formulations and theorems are cumulated on the basis of older versions in efforts to enlarge the scope and increase the depth of existing theoretical models. On the other hand, as economists we have at the same time a strong conservative leaning to stick to the theoretical tools we have learned to handle, and to apply them to ever changing issues. Old theories are hardly ever effectively killed off by a process of "creative destruction."

The degree to which eventual contradictions between theory and economic reality do exist and are serious may to some extent be judged from the viewpoint of whether and to what extent the conjunctures and corresponding instability issues are significantly different when we compare the interwar with the postwar period, or when we compare the instability situations of various countries. In fact this question of the applicability of old and new tools of analysis turns up in several chapters and is especially dealt with in Chapter 2.

Looking at the types of theories actually applied for analyzing conjunctures over the period 1920–64, we find conservation and radical change side by side. Over the whole period we find use of various versions of the quantity theory of money and of rather simple overcapacity and underconsumption formulations of business cycle theory. Keynesian approaches to analyzing changes of demand are fundamental for defining the problems both of deficit and excess demand. We shall also find Wesley C. Mitchell's notions of the changes in income distribution over the business cycle, especially as to the squeeze of profit margins during the later stages of a boom, useful for understanding the ensuing instability. But there are also very important developments and innovations that have occurred since the Second World War.

THE STATISTICAL REVOLUTION

The most important of the new developments relates to the statistical revolution that in most countries had its origin during the war. The development of systematic national income accounting implied a revolution in observation techniques. During the 1920s there was in a way much more freedom in interpreting economic change; available statistics could be picked out to confirm an assertion, or statistical testing could be omitted completely because relevant data were nonexistent. Thanks to the ever increasing flow and improvement of current time-series statistics in general, and well-developed national accounts in particular, there now exists in all Western countries a relatively well-organized statistical universe to which our notions of development and stability refer. Furthermore, not only does there exist a large supply of data, but—as citizens, politicians, or economists—we take these statistical observations seriously. Economic reality is a product of systematic statistical observations in a more serious sense today than it was during earlier decades. Unemployment at 1.5 per cent rising to 2.5 per cent would in most countries be taken during the postwar period as a serious indicator of disequilibrium and as a deviation from a policy target. We also take seriously a retardation of the rate of growth of GNP—an observation that was scarcely ever made during the interwar period—and regard a deterioration from a 5 per cent to a 3 per cent rate as an important economic change.

At many points in this volume there will be opportunities for warning the reader against taking this statistical world *too* seriously. There are great dangers in comparing a country's savings ratios, productivity changes, unemployment rates, and so forth, over longer periods—or sometimes even from year to year. The difficulties are still greater when different countries are being compared. Such warnings, and of course especially any evidence that the errors might be big, should be kept in mind when studying growth rates and other measures derived from the national income statistics. But a critical attitude in these respects should not be allowed to be so destructive that the interpretation of economic reality or the testing of hypotheses seem meaningless. Our techniques of statistical observation, not least our methods of putting the results into national accounts, is a fundamental and necessary way of communication, a language for expressing the common consciousness of economic reality. One may say that modern statistical observation techniques have become our sixth sense organ which—although quite as imperfect as the other organs in providing an unbiased picture of reality—is generally good enough for useful communication and policy decisions.

Another rather new development in our ways of trying to understand conjunctural movements comes from econometric techniques of analysis. After Tinbergen's pioneering study, at the end of the 1930s, of the United States business cycle, econometric model building has shown, all in all, an impressive development during the postwar period. Econometric techniques of testing theories and giving quantitive precision to the marginal importance of strategic variables refer both to the measurement of various partial relationships (as for instance the consumption function or the relation between changes in wage rates and in unemployment) and to total models describing the short-term mechanism of an entire economy.

There is no doubt that econometric research has contributed in an impressive way to an understanding of the conjuncture mechanisms of some countries. It is therefore natural that this type of analysis is discussed in various places in the following chapters. Again there is no question here of giving a systematic presentation of the techniques of analysis. Our concern is to study how and to what extent econometric research seems to help, and not least to warn against exaggerated claims of quantitative precision. These warnings refer not only to the sometimes very uncertain time-series statistics that have to be used, but mainly to the ever changing conjunctural situations that may not contain a sufficient degree of repetitiveness of similar constellations in order to give the econometric methods of analysis a good enough chance to discovering the "true" strategic relations.

On the other hand it is our view that econometric analysis and model building is extremely stimulating for further research and deeper probing into the material problems of the working of "conjuncture mechanisms." The econometric technique implies a systematic way of arranging the statistical material, and electronic computers make possible the quick "testing" of a great number of alternative hypotheses. The results under most conditions mean a stimulating challenge to accept or not accept the results, to scrutinize the methods and the economic theories involved, and to judge the reliability of the statistical data used. As will be shown in the following chapters, results of econometric research are frequently used for an appraisal of various issues.

A critical attitude as to the possibilities of reaching precise and stable quantitative relations within a model of a conjuncture mechanism has affected the layout of the book. It is this mixture of a certain measure of repetition and a considerable amount of diversity in every sequence of conjunctural situations that creates the challenging difficulties which we try to bring out as clearly as possible, both by studying a number of problem cases over a long period and by looking at the experience of a number of different countries.

GOVERNMENT POLICIES AND COUNTRY STUDIES

Government policy is an important factor in causing business cycle patterns to change. One of the themes of this book has to do with the difficulty of isolating a changing "conjuncture mechanism"—in some ways embodying the built-in reaction patterns of the economy—from the direct impulses of policy changes. Over the whole period covered, actual economic changes have been more or less strongly influenced by the introduction of government policy measures designed to achieve stabilization. The business cycles actually observed cannot be understood without paying attention to current monetary, fiscal, and other governmental stabilization policies. Stress has therefore been laid on the aims and means of stabilization policy, the shifts in modes over a period of time, the lags in application, and the possible effects on stability. In this field there is much need both for effective statistical observation and for good theory to help in analyzing the effects of policy measures.

Not least with regard to the importance of studying current government policy changes, there is a need for country studies. There is much idiosyncrasy in government reactions to instability situations—not so much as to the policy targets established as to the policy measures actually applied. By taking up a number of conjuncture situations in a number of countries over a considerable period of time we ought to be able to cover quite a variety of instability cases, including a diversity of government policy reactions. In this way we hope to give the reader an impression of the rich variety of conjuncture developments with which policies interfere, and of how difficult it must be to make generalizations about, for instance, the effectiveness of various types of stabilization policies.

These country studies are made against the background of a broad international survey of instability experiences during the interwar and postwar periods (Chapters 2 and 3). In these chapters we present in a systematic way the problems of instability and how they are transformed over time and take different forms in the individual countries. Various measures of instability are discussed and presented together with a survey of the main differences in conjuncture experiences between the interwar and postwar periods. All this gives a background for the following more intensive study of country experiences during the postwar period up to 1964.

It must be strongly emphasized that both the selection of countries and the choice of problems for each country has been rather arbitrary within wide limits. The main guideline has been the desire to cover the main types of interesting instability cases that have occurred during the postwar period. These case studies should help to clarify the set of instability issues raised in Chapters 2 and 3. The approach means that the chapters on specific countries (Chapters 4 through 8) should not be read as systematic studies of the business cycle history of these countries. In fact, the emphasis on periods and problems changes from country to country just because of this concentration on what is taken as the conjuncture specialities of the selected countries. In order to clarify this approach, let us examine, very briefly, some examples of such specialities:

The United Kingdom (Chapter 4): the sequence of balance of payments disturbances; the repeated stagnation periods; the interdependence of the stop-go policies and retarded growth.

Holland (Chapter 5): the intensive use of econometric model building for forecasting, policy planning, and analysis; the application of wage policy; an internal cyclical mechanism determining instability of investment.

Sweden (Chapter 6): a high degree of stability related to ambitious government policies; no balance of payments disturbances; the experience of active labor market policies and some other policy innovations.

Japan (Chapter 7): possible relations between very high rates of growth and the short duration of the recessions; the effectiveness of monetary policy to dampen investment booms and reestablish balance of payments equilibrium.

United States (Chapter 8): the extended periods of deficit demand; relations between planned savings and investment during fast and slow expansion; the discussion of the effects of fiscal and monetary policy.

Canada (Chapter 8): the problem of close dependence on the United States economy; the experiences and potential possibilities of floating exchange rates; problems of international capital movements.

This presentation of some instability issues of special interest with regard to the selected countries is of course very schematic and may give an impression of more narrow treatment of the country experiences than is actually the case. Our intention in this enumeration is, however, not only to give some defense for the choice of the countries mentioned—supplying us with these and other issues—but also to announce the kind of emphasis that the corresponding chapters contain. It should be added that Chapters 2 and 3 also contain references to the stability experiences of a number of countries other than the ones explicitly mentioned above.

2 INSTABILITY ISSUES OF THE INTERWAR PERIOD

MAIN DIFFERENCES FROM THE POSTWAR PERIOD

It is customary to consider the favorable economic developments since the end of the Second World War against the dismal experiences of the two decades that followed the end of the First World War. The contrast between the interwar period's stagnation combined with severe business contractions on the one hand, and the rapid and relatively smooth growth of the postwar period on the other, provides an opportune starting ground for a discussion of factors and interrelations that appear to have determined the relatively good postwar record. One can point out a number of factors and interrelations that apparently had strong destabilizing effects during the interwar period, and then investigate the reasons for the absence—or at least the lesser importance—of these factors and interrelations in all countries during the postwar period. This method of presentation is certainly clarifying and pedagogic. We shall thus have good reason to refer frequently to the interwar background when discussing postwar experiences.

For a change, however, it may be useful to look back upon the interwar experiences with a reversed perspective, that is, to take the documented possibilities of sustained, relatively stable and rapid growth after a devastating war for granted and to ask ourselves why and how the large fluctuations and the low overall pace of economic activity during the interwar years came about. Whether we look at the interwar events in the latter way or the former is of course a relatively trivial matter of disposition and emphasis. Nevertheless, the latter way of presentation provides us with a convenient opportunity for concentrating on the strategic issues without having to present a detailed and relatively complete chronicle of events.[1] Thus, we shall emphasize the instability and stagnation issues that seem interesting and surprising in the light of postwar experiences. From such a discussion we also hope to improve our understanding of how and why the different countries up to now have succeeded so much better in most relevant respects during the postwar period.

In the following, we have attempted to outline some basic traits of the course of economic activity in the interwar period that stand in contrast with the comparable postwar features. This is done mainly in the form of enumerating and discussing a number of apparently relevant points of difference. The characterization is intended as an introduction to the following sections which focus on the differences in cyclical behavior patterns and their possible causes.

Taking the postwar development as a standard of reference, the interwar developments can be characterized by the following distinctive features:

1. The slow rate of growth
2. The imprint of severe cyclical setbacks
3. The United States economy as the engine of business cycles
4. The high instability of international trade
5. The deflationary tendencies
6. The high rates of unemployment

1. There are at least three illuminating and comprehensive surveys available, but they all concentrate on only a few countries: W. A. Lewis, *Economic Survey 1919–1939* (Philadephia, 1950); H. W. Arndt, *The Economic Lessons of the Nineteen-Thirties* (London, 1944); J. A. Schumpeter, *Business Cycles* (New York and London, 1939), Vol. 2.

7. The disorganization and overcapacity problems
8. The destabilizing conditions regarding international and national systems of credit and finance
9. The low scale of government operations
10. The weak role of economic policy

1. The interwar period as a whole was characterized by much slower rates of growth of GNP and industrial production, as Table 2.1 illustrates. Western Europe's combined GNP only grew approximately half as fast during the interwar period as during the postwar period. The average annual growth rate of GNP in the United States also was only about two thirds of the rate experienced since the end of the Second World War. Similar generalizations hold for the growth of industrial production. The contrast between the growth rates of the two periods would be still greater if the rates were expressed per unit of the labor force. Since Europe's combined production levels fell below their respective prewar peak levels as a consequence of the world wars, both the interwar and the postwar average growth rates include a catching-up effect. Adjusting for this effect of course reduces Europe's average growth rates, but it also enhances the indicated difference in the overall pace of economic activity between the two periods. It took about six years after the end of World War I until the prewar levels of GNP and industrial production were reached again, whereas it took only about four years to pass the corresponding bench mark after World War II. (The adjusted rates are under A′ and B′ in Table 2.1.) The table shows clearly that the experience of slow economic growth during the interwar period mainly refers to the stagnation of the 1930s. As a matter of (statistical) fact, growth in the 1920s is rather comparable to growth in the first part of the postwar period (1948–55).

2. The interwar period carried the imprint of severe cyclical setbacks around 1921, 1930–33 in North America and in Europe, and 1938 in North America, whereas the postwar period has been subject to minor recessions only, which in

TABLE 2.1

Compound Annual Growth Rates of Gross National Product and Industrial Production

Western Europe	1920–29	1929–37	1920–37	1948–55	1955–62	1948–62
A GNP[a] excl. Germany	3.7			4.1		
incl. Germany	4.0[b]	1.4	2.8[b]	6.0	4.4	5.3
A′ GNP above 1913 peak (19 years after end of WW I)			2.0			
GNP above 1938 peak (17½ years after end of WW II)						4.0
B Industrial production	5.1	2.2	3.7	8.3	5.2	6.8
B′ Industrial production above 1913 peak			2.1			
above 1937 peak						5.6
United States						
A GNP:	4.0	0.6	2.4	4.3	2.2	3.4
B Industrial production	3.9	0.5	2.2	4.4	3.0	3.7

a. Belgium, France, Netherlands, Sweden, Norway, United Kingdom.

b. Calculated under the presumption that Germany's GNP in 1920 was 70 per cent of the 1913 level.

Sources: GNP: Underlying data from Angus Maddison, "Growth and Fluctuations in the World Economy, 1870–1960," *Banca Nazionale del Lavoro, Quarterly Review* (June 1962), Appendix.

INDUSTRIAL PRODUCTION: Organization for European Economic Cooperation (OEEC), *Industrial Statistics 1900–1959; General Statistics.*

some instances are hardly noticeable on a trend chart. The 1921 slump has no counterpart after the Second World War. The 1949 recession in the United States was at the time just a weak reminder of the existence of a cyclical instability problem. In Europe, there was hardly any such reminder at all in the late forties, at least not with regard to the development of output.[2] From 1920 to 1938, annual GNP fell below the level it had attained a year earlier six times in the United States and four times in Europe. The maximum decline from peak to trough year amounted to 29 per cent and 7 per cent respectively. From 1947 to 1964, there were only three years when the GNP of the United States fell below the previous year's level, the largest decline amounting to 1½ per cent, and there was no year when the combined GNP of Europe fell below the preceding year's level. The general impression remains substantially the same if, instead of looking at the combined GNP of Europe, we look at the development of GNP in the individual countries. During the interwar period, GNP in the various countries fell on average one year out of four, during the postwar period about one year out of twenty-five. The highest maximum decline realized in any country after World War II was still much below the lowest maximum decline experienced anywhere in the prior period.

3. With the interwar experience in mind, Europeans have for a long time in the postwar period tended to fear the United States economy as the engine of international business cycles. But actually, as it has turned out, deflationary shocks from the United States have remained small enough to leave Europe largely to its own generation and timing of recessions and inflations. Only around 1958 have both continents been in recession at the same time, and it would be difficult to demonstrate that either recession was mainly foreign-generated rather than home-produced. Of course, within Europe and within North

2. Switzerland seems to have been the only country to experience a drop in GNP in 1949. See Chapter 3 on the postwar period.

America, transmission of cyclical impulses still played an important role in several instances, but the uncomfortably strong link of Europe to the United States cycles observed in the interwar period has been greatly weakened. It is left to another chapter to discuss whether this reflects a fundamental change in the mechanism of transmission of cyclical impulses between America and Europe rather than the fact that United States postwar recessions have all been much milder than the interwar recessions of 1920–21 and 1929–33, when synchronization between the two continents was mainly observed.

4. International trade has been subject to relatively high instability during both periods. The difference mainly refers to the growth experiences. In the postwar period, international trade has expanded very rapidly. The volume of imports and exports since 1948 has generally been rising about twice as fast as real GNP in the case of Western Europe and about as fast as real GNP in the case of the United States. In the interwar period, on the other hand, the volume of international trade grew as slowly as GNP in Western Europe and more slowly than GNP in the United States. The unfavorable development in the interwar period, however, relates also in this respect mainly to the 1930s rather than to the entire period. After the catastrophic decline in the early 1930s, the trade volume of both areas did not recover the 1929 level in any one of the remaining years of the decade.

5. During the postwar period inflationary conditions have predominated; rising price levels have been taken as a natural phenomenon in most countries. With these experiences in mind, among the outstanding features of the interwar period are the deflationary tendencies.

For price-level changes, the movements of the GNP-deflator would actually be most representative. Such data are, however, available for most countries only with regard to postwar years. We therefore were able to follow this indicator over both periods only for four European and the two North American countries. In the first period, the general price level of these countries fell on average in over half of the years, whereas in the later period it fell in about one year per twenty-five (country-)years covered, on average, and in most countries not at all. In addition, the declines of the latter period in no instance exceeded 3 per cent, whereas the declines of the former period exceeded that figure in about three fifths of the cases, the largest declines ranging between 8 and over 20 per cent. As far as price increases are concerned, there is no obvious difference in the magnitude of the increases between the two periods. Very high increases of roughly the same order of size occurred in 1920 and in 1951. In 1937, there was a sharp rise in some countries, but in others the rise was not unusually large.

As far as the behavior of money wages is concerned, the widespread and substantial declines that occurred around 1920–21 and 1929–33 have no counterpart in the postwar period. For example, hourly money wage rates fell by some 20 per cent in Germany and the United States in connection with the Great Depression, whereas the least favorable change in the postwar period was still an increase of some 2 per cent. However, it would be rash to conclude from this evidence that there was significantly more downward flexibility of wage rates during the earlier period, since few downward adjustments took place even during that period in connection with minor setbacks in economic activity. In those cases where wages actually did fall in connection with (primarily major) economic setbacks, the downturn in wages lagged substantially —usually around a year or more—behind the general downturn. Three major reasons for this lag have been mentioned: the difficulty of quickly identifying the occurrence of turning points, the existence of contractual obligations, and the unpopularity of wage-rate reductions[3] which made wage cuts

3. The frequency of labor disputes over the issues of wage reductions in circumstances of high unemployment in the 1920s is evidence of both strong pressure for and strong resistance against wage cuts. See, for example, W. A. Lewis, *Economic Survey,* p. 44.

TABLE 2.2

Cyclical Setbacks in Annual GNP and in Industrial Production

A: Years covered
B: Maximum percentage decline from peak to trough
C: Years of decline as a percentage of years covered

		Interwar Period			Postwar Period		
		A	B	C	A	B	C
Belgium	GNP	1920–38	n.a.	n.a.	1948–64	1.8	12
	I P	1920–38	27.1	28	1948–64	6.4	12
Canada	GNP	1920–38	29.3	33	1948–64	2.9	6
	I P	1920–38	32.3	33	1948–64	0.0	0
Denmark	GNP	1920–38	11.8	22	1948–64	0.2	6
	I P	1920–38	22.2	28	1948–64	4.0	6
France	GNP	1920–38	19.3	50	1948–64	0.0	0
	I P	1920–38	25.6	44	1948–64	1.0	6
Germany	GNP	1924–38	16.1	36	1948–64	0.0	0
	I P	1920–38	40.8	28	1948–64	0.0	0
Italy	GNP	1920–38	5.4	28	1948–64	0.0	0
	I P	1920–38	22.7	33	1948–64	0.0	0
Netherlands	GNP	1920–38	12.1	28	1948–64	0.0	0
	I P	1920–38[a]	(16.9)	(15)	1948–64	0.0	0
Norway	GNP	1920–38	8.0	17	1948–64	0.2	6
	I P	1920–38	21.3	17	1948–64	1.1	6
Sweden	GNP	1920–38	13.3	17	1948–64	0.4	6
	I P	1920–38	21.4	17	1948–64	2.0	6
Switzerland	GNP	1924–38	8.0	28	1948–64	2.2	12
	I P	1920–38[a]	(37.7)	(39)	1948–64	n.a.	n.a.
United Kingdom	GNP	1920–38	13.2	17	1948–64	0.5	12
	I P	1920–38	32.4	39	1948–64	3.1	12
United States	GNP	1920–38	28.9	39	1948–64	1.6	19
	I P	1920–38	44.7	39	1948–64	7.7	19

a. Ingvar Svennilson, *Growth and Stagnation of the European Economy* (Geneva, 1954), p. 304.

Sources: See Table 2.1.

feasible only in case of a pronounced deterioration in employment and profit conditions. The same factors help to explain why wage rates usually were not reduced in connection with brief and mild contractions.[4] The complete absence of widespread money wage reductions following postwar minor downturns can be explained by the strong postwar upward trend in wage rates in nonrecession periods. This strong positive trend and the moderate negative cyclical forces resulted generally only in a considerable slowdown in the rate of wage increase.

For the interwar period as a whole, money wage rates have tended to rise more slowly than output per man-hour, a development that was clearly reversed during the postwar period. A considerable decline in living costs from 1920 to 1937 and a substantial rise from 1948 to 1964 were generally connected with these contrasting trends.

6. In trying to compare interwar and postwar unemployment rates derived from customary sources, one is likely to note a much higher variability of interwar rates in connection with the much more severe output fluctuations of that period and to be perplexed by, in general, much higher interwar rates even in relatively prosperous years. Let us discuss the latter point first.

According to well-known sources, unemployment rates above 10 per cent seem to have been the rule rather than the exception even in the 1920s in some European countries.[5] However, the data refer only to a part of the labor force that

4. For a presentation and analysis of cyclical wage developments in the interwar period in Germany, the United States, and Great Britain, see Gerhard Bry, *Wages in Germany 1871–1950* (National Bureau of Economic Research [NBER hereafter], Princeton, 1960), especially pp. 290–94.

5. See for example, Ingvar Svennilson, *Growth and Stagnation of the European Economy* (United Nations Economic Commission for Europe, Geneva, 1954), p. 31; Walter Galenson and Arnold Zellner, "International Comparison of Unemployment Rates" in *The Measurement and Behavior of Unemployment* (NBER, Princeton, 1957).

has a much higher unemployment risk than the labor force as a whole, including employers and self-employed. Postwar unemployment statistics are usually much more comprehensive; a direct comparison between the data for the two periods is therefore not very meaningful. There are, however, some recent studies in which a standardization of unemployment rates around a uniform and comprehensive concept was attempted.[6] Whereas in general only relatively small adjustments were considered necessary for a standardization of postwar national data, the interwar figures were in several cases scaled down rather drastically in order to achieve approximate intertemporal and international comparability.[7] According to Table 2.3, the 1920s do not stand out as a decade of such severe unemployment except in the case of the United Kingdom. For the United States the "degree of full employment" should have been as high in the 1920s as in the 1950s. However, these calculations for the interwar decades are uncertain within wide margins and, in particular for the 1920s, probably considerably downward-biased.[8] Nevertheless, for the 1930s high average levels remain even after the large downward adjustments.

6. President's Committee to Appraise Employment and Unemployment Statistics, *Measuring Employment and Unemployment* (Washington, D.C., 1962), Chap. 10 and Appendix A; Angus Maddison, "Economic Growth in Western Europe 1870–1957," *Banca Nazionale del Lavoro Quarterly Review* (March 1959); Angus Maddison, *Economic Growth in the West* (New York and London, 1964), Appendix E. The first-mentioned study is relevant for the postwar period; the others provide adjustments for both the postwar and the interwar period.

7. The quoted attempts at standardization of historical unemployment rate statistics deserve praise for tackling an important and difficult problem. However, at least with regard to the interwar period, both the methods applied and the results obtained warrant a skeptical attitude which only a more intensive study can clear up.

8. An unpublished study made by F. Ettlin on the basis of the Swedish unemployment census of 1936 reported trade union unemployment rates and other evidence suggests unemployment rates for the 1920s which are at least 30 to 50 per cent higher than those given in Table 2.5.

TABLE 2.3

Average Unemployment Levels 1921–29, 1930–38, and 1950–60. According to "Standardized" Data[a]
(Average Unemployment Rates Among Industrial Workers[b] in Parentheses)

	Average 1921–29	Average 1930–38	Average 1950–60
Belgium	1.5 (2.3)	8.7 (14.0)	5.3
Denmark	4.5 (17.1)	6.6 (21.9)	4.3
Germany	4.1 (9.3)	8.8 (21.8)	4.1
Italy		4.8	7.9
Netherlands	2.4 (8.3)	8.7 (21.9)	1.9
Sweden	3.4 (14.2)	5.6 (15.8)	1.7
Switzerland		3.0	0.2
United Kingdom	6.8 (12.1)	9.8 (16.5)	2.5
Canada	3.5 (5.5)	13.3 (18.6)	4.5
United States	4.9	18.2	4.5

a. Angus Maddison, *Economic Growth in the West* (New York and London, 1964), Appendix Table E-1, p. 220.

b. Walter Galenson and Arnold Zellner, "International Comparison of Unemployment Rates" in *The Measurement and Behavior of Unemployment* (NBER, Princeton, 1957), pp. 455–56.

As far as the cyclical variability of annual unemployment rates is concerned, the shocking increases that occurred in connection with the Great Depression exceeded 10 per cent of the total labor force in six out of ten countries for which we have presumably comparable data. In the United States the increase even exceeded 20 per cent. Most countries had experienced a sharp rise in unemployment around 1921 which by far exceeded any increases after World War II. The rise in annual unemployment rates in connection with postwar recessions exceeded some 2½ per cent only in one instance and was usually around 1 per cent or below.

7. The interwar stagnation tendencies in European countries have been persuasively related to the economic disorganization, dislocation, and postponed adaptation to fundamental changes caused by the First World War and the consequent peace settlements.[9] Although Svennilson admits

9. Ingvar Svennilson, *Growth and Stagnation,* esp. pp. 16–52.

that an insufficient level of aggregate demand may be part of the reason for the slow recovery after the First World War, he puts the weight of his argument on the faulty and sticky distribution of resources in relation to the changed distribution of actual and potential demand at home and abroad, which resulted in overcapacity problems in a number of traditional European key industries, in particular, coal mining, steel, shipbuilding, and cotton textiles. The troubles in the coal mining industry were partly the result of stagnating demand due to technical substitution, mainly by oil and hydroelectricity, and partly the result of the relative stagnation of a number of industries that were heavy coal consumers: steel production, shipping, and textiles. The overcapacity problems of the European steel industry in the 1920s can be seen as a consequence of the wartime expansion of the steel industry in some countries, the construction of new plant to compensate for losses through territorial changes, and the resistance by private industry to reduce the number of local units when the optimal plant size was growing. Wartime building of ships had resulted in a large increase in the world merchant fleet. This increase in the size of the fleet in combination with the slow expansion of international trade in the 1920s relative to the prewar level meant that the freight market was weak and the demand for new ships low. The resulting overcapacity problems of the European shipyards were compounded by the sharp drop-off in the demand for warships. The overcapacity problems in the cotton textile industry were primarily a British phenomenon. Britain had lost a large part of its traditional overseas markets as a consequence of the war, which had stimulated a rapid development of overseas sources of supply.

It is easy to agree that trouble spots of this nature have strongly influenced the growth record of the 1920s and contributed to the sensitive European response to the United States depression. However, it should be observed that worse disorganization and dislocation problems existed again after the Second World War. Apparently, this time they were resolved rather smoothly and rapidly.

Problems of overcapacity and of sick industries were much more common occurrences in the interwar years than in the period since 1945, which was, instead, characterized by problems of bottleneck and even general inadequacy of capacity. Of course, problems of the latter type were not entirely unknown even in the earlier period, but in most countries there seems to have been only one instance, around 1919–20, when they presented a strong and truly pervasive phenomenon. Similarly, there were some experiences of excess capacity and of industries in serious trouble also in the postwar period. For example, industries in North America started to suffer from rather widespread though limited surplus capacity around 1956–57; the coal industry both in Europe and in America has for several years been faced with unfavorable trends in demand; and the steel industry and paper and pulp industry were confronted, from the late fifties onward, with the effects of overexpansion. And yet, except in connection with the brief and relatively mild recessions, such phenomena have in the postwar period either been too sporadic or too weak to seriously affect the forces of strong, pervasive, and continued expansion. During the first interwar decade overcapacity and sick industries appear to have presented serious problems in countries other than the United Kingdom, even though these questions became most widely discussed there. But the fundamental difference between the interwar and postwar period relates, of course, to the 1930s.

8. The extent to which the international dislocations of production and trade that followed the world wars implied serious disturbances of economic developments depended partly on the conditions of the systems of international exchange and finance. The first interwar years, characterized by inflation, devaluations, and deflation, enforced belief in the good stabilizing powers of the old gold standard rules. Much has been written about the failures of the gold and gold exchange standards during the period 1924–31, for example how and why the new exchange parities meant gold flows

mainly concentrated to the United States and France, accompanied by deflationary tendencies instead of expansionary impulses in the gold receiving countries.[10] Again, however, we can maintain that it was not mainly an international currency system with fixed exchange rates that was "creating" instability in the form of deflationary tendencies. During the postwar period a system with mainly fixed exchange rates has been functioning fairly well, in particular if we disregard the persistent inflationary conditions. The blame, therefore, should instead be laid on the unstable international financial conditions that existed during the interwar period, and to quite inadequate government policies (discussed under 10).

By desisting from huge reparations claims and by granting large gifts and long-term loans—of which Marshall Plan aid is a telling example—the United States government contributed strongly to the reconstruction of a prosperous and resistent world economy after World War II. Off-shore purchases and other expenditures abroad in connection with the continued maintenance of large military contingents in Europe and the Far East, particularly during the Korean war, further enhanced this effect. The United States government had made very substantial loans also in 1919 and 1920, but during the 1920s it was the flow of private capital from the United States that not only enlivened the pace of recovery and development in the European economy but also stimulated development in other areas of the world. In 1927 and 1928 about one fifth of the supply of dollars was provided by private capital outflow.[11] Unfortunately, this turned out only to be a fair-weather method for balancing the international accounts. In time of disruption there was nothing to prevent

10. Still the best survey and analysis of the exchange developments and policies during the interwar period is Ragnar Nurkse, *International Currency Experiences* (League of Nations, Geneva, 1944).

11. Hal B. Lary and Associates, *The United States in the World Economy* (Washington, D.C., 1943), p. 174.

the large capital movement from eventually being reduced, stopped, and reversed. Curtailment of United States private net foreign investment started in 1929 in connection with the New York stock market boom. The violent turndown in the economic activity of the United States, its immediate impact on the internal and external liquidity of debtor countries, particularly agricultural ones, and the consequent increased risk of default, financial insecurity, and crises in America and in Europe, resulted in a rapid dwindling of the capital outflow from the United States. The further worsening of the economic situation in the rest of the world, which was partly the result of the said reduction in the outflow of capital from the United States, finally resulted in a reverse flow of capital into the United States.

The post World War II net flow of capital from the United States, as was the case in the 1920s, helped to promote world prosperity, but thanks to its lesser importance for the supply of dollars in the postwar period and to the absence of severe deflationary shocks on the world economy, there has not been—and is not likely to be—anything like the catastrophic reversal of the 1930s. In the postwar period there have certainly been instances of destabilizing private capital movements; in particular the situation of the pound sterling has repeatedly been aggravated by exchange speculation. In other instances, it is more difficult to judge the stability impact of capital movements as, for example, with regard to the large capital movements into Germany and Switzerland.

International financial cooperation during the postwar period—not least between the central banks of the various countries—has been supported by relatively stable national credit systems. During the postwar period there have been no financial crises or panics of the kind that occurred after the 1929 debacle, when the credit system, especially in the United States but also in other countries, functioned in a destabilizing way, giving active support to the cumulative deflationary processes. Of course, the differences in this respect between the periods are closely interrelated with the government policies carried out. (See point 10.)

9. Postwar government activity contrasts with the interwar background not only in regard to the goals and the range and precision of instruments of economic policy aspects, which are discussed below, but very importantly also in regard to the relative scale of government financial operations. Even more than in 1914–18, the world war of 1939–45 brought a very large increase in the public sector within the economy, which was only partly reversed after the end of hostilities. The average share of government expenditures on goods and services, exclusive of public enterprise investment, has risen from around 10 to 14 per cent during 1920–38 to around 16 to 20 per cent during 1948–58. Concurrently, there was also a large rise in government transfer expenditures. The average ratio of tax receipts to GNP has risen from about 12 to 21 per cent in the interwar period to some 24 to 35 per cent in the postwar period. The larger share of government purchases of goods and services has directly tended to promote greater stability of GNP and resistance of GNP to fluctuations in private investment. The larger relative importance of taxes and transfer payments have indirectly promoted greater GNP stability via the stabilization of consumer incomes.

10. The last and perhaps most important point of difference between the interwar and the postwar period which we choose to list concerns the role of government economic policy. The goals of economic policy and the ability to implement them have changed fundamentally.

In the postwar period, the achievement of full employment and rapid economic growth have become a primary concern and responsibility of national governments. Such policy targets certainly did not—nor were they expected to—guide government activities during most of the interwar period. Instead, particularly in the 1920s and the crucial first years of the following decade, there were various policy aims that today would largely be considered as either intermediate, secondary, irrelevant, or irrational targets, such as the restoration or preservation of a specific exchange rate, the annual balancing of the government budget, and the stability of the price level at a prevailing or a previously reached niveau. True, during and after the calamities of the Great Depression other aims for economic policy gained in importance. First, there were the basically passive and as such still terribly inadequate efforts to reduce the plight of the unemployed. Later, the creation of employment and the establishment or improvement of various social security programs signified the beginning of a more active government approach with regard to the problems of economic stability and security. Unfortunately, even at this late stage such action tended to be tardy and inadequate, until rising military expenditures and other preparations for war provided a strong stimulus to the economies of a number of countries.

The tardiness with which the achievement of higher and finally full employment became accepted as a government responsibility, and the first government efforts to implement such a goal, must in part be blamed on the economic profession. Economists, with too few exceptions, had for too long shown a lack of awareness of or concern for the existence and the problems of unemployment. When finally the disaster of the Great Depression made even blind men see unemployment as a serious economic and social problem, and the previous doctrinal faith in the speed and strength of self-adjusting processes was finally shaken, not only did traditional economic theories and advice prove utterly inadequate or even wrong, but it took time for more adequate theories and their policy implications to be developed and to become sufficiently accepted and understood by economists, politicians, and the public. Actually, the needed fundamental change in opinion and attitude took hold, in most countries, only during World War II and the first years thereafter. Since then policy theories have been generally based on Keynesian economics, the term being used in a very broad sense to include all types of analysis focusing on the size and development of total demand.[12] At the same time we have become accustomed to the application, with varying degrees of sophistication and success, of a much wider and still growing range of stabilization policy instruments.

In comparison with the postwar set of policy instruments, the official tools of the interwar period seem to have been much less advanced and were utilized with less foresight and skill. During the 1920s, the discount rate was generally the central tool of stabilization efforts, and in most countries it was applied roughly in accordance with the automatic signal system of the traditional gold standard. Efforts in the direction of a more active monetary policy appeared first in the United States; in fact monetary policy was regarded as quite successful in controlling business cycles during the 1920s.[13] In most other countries the scope for more independent monetary action remained limited for another decade. The gold sterilization policy in the United States—and also since 1928 in France—meant deflationary pressure and little room for the independent monetary policies of other countries.[14] Disappointment with the working of monetary policy from 1929 on was so great that out of the bad experiences of the 1930s came the doctrine of the inefficiency of monetary policy that lasted up to the beginning of the 1950s.

Something similar to systematic fiscal policy, in the postwar

12. For example, the policy debate in Sweden during the 1930s had its origin in the writings of Knut Wicksell rather than in Keynes' *General Theory*.

13. For a summary of the discussion see, for instance, Chapter 6 of Milton Friedman and Anna Jacobson Schwartz, *A Monetary History of the United States, 1867–1960* (NBER, Princeton, 1963).

14. In fact, as Ragnar Nurkse has shown in *International Currency Experiences,* Chap. 4, there was nothing automatic about the mechanism envisaged in the gold standard rules of the game. There was instead an automatic tendency of neutralizing the effects on the monetary systems arising from the gold flows, so that rather an active policy was needed to establish offsetting reactions.

sense, hardly existed even in theory. But, of course, there was a lot of fiscal policy action in the passive and largely perverse form of adjusting expenditures and tax rates in order to reach or approximate some balance of the budget. Fiscal deficits were usually conceded most reluctantly only under the pressure of circumstances. The emergencies of the 1930s also led to changes in the exchange rates, which for a number of countries was an effective yet hardly voluntary measure. The devaluation of the United States dollar, for which there was little justification, later reduced the efficacy of this tool by causing the devaluation movement to become general. In the 1930s, frequent recourse was also taken to import restrictions and exchange control—measures which in the postwar period generally came into disfavor. Government tactics in favor of wage and salary cuts during depressions did not reemerge after the war. On the other hand, the latter period witnessed an increased government concern with the inflationary consequences of wage and salary increases.

The change in the opinions and attitudes among economists and politicians with regard to the problems of cyclical instability was reflected not only in the aims and instruments of economic policy. It was accompanied also by improvements in the assessment of the economic situation and of the potential or actual impact of government measures—both also prerequisites for successful policy action.

A beneficial mutual interaction between improvements in the production and evaluation of economic statistics on one side and the development and refinement of economic theory on the other started in the 1930s. The number of government and private institutes with resources for observing and analyzing current economic trends rose considerably. But only during the Second World War and the first years thereafter did it become common to compile and utilize comprehensive national accounts as a basis for the assessment of the current and near-future state of the economy and for the necessity of policy intervention. Nowadays, we have become so accustomed to the use of gap analysis and national budgets in order to get some notions of the interdependence and the relative size of relevant factors that we have nearly forgotten the primitive ways of the 1920s. At that time, there was hardly any direct reference, except by a few people considered as "cranks," to total demand as a strategic factor in explaining overcapacity, unemployment, deflation, or inflation. The policy debate—both among politicians and economists—mostly turned around the price level and wage formation problems.[15] Disequilibriums in price and wage relations within and between countries caused by monopolies and labor unions were considered as the main factors explaining maladjustments in production developments, too high or too low profits, and balance of payments disequilibriums. There were, however, also some more sophisticated references regarding the effects of changes in monetary policy on prices and international capital movements, the effects on the price level being considered by means of various versions of the quantity theory.

In later chapters describing and analyzing postwar growth and instability it will be necessary to devote a great deal of attention to the role of government—including that of the central bank. It is a major problem to determine to what extent government measures—with and without stabilization intent—are to be given credit for the higher degree of stability in the postwar period. After all, there had also been a lot of policy action with stabilization aims in the interwar period. For example, the deflationary policies carried out in a number of countries in the 1920s, the budget pruning resorted to during recession in the interests of "confidence and the soundness of public finance and of the currency," and the exchange rate

15. For example, in the United Kingdom the restoration of the pre-World War I price level and exchange rate by deflationary monetary policy, and with high unemployment sometimes accepted as a means, was seriously advocated by highly reputable economists. See Keith Hancock, "Unemployment and the Economists in the 1920s," *Economica* (November 1960).

variations adopted in the 1930s were all important policy measures with a strong impact not only on the economies directly concerned. But it can very plausibly be maintained, at least from a relatively enlightened postwar point of view, that the measures taken were more inappropriate, more badly timed, or more obviously wrong than most measures of similar importance adopted in the postwar period.

Finally, the dynamic setting of the two periods should not be forgotten: the postwar period came *after* the interwar period, which through its deeply frustrating experiences promoted radical changes in the aims and means of economic policy. The clearest manifestation of this metamorphosis in attitude was the announcement of full employment goals by a number of governments during the last years of World War II and the first years thereafter. At the same time, there existed—unlike the 1920s—no superstitious ambitions of any importance in favor of returning to some prewar price level or exchange parity. In general, there was no temptation to look back upon the prewar conditions as an ideal to be reattained in contrast to the climate of opinion that had dominated economic thinking and government policy in the 1920s. Whereas the return to pre-World War I normalcy had been a widespread expectation among businessmen far into the 1920s, after World War II prewar (interwar) conditions were not remembered at all as good old times—except perhaps by small groups of high-income taxpayers.

SOME QUESTIONS CONCERNING THE FUNDAMENTAL BEHAVIOR WITHIN THE PRIVATE SECTOR OF THE ECONOMY

In the preceding, we have stressed differences rather than similarities in important features between interwar and postwar economic life. Primarily, the differences pointed out were of two kinds: changes in the pace and instability of actual economic development, and changes in the economic role of government. As far as behavior patterns *within* the private sector of the economy are concerned, similarities rather than differences between the interwar and postwar period seem in a general sense to predominate. It can be argued that the basic mechanisms of response by producers and consumers have remained about the same, while the outside conditions to which producers, dealers, and consumers respond have been quite dissimilar during the two periods. It appears that such fundamental factors as profit motives, competitive conditions, price formation, investment decisions, and financing should have been occurring along broadly unchanged patterns. The reaction of households with regard to the disposal of their incomes appear also to have undergone little change, except for periods of rationing.

It has to be admitted, however, that such statements have largely to be impressionistic rather than based upon well-founded investigations. But such investigations as do exist (they mostly refer to the United States) on the whole support our contention. We might derive some support from the fact, for example, that Klein and Goldberger, with regard to the United States economy, and the Central Planning Agency of the Netherlands, with regard to the Dutch economy, have based the coefficients of their original postwar econometric forecasting and policy models largely on interwar data. Since statistical data are not very adequate, particularly for the earlier period, even a better exploitation and evaluation of the available material will hardly succeed in determining convincingly if the consumption and investment functions, which are fundamental parts of any relevant conception of a conjuncture mechanism, have changed significantly since the interwar years. This difficulty is enhanced by the fact that even with regard to postwar data none of a number of competing hypotheses on investment behavior has yet proved to be truly satisfactory.

The issues involved here ultimately refer to the kind of business cycle models that seem adequate for explaining the cyclical behavior of the economies during the two periods. If we disregard the public sector, including the policy changes, the pertinent question is, can we use the same basic model in accounting for the main instability experiences of both periods? If the answer is yes, it would imply that fundamental properties of the private sector of the capitalist market economies have remained unchanged, that *potentially* the fluctuations could have been as big during the postwar period as during 1919–39, and that the much better performance of the economies after the Second World War should be explained by outside factors and conditions, such as stabilizing effects of the larger government sector and active stabilization policies. It is sad that we cannot give clear-cut answers to such a question; we can only assert that there might be a good deal of truth in the suggestion, and then discuss why the evidence is not sufficiently clear and significant.

The first problem concerns the meaning of the proposition that the same basic model can be successfully applied to the two periods. The simplest claim is that the models to be applied at least *qualitatively* contain the same type of relations. In a general way we can, for instance, maintain that the cyclical changes in both periods have in the main been due to variations in total demand; changes in the price level concurrent with the total volume changes may be taken as good enough evidence.[16] Supply conditions may in both periods be taken into account by introducing ceiling restrictions during some of the boom periods. In order to explain demand variations there is the same necessity with regard to both periods to distinguish between private consumption and investment demand. It is possible to apply consumption functions and use multiplier approaches. Concerning investment, there is the same need to distinguish between fixed business investment, residential construction, and inventory changes. At the side of these basic demand functions, that give the main structure of

16. See R. C. O. Matthews, *The Trade Cycle* (Cambridge, 1959), Chap. 1.

the model, we have in both periods to pay attention to balance of payments reactions and price-wage determination. Especially with regard to the monetary factors (that is changes in interest rates, money supply, bank advances) we seem to have the same type of questions for both periods: what role in specific phases of the cycle have the partly endogenous changes of these variables played? As will be discussed in various parts of this book, the problem has a position of "strategic uncertainty" during both periods in most of the countries studied.

We certainly move on a very high level of abstraction when we try to isolate "a pure mechanism" of the private economy, separating it from changes in the surrounding conditions, in particular from the much higher degree of government influence and from a strongly changed set of international relations during the postwar period. As discussed in the following chapters, the postwar cyclical changes in production and demand may in several countries seem to be so closely determined by the frequent policy reactions of the government that there will not be much chance for the behavior patterns of the "pure system" to show their character before new government disturbances occur. Especially, the postwar downward movements of incomes, profits, consumption, and investments have been neither deep enough nor sufficiently prolonged to give us a fair chance to determine whether there would be significant differences in behavior patterns in response to "outside" conditions that are much more unfavorable and thus more comparable to the "outside" conditions that characterized the severe setbacks in the 1920s and 1930s. The relatively passive and unsuccessful government policies during the interwar period permit us to study contraction movements in the private sector that not only ranged much more widely but presumably also are freer from outside interference. But with regard to the opposite end of the cyclical range, the postwar developments of many countries offer us better opportunities to study the behavior patterns of the private economy around and above full use of capacities—although, again, the reactions are heavily disturbed by government policy actions. The interwar experiences offer corresponding evidence only to a very modest extent; only the very specific conditions during the 1920 boom give some evidence, but even that does not seem to be very helpful. We are not quite sure, however, if the absence of full-employment booms (except possibly for 1920) during the interwar period should be explained by intrinsic characteristics of the capitalist system, that can be accounted for by a business cycle model, or should be partly explained by restrictive monetary policies (especially in the United States) or by other outside influences (for instance decline of exports for Western European countries). To these difficulties of interpretation we have to add the poor state of statistics concerning the interwar period that makes direct comparisons with the postwar period uncertain within wide limits.

Having mentioned some of the difficulties of an attempt to compare the interwar and postwar "cyclical mechanisms," we intend merely to offer some simple observations about the strategic relations in question. This is done only to mark out and emphasize some interesting problems in model construction that ought to be discussed. The discussion mainly refers to United States experiences, where we find the best statistics and perhaps also the least degree of policy disturbances. The conclusions are mostly left open. The main emphasis in the following sections is instead put on a discussion of the changing conditions for the working of the business economies.

The most strategic relations of a business cycle model refer to *investment demand*. With regard to our problem in this section, it is quite fatal that our knowledge of the interwar period is in this respect very imperfect. It matters a lot for the properties of the model if we put the emphasis on past and current business profits or use various forms of the acceleration principle [or the capital stock adjustment process] in order to account for the variations in business *fixed investments*. The available yearly statistics are too blunt to give enough guidance for a choice. The relative importance of interest rates and credit availability can be given varying weights without statistical inference offering enough of a guiding hand in the search for the most correct of a number of plausible interpretations.

In this connection, it may be instructive to have a brief look at some econometric models of the United States.[17] Tinbergen, in his pioneering model for the period 1919–32, and Klein and Goldberger, in their model for the years 1929–41 and 1946–52, relied heavily on profits for explaining investment variations. It is lagged profits (the lag of investments behind profits is half a year in Tinbergen's model and one year in the model of Klein and Goldberger) that seem to present the chief explanatory variable of changes in investment in plant and equipment. But upon closer inspection it appears that these relationships mainly show the close parallel movement of current profits and investment. Klein and Goldberger's investment equation misses practically every turning point by one year, and Tinbergen, whose equation was more successful with regard to turning points, introduced current profits by the back door since he derived his profits series by averaging the profits of the current and the previous year.

The equations, in fact, do not represent much more than the well-known tendency of profits to be high when investment is high or low when investment is low; they can hardly be said to provide a valid explanation of investment fluctuations.

The investment functions applied to the interwar experiences seem very primitive in comparison to some of the sophisticated approaches used to account for the postwar developments. Of course this does not mean that there are corresponding differences in behavior mechanisms. We simply observe the progress in econometric research in combination with great improvements in the availability and the quality of economic

17. Jan Tinbergen, *Business Cycles in the United States of America, 1919–1932* (League of Nations, Geneva, 1939); L. R. Klein and A. S. Goldberger, *An Econometric Model of the United States, 1929–1952* (Amsterdam, 1955).

statistics. But there does not seem to be enough evidence and analysis to judge if there is a significant difference in the business investment behavior between the interwar and postwar periods.

Since for most countries other than the United States fairly comprehensive data on *inventory investment* during the interwar period are nonexistent—even postwar movements in many European countries are still largely derived by the unsatisfactory residual method—it would be even more difficult to prove if the determination of inventory investment has fundamentally changed since the time before World War II. The average inventory-sales ratio in the United States has declined since the interwar period, and there is some evidence of a similar development in some European countries, too. The decline can be considered a consequnce of faster communication and transportation and the adoption of better inventory management techniques. But, as the example of the United States demonstrates, this downward shift does not necessarily imply more cyclical stability of inventory investment, particularly as the proportion of inventories held by the durable goods sector has increased since the interwar period. We may observe, however, that whereas the average reference cycle pattern of inventory investment relative to GNP in the United States shows a lag at the turning points of the earlier period, this lag no longer appears in the corresponding pattern of the postwar period.[18] Instead, there appears a fast rebound in the early stages of expansion, followed by a slight decline to the reference peak, and a fast decline thereafter; but the relative amplitude seems, according to Gordon, to be of about the same size during the minor cycles of the 1920s as during the postwar period. It is still uncertain, however, if the differing pattern reflects a change in the reaction mechanism or if it is due to special factors, in particular the Korean war experience. As

18. R. A. Gordon, *Business Fluctuations* (2nd ed. New York, 1961), p. 281.

far as the sharp rise and consequent fall of inventory investment during 1950–52 is concerned, it can be considered typical business behavior in response to a sudden acceleration of basic material prices; in this respect the 1950–52 development was rather similar to the interwar experiences during 1919–22 and 1936–38. It is important to remember that the character of inventory-changes during the cycles—and this especially refers to purchased materials—very much depends on current and expected supply conditions,[19] implying another and smoother development during the expansions of 1954–57 and after 1961 than during the earlier postwar booms. It should also be kept in mind that statistics of realized inventory changes tend to underestimate the contribution to instability from this source.

In North America and a number of European countries, including France and Germany, investment in *residential construction* fluctuated much more during the interwar period than after World War II. With the exception of the United States, the greater instability refers to the years of the Great Depression only. To judge from the indicators of residential construction, it would seem difficult to point out general changes in the overt pattern between interwar and postwar minor recessions. However, it seems—judging from the average reference cycle patterns—that in the postwar period residential building in the United States has turned up earlier in the recessions and also turned down earlier during the expansions than during the cycles of the 1920s.[20] With regard to the major fluctuations, the big United States wave is in sharp contrast to the development in the United Kingdom, Sweden, and Norway. In a country like Sweden there was no real setback in residential construction in connection with the 1929 crisis; on the contrary a boom occurred in 1930–31, and the interruption in 1932–33 was mainly due to a big building strike,

19. Thomas Stanback, *Postwar Cycles in Manufacturers' Inventories* (NBER, Princeton, 1962), puts special emphasis on the importance of the development of unfilled orders. See especially Chap. 8.

20. See Gordon, *Business Fluctuations,* p. 275.

which was followed by a rapid expansion during the rest of the 1930s, largely the result of expansionary policies and low interest rates. Again we find a contrast with such countries as France, Holland, and Denmark, where deflationary policies and exchange restrictions implied stagnation on a low level of residential construction during the 1930s.

During the postwar period, the underlying atmosphere with regard to the market for new housing has fundamentally changed. Particularly in European countries, the postwar years were characterized by a persistent shortage of housing on the one side and virtual government regulation of the volume of housebuilding by various kinds of financial supports on the other.[21] The minor setbacks that have occurred in residential construction—partly only in the form of a slowing down in the rate of expansion—can be directly attributed to restrictive policy measures. Also in the United States, the contrast in the underlying conditions for dwelling construction is large between the interwar and the postwar period. The tremendous decline of residential construction in the earlier period seems to have been relatively independent of general business conditions at least up to 1929. There occurred a growing surplus of new dwelling units over new household formation from the mid-1920s to the mid-1930s in spite of an extreme concurrent decline in the number of new dwelling units started. This meant that investment opportunities for residential construction were very unfavorable. Later the atmosphere was greatly improved,

21. The percentage of new dwellings for which public financial assistance was granted ranged between 50 and almost 100 per cent in most European countries around the mid-1950s. At the same time the percentage of housing expenditure financed from public funds amounted from 28 to 75 per cent. Among the countries of Western Europe covered in this study, only in Switzerland and Italy was public finance for housing much less important. See the United Nations Economic Commission for Europe, *Financing of Housing in Europe* (Geneva, 1958).

when in the decade of the 1940s a very large surplus of new households over new dwelling units accumulated, which in spite of the high construction rates in the following decade still amounted to some three million units at the beginning of the 1960s.[22] Furthermore, even if investment opportunities for residential construction would once more become unfavorable, much of the interwar debacle would not recur because of the improved financial structure, built on the fully amortized government-insured and government-guaranteed mortgages.

Since in Europe, interwar data on total *consumer expenditures* and disposable income exist for only a few countries, it is not easy to make empirical generalizations regarding consumption behavior during that period. Inspection of the available statistics suggests that the concept of a stable and passive Keynesian consumption function has only limited validity in explaining the actual changes in consumption which are associated with short-period changes in income. In the United States, consumption has tended to vary in a relatively stabilizing manner during both interwar and postwar cyclical setbacks. When GNP fell, consumption either continued to grow or declined less, and when GNP advanced unusually slowly, consumption advanced faster. When comparing the interwar and postwar periods there is no clear indication of higher or lower short-term stability in private consumption during the minor recessions.[23] The stabilizing pattern of private consumption derives partly from the action of automatic stabilizers on disposable income and partly from a reluctance to reduce consumption standards in the face of short-run declines in per capita disposable income. It may be generally true— as seems

22. Bert G. Hickman, *Growth and Stability of the Postwar Economy* (The Brookings Institution, Washington, D.C., 1961), p. 314 (diagram).

23. For United States data on the relationship between changes in GNP and disposable personal income during interwar and postwar years of minor recession, see Hickman, Table 38, p. 230.

to be the case with regard to the United States economy[24]—that disposable income has become more stable in relation to GNP; that is it rises and declines less for a given change in GNP during the postwar period than in the interwar period. This effect seems mainly to be due to higher marginal tax rates as well as to the greater importance of transfer payments in general, including a more generous response of unemployment compensation during recessions. The stabilizing effects on consumption of gross business profits should be about unchanged when comparing the 1920s with the postwar period. The dampening effect of (retained) profits seems to be especially important during short recessions, when employment and labor costs are only moderately affected and business profits will act as the main shock absorber.

In a major depression such a shock absorber will not work effectively; employment, wages, and so on will have to be adjusted downward with the declining profits, and the multiplier effects will be larger. That was what happened in many countries during the post-1929 depression.

It is not surprising that for the depression-torn 1930s the usual type of regression between levels of consumption and disposable income should result in a lower slope than for the more prosperous 1920s or 1950s. Since the lowering of the slope of the consumption function was accompanied by an upward shift of the function's intercept, it would be misleading to talk about a destabilizing (autonomous) shift of the consumption function during the 1930s. United States consump-

24. Gordon, *Business Fluctuations,* p. 99, arrived at the following regression functions between annual consumption expenditures and disposable income (both variables expressed in 1954 dollars):

$$1929\text{–}40: C = 20.7 + .80\, Y_d$$
$$1948\text{–}57: C = 10.5 + .89\, Y_d$$

Hickman, *Growth and Stability,* p. 224, on the basis of undeflated data, came to the following results for the 1920s and the postwar period:

$$1921\text{–}29: C = 2.3 + .93\, Y_d$$
$$1947\text{–}58: C = 12.8 + .88\, Y_d$$

tion expenditures in the depressed 1930s were in fact much higher than at the corresponding levels of GNP and disposable income in the prosperous 1920s, and thus had a stabilizing impact on aggregate demand. Of course, extrapolation of the regression line for the 1930s beyond the 1929 level of income would suggest a decline of consumption compared with the levels corresponding to an extrapolation of the regression line for the 1920s. But the clockwise shift around the 1929 observation was hardly an independent shift; if "autonomous" expenditure on investments and by government had continued to grow beyond the 1929 peak level, then most likely consumption would have approached levels indicated by the extrapolation of the regression line for the 1920s.

In the case of the few European countries for which we have interwar data on consumption expenditures, stabilizing shifts in consumption during years of depression are also observable. The characteristics of consumer behavior in minor recessions will be discussed in the next chapter.

The behavior of aggregate consumption in Germany in connection with the large decline of GNP and disposable income between 1928–29 and 1932 could also be interpreted as a stabilizing clockwise shift around the peak income level, although it is more difficult than in the case of the United States to indicate quantitatively the extent of the shift since the data are available only from 1925 on, and for the first two years the consumption ratio was exceptionally low, probably still in consequence to the previous hyperinflation.[25]

The *volumes of exports and imports* have usually fluctuated more widely than GNP during both the interwar and the postwar period. Foreign trade represents both an impulse mechanism and a response mechanism, with export changes to be considered, at least in the short run, mainly as foreign-generated impulses and with import changes to be considered

25. See G. Gehrig, *Eine ökonometrische Analyse des Konsums von 1925 bis 1938 und 1950 bis 1957,* Schriftenreihe des Instituts für Wirtschaftsforschung, Nr. 52 (Berlin-München, 1963).

largely as endogenous responses of the domestic economy. The slow expansion of trade in the interwar period reflected not only the slow average pace of economic growth, but also low elasticities of import demand with regard to the growth of GNP. Among eleven countries in Europe and North America, only four had a percentage growth of imports that exceeded the growth of GNP between 1924 and 1937. In the postwar period, on the other hand, imports grew faster than GNP in each one of these eleven countries. The differential development has to be explained by the contrast in regard to capacity utilization—which was generally much lower in the earlier period—and by the increase of trade restrictions in the 1930s and the successive elimination of such restrictions in the 1950s. It is worth noting that the growth of imports in relation to the growth of GNP during the 1920s (1924–29) was roughly the same for the countries in question as during the 1950s.

TABLE 2.4

Ratios of the Percentage Growth of the Import Volume to the Percentage Growth of GNP, Interwar and Postwar Periods

	1924–29	1924–37	1950–62
Belgium			2.2
France	0.9	0.8	1.6
Germany	3.0	0.4	1.7
Italy	2.4	0.0	1.8
Netherlands	1.3	0.4	1.4
Norway	1.2	1.3	1.7
Sweden	1.8	1.5	2.1
Switzerland	0.5	0.3	1.3
United Kingdom	0.9	0.6	1.8
Western Europe	1.3	0.5	1.6
Canada	2.1	1.5	1.3
United States	2.5	1.5	1.2

CHANGES IN GENERAL CONDITIONS

No conclusive evidence about differences in the "conjuncture mechanisms" as between the interwar and postwar periods can be reached from the discussion in the previous section. Though we can expect some differences in the investment and consumption functions, we could only in a rather unprecise way discuss the existence of systematic deviations even if we would consider only the relatively well-documented United States experiences. This inability can be explained not only by referring to the previously mentioned difficulties, but also by referring to the possibility of significantly differing mechanisms being relevant for the cycles within each of our periods. There are likely to be greater differences between the appropriate model structures for the cycles of 1919–21 and 1927–33 than between the minor fluctuations during the 1920s and the ones during the period 1948–64. Because average behavior patterns are the basis of econometric analysis, they must necessarily conceal interesting characteristics of the various cycle—as well as the successive transformation of the structures over a period of time. As pointed out before, a one-way learning process is proceeding all the time, and only in a very approximate way do "pure" phenomena of repetition seem to exist.

From this point of view the study of certain features of the conjunctural structure needs to be complemented by a wider discussion of *changes in general conditions* that according to our view should have influenced the instability patterns. We shall here direct our attention to two such aspects of a more institutional character that may illustrate the relevance of this type of problem. The one aspect refers to a rather mechanistic approach to the analysis of cyclical variations within the private sector. We know that the instability tends to be larger within certain sectors of the economy than within others, perhaps also that certain types of firms or organizations tend to show greater short-term stability than other types. From this point of view, a significant change in these respects of the structure of the economy from the interwar to the postwar period could matter with regard to the cyclical sensitivity. The other aspect refers to a traditional but central issue: the changing importance of price and wage formation during the business cycle. In the type of business cycle model we referred to in the previous section, price and wage developments had no explicit roles, as the investment and consumption functions were given in real terms, and prices and wages were not mentioned among the explanatory variables. There are certainly important aspects of cyclical instability that will be neglected when we abstract from price and wage changes. In any reasonable account of the current state of the business economy —referring to the interwar as well as to the postwar period —we are apt to find some emphasis laid on the relation of price to wage development, for instance with regard to effects on profit margins or international price and cost developments.[26] Our objective is to discover if there are eventually some significant indications of changes in the patterns of price and wage formation over the relevant periods.

Structural differences—We have already in the first part of this chapter briefly discussed—and dismissed—the problems of war-induced distortion and dislocation in the balance of resources between countries and industries as an essential point in the explanation of the relatively poor economic record of the interwar period. Similar developments also accompanied the Second World War, and paradoxically enough they are often quoted as an essential point in the explanation of the excellent postwar economic record of western Europe.

Various kinds of structural changes have occurred since the beginning of the interwar period. But their extent and their impact on the business cycle are usually not yet sufficiently known. Since the cyclical sensitivity of output and employment differs greatly between various sectors of an economy, differential long-term growth patterns between the more cycle-sensitive and the less cycle-sensitive sectors could conceivably have

26. Wesley C. Mitchell, in his pioneering works on the business cycle, stressed the strategic position of price relations, especially via their effects on profit margins.

altered the overall instability characteristics. Output and particularly employment in mining, manufacturing, and construction have typically fluctuated more widely than in agriculture, trade, finance, insurance, government, and personal services. Actually, the cycle-sensitive sectors have either about kept their share of the total employment since the early interwar period or increased it. Thus, in spite of the well-known tendency of the service sectors to increase in relative importance, the part of the economy that is less prone to cyclical fluctuations has in most countries either remained roughly the same or even decreased since the early interwar years. This result is due to the usually pronounced relative decline of agriculture. However, no far-reaching conclusions can be drawn as to stability-effects of such changes in the composition of big aggregates. For instance within these aggregates we have to pay attention to the rising share of durable goods that has occurred in all countries over the whole period. This shift is in itself not very dramatic: durable consumer goods have in most countries increased their relative importance by only some few percentage points of GNP since the 1920s. Indirectly, especially with reference to the holding of inventories in durable-goods industries, the impact of this shift on instability will be relatively more important. We may from another angle also consider the rising share of gross investments from the interwar to the postwar period as a structural shift that should imply higher potential instability. However, insofar as this rise largely refers to government investments or government-controlled investments, it should not imply higher cyclical sensitivity of the private sector.

Shifts in employment patterns may have a cyclical impact. The tendency for salaried or "white collar" employees to grow in numbers relative to the total number of employees, which in recent years has been observed both in American and European manufacturing, has had the consequence of somewhat reducing the impact on employment of fluctuations in demand, since salaried employees may enjoy greater job security. We can also observe a significant general tendency of higher stability of employment during the recessions in the postwar period than during the earlier periods of declining demand for workers. Entrepreneurs seem generally to be slower in their lay-off reactions during the postwar period than earlier. It is of course very difficult to judge to what extent this change in reaction patterns, which seems to be quite general, has to do with structural shift, or if it is simply to be considered a function of the full-employment experiences in the postwar period. When entrepreneurs expect reduced demand to be very temporary, expecting government full-employment policies to mean difficulties in reemploying discharged workers in a revival, then this relative employment stability should be considered a consequence of successful government policy. But potentially a setback of interwar proportions might have similar employment consequences. The distinction between cycle and structure in this respect is in fact nontestable. We might, however, assert that higher *short-term* stability in employment policies within the private sector might have stabilizing effects on income and consumption and therefore imply a built-in stabilizer that is more important now than during the interwar period.

Within industry and trade the attitudes and policies of the firms with regard to short-term instability may in some ways have been rather different in the interwar period as compared with the reactions after the war. A number of indicators as to such differences are mentioned in the discussion,[27] such as the growing importance of corporate in relation to noncorporate enterprises; the tendencies to higher degrees of concentration in various fields of business and corresponding tendencies to forms of oligopolistic and monopolistic competition. Here we meet extremely difficult problems of interpretation. Even if it were true that such tendencies exist and that in most

27. See, for instance, Arthur F. Burns, "Progress Towards Economic Stability," *American Economic Review* (March 1960).

countries there would be significant differences in this respect between the interwar and postwar periods, we cannot be certain as to the type of effects on the "conjuncture mechanism." There are some indicators of alterations in behavior patterns from the interwar to the postwar period that may be due to such changes: higher stability (or less downward flexibility) in prices and wages; greater foresight and more long-term planning in decisions on fixed investments; less speculation and more rational adjustments with regard to inventories; more general financial stability owing to a higher degree of consolidation and greater liquidity, at the same time that credit markets and institutions have shown higher degrees both of stability and flexibility.

Generalizations of the type exemplified above are easily made and may even be true in some unknown degree, but they are rather useless for understanding eventual real differences in the "conjuncture mechanisms." We have made these very general statements in order to point out essential problems that should or could be analyzed for the individual countries but about which we so far have very limited factual knowledge. One of the main difficulties is simply that we cannot easily compare the postwar and interwar "conjuncture mechanisms" under even approximately equal conditions. The pressures on the financial systems as well as on wage and price formation were so much heavier in the depressions of 1921 and the 1930s that we do not know how the postwar systems would have behaved under "equal" circumstances.

The share of total business output produced by corporations has almost certainly increased since the interwar period in most countries under review. Two major consequences of an increase in the relative size of the corporate sector concern the stability of consumer income and expenditure on the one side, and the stability of corporate cash flow and investment on the other.

The fraction of total net corporate profits distributed to the shareholders tends to vary countercyclically. This may be the result of an active policy of keeping dividend payments relatively stable, that is a conscious attempt to determine dividend payments on the basis of a longer-term concept of profits. This seems to be an important corporate policy in the United States.[28] The lesser variability of total dividend payments compared to total net profits could, however, also be the result of (proportional) dividend payments by corporations with positive net profits, and no dividend payments by corporations with negative net profits. Since even at the bottom of a deep depression many corporations still have positive profits, although total net profits for all corporations are negative, the dampening in the variation of aggregate dividends in relation to aggregate net profits would result. This explanation would agree rather well with, for example, German estimates for the years 1925–33 when dividends remained a rather steady percentage of the net income of the corporations with positive profits.[29] Even for the United States in the interwar period the second explanation seems to be much more relevant than the first explanation of an active effort to stabilize the amount of the dividend.[30]

As far as the effect on disposable income and consumer expenditure is concerned, it matters little if a given stabilizing pattern of dividend payments is itself the result of either the first or the second type of process. On the basis of the widespread practice of considering aggregate current disposable income as the main determinant of consumer expenditure, on the one side, and of counting all noncorporate business income into disposable income, on the other side, one might be tempted to conclude that the relative growth of the corporate

28. John Lintner, "Distribution of Incomes of Corporations Among Dividends, Retained Earnings and Taxes," *American Economic Review Papers and Proceedings* (May 1956).

29. See the data on the balance sheets of corporations in *Statistisches Jahrbuch für das Deutsche Reich;* various years.

30. See Neil H. Jacoby and J. Fred Weston, "Financial Policies for Regularizing Business Investment" in *Regularization of Business Investment* (NBER Conference Volume, Princeton, 1954), p. 398.

business sector promotes the stability of consumer expenditure and thus of aggregate demand. But if current consumption expenditure of noncorporate business households should to an important extent be determined by longer-term considerations, along the lines of the permanent income hypothesis,[31] then the net effect on total consumer expenditure of a relative increase of the corporate sector would be rather uncertain as to sign and probably unimportant as to its magnitude.

Changes in the relative size of the corporate sector could nevertheless still have affected the cyclical stability properties of the economy given the fact that there was an important difference with regard to fluctuations in investment between the corporate and the noncorporate business sector. For example, the countercyclical variations in the aggregate dividend-earnings ratio discussed above may imply an accentuation of the cyclical fluctuations of retained earnings and thus of internal funds available for capital formation in the corporate sector. But we have also suggested that retained earnings in the noncorporate sector, in fact, may fluctuate rather similarly, so that any net effect of a change in the relative size of the two sectors would be relatively minor. In the absence of any strong evidence to the contrary, it seems reasonable to assume that there is no important difference in investment fluctuations between the two sectors, so that even large changes in relative sector size could not have affected the instability of total business investment.[32]

31. Milton Friedman, *A Theory of the Consumption Function* (NBER, Princeton, 1957). It should perhaps be pointed out that Friedman's consumption concept differs from the usual consumption expenditure concept by including the services from the stock of consumers' durables instead of the current purchases of consumers' durables. Furthermore, we remain skeptical as to the complete unimportance of transitory income on which he insists.

32. For example, a comparison of the relative instability of fixed capital expenditures in United States manufacturing, 1915–40, showed no basic difference between small (noncorporate and corporate) firms on one side and large (corporate) firms on the other. See Millard

It appears that long-term investment planning or capital budgeting has gained in importance in the postwar period for various reasons, among them the wider adoption of improved management techniques in general, confidence in the prospects for long-term growth and in the success of government policy in avoiding deep and prolonged cyclical setbacks, and, in some countries, long-term economic "plans" initiated by the government. Long-term capital budgeting could be thought of as having a stabilizing effect on investment demand by smoothing its flow and by making investment more successful on average. However, it should be remembered that such budgeting refers only to the projection of investments and not to commitments for capital expenditure, and such plans can thus be quickly changed, not least under the impact of cyclical fluctuations. The considerable discrepancies between planned and realized investment even on a relatively short annual perspective in the United States and Sweden suggest that at least the direct stabilizing importance of investment planning might easily be exaggerated. There still remains, however, the possibility that the projections help to improve the short-term forecasts which play an important role for the determination of government stabilization policy. A major expert in the field of capital budgeting even concluded that improvements in the management of capital expenditures were more likely to accentuate cyclical fluctuations in investment than to smooth them.[33]

A closely related question refers to the shift in emphasis from profitability to liquidity and solvency considerations in the face of an expected or actual downturn in economic activity. It is impossible to determine if and to what extent such considerations have become less important since the

---

Hastey, "The Cyclical Behavior of Investment," in *Regularization of Business Investment,* pp. 20–24.

33. Joel Dean, "The Concept and Economic Significance of Regularization of Business Investment," in *Regularization of Business Investment,* pp. 52–63.

interwar period. Postwar economic setbacks have only been of a minor kind, which means not only that cyclical shifts in liquidity preferences have either been moderate or that they have been largely countered by government policy, but it also means that the business community has not really been put to a serious test.

Market Structure and Price Reactions—How have changes in the *competitive structure* of labor and commodity markets of the various countries affected the cyclical mechanism since the interwar period? Probably the best tentative answer would be that any such changes can have been of minor importance only. First of all, for most countries under review it would be rather difficult to generalize about the nature and extent of differences in the competitive structure of commodity and labor markets between the interwar and postwar period. Such operational measures as the percentage of wage and salary earners who are members of labor unions, or concentration ratios (that is measures of the percentage of an industry or a commodity market supplied by a specified number of large firms), are not necessarily good indicators of changes in the degree of competition. Furthermore, the comparison of concentration ratios between an interwar and a postwar year for a large number of manufacturing industries indicates that even the availability of concentration ratios would hardly permit a valid generalization about the overall direction of change in concentration.[34]

Rather than finding significant differences in the behavior of prices between our two periods, the general similarities might seem more apparent. For instance we find for both periods the typical scissor development of prices for finished manufactured goods in relation to the prices for raw materials and

34. See, for example, Report prepared by the Bureau of the Census for the Subcommittee on Antitrust and Monopoly, *Concentration Ratios in Manufacturing Industry 1958* (Washington, 1962), Part I, Tables 2, 2A, and 3.

primary products. There are periods both during the interwar and postwar periods when the prices of primary products were declining considerably in relation to manufactured products. The corresponding movements of the terms of trade of primary producing countries have had destabilizing effects on the balance of payments and exchange situations of these countries, with repercussions back on the export markets and conjunctures of the industrialized countries of Western Europe and America. We cannot tell if there has occurred any other change in the potential working of this mechanism than that the actual fluctuations (downward) have been much milder since 1951 than during the interwar period. Potentially this type of transmission mechanism is still as destabilizing now as previously. But of course the international financial and exchange organization provide, as pointed out above, a more powerful resistance to such disturbances than before World War II.

As far as the labor markets are concerned, changes in market power since the interwar period are more obvious and mostly point to an increased strength of labor. The greatly enhanced importance of collective bargaining in the postwar period is often considered to be such a fundamental change. In practically all countries, labor unions have become stronger through increased membership, improvements in their legal and social status, and often also through consolidation. Furthermore, the emphasis in their policy aims has partly shifted. Wage-rate reductions and slower growth of the trend in wage rates than of the trend in productivity, such as repeatedly occurred in the interwar period, would not be likely to recur even if the recessions became deeper and more prolonged. That is, of course, a hypothetical assertion only, since severe contractions have been entirely absent from the postwar scene. As far as the short and shallow recessions are concerned, the greater strength of labor may not be so significant, since even in the smaller recessions of the interwar period wage cuts were not customary (except in the United Kingdom). The cumulative processes of declining wage-price spirals during the depressions starting in 1920 and

1929 correspond in a way to the cumulative rising spirals during the postwar period. We may consider the one type of reaction pattern to be as destabilizing as the other—from the point of view of a norm of general price-level stability. It is likely that our economies on the one side contain more "built-in" resistance to downward cumulative wage-price spirals nowadays than during the interwar period, but on the other side less resistance to corresponding inflationary spirals. But again this statement is largely hypothetical—there has been no chance during the postwar period of testing the resistance of the economies to strong downward pressures. There is ground for being rather skeptical about the effects of general wage movements on internal economic stability. The pronounced changes in wage rates initiated by government in Germany (1931), the United States (1933), and France (1936–37) failed to have any noticeable effect on employment and output. These failures can be taken as confirmation of our view. It should be added that from a general stabilization point of view, downward flexibility of the wage level and price level might be a good thing—ceteris paribus—under the interwar type of deflationary conditions, when exchange rates were kept fixed. The contrasting examples of Japan on the one hand and the United Kingdom on the other illustrate this point. The wage and price levels of the first country declined quickly, apparently with a minimum of friction, in the 1920s, while this was not the case in the United Kingdom. The contrast in the expansion of exports as well as GNP between the two countries is apparent.

It is difficult to assess the importance of the strength of labor unions in boom conditions, since such experiences were frequent in the postwar period only. In fact, views are divergent as to whether strong labor unions have actively helped to push up wages[35] in times of excess demand for labor, or if they—as

35. This is, for example, the view regarding the United States taken by W. G. Bowen, *Wage Behavior in the Postwar Period: An Empirical Analysis* (Princeton, 1960).

is maintained in the Swedish discussion—have worked to hold back potential further wage claims in situations of excess demand for labor. Whereas a number of writers would explain the different behavior with regard to wage rates in the two periods by differences in the state of unemployment,[36] others, although not denying some influence of this type, have found that small changes in unemployment have had little effect on the pace at which wages increase, and that at given levels of unemployment, wages have on average gone up faster in the postwar period than in earlier years.[37]

Even if the nature and extent of changes in the competitive structure of product and factor markets were known for most industrial western countries and pointed clearly in one direction, not much would be gained for our understanding of the differences between the economic fluctuations of the interwar and postwar period. Although many economists have in the past held very strong views on the influence of the degree of competition on cyclical fluctuations,[38] professional opinion today is in general much more doubtful on that point.

W. A. Jöhr, who has made a careful theoretical analysis of the problem, came to the conclusion that any influence of

36. A. W. Phillips, "The Relation Between Unemployment and the Rate of Change of Money Wage Rates in the United Kingdom, 1861–1957," *Economica* (November 1958); R. G. Lipsey, "The Relation Between Unemployment and the Rate of Change of Money Wage Rates in the United Kingdom, 1862–1957: A Further Analysis," *Economica* (February 1960).

37. See Chap. 2 of W. G. Bowen's empirical study for the United States.

38. It was usually held that depressions may be caused, or at least considerably deepened, by restrictive market practices. For such a view, see, for example, Henry C. Simons, *A Positive Program for Laissez Faire: Some Proposals for a Liberal Economic Policy* (Chicago, 1934), p. 14. However, an opposite view was put forward by, for example, Schumpeter, who pointed to the lesser ability of a perfectly competitive industry to counter the impact of contractionary forces: Joseph A. Schumpeter, *Capitalism, Socialism, and Democracy,* 2nd ed. (London, 1943), p. 106.

market imperfections on economic fluctuations are likely to be minor on balance.[39] On the empirical side, A. C. Neal has studied the relationship between prices, costs, and concentration during the 1929–33 depression in the United States. He found little or no correlation between price declines and concentration. However, the relationship between changes in prices and in costs was very close. "Pricing in concentrated industries is based upon costs, and apparently these industries pass along lower costs for materials and labor about as well as non-concentrated industries."[40]

Actually, there is a considerable body of evidence to support the view that, in manufacturing, prices are set by reference to costs at some normal level of capacity and are not sensitive to moderate fluctuations in demand. Full cost or "target" pricing may, however, be abandoned when demand is abnormally strong or weak.[41]

Grossly neglected as a factor in economic theory but highly important in practice is adjustment to fluctuating demand by changing order books and delivery lags as an alternative to flexible prices. Under this type of cyclical adjustment, new orders in excess of the current rate of production are absorbed, first partially, and once capacity production is reached entirely, by the lengthening of order books. These order backlogs can be drawn upon to sustain production later on when new orders decline below the current rate of production. On the basis of interwar and postwar interindustry data for the United States, it has been pointed out that backlog changes may have

39. See his thorough treatise of the business cycle: W. A. Jöhr, *Die Konjunkturschwankungen: Theoretische Grundlagen der Wirtschaftspolitik,* Band II (Zürich and Tübingen, 1952), in particular Chap. 9.

40. "Pricing Aspects of Business Cycle History" in Chamber of Commerce of the United States, *Pricing Problems and the Stabilization of Prosperity* (1947), p. 37.

41. See in particular R. R. Neild, *Pricing and Employment in the Trade Cycle* (National Institute of Economic and Social Research, Cambridge, 1963), and the studies mentioned there.

a strong stabilizing effect in many industries, whereas changes in finished stocks have relatively weak stabilizing effects.[42] A similar conclusion emerges from industrial computer simulation studies.[43]

However, we cannot be quite sure even in theory that we are able to make probable that a branch of industry with many individual units in relatively effective price competition will have a more unstable output development than another branch with high concentration and an oligopolistic type of price formation. Take two simple "ideal types" as models: (A) A textile industrial branch with a great number of firms in such effective price competition that there will never arise excess or deficit demand positions; changes of prices up as well as down occur so quickly that demand and supply will be in continuous equilibrium. (B) A branch of machinery production with nearly constant prices over the cycles so that an increase of demand at full capacity level will be reflected predominantly in larger order backlogs and longer delivery times, whereas in the recession prices will be kept relatively stable.

It will be quite possible to argue that the type-A industry—under otherwise equal conditions—will have a more unstable development than B. The equilibrating mechanism of strongly fluctuating prices will tend to create destabilizing tendencies in investment and production both during the expansion and the contraction phases of the cycle. Expectations of continuing price rises will motivate purchases above current consumption and magnify the movements of ultimate consumers' demand from one stage to the next. Optimistic profit expectations may tend to give extra incentive to higher investments in stocks (at all stages) and probably also to fixed investments in enlarged plant capacity. Numerous examples can be cited both from the

42. Victor Zarnowitz, "Unfilled Orders, Price Changes, and Business Fluctuations," *Review of Economics and Statistics* (November 1962).

43. J. W. Forrester, *Industrial Dynamics* (New York and London, 1961).

interwar and postwar periods of how short-term price booms have misled producers to commit overinvestments—with following drastic declines in investment and production. Excessive inventory investments during the price inflation booms of 1919–20, 1936–37, 1950–51 are similar in type, as well as the following reactions. The declining prices after the upper turning point will tend to create a combination of increased sales pressure (to get rid of surplus stocks) and buying resistance that may be aggravated by profit declines and liquidity difficulties, being especially hard on marginal fringes of producers and traders. It is easy to make plausible that branches of industry with "effectively" working price formation systems will be characterized by high "built-in" instability.

It is also easy to point a contrasting picture of the "orderliness" of an oligopolistic branch with sticky pricing policies, that is with prices that do not react effectively to demand changes. The accumulation of orders during the boom, after more or less full use of capacity has been attained, will imply stable production some period after the turning point; the excess demand situation before the turning point will be choked off and the extra steam saved for the recession when capacity is available. Destabilizing fluctuations will be reduced, and changes in profits and liquidity should consequently also be less than in type-A cycles.

As said above, it is difficult to test the significance of such hypotheses by observing the statistical reality. Very little can be inferred, either by comparing the "conjuncture mechanisms" of different branches of industry with significantly different competitive structures and price behavior or by studying differences in cyclical behavior between postwar and prewar economies.[44]

44. It has been demonstrated how in durable goods industries exposed to heavy cyclical demand fluctuations the existence of relatively large and variable backlogs of orders will act as effective shock absorbers. (See Zarnowitz, "Unfilled Orders, Price Changes and Business Fluctuations.") New orders as expressions of demand will fluctuate heavily,

The assumptions underlying these tentative conclusions are very doubtful, however. We could as well assume that a system with varying order stocks and a minimum of price flexibility or price-change disturbances may contain pronounced destabilizing elements. Accumulation of orders during periods of rapid expansion may—as well as rising prices—be grossly misleading for entrepreneurial decisions. The widespread practice of double ordering may give entrepreneurs a false and exaggerated picture of the strength and permanence of the demand pressure and lead to overinvestment tendencies that may be assumed to be more destabilizing than if "corresponding" price increases had occurred. After the upper turning point, order backlogs may quickly evaporate—as often occurs in reality—and will therefore only to a limited extent support production during the contraction phase; a very slow adjustment downward of sales prices in a market characterized primarily by order-book adjustments may postpone the adjustment process and make the contraction longer than if a quick cutting down of prices had created expectations that in the near future prices would rather go up than down. That ideal type of reaction would imply such equilibrating price increases during the expansion phase

---

while prices and shipments as well as production will be much more stable. Zarnowitz shows, with a statistical material covering the period 1913–38, how for a number of branches changes in delivery periods and backlogs of orders had very strong stabilizing effects on shipments and production over the cycles. This was significantly much less the case in branches (like textiles and paper) where prices were more flexible and order backlogs relatively unimportant in relation to inventories of finished goods. It should be observed, however, that these effects are not directly related to our question of stabilization. The big variations in unfilled orders are partly a result of the weak price response to changes in demand and to the difficulties or unwillingness to hold stocks in the branches in question. In other branches, where prices are more flexible and there are relatively big inventories, there will be less stabilization effects between orders and shipments, but also as a consequence less order stock variability.

that demand is effectively choked off and purchases postponed to times of expected lower prices.

A GENERAL VIEW OF THE INTERWAR EXPERIENCES

It is impossible to catch the specific features of the interwar instability experiences by stressing a few strategic factors and relations, and it would not help much to put down some model system of equations. We are dealing with a most complicated historic process, starting with the Versaille treaty and ending with Hitler's war, a process in which political and economic developments were closely integrated in a sequence of minor and major events. Although the futility of supplying simple answers is obvious, we have an irresistible urge to make sweeping generalizations that go beyond the rather unconvincing method used above of pointing at interesting features or observations. We shall end this chapter, therefore, by committing the sin of making rather large and simple, and on the whole non-testable, generalizations, trying to judge the failures of the interwar period against the background of the much better performances of the economies during the postwar period.

The conclusion implied in the previous sections is that there is little clear evidence indicating that the working mechanism of the private-enterprise sectors of the Western economies has changed fundamentally since the interwar period. The big post-war depression *could* have occurred in the 1950s, if all the important conditions "around" the capitalist system has been the same as after 1918. The early forecasts made around the end of the Second World War might not have been fundamentally wrong in their prognosis of a coming United States depression, and about its repercussions on Western Europe, if "fundamentally" merely means neglecting the all-important new political and institutional preconditions.

It is in a way self-evident that sufficiently expansive government policies, which had begun in 1920 and had been carried out in all the countries, could have prevented the deflationary tendencies of the 1920s. If government expenditures had not been cut down so radically from 1919, and monetary policy had not been so restrictive in a number of countries during most of 1920, the deflation crises of 1920–21 would have been much milder. If the deflationary policies in the United Kingdom and some other countries had not been so strong, motivated as they were by the irrational target of returning to prewar parities (compare the devaluations of 1949), then the 1920s could have looked very different from the factual development of deflation and unemployment.

When we look at the interwar period from the perspective of our recent experiences and ambitions, we naturally must miss such things as a Marshall plan for helping to clear up international financial discrepancies following a world war, as well as all the expansionary government policies needed for keeping high employment in the national economies, letting the exchange parities be secondary matters. In fact, such a perspective on the interwar period is only some degrees different from, for instance, a Swedish interpretation of why the American economies between the middle of the 1950s and the beginning of the 1960s have been so sluggish.

Now the above type of apparently truistic generalization about the absence of expansive government policies being a fundamental cause of the unbalanced development of the 1920s may not be so self-evident as it looked at the first moment. The statement implies that, given the historical reaction patterns of government policies, the capitalist systems of the Western world had a built-in propensity for unbalanced development, with the cyclical swings eventually getting worse and ultimately ending in the post-1929 catastrophe. With mathematical models along the lines of Hicks and Kalecki it is easy to demonstrate the probability of such a cyclical propensity of a capitalist system with no essential stabilizing government interference. With such business cycle models in the back of our minds, we shall instead concentrate our attention on some essential issues around the instability problems of the real world, consisting of a number of countries with varying structures and working under different conditions as compared with those assumed in the cycle models. It is natural that we focus attention on the causes of the 1929 breakdown.

Table 2.5 gives an impression of interesting differences between the various countries during the conjunctures of the interwar period.

TABLE 2.5
Declines of Industrial Production (IP), GNP, and Export Volume (X) During Interwar Contractions (annual data)

		Contraction around		
		1920–21	1929–32	1937–38
	IP	−21%	−12%	+ 1%
Sweden	GNP	−12	−13	+ 4
	X	−21	−33	−16
	IP	− 5%	−26%	− 7%
France	GNP	− 7	−19	− 1
	X	− 3	−42	+ 8
	IP	−32%	−14%	− 7%
U.K.	GNP	−13	− 2	+ 1
	X	−30	−37	−12
	IP	−23%	−45%	−21%
U.S.	GNP	− 2	−29	− 5
	X	−25	−49	− 0

There are considerable variations in the degrees of instability when comparing the countries. As during the postwar period, the United States and Canada show instability far above the other countries. A considerable part of the interwar instability refers to the existence of stagnation periods with production far below potential. There is a rather close synchronization of the upper turning points during the interwar period. Most of the turning points for these countries in 1920 and 1929–30 fall within half a year. There was considerably less synchronization during the interwar period as to the corresponding lower turning points, during 1921–23 and after 1931, when compared with the upper turning points, and the same is true about the minor cycles, where the lack of covariance seems to be at least as large as during the postwar period.[45]

It is more or less generally accepted that it was the internally generated contraction in the United States which took the rest of the world along into depression. But the impulses generated by the United States economy affected an outside world which, due to a number of weaknesses we shall discuss below, was at the time readily and vigorously predisposed to respond.

Although there is consensus that the Great Depression in the United States was internally generated, professional views on the basic cause or causes of the breakdown are even today by far less than unanimous. Perhaps the most widely accepted view stresses the tendency toward "capital saturation." As far as housing is concerned, the evidence for such a view is indeed strong. Residential construction had already reached a peak around 1925–26, and fell by some 15 per cent over the next two years and another 25 per cent from 1928 to 1929, despite the continued rise of national income. The early and rapid decline of this important component of gross fixed private investment was clearly related to a weakening of demand. The formation of new households, which had been rising rapidly since the end of the war, reached a peak in 1923 and then declined by some 40 per cent until 1929. The construction of new dwellings had in 1923 already exceeded the rate of household formation, and there does not seem to have existed either a shortage of dwellings substantial enough, or sufficient income elasticity of demand, to justify the construction of new dwellings much in excess of household formation throughout the rest of the 1920s. Thus there was probably already some overbuilding in the late 1920s despite the rapid decline of residential

45. See Oskar Morgenstern, *International Financial Transactions and Business Cycles,* NBER, Princeton, 1959), Chap. 2, where the problem of the covariance of the cycles of various countries is extensively discussed.

building construction. Rents declined by 7 per cent between 1925 and 1929 whereas the remaining components of the index of consumer prices fell by only some 2 per cent. Clearly, the demand for new residential construction was weak even before the downturn in general economic activity in 1929. It is not unlikely that dwelling construction would have continued to decline into the early 1930s even in the absence of a general economic decline, but unquestionably any such decline would have been much more moderate than it actually turned out to be.

How about capital saturation in other branches of activity? As far as plant and equipment as a whole is concerned, it would be rather difficult to find satisfactory evidence of widespread overinvestment before the downturn in 1929. On the other hand, before that downturn there were already overcapacity problems in some individual industries, particularly in the automobile and textile industries. But these trouble spots represent too narrow a basis for a belief in general, or at least widespread, overinvestment in plant and equipment, since it is not unusual that individual industries are either in trouble of their own or turning down early in periods of high prosperity. In this respect it can indeed be questioned if the situation before and around the downturn in 1929 was so very different from the corresponding situation in 1957, for example.

The general statistical studies of the developments of real capital stock and production (within the business sector) do not give the impression that 1929 is an exceptional year. The analysis (on this basis) of potential production capacity in fact indicates that 1929 is quite a normal year, more or less like 1925 or 1957.[46] However, this is too paradoxical to be

46. In his account of the turning point in 1929, Gordon stresses important elements of weakness in the business situation. Production and investments, in stocks as well as in fixed equipment, had in various lines been rising at a rapid rate that could not possibly be maintained. "Excess capacity was developing in a number of lines, and this meant a decline in demand for further capital goods." (*Business Fluctuations*, p. 426.)

quite true. Generally declining prices before 1929—and the exceptionally rapid falloff in business investments during 1930—are indicators that there was something very wrong with 1929. In a modern formulation of investment theory, the old problem of whether there was capital saturation around 1929 should, however, be formulated in terms of a capital adjustment process. If this could be done with regard to fixed business investment, the result might show a relatively big decline in the gap between desired and actual stock of capital from 1923 or 1925 to 1929. There would not need to be any general "overcapacity," only a lower average degree of incentives to increase capacity in relation to earlier years.[47] That would be enough to cause a rising degree of *vulnerability* to outside shocks—coming from many sides of the unbalanced world of the late 1920s. On this point any decisive testing seems impossible, because of the uniqueness of the 1928–30 constellation. It is from this point of view quite possible to put much emphasis on monetary and financial factors as many economists have done, lately and most vigorously Milton Friedman. Federal Reserve policy became restrictive from the beginning of 1928 in order to check the tremendous bull market in stocks. The result of this restrictiveness with regard to interest rates does not seem impressive but—as Friedman points out—the volume of money[48] stopped rising sixteen months before the turning point, according to him an indication of exceptional restrictiveness. It can be argued that in a vulnerable investment situation there need not be much of a monetary disturbance to tip the balance. The unfortunate fact is, however, that several other factors can claim this questionable honor, not least the general evaporation of business confidence following the stock market crash.

47. James W. Knowles, "The Potential Economic Growth in the United States," Study Paper No. 20 of the *Study of Employment Growth and Price Levels* (U.S. Congress, Joint Economic Committee, Washington, D.C., 1960), pp. 21 and 36.

48. Defined in the extensive sense including time deposits.

Perhaps it would be most fruitful to divide the problem of the American contraction starting in 1929 into two separate questions. First, it should be asked why economic activity declined so steeply from 1929 to 1930; and second, why the contraction was not stopped and reversed either in 1930 or at least in 1931. The 6 per cent growth of GNP in 1929 was entirely accounted for by the growth of consumption and inventory investment. The growth of consumption was unusually large in relation to the growth of nonconsumption expenditures. The high capital gains on stock market transactions are an obvious explanatory factor for this extra boost to consumption. After the fall of 1929, this extra stimulus to consumption not only disappeared but gave way to a possibly even greater drag to consumption in 1930. The high rate of inventory accumulation in 1929, on the other hand, could hardly be expected to continue for another year; on the contrary, a reversal of the high rate of accumulation was likely to follow according to experiences made before and since the Great Depression. This reversal from 1929 to 1930 was considerable but not unusually large; actually, the negative stimulus from inventory investment was less only in one of the other interwar cyclical setbacks. Nevertheless, this relatively moderate inventory setback in conjunction with the autonomous decline in consumption (to be kept separate from the stabilizing cyclical shift in the consumption function which partly hides the above autonomous shift), and the continued rapid decline of residential construction, were sufficient to generate alone a decline of GNP of some 5 to 6 per cent without taking account of multiplier effects. That in face of such strongly depressing forces nonresidential fixed investment also declined substantially is not surprising. The total effect was a 9 per cent decline of GNP in 1930.

There remains the question of why the contraction of GNP was not reversed in late 1930 or at least in 1931, but instead deteriorated by another 6 per cent in 1931, and 15 per cent in 1932. In 1931, the decline of nonresidential fixed investment accelerated and accounted for about half of the further GNP decline. The decline of consumption was, at least temporarily, slowed down in 1931 and the change in inventory investment was only slightly negative. In fact there were clear indications of revival in the spring of 1931. Thus we can put our second question more precisely, and ask why the decline of investment in plant and equipment accelerated after the first year of decline instead of turning up again as in 1922 and in 1939? One explanation would be that the decline of GNP in 1930 was almost four times, respectively twice as large, and thus the depressionary shock to the system much stronger—on profits as well as on demand. But most likely a more precise and more satisfactory explanation has to take account of the catastrophic state of the country's financial mechanism highlighted by the banking crises of late 1930 and early 1931. The further deterioration of the economic and financial situation could have been prevented, at least partially, by a more adequate monetary policy even at this late date.[49]

If this represents an acceptable account of the instability development in the United States shortly before and during the Great Depression, what about the instability development in the other economies? We have already previously accepted the view that the American depression was in various ways transmitted to the rest of the world, which was predisposed to react strongly to the series of shocks coming from the United States economy. The sensitivity of the economies of other countries referred less to the internal economic mechanism of these countries than to their international payments structure, which depended on a continuous and increasing supply of dollars from the United States in order to maintain a precarious international financial balance. The diminished net outflow of capital from the United States had already in 1929 brought

49. For an interesting discussion of alternative monetary policy measures at different stages of the contraction and their potential effects, see Friedman and Schwartz, *A Monetary History of the United States,* particularly pp. 391–419.

difficulties to a number of countries, and the tremendous decline of imports accompanying the American depression loosened the basic pillar in the international payments system and as a consequence the scaffold practically collapsed, pulling down a large part of the economic structure itself in the process.

We have previously mentioned the case of "sick" industries in a number of European countries in the 1920s. The depressing effects of these trouble spots, which had partly the character of postwar dislocations in specific fields of activity, were, however, largely compensated by branches of activity for which the 1920s marked the beginning of a promising long-run expansion. Among such branches we like to mention the automobile and associated industries, the radio and the chemical industries, as well as the housing sector.[50] In a country like Sweden there were no apparent tendencies of general weakness of the conjuncture during the years up to 1929. This appears obvious from the fact that consumption and investment continued to increase rapidly in 1929–30, and housebuilding even up to 1932 in spite of an immediate considerable decline in export prices and volume from 1929 on and increasingly severe import competition. The Swedish case was certainly not unique; the same tendencies were apparent in the United Kingdom. In France the strong conjunctures of the second half of the 1920s were carried up to 1930. However, not all countries followed the British and Swedish patterns of

50. As far as housing is concerned, the early downturn of construction in the United States appears to have been a unique event. As far as the timing of the downturn is concerned, only the United Kingdom comes close to the United States case; and as far as the amplitude of the declines is concerned, only France and to a lesser extent Switzerland are roughly comparable to the United States, but their contractions did not begin until 1931 and 1933, respectively. The renewal of the rise in residential construction from a still relatively high level in the United Kingdom and Sweden, after 1932 and 1933 respectively, contributed importantly to the comparatively favorable development of these countries in the 1930s.

internal stability. Disregarding a number of primary producing and exporting countries (including Australia and New Zealand) which had already gotten into export difficulties and narrow balance of payments constraints before 1929, and therefore experienced an early dampening of conjunctures, we can take Germany as another interesting case of deviation.

The contraction in Germany represents an interesting case in several respects. The peak of economic activity had already been reached in 1928. GNP declined by 0.5 per cent in 1929 and this was more than fully accounted for by a decline in nonresidential investment. Although data on inventory investment are lacking, it appears from the behavior of the available expenditure components of GNP that inventory investment contributed to the early downturn. It is rather likely that this early downturn, at a time when exports were still rapidly rising, was caused by *capital scarcity,* that is by an insufficient supply of loanable funds. Both the very high interest rates and the heavy dependence on capital imports, and their rapid decline after 1927, support the above view.[51] With gold and foreign exchange reserves corresponding to less than one month's worth of imports, there would have been little leeway for independent monetary action even without the drag of tremendous annual reparations and interest and dividend payments abroad. Unwilling to devalue for internal and external reasons, Germany had to revert to exchange control and domestic deflation in a series of rather hopeless attempts to maintain its external solvency. It is thus not very surprising that the country should have experienced the deepest contraction among the countries of Western Europe.

51. According to very approximate calculations, the order of size of capital imports to Germany at the end of the twenties corresponded to about 50 per cent of German net savings. The current supply of foreign (American) long- and short-term credits was an important distinctive element of the German conjuncture that made it look very different from the United States model. See Carl T. Schmidt, *German Business Cycles 1924–33* (NBER, New York, 1934).

We do not intend to enter deeply into a discussion of the very specific conjunctural conditions relevant in the years after the contractions in economic activity had ceased in the various countries. As a pedagogic device we can use the development of the 1930s as a contrast to the 1920s. In the United Kingdom, Japan, and Sweden, for example, it was the radical devaluation of the currencies that provided both stimulus to expansion and space for other expansionary measures, in particular easy credit policies. Investment revived, partly under protection from foreign competition. It should be emphasized that the revival of economic activity owed relatively little to expansionary fiscal policy, not even in Sweden.[52] Actually, the only country where fiscal policy was already an important expansionary force before the late 1930s was Germany (although for other reasons than peaceful expansion). By the late 1930s, the European economies had gained enough momentum to respond to the severe American contraction of 1937–38 either with only a slowdown in the rate of growth of GNP and industrial production or a relatively moderate decline in total and industrial production. The character of this minor recession in Europe was largely comparable to the European postwar recessions. The protracted stagnation experiences of the gold bloc countries (Belgium, France, Italy, the Netherlands, and Switzerland) show how overvaluation of the exchange rate in combination with restrictive monetary policy can effectively check the possibilities for expansion. Thus, in 1937 for example, French real national income and industrial production were still some 15 and 11 per cent *below* their 1929 peak levels, whereas in Sweden the corresponding figures were about 16 and 55 per cent *above* the previous peak levels, and in the United Kingdom they were about 16 and 38 per cent above. The Blum inflation experiment of 1936–38 succeeded in rapidly driving up wages and prices (industrial wages by more than 50 per cent, the cost

52. See Erik Lundberg, *Business Cycles and Economic Policy* (London, 1957), Chap. 2.

of living by more than one third). But production responded much more modestly; in fact the small gain in 1937 was largely wiped out again in 1938.

The type of business cycle model most useful for interpreting the developments of the 1930s may not be the same one that is most useful for interpreting the developments of the 1920s. Furthermore, important conditions differed from country to country, and have to be taken into consideration. For a number of countries, the devaluation of 1931 seems to mark out a "structural divide" followed to a certain degree by new and more stable tendencies of production and demand. But, on the other hand, in a more general framework this structural change may be considered as a function of the undervaluation of the currency and expansionary monetary and fiscal policies.

There were obviously large differences between some of the more successful countries on one side and some of the less successful ones on the other side with regard to underlying conditions and outside stimuli, but probably the major determinant of the unequal overall success must be sought in more or less fortunate policy measures.

The failure of the American economy to reattain a satisfactory utilization of resources in the late 1930s, even plunging into another serious setback in 1938, should be attributed to unsatisfactory government policy measures. The attitudes toward fiscal policy had become somewhat more enlightened after 1933. Federal government expenditures rose rapidly—and, though some tax rates rose too, deficits grew larger up to 1936—at the same time as GNP at current prices rose some 14 per cent per year, and GNP at constant prices by some 10 per cent per year, on average. Yet the expansionary spending measures were not impressive; aggregate public works, federal, state, and local, were not back at their predepression level even by 1938.[53]

53. See Alvin H. Hansen, "Was Fiscal Policy in the Thirties a Failure?" *Review of Economics and Statistics* (August 1963).

Fiscal policy has to be strongly blamed as a major cause of the 1937–38 contraction under the conditions of insufficient revival of private investments, especially all forms of private construction. Easy monetary policy and extremely low interest rates did not help when widespread excess capacity excluded needed investment incentives. The background was an inflationary boom which had started in late 1936, not least as a consequence of increasing fiscal stimulation in which the large transfer payments to veterans was particularly outstanding. Large inventory investment carried the rapid advance of GNP into 1937, but the premature balancing of the budget at a time when some 14 per cent of the civilian labor force were still unemployed helped in turning vigorous expansion into vigorous contraction. Thus, the explanation of the 1937–38 contraction differs clearly from the explanation of the 1929–30 contraction. In comparison to this latter downturn, consumption was well maintained in 1938. To the differences in the succeeding recovery conditions we have already previously referred.

When we look at the general experience of the 1930s and observe the lack of international conformity of the conjunctures, we must attribute a good deal of this to fundamental differences in the attitudes and policies of the respective governments. However, differences in the response mechanisms of the various economies continued to play a role. For example, in Japan there was apparently a much more flexible price and wage system than in practically all the other economies, and consequently the deflationary policies following the repercussions of the United States contraction, up to the yen devaluation in September 1931, did not create such calamities as in the other countries where similar measures were applied. Prices and wages declined effectively, and production fell less from 1929 to 1931 than it did in most other countries. The strong undervaluation of the yen—the devaluation was about one and a half times as large as in the United Kingdom—did not give way to inflation but instead gave rise to a rapid expansion of production amounting to some 50 per cent between 1932 and 1937. An outstanding feature was the tremendous increase in profits that came about thanks to a high mobility of labor, stable wages, and rapidly rising productivity. The rapid rise and high level of profits must in turn explain the large rise of private investment. This development pattern is in fact quite similar to the one we can observe during the postwar period. (See Chapter 7.)

It is of great interest to compare the Japanese case of very effective price reactions with the failures of the French and United States economies to react strongly to reflationary impulses. The long-term expectations were apparently not affected in such a way that stable accelerator-multiplier reactions got the floor. Instead, short-term fluctuations in inventory investment came to dominate the scene at the same time as wage increases and immobility of labor explained short-term inelasticity of supply. It is a paradox that the postwar economies exposed to inflations at full employment and near full use of production capacities give the impression of greater resource flexibility than seems to have been the case in some of the economies during the 1930s when there was very much of surplus capacity with regard to both labor and capital.

3 GENERAL SURVEY OF POSTWAR ECONOMIC INSTABILITY

MANIFESTATIONS OF ECONOMIC INSTABILITY

In the present chapter, we shall describe and compare some important general features of postwar economic development in the industrialized countries of Western Europe, North America, and Japan. This comparative survey should not only give us an overall perspective on postwar economic instability, but also provide some helpful guidelines for the selection of the more specific problems to which we shall turn our attention in the country studies that follow this chapter.

In Western Europe, the striking feature of the course of economic development during the postwar period has been the rapidity rather than the instability of the growth of total output. From 1948 to 1964, the real GNP of the area rose on average at a rate of about 5 per cent per year, and deviations from this average rate were rather limited. Even in 1952 and 1958—years that are generally considered to be periods of recession for most individual member countries—the combined rate of growth was still around 2.5 per cent. Among the years with faster than average growth, only 1950 stands out with its rate of over 8 per cent.

The yearly index of industrial production of the Western European countries combined conveys the same impression of fast and relatively smooth growth. The annual aggregate increased at a rate of about 7 per cent, and it continued to

TABLE 3.1

Annual Rates of Growth of Real GNP (1950–64)

	1950	*51*	*52*	*53*	*54*	*55*	*56*	*57*	*58*	*59*	*60*	*61*	*62*	*63*	*64*	*Average 1950–64*	*Average Variation*[b]
Austria	10.4	6.9	0.3	3.9	8.6	11.1	5.1	5.9	4.1	2.8	8.3	4.6	1.6	4.4	6.0	5.6	2.4
Belgium	5.0	5.7	−0.9	4.0	3.7	5.5	2.9	2.6	−1.0	2.6	5.6	4.7	5.0	4.8	5.2	3.7	1.6
Denmark	8.8	−0.2	1.6	5.8	2.8	0.1	2.1	5.0	2.8	7.2	6.6	6.4	5.7	1.7	7.8	4.3	2.5
France	7.7	6.0	2.5	3.0	4.8	5.8	5.0	6.0	2.6	3.0	7.4	4.4	7.1	4.7	5.5	5.0	1.4
Germany (F.R.)	14.3	10.5	8.3	7.5	7.4	11.5	6.9	5.7	3.2	7.0	8.8	5.4	4.2	3.2	6.5	7.4	2.2
Italy	7.1	7.6	2.9	7.6	5.1	6.7	4.2	6.1	4.4	7.3	6.8	8.3	6.3	5.3	3.0	5.9	1.4
Netherlands	3.7	3.0	2.0	8.5	7.3	7.7	3.4	3.2	−0.1	5.2	8.9	3.5	3.8	3.1	8.2	4.8	2.3
Norway	5.3	3.0	4.1	4.2	4.3	2.3	5.1	2.7	−0.7	3.7	5.6	6.4	3.0	5.0	6.9	4.1	1.4
Sweden	5.3	−0.4	2.8	3.6	6.5	3.6	3.4	3.5	1.1	5.5	3.6	5.6	3.7	5.0	7.2	4.0	1.5
Switzerland	7.2	8.1	0.8	4.5	5.6	5.3	6.0	2.9	−1.8	7.2	5.8	7.3	5.1	4.6	5.1	4.9	1.8
United Kingdom	4.4	1.9	−0.3	4.3	4.1	3.0	2.2	2.0	0.7	4.3	4.7	3.4	1.1	4.6	5.2	3.0	1.4
Western Europe[a]	8.3	5.4	2.7	5.1	5.3	6.1	4.7	4.3	2.0	4.6	6.6	5.1	4.6	4.8	5.7	5.0	1.0
Canada	7.0	6.1	8.0	3.8	−2.9	8.6	8.7	1.2	1.3	3.3	2.5	2.5	6.7	4.6	6.5	4.5	2.7
United States	9.6	7.9	3.1	4.5	−1.4	7.6	1.8	1.4	−1.1	6.4	2.5	1.9	6.6	3.8	5.0	4.0	2.6
Japan	11.7	13.6	10.9	6.7	3.3	11.2	8.7	7.0	3.4	17.5	14.1	15.3	5.0	11.9	11.1	10.1	3.5

a. OEEC or European area of OECD at constant prices and 1954 exchange rates up to 1955 and 1958 exchange rates thereafter.

b. GNP—variation index: average deviation of annual percentage rates of growth from their average.

rise at a rate of about 1 per cent even during the most unfavorable years 1952 and 1958. This picture incorporates, however, a substantial bias in favor of stability, since annual data reflect only poorly the cyclical impact of brief recessions. The regional aggregation over the European area further adds to the bias if, as it happened, the turning points in individual countries are less than fully synchronized.

We may receive a first impression of the general instability of growth in the selected countries from Table 3.1, showing the annual rates of change of real GNP during the years 1950–64. The variation of these rates is quite considerable for some of the countries (for instance the United States, Canada, Belgium, Denmark) and less pronounced for other countries (Germany, Italy, Norway, Sweden). We must of course remember that yearly changes tend to underestimate the current alternations, as peaks and troughs in production activity tend to be flattened out over the calendar years. A more vivid impression of cyclical swings comes out of the diagram of industrial production (Figure 3.1) presented below. Nevertheless, the yearly and quarterly variations in production, as well as the variations of unemployment rates, seem rather insignificant against the background of the interwar experiences. It may even seem futile or pedantic to devote so much attention to the postwar irregularities of growth that mostly, with regard to yearly changes of real GNP, refer only to retardations and accelerations of these rates. Only in relatively few cases (the United States, Canada, Switzerland, and Belgium) can we register significant absolute declines in one or more years. However, we must refer these instability experiences to the much greater postwar ambitions with regard to full employment, as well as to the new ambitions of rapid and stable growth, that have become accepted more or less explicitly by all countries after the war. From this point of view a retardation of growth from a normal rate of 5 per cent to 1 per cent is regarded as quite a serious affair, implying perhaps a doubling of the unemployment rate (say from 2 to 4 per cent) and serious troubles for the most exposed branches of activity, often rather highly dependent on export trade. Excessive price and wage movements as well as balance of payments troubles also belong to instability experiences that are taken seriously. As an additional issue let us not forget that we also are looking for explanations as to why the postwar development has so far been so highly stable.

There is a limited degree of synchronization of the general growth rate variations between the countries. The individual countries' weakest performances cluster around 1951–52 and 1957–58, and to some extent around 1962–63 in the case of Western Europe, and around 1949, 1954, 1957–58, and 1960–61, in the case of North America and Japan. Cyclical fluctuations in the sense of oscillations around the trend of overall activity may thus be indentified. But if we define the cyclical characteristic more stringently in the sense of fairly regularly recurring interruptions of the growth in total output by periods of substantial absolute decline, then on the basis of the country tables only for the United States, Belgium, and Switzerland, could a (rather moderate) business cycle pattern be identified. However, this may partly be the result of the inadequacy of annual data to reflect satisfactorily absolute declines of relatively short duration rather than the consequence of an actual complete absence of such declines in all the other countries.

Comprehensive output measures for a systematic comparative analysis in terms of time periods shorter than one year exist in the form of quarterly and monthly indices of industrial production in all but one of the countries studied.[1] Figure 3.1

1. The exception is Switzerland where an index of industrial production for the years before 1958 is entirely lacking. Output originating in manufacturing, mining, and quarrying, which is represented by the indices of industrial production, only accounts for between about one quarter and close to one half of the total output of the countries investigated. But since cyclical instability in advanced countries centers around the industrial sector primarily, the less comprehensive measure is quite adequate at this point of the study. The instability of the indus-

FIGURE 3.1
Index of Industrial Production, Percentage Deviations from Trend of Seasonally Adjusted Data (monthly 1951–61, quarterly thereafter)

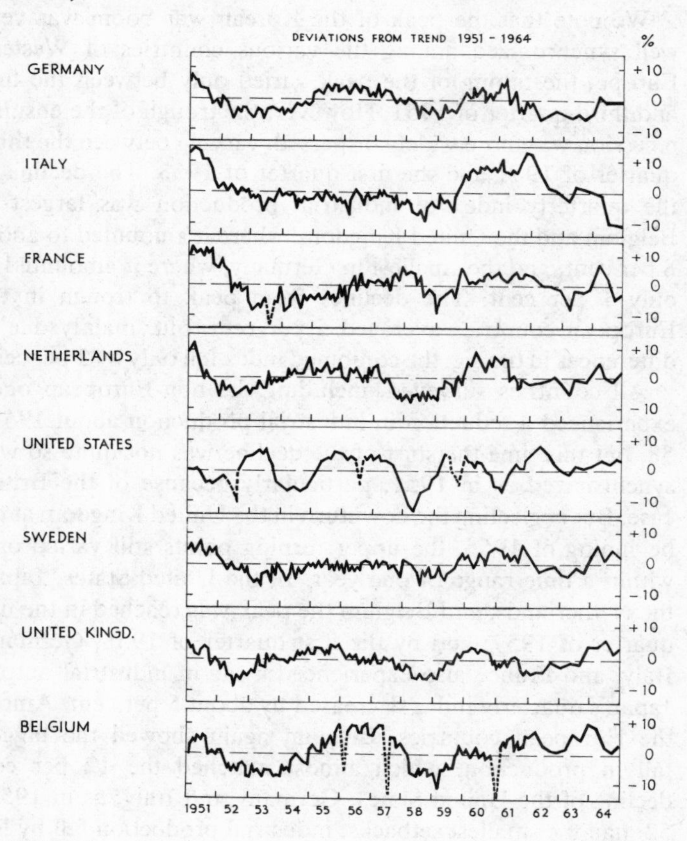

illustrates the deviations from trend of the seasonally adjusted monthly (quarterly after 1961) index of industrial production for the majority of the countries studied.

We note that the peak of the Korean war boom was very well synchronized among the various countries of Western Europe; the timing of the peak varied only between the first and third quarter of 1951. However, the trough of the ensuing recession was more widely dispersed, varying between the third quarter of 1951 and the first quarter of 1953. The decline in the quarterly index of industrial production was largest in Belgium and the United Kingdom, where it amounted to about 8 per cent, and the smallest in Germany, where it amounted to only 1 per cent. The declines from peak to trough in the European countries averaged 5 per cent, but, mainly due to differences in timing, the combined index fell only by 2 per cent.

All countries surveyed, including the non-European ones, experienced a reduction in industrial production about 1957–58, but this time the start of the decline was not quite so well synchronized as in 1951, particularly because of the British case. But neglecting the downturn in the United Kingdom at the beginning of 1956, the upper turning points still varied only within a time range of one year. In the United States, Japan, the Netherlands, and Belgium the peak was reached in the first quarter of 1957; and by the first quarter of 1958, Germany, Italy, and France also experienced a sag in industrial output. Japan's quarterly index decreased by about 5 per cent. Among the European countries, Belgium again showed the biggest fall in production, which almost matched the 12 per cent decline of the United States. Germany and Italy, as in 1951–52, had the smallest setbacks: industrial production fell by less than 1 per cent. The weighted average of the declines in the

---

trial sector has been approximately matched in importance only by the construction sector in the case of Belgium, and largely for reasons independent of the business cycle, the agricultural sector in the case of Canada.

quarterly indices of the individual countries of Western Europe amounted to 2 per cent, whereas the combined index for the Western European area dropped by only about one third as much. The 1957–58 recession was followed by rapid expansion in Japan and Western Europe as well as in North America. In the latter area, however, this upswing of economic activity was rather short lived, as industrial production in the United States as well as in Canada had already reached a new upper turning point in the first quarter of 1960.

The downward pull of the new recession, which lasted in both countries for a year, was milder than on previous occasions. But in view of the fact that full employment had not been attained at the peak, the recession helped to create a set of problems that were at least as serious as on previous occasions. In Japan and most of the industrialized countries of Western Europe, the expansion proceeded unimpeded up to 1961. Besides the United Kingdom, where a new pause in industrial growth set in from mid-1960, there was, as the diagram indicates, some dampening of the growth performance during some of the following years (mostly 1962 or 1963).

Concentration of the conjunctural movements to a rather limited number of branches of industry seems characteristic for the postwar period. Thus we find quite impressive variations in production, orders, prices, sales (especially for exports) as well as investments in fixed capital and inventory investments within such branches as iron and steel, iron ore, pulp and paper, textiles, shipbuilding, and certain subbranches of machinery production. Each of these branches usually shows much more international synchronization of cyclical development than total GNP growth. In such branches of industry, international trade plays a strategic role in most of the countries, and there is therefore an international price system having a common impact on profits, production, trade, and investment. Even if such branches have heavy weights in total industrial production, their relative importance in GNP is more limited, so that there will be much room for independent movements of other sectors within the economies. The specific cycles of various industrial branches can only be touched upon in this connection; it is a big field of research that cannot be covered in this study.

Before we look more closely at the experiences of the various countries as they appear in the form of varying growth rates, it is necessary to point out the narrow limitations and the deficiencies of instability measures that only pay attention to the variations of the growth rates. It is, for instance, evident that a higher than average rate of growth of GNP following a lower than average rate should not necessarily be taken in itself as contributing to instability, as will be the first impression from the table. On the contrary such a reversal to a rate above the average may make a contribution to stability. If the downward deviations were not quickly followed by such reversals, the result would be larger deviations from the growth trend which the full employment of labor and capital would generate.

This comparison demonstrates the point that there are several dimensions to the conception of short-term instability in economic growth. A measure of the variation of the growth rate is just one possibility that gives a specific aspect that may or may not be interesting when making comparisons among countries. Let us put down some of the criteria for the choice of measures that would be significant for making such comparisons. (For a general discussion of this issue, see Chapter 1.)

When looking at the development of total real GNP one important aspect refers to the deviations from full-employment growth. These deviations can be measured in various ways. A summary account of the results over a period can be ascertained as a surface below (and above) the full-employment trend. Inevitably there will be a certain degree of arbitrariness. There is nothing objectively given as to the concept of full-employment growth; explicit assumptions must be made, and the results depend upon them. There are two main alternatives as to the choice of such assumptions: to draw the trend either with full attention paid to the target norms of development as accepted in the country in question or by stipulating a certain standard norm for all countries compared.

The first alternative would mean that the full-employment trend for the United States economy should be drawn under the assumption of a 4 per cent unemployment rate as the—at least until recently—generally accepted norm, while the corresponding norms for most Western European countries, although in general not stated as clearly as in the United States, lie between 1 and 2 per cent unemployment. For international comparisons it seems preferable to apply the same norm for calculating the full-employment trend (implying, for instance, an unemployment rate of 2 per cent). This is admittedly an arbitrary assumption, but this type of arbitrariness seems necessary for reaching comparable instability measures. When trying to refer the instability concept to a full-employment trend there are, besides this choice of an "optimal" unemployment rate, other kinds of arbitrariness involved. Deviations below the trend will have implications for labor force participation, and productivity via capital formation, intersectoral shifts, and so forth, the quantitative effects of which in the current state of economic knowledge must still be largely guessed at. It is possible that a relatively high degree of variation of the growth of total production or a high frequency of balance of payments difficulties (as in the United Kingdom and Denmark), may have a retarding effect on the rate of private investment and therefore indirectly on the full-employment trend, that is capital accumulation and entrepreneurial activity would be below the level which would have been achieved under more stable conditions. These remarks should be sufficient as a warning of the unavoidable arbitrariness of any measure of this kind.

It should also be observed that we are here referring to deviations of actual output from potential output as just one dimension of instability. We might, as discussed in Chapter 1, find it interesting to direct attention to the instability of *total demand*. During boom years, with more or less full utilization of an economy's potential, there might be excess demand for goods and services as well as for labor. The real GNP series may therefore give a significant underestimate of the variations in total demand. Variations in the rate of growth of nominal GNP would perhaps in some way come closer to this type of instability measure, although even so some major aspects would be excluded. Eventually, we might in comparing the countries take changes in the price and wage level, and respective deviations from some price stability norms, as indicative of demand instability. The total change of the price level over a period might thus serve as an indicator of cumulated excess demand. However, particularly due to cost-inflation phenomena, such an indicator would be an imprecise measure of demand instability. Variations in the intensity of the demand for labor can to a certain extent be accounted for by changes in the rate of unemployment; short-term changes in the work week as well as changes in vacancies and quit rates give additional information on the state of the labor market.

We should also remember that any summary account of the instability of annual GNP growth can convey only a limited picture of the fluctuations in the state of economic activity. We may want to know a lot about the timing and amplitudes of the variations, as well as about the variations in the composition of the changes in total GNP, in order to comprehend some of the important differences between countries. We would, for instance, like to know how the GNP variations in one country reflected variations in the growth of investment, consumption, exports, and so forth, or to what extent the variations were concentrated on specific industries.

The exploration of a number of such dimensions of instability tends to make comparisons difficult to survey. A more direct method of studying comparative instability experiences and a highly ambitious goal to aim at in a study of the present type would be to compare the exogenous postwar disturbances in combination with the relevant reaction patterns of the respective economies. By putting the issue in this way we realize the tremendous difficulties in finding criteria for meaningful international comparisons of cyclical instability. The set of countries chosen for comparison have, during the postwar period, been exposed to shocks and disturbances of quite different kinds and in varying degrees. In fact, we would like to compare sensitivities of the economies with regard to shocks of the same kind and relative order. The trouble is that there is a rather vague and arbitrary line of division between what should be called external disturbances and the reaction patterns of the economies. May we, for instance, say that the United Kingdom and Denmark have been affected more frequently and deeply by balance of payments disturbances than Sweden, Germany, and Switzerland, or do most balance of payments disturbances belong to the setup of behavior relations characteristic for the economies in question? This kind of problem is, of course, especially pertinent with regard to government policy reaction. The actual postwar instability patterns in the various countries may be heavily influenced by policy changes, taken as exogenous factors or regarded as responses to actual or expected deviations from certain targets or norms.

Whatever the method used for making instability comparisons, a number of doubtful and arbitrary assumptions must be explicitly or implicitly admitted. One of our comparative measures of instability concentrates simply on the variations in the growth rate of GNP. Besides its simplicity, the approach has the advantage that it can easily be extended to the major components of GNP in order to establish their respective contributions to the variations of total GNP growth. These measures need, however, to be complemented by indicators of the deviations from full-employment output, since the former type of instability measure does not systematically take account of differences in the levels and slopes of the trends of actual and potential output. Furthermore, a deviation of the growth of GNP from the average rate of growth, which will be recorded as instability by the former type of measure, may be stabilizing from a relevant point of view if it brings the economy closer in line with the path of full-employment growth. But as a comparison of these two types of instability indicators will show, this point appears, in the case of most countries, to be of secondary importance as far as the ranking of the countries with regard to their average instability of GNP growth from 1950 to 1964 is concerned.

DEVIATIONS FROM POTENTIAL OR FULL-EMPLOYMENT OUTPUT

We start with the presentation and application of the last-mentioned approach, which defines and attempts to measure economic instability as the deviations of actual output from potential or full-employment output. Potential or full-employment output of a country may be defined as the amount the economy could produce at some stipulated rate of use of the labor force and of capital which would neither imply excess strain nor wasteful slack in the economy.[2] Thus, an estimate of potential or full-employment output is not intended to represent the maximum level of production from the short-run point of view, but tries instead to indicate the result of a high rate of utilization of a country's productive resources which can be sustained for a long time.

Although the definition aimed at above implies a low level of unemployment, say somewhere within the range of 1 to 4 per cent of the labor force, it is by itself too vague for choosing a feasible minimum unemployment rate within this range. A certain amount of short-run frictional unemployment is a necessary feature of a dynamic economy where, in a continuous flow, new entrants and reentrants into the labor force have to find appropriate job openings, and where more or less voluntary movements between jobs are the result of changing market forces and technology as well as personal choice on the part of employees and employers. To the minimum rate of frictional unemployment, some minimum of structural unemployment has to be

2. Knowles, "The Potential Economic Growth in the United States," pp. 6–8.

added. The latter concept refers to unemployment on account of long-run declines in the demand for labor of a certain type, which is usually concentrated in specific geographical areas; such declines in demand in combination with economic and psychological factors delaying the necessary occupational and geographical mobility can result in long-lasting unemployment even in the face of excess demand for labor in other occupations and geographical areas.

The minimum amount of such frictional and structural unemployment is likely to differ to some extent both internationally and intertemporally, not least on account of marked differences in the age-composition of the labor force and in the degree of legal and social job protection. Improved information about job opportunities would tend to reduce the feasible minimum rate of frictional and structural unemployment in a given country, and so would various labor market policies intended to facilitate the geographical and occupational mobility of the unemployed. The minimum rate of unemployment has to include also an allowance for a certain minimum amount of seasonal unemployment.

The feasible minimum level of unemployment in a given country will not only depend upon the particular concepts and measures of labor force and unemployment used; policy targets and possibilities in a given country should also be considered. To the extent that the feasible minimum level of unemployment is below the level that is taken as compatible with a target of price-level stability—which seems to be the case in all countries—the *desired* minimum level of unemployment also depends upon the conceived trade-off possibilities between the target variables and the comparative political valuation of the conflicting aims. But we have decided to keep such considerations in the background only, not least in view of the well-known difficulty of establishing quantitatively the respective elements of a country's social welfare function and the actual trade-off possibilities between small differences in the unemployment percentage and the general price level.

Opinions differ as to what specific level of unemployment closely represents the feasible minimum unemployment rate in individual countries; they tend to be strongly influenced by what minimum levels have actually been achieved in the past. For example, for a long time during the postwar period there has been a wide consensus in the United States that the feasible minimum rate was around 4 per cent of the labor force. In recent years, however, not entirely independently of the much lower rates achieved in many industrialized countries outside North America, a Senate subcommittee[3] has recommended a target rate of unemployment not higher than 3 per cent, and an independent study by a prominent American economist has come up with a minimum rate of just slightly over 3 per cent.[4] Similarly for Canada, a feasible minimum rate of 3 per cent was arrived at in an official study.[5]

On the basis of postwar experiences outside North America, we are strongly tempted to consider even a 3 per cent rate as being unnecessarily high also for the United States and Canada. The empirical methods employed in the above-mentioned studies, although quite different from each other, rely heavily on actual national unemployment data for postwar years when unemployment, according to the experiences of the respective country, was at its lowest. Actually, the last-mentioned United States study implies that 1953, when unemployment was lowest and averaged 2.9 per cent (respectively 2.6 per cent if the recessionary rise toward the end of the year is discounted), was a year of overfull employment even though prices were

3. Subcommittee on Employment and Manpower of the Senate Committee on Labor and Public Welfare, *Toward Full Employment: Proposals for a Comprehensive Employment and Manpower Policy in the United States* (Washington, D.C., 1964), p. 40.

4. R. A. Gordon, "Full Employment as a Policy Goal" in Arthur M. Ross, ed., *Employment Policy and the Labor Market* (Berkeley and Los Angeles, 1965), particularly pp. 49–55.

5. Frank T. Denton and Sylvia Ostry, *An Analysis of Post-War Unemployment*, Staff Study No. 3, Economic Council of Canada (Ottawa, 1964), particularly p. 18.

quite stable. We, on the contrary, consider this experience as specific evidence that the minimum feasible rate of unemployment in the United States should lie well below 3 per cent. This view does not of course deny the fact that at an unemployment rate below 3 per cent there will tend to be excess demand for labor both in individual sectors, occupations, or geographical areas in Europe and North America. Canada reached a 2.6 per cent rate in the Korean war boom year of 1951.

In particular the much lower unemployment rates achieved in most European countries has induced us to choose 2 per cent of the labor force as the minimum feasible unemployment rate to be applied uniformly for calculating the potential or full-employment labor force in all countries studied. According to the considerations given above, there has not been sufficient ground for a differentiation between North America and the other countries. Although the uniform application of this 2 per cent norm certainly is rather arbitrary, we feel that it is sufficiently close to the feasible minimum rate of practically all countries in question as not to distort the picture seriously. The choice of a uniform computation norm is also justified from the point of view that fairly precise independent norms for the individual countries are lacking because of the well-known reluctance of governments to commit themselves to precise targets. Finally, as emphasized above, for the sake of international comparability a uniform minimum unemployment rate seems not only convenient but preferable. The specific choice thus means that the potential output measure will be built upon the assumption of 98 per cent of the available labor force being employed.

There remains, of course, the nasty problem of the international comparability of the statistical concepts and measurements of unemployment. It is well known, but nevertheless often forgotten, that differences in the concepts and particularly the methods of counting unemployment may make international comparisons of the absolute levels of the unemployment percentage strongly misleading. Fortunately, particularly during the last years, attempts have been made to standardize the unemployment percentages by adjusting them in the direction of the concepts applied in the United States.[6] Although we are well aware that the unemployment percentages we finally used for the various countries studied are approximations, and may in some cases not yet be strictly comparable, we nevertheless consider their use as worthwhile, since the tentative description and provisional appraisal of important aspects of comparative economic performance is definitely to be preferred to the complete lack of such description and appraisal.

Potential employment is thus assumed to correspond to a 98 per cent utilization of the available labor force. For a measure of the available labor force we have relied on the actual data on the size of the labor force when unemployment was relatively low.[7] It might have been more appropriate for the present purpose to try to determine what the labor force would have been if unemployment in each country had been successfully kept at the 2 per cent rate chosen as a norm. But preliminary investigation did not suggest any obvious aggregative adjustments, and what the exact consequences for the labor force participation of various groups are when the economy is

6. We are thinking here of the efforts by Angus Maddison, *Economic Growth in the West,* Appendix E; by OECD in assembling the figures in *Manpower Statistics,* published first in 1963; and finally of the revisions made by the United States Bureau of Labor Statistics, which are the most comparable estimates available, but unfortunately cover only a limited number of countries and years. For the latter see the President's Committee to Appraise Employment and Unemployment Statistics, *Measuring Employment and Unemployment* (Washington, D.C., 1962), Chap. 10 and Appendix A, giving revised estimates for 1960. Also Robert J. Myers, "Unemployment in Western Europe and the United States," in Arthur M. Ross, ed., *Unemployment and the American Economy* (New York, 1964), giving figures adjusted to United States definitions for 1961 and 1962.

7. In all cases where it is possible, we use the figures in OECD, *Manpower Statistics,* 1950–62 and 1954–64.

operated with varying degrees of strain or slack remains unresolved.[8]

Full-employment output at the chosen 98 per cent rate of utilization of the labor force will further depend upon the normal average number of hours worked per man-year and the potential average output per man-hour. The normal average number of hours worked at the 98 per cent employment norm could in principle be determined on the basis of quantitative information on normal vacation, holidays, and weekly hours in different sectors of the various economies. The determination of potential average output per man-hour could be approached by means of appropriate production functions which would take account of the major factors affecting the (total) productivity of the labor input.[9]

For the present comparative study we have chosen a less elegant shortcut method that avoids most of the data problems with which we otherwise would have to contend. We hope, nevertheless, that this simpler approach yields, at least roughly, the same basic results. The method consists basically of the following steps. First, the actual figures for real GNP in years of relatively high economic activity are adjusted by the difference in percentage points between the actual (standardized) unemployment rate and the 2 per cent norm. In the case of some countries the figures were further adjusted for crop fluctuations.

8. For evidence of a systematic relationship between changes in the labor force and the demand for labor, see Alfred Tella, "The Relation of Labor Force to Employment," *Industrial and Labor Relations Review* (April 1964); as well as William G. Bowen and T. A. Finegan, "Labor Force Participation and Unemployment," in Ross, ed., *Employment Policy and the Labor Market,* pp. 115–61.

9. This elaborate type of approach was chosen by Knowles, "Potential Economic Growth," in a commendable attempt at estimating what the potential economic growth in the United States is. Even if an equivalent set of data was available also for the other countries included in the present study, we could not, in the present context, hope to be able to apply his elegant but laborious type of technique even to a limited number of the countries.

Second, at least two and at most four such adjusted figures (some of which are the average of the adjusted figures for two consecutive years) were selected for determining the trend of potential output. Third, potential output in the remaining years is determined by log-linear interpolation between the selected points and in some instances (for example, Belgium 1956–61, Germany 1957–60, Canada 1956–64) by extrapolation beyond selected points. In connection with such extrapolation, account was taken of significant differences in the growth of the labor force between subperiods. Obviously the suggested method involves a considerable degree of arbitrariness and subjective judgment, particularly in the case of countries where actual unemployment did not fluctuate closely around the stipulated 2 per cent norm during at least the first half of the 1950s.[10] With the help of the resulting potential output path, the instability of real GNP can then be expressed as the percentage deviations of actual real GNP from potential GNP. Other methods of weighting the deviations are of course also conceivable; for example larger deviations might be given greater than proportional weight, and variations within a certain limited range around potential GNP might not be counted as instability.

The result of the described procedure is presented in Figure 3.2 in a series of graphs giving the development profiles of our countries. For each country and each year covered we are now able to see to what extent actual output exceeded or fell short of the potential output which would presumably have accompanied a not unfeasible steady 98 per cent utilization of the available labor force. Canada, the United States, Italy, Germany, Denmark, Belgium, and the United Kingdom show periods of negative gaps, which would primarily reflect an

10. We feel that for present purposes our method of trend selection, which is based on some knowledge of underlying relationships and circumstances, is preferable to trend selection on the basis of purely statistical criteria, such as a least-squares fit. We have also tried to adjust the fix points for large crop fluctuations in the agricultural sector wherever it seemed necessary (Canada).

FIGURE 3.2
Development Profiles: Growth of Actual and Potential GNP at Constant Prices (actual GNP in 1950 = 100)

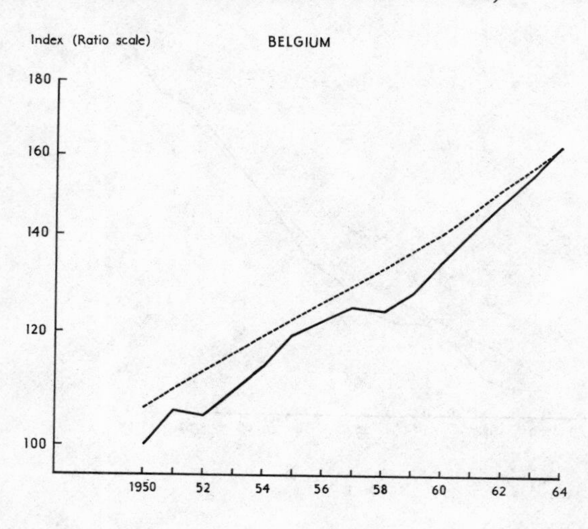

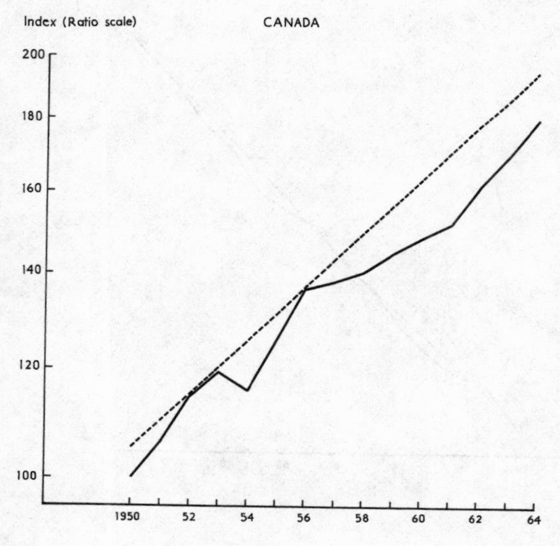

FIGURE 3.2—*Continued*

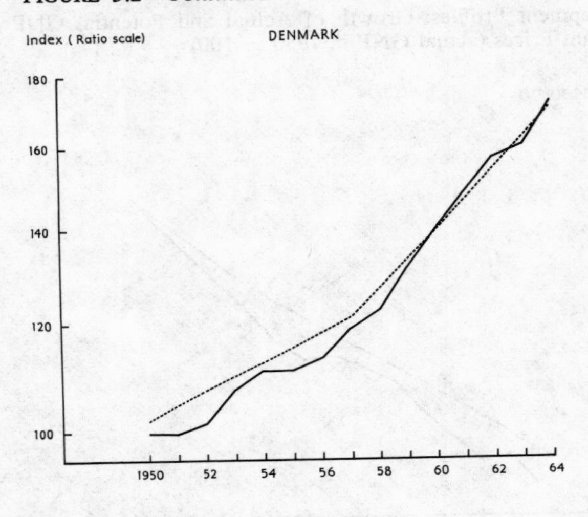

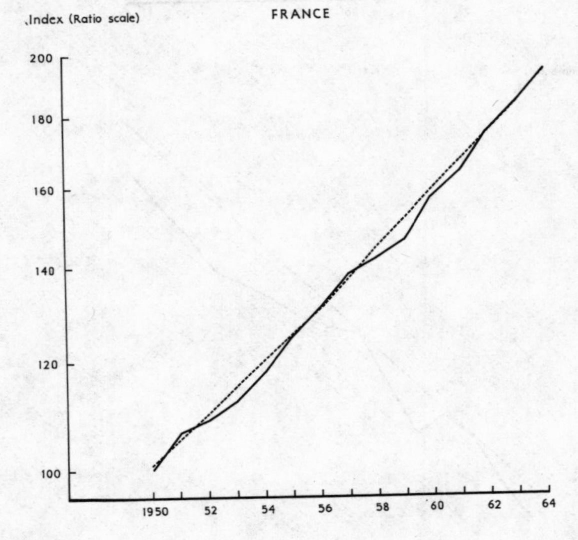

FIGURE 3.2—*Continued*

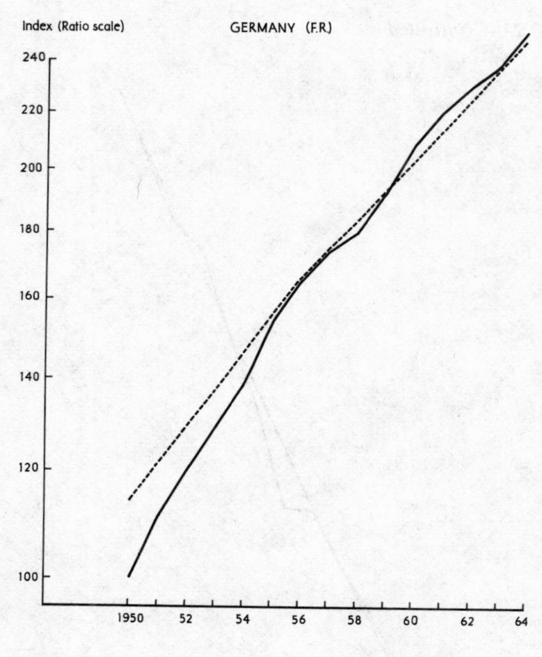

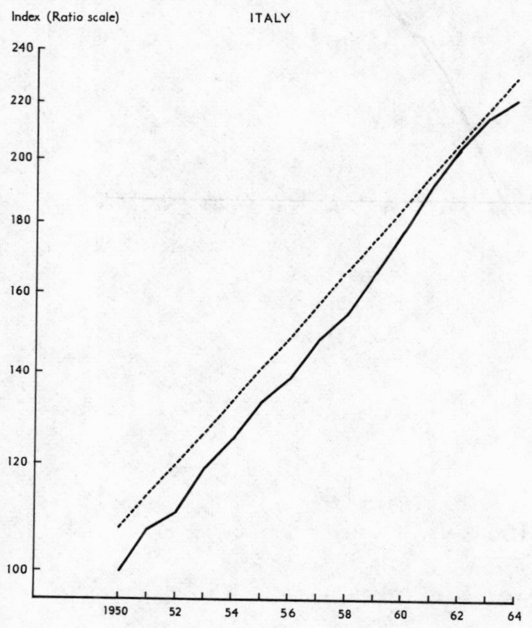

FIGURE 3.2—*Continued*

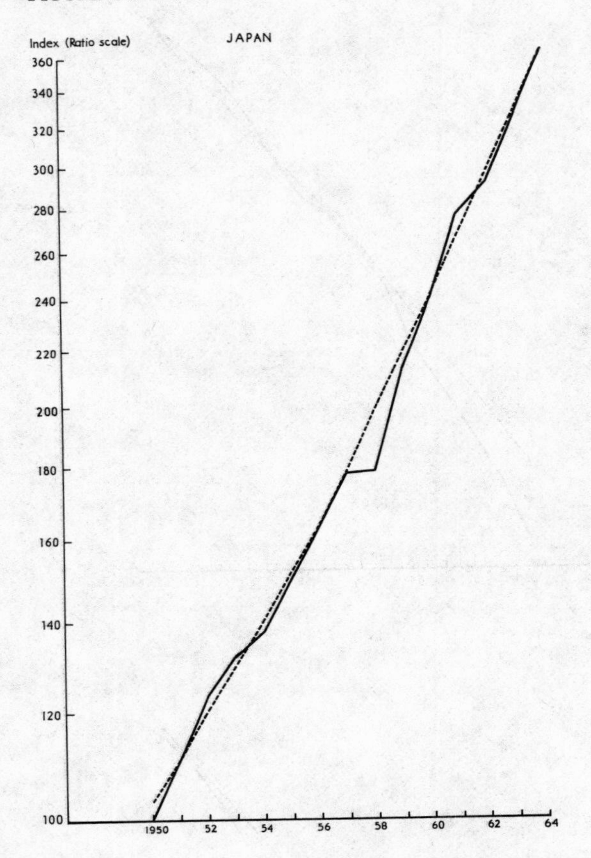

FIGURE 3.2—*Continued*

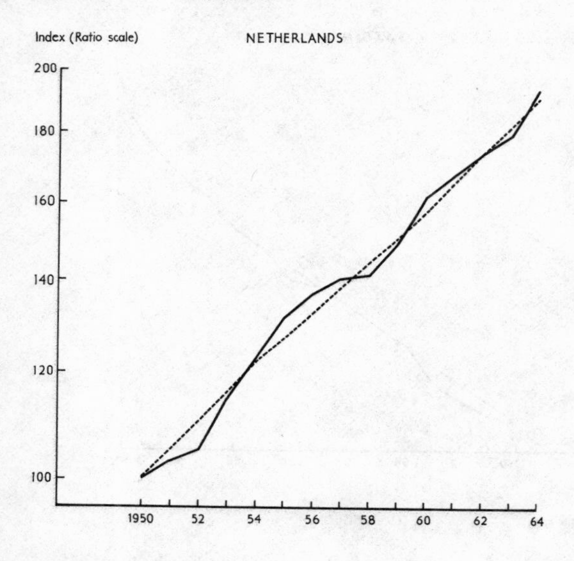

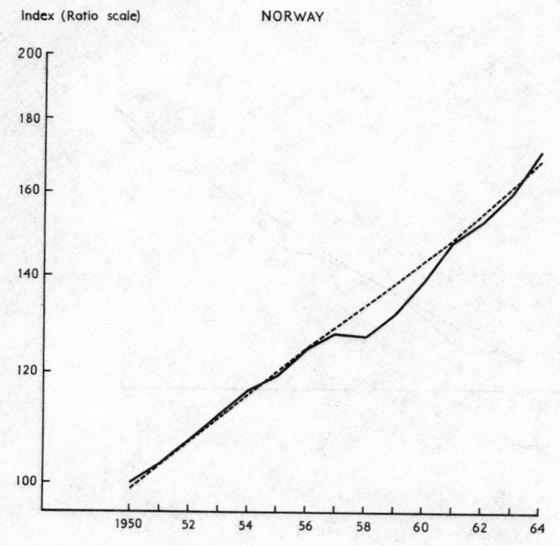

FIGURE 3.2—*Continued*

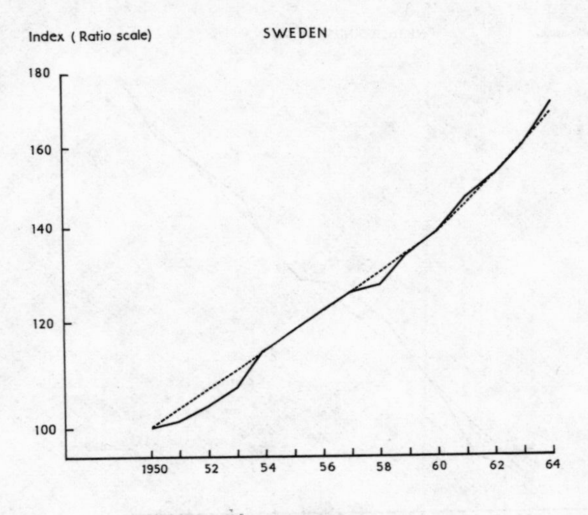

Index (Ratio scale)
UNITED KINGDOM
180
160
140
120
100
1950
52
54
56
58
60
62
64

FIGURE 3.2—*Continued*

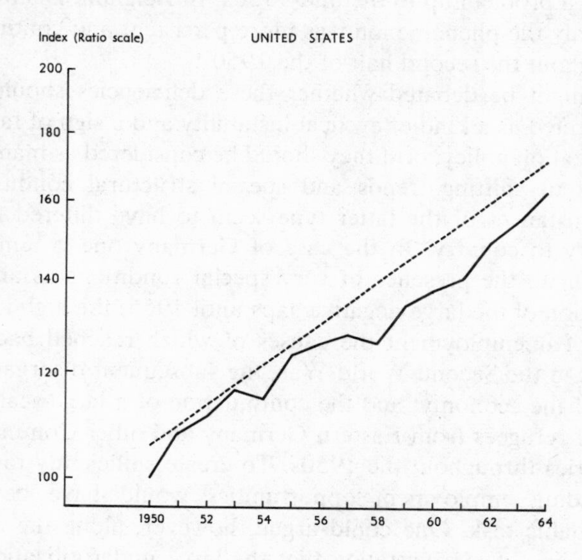

inadequacy of total demand. The inadequacy of demand, which partly may be regarded as a short-run business cycle phenomenon and partly may reflect longer-run demand deficiency, caused a shortfall of actual output. These shortfalls in the case of the United States added up to about a year's total GNP over the fifteen-year span. The cumulative loss of output in Canada, which appears to have been of similar order of size, partly reflects difficult-to-avoid problems on account of the developments in the dominating economy of the United States and partly reflects failures in the conception and execution of economic policy. (See Chapter 8.) In contrast to the experience of these countries, where the problem of a longer-run inadequacy of total demand became acute mainly during the second half of the 1950s and the first years of the 1960s, the underutilization of potential output in Germany was primarily a problem up to the mid-1950s. In Belgium, Denmark, and Italy the phenomenon was more persistent and continued throughout the second half of the 1950s.

It might be debated whether these deficiencies should be interpreted as a kind of cyclical instability and a sign of failing stabilization policy, or if they should be considered as manifestations of shifting trends and special structural conditions. Circumstances of the latter type seem to have differed from country to country. In the case of Germany one is tempted to point to the presence of very special conditions as an explanation of the large negative gaps until 1955: the high initial level of unemployment the causes of which reached back to defeat in the Second World War; the subsequent disorganization of the economy; and the continuation of a large-scale influx of refugees from Eastern Germany and other Communist countries throughout the 1950s. To create sufficiently rapidly expanding employment opportunities would have been a formidable task. One could argue, however, along the alternative line of interpretation that the large underutilization of the existing capital stock in the first years of the 1950s as well as the rapid accumulation of the gold and foreign exchange reserves after 1950 would suggest the possibility that excess unemployment could have been eliminated more quickly by means of stronger demand pressure.[11] The negative GNP gaps in Denmark seem more clearly to be indicators of inadequate demand referring to balance of payments and policy restrictions. Toward the end of the 1950s, partly thanks to structural changes giving the necessary balance of payments space, the gaps disappeared in connection with more expansionary policies. The considerable underutilization of the country's potential output in Belgium, during the 1950s, might be blamed on governmental attitudes and policies which in particular in

11. For supporting evidence, see Ferdinand Grünig, *Die makroökonomischen Determinanten des Wirtschaftspotentials,* herausgegeben von Klaus Dieter Arndt und Rolf Krengel (Deutsches Institut für Wirtschaftsforschung, Sonderhefte N.F. Nr. 52, Berlin, 1960).

the first half of the 1950s were primarily concerned with inflation at the cost of full employment as a policy goal.[12] Italy's underachievement with regard to potential output was more clearly linked to structural unemployment, particularly in the underdeveloped south, than the corresponding gaps in any of the other countries mentioned.[13]

These six countries here mentioned not only showed a preponderance of negative output gaps but also had the largest average gaps between potential and actual output. However, it should be pointed out that the positive deviations of actual output from the trend of potential output are necessarily limited as to size because of the closeness of various types of supply limitations, whereas no such limitations exist for movements below the trend. Of course, this does not mean that negative gaps have to be larger than positive ones; total demand, though deficient, may still be sufficiently close to the level that would be adequate so that a low average gap may result. The group of countries which at least recurrently achieved or exceeded potential output includes the Netherlands, Sweden, Norway, France, and Japan.[14] The significance of the small differences in the average GNP gaps of these countries should not be ex-

12. L. Morrissens, "Economic Policy in Belgium," in E. S. Kirschen and Associates, *Economic Policy in Our Time* (Amsterdam, 1964), Vol. 31, p. 24.

13. George H. Hildebrand, *Growth and Structure in the Economy of Modern Italy* (Cambridge, Mass., 1965).

14. The application of the standard procedure for calculating potential output would have met particular difficulties in the case of Switzerland. The calculated gaps would therefore be even more arbitrary and tentative in that case. The published data for registered unemployment remain below 0.5 per cent of the labor force during each of the fifteen years covered. Even after upward adjustment of the data on the basis of the censuses of 1950 and 1960, the figures remain below 0.5 per cent of the labor force. Enumeration of the basis of the concepts and procedures applied in the United States would probably raise these figures but, one suspects, still yield very low unemployment percentages. Further difficulties arise out of the high responsiveness of the annual

aggerated in view of the many practical problems involved in the present application.

In some countries, a considerable part of the positive deviations of actual from potential GNP refers not only to a temporary rate of employment exceeding the chosen norm of 98 per cent of the labor force but also to what may be considered as an accompanying rise of man-year productivity above its potential path. A large part of these increases is likely to be the result of a temporary rise in working hours. It would of course be possible to argue that any positive deviations of actual from potential output, on account of either an "abnormal" rise of employment or man-year output, should not be considered as representing instability. Potential output would, according to this view, be interpreted as the lower limit for the magnitude that actual GNP should reach but that may be exceeded without being considered as instability. This consideration would mean that the instability index scores of the second group of countries mentioned would become still smaller in relation to the scores of the first group.

But what about price stability as another goal of economic policy? There is a widely accepted view that price-level changes and the degree of excess demand are rather closely related. If it can be assumed that the calculated GNP gaps are reasonably good proxy variables for changing demand pressure during the period surveyed, price-level changes and GNP gaps should be expected to show a clear positive correlation. The observations for the individual countries, covering as a rule fifteen pairs of annual observations for the period 1950 to 1964, show surprisingly little evidence of the expected positive relationship, however. Still, it is plausible and even probable that price-level changes in individual countries are somewhat more strongly related to the variations in demand pressure

---

rate of immigration of foreign labor to the pressure of demand in Switzerland throughout the 1950s and the first years of the 1960s before the introduction of restrictive government measures.

FIGURE 3.3
Average Annual Change of GNP Deflator Related to the Average GNP Gap, 1950–64 (percentages)

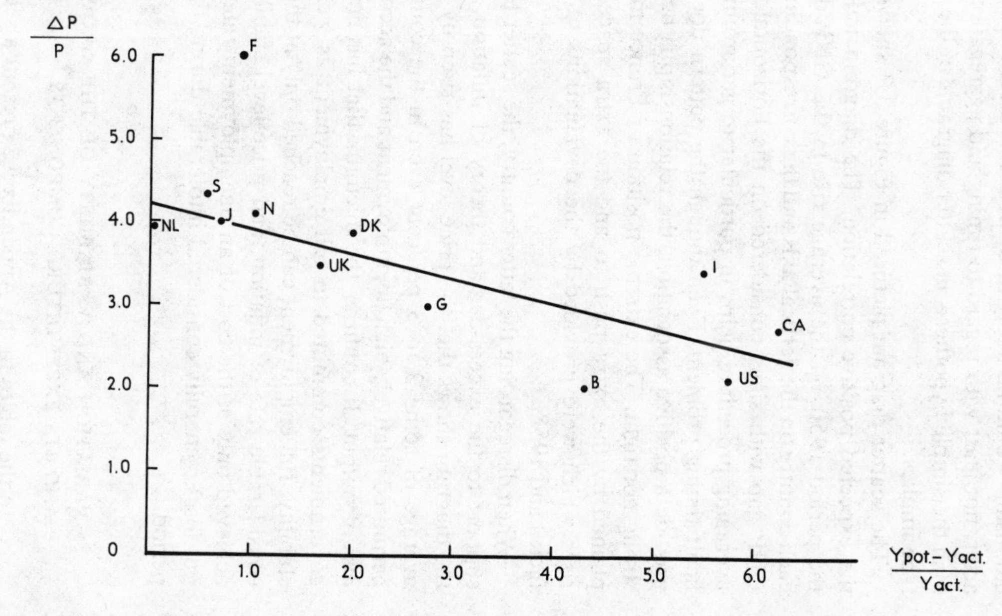

indicated by the calculated GNP gaps; but any such causal relationship would be likely to be of much more complex character, not least with regard to timing and aggregation aspects, than the simple hypothesis in scatter diagrams of the suggested type implies.

The scatter diagram pictured in Figure 3.3 shows more of the expected positive correlation. The diagram indicates for the period 1950–64 the average rise in the GNP deflator of each country on the vertical axis and the corresponding average GNP gap with signs considered on the horizontal axis. The averaging procedure helps in particular to get around the difficult timing problem. Even though the pattern does seem to provide a positive association, the relationship is neither very strong nor tight. The extreme position of France may be explained by the extra push to and the extra space for price rises which were provided by the devaluations of 1957 (de facto) and 1958.

When disregarding the latter country, the scatter lends some support to the excess-demand theory of inflation. However, the diagram shows that the price level has risen by an annual average of some 2 to 3 per cent even in the countries that permitted relatively high unemployment and the accompanying loss of output. It confirms the dilemma that has embarrassed governments committed to full employment as well as price stability: full employment can be reached only at the cost of a considerable rate of inflation, and price-level stability can be achieved only at the cost of an unemployment rate (and output loss), generally considered intolerable during the postwar period.

VARIATION AND VARIABILITY OF THE GROWTH RATE AND ITS EXPENDITURE COMPONENTS

In the tables in the Appendix we present a second set of instability measures. Each table shows for a specific country the actual rate of growth of real GNP and its expenditure composition, both annually and as an average for the period 1950–64. The second to last column on the right-hand side of each table indicates the average deviations of the annual percentage rates of growth of GNP and its expenditure components around their respective mean rate of growth given in the third to last column. The *average* deviation of the annual percentage rates of growth of GNP—the mean variation of the GNP growth rate—serves as our second measure of overall economic instability; it is sometimes referred to in this book as the *GNP-variation index* in contrast to the previously discussed *full-employment gap index*.

Finally, the last column on the right-hand side of the tables shows the ratios of the average deviations and the respective mean rates of growth. These ratios represent a measure of the average variability or volatility of the growth of GNP and its components; they are of interest to us primarily as a measure of the average variability of the components. As can be seen from the tables, this sort of presentation of the GNP accounts—which concentrates on the first differences of the variables and expresses these first differences as percentages of the previous year's GNP—represents a convenient summary of some of the most basic manifestations of economic instability in an individual country. It also greatly facilitates meaningful international comparisons of instability patterns. In a given country each year's percentage rate of growth of GNP is thus decomposed into changes in expenditure on private consumption, government purchases, total fixed private investment, inventory investment, total exports, and total imports, with the changes in the component variables all being expressed as percentages of the preceding year's GNP at constant prices. In this way the relative importance of the yearly changes in these items for the total GNP change can be immediately read off in the table and compared with the corresponding changes in other countries.

Table 3.1 in the beginning of this chapter shows from each of the above-mentioned country tables in the Appendix the annual rates of growth of GNP, their average, and their average variation for the fifteen-year span from the beginning of 1950 to the end of 1964. These indicators are not to be identified with cyclical changes only. The measures are in a way more general and permit us to observe irregularities in the growth process without "cyclical preconceptions." Nevertheless, the strong retardations or absolute declines around the recession years and, to a more limited extent, the spurts during recovery explain a considerable part of the instability as recorded; actually, differences in the frequency and the size of such specific changes in GNP growth explain the main part of the international differences in the size of this second instability measure.

The ranking of the countries according to our first measure of instability—the full-employment gap index—is in most cases not changed much. Canada and the United States have a high degree of instability, even according to the new index; Sweden, Norway, and France remain at the other end of the list. The order is radically changed only in the case of Italy and Japan; the first country shifts from the high instability end of the list to the other end, and the latter country from low instability according to the full-employment gap index to the top of the list according to the GNP variation index. Given the actual differences in the growth patterns and the conceptual differences of the two methods of measuring instability, such shifts are unavoidable.

We have already mentioned that we do not intend to put much emphasis on the variability ratio of GNP which is the result of dividing the GNP-variation index by the average rate of growth of GNP. This is because of conceptional reasons, since the undesirable aspects of overall economic instability (aside from questions of differences between the trends of actual and potential GNP) seem to be somewhat more clearly related to the variation of GNP growth rather than its variability.[15]

15. In practice, as long as it is only a matter of ranking according to the size of the measure of GNP instability, the order would not be

When we look at the expenditure components of GNP as given in the above-mentioned country tables in the Appendix, new problems arise. Even apart from questions of functional relationships, it is not easy to get a clear picture of how the observed output instability—the variation of the GNP growth rate—and the instability of its expenditure components are related, since the variations in the growth of the components cancel or reinforce each other to a varying extent. Nevertheless, it may still be worthwhile to try to compare at this relatively general level the instability patterns of these components in the different countries in order to establish some basic similarities or dissimilarities between the instability of GNP growth on one side and the instability of the growth of the GNP components on the other side.

The arithmetical relationship between the average variation of GNP growth and its components can be said to depend upon how much the growth of the components fluctuates, how much the growth of the components on average contributes to the growth of GNP, and to which degree the weighted fluctuations of the components are synchronized with each other. The variability ratios of the components in the last column of the country tables in the Appendix provide an answer to the first question; the third-to-last column an answer to the second

---

modified much, except for Japan with its extremely high growth rate, where the relative instability score would thus greatly decrease, and the United Kingdom with the lowest growth rate, where the score would greatly increase. It is in particular the contrast between these two extreme cases that causes one to realize that an equal variation of, say, three percentage points in a country growing at some 10 per cent on average and one growing at less than 3 per cent on average may represent a less serious problem in the first country. This example could be interpreted in favor of the variability ratio. On the other hand, it is not in any way clear why an equal variation in the growth rate should be counted only one third as much in the first country as in the second, which would be the implication of applying the variability ratio in this example.

TABLE 3.2

The Variability of Growth of the Expenditure Components and the Variation of GNP Growth (1950–64)

	Variation[a] of	*Variability[b] of growth of*					
	GNP growth	*Consumption*	*Government expenditures*	*Gross fixed private investment*	*Inventory investment*	*Exports*	*Imports*
Japan	3.5	0.4	0.6	0.8	5.4	0.4	0.8
Canada	2.7	0.3	0.9	1.6	12.9	0.9	1.1
United States	2.6	0.5	1.5	1.8	5.5	1.6	0.7
Denmark	2.5	0.8	0.5	0.9	16.2	0.4	0.9
Austria	2.4	0.3	0.6	1.2	3.1	0.5	1.0
Netherlands	2.3	0.7	0.8	1.2	8.1	0.4	0.8
Germany (F.R.)	2.2	0.2	0.4	0.5	30.7	0.4	0.3
Switzerland	1.8	0.4	0.9	0.5	5.7	0.3	0.7
Belgium	1.6	0.6	0.8	1.7	64.0	0.4	0.6
Sweden	1.5	0.4	0.4	0.7	83.0	0.6	0.7
United Kingdom	1.4	0.5	0.9	0.7	7.5	0.8	1.0
Italy	1.4	0.3	0.5	0.6	7.7	0.4	0.7
Norway	1.4	0.4	0.5	1.1	28.6	0.4	0.4
France	1.4	0.3	0.8	0.6	21.0	0.8	0.7
Unweighted average	2.0	0.4	0.7	1.0	21.4	0.6	0.7

a. See note to Table 3.1, p. 86.

b. Variation of the component's annual rates of growth divided by the component's average rate of growth.

question; and, finally, the second-to-last column contains a partial answer to the third question.

Table 3.2, which reproduces the last column of each country table, shows, at least within the range of experience of one and a half decades and fourteen countries, that the degree to which the growth of the individual components fluctuates on average has in general no clear association with the degree of variation of the GNP growth rate. The table does confirm rather convincingly that the growth rate of inventory investment is by far the most volatile, and that the growth rate of consumption is on average most stable. The growth of private fixed investment tends to be roughly twice as variable on average as the growth of consumption and total GNP.

Taking account not only of the variability of the growth of the components but also of the components' share in the longer-run growth of GNP, which is shown in Table 3.3, represents the second step in our attempt to outline the (arithmetical) relationship between the instability of GNP growth and its components. Finally, Table 3.4 indicates the combined effect of the first two factors.

This is a good opportunity to clarify a widespread misconception about the relative stability of consumption. As can best be seen from the average given in the first column in Table 3.4, the consumption part of GNP growth tends to show quite high instability and is thus not the least unstable of the major expenditure items. This is the consequence of the very large average share of consumption in GNP growth which swamps the effect of the low variability of consumption growth. Similarly, the extremely high variability of the growth of inventory investment is moderated in its impact on the GNP growth rate by a generally very small share of inventory investment in long-run GNP growth. Nevertheless, it still remains on average the most unstable part of GNP growth, although the difference to the corresponding average figure for imports is minor.

Although Table 3.4 suggests some positive association between the variation of GNP growth and the variation of some of

TABLE 3.3

Relative Contribution of Expenditure Components to the Growth of GNP (1950–64)

	Consumption	*Government expenditures*	*Gross fixed private investment*	*Inventory investment*	*Exports*	*Imports*
Japan	0.46	0.19	0.27	0.06	0.20	−0.18
Canada	0.65	0.18	0.17	0.02	0.22	−0.25
United States	0.59	0.24	0.12	0.05	0.02	−0.02
Denmark	0.56	0.21	0.25	0.03	0.61	−0.66
Austria	0.64	0.12	0.26	−0.11	0.46	−0.37
Netherlands	0.53	0.16	0.24	0.05	0.98	−0.96
Germany (F.R.)	0.57	0.18	0.24	0.00	0.38	−0.37
Switzerland	0.53	0.12	0.29	0.07	0.45	−0.55
Belgium	0.60	0.21	0.15	0.00	0.71	−0.66
Sweden	0.53	0.26	0.23	0.01	0.47	−0.50
United Kingdom	0.58	0.16	0.24	0.05	0.27	−0.29
Italy	0.57	0.16	0.24	0.01	0.30	−0.29
Norway	0.47	0.23	0.22	−0.01	0.81	−0.72
France	0.65	0.15	0.19	0.01	0.21	−0.20

TABLE 3.4

Variation[a] of the Expenditure Components of GNP Growth (1950–64)

	Consumption	*Government expenditures*	*Gross fixed private investment*	*Inventory investment*	*Exports*	*Imports*	*Ratio of gross to net variation of GNP growth*
Japan	1.9	1.2	2.1	3.1	0.9	1.5	3.0
Canada[b]	0.9	0.7	1.2	1.4	0.8	1.3	2.4
United States	1.1	1.4	0.9	1.0	0.4	0.2	1.9
Denmark	1.9	0.4	0.9	1.9	1.0	2.5	3.5
Austria	1.0	0.4	1.7	1.9	1.3	2.0	3.5
Netherlands	1.7	0.6	1.4	1.9	1.7	3.7	4.7
Germany (F.R.)	0.9	0.5	0.8	0.9	1.0	0.8	2.7
Switzerland	1.0	0.5	0.9	1.8	0.7	1.9	3.8
Belgium	1.4	0.6	0.9	0.6	1.1	1.6	3.7
Sweden	0.8	0.5	0.7	1.7	1.1	1.3	4.0
United Kingdom	0.9	0.4	0.5	1.2	0.7	0.9	3.3
Italy	1.1	0.5	0.8	0.5	0.7	1.2	3.4
Norway	0.8	0.4	1.0	1.4	1.3	1.2	4.6
France	1.0	0.6	0.6	0.8	0.8	0.7	3.3
Unweighted average	1.2	0.6	1.0	1.4	1.0	1.5	3.4

a. Deviation of the respective rates of change, expressed as percentages of the previous year's GNP, from their average. Signs disregarded.

b. Variation of residual error not reproduced. See table in the Appendix.

the components in some countries, the conclusion must clearly be that the instability of the growth of GNP depends most of all on the extent to which the fluctuations in the growth of the components reinforce or cancel each other. This is confirmed by the last column in the table comparing the *gross and net variation of GNP growth*. The gross variation of each country is equal to the sum of the average variations of the growth of the six GNP components (as given by the first six columns in the table). The net variation of each country is simply the figure for the average variation of the growth of total GNP.

Obviously, the gross variation tends to be larger for the smaller countries in the group. The Netherlands, Canada, Denmark, Sweden, Belgium, and Norway have experienced relatively larger variations in the growth of the various GNP components than have the United Kingdom, the United States, Germany, France, and Italy. But the variations in the growth of the components tend to offset each other to a greater extent in the smaller countries.

Notice, for example, the contrast in the size of the ratio between the gross and net variation between Sweden and the United States. Should this be interpreted that there are more stabilizing forces in the Swedish economy than in the United States economy? Or is the contrast mainly a result of differing stabilization policies? Actually, part of the much larger degree of offsetting among the growth variations of the components in the Swedish economy is due to the operation of the economy much closer to potential output and the limits of total supply. A further part of the difference in the degree of mutual compensation among the variations in the growth of the components refers to the difference in the importance of foreign trade, since variations in the growth of exports and imports tend to be mutually offsetting rather than additive. This is shown by a comparison of export and import developments in the country tables in the Appendix.

The gross instability coefficient for Western Europe, although not reproduced in any of the tables here, is lower than the corresponding figure for any of the individual countries. The net instability coefficient is slightly below the lowest corresponding figure for the individual countries. How much of the lower instability in Western Europe as a whole compared to the United States is due to a lesser degree of synchronization between regions within the first area, and to what extent is this due to a higher degree of policy independence of the individual countries?

TRENDS AND FLUCTUATIONS

Is it plausible that the faster growth rate of Western Europe, where real GNP increased on average by 5 per cent per year and industrial production by 7 per cent over the period 1950–64, may help to explain the lower degree of variation of GNP growth of this area compared to the United States, where both real GNP and industrial production rose on average by 3.8 per cent per year over the same period? As mentioned above, we may hope to be able to find some guiding evidence about the relevance of such a hypothesis by looking at the empirical relationship between growth and instability in the case of individual countries and industries. We find, for example, that the low growth rates of Belgium and the United States have been associated with relatively high instability regardless of the method of measuring instability. But for the other countries the case is not at all so clear-cut, and depends largely on the type of measurement of cyclical instability one chooses to adopt. If one measures instability in terms of the mean (or root-mean-square) deviation from trend, then no clear relationship can be detected in either the annual GNP data of the country tables in the Appendix or the monthly data of industrial production (shown in Figure 3.1). On the other hand, if we adopt a measure of instability that refers to the number of quarters below previous peak levels of activity or to the cumulated declines below peak levels, then a negative correlation emerges, a result which is hardly very surprising.

With *given* fluctuations around the trend line, clearly, this second way of measuring instability will result in a higher index of instability the slower is the rate of growth.

It should be added that neither one of these measures of cyclical instability may be satisfactory for the case of deep depressions or of a failure of peak levels of activity to reach the level attainable at full employment. But this aspect has already been treated in connection with the measurement of the gaps between actual and potential output.

We need also to remind ourselves that instability taking the form of excess demand or overfull employment is not adequately reflected by any one of the measures discussed here. In this respect, by only observing actual output variations we may certainly be underestimating the instability of total demand in several European countries as compared to the instability of total demand in North America.

When we compare the countries of Western Europe and Japan with those of North America with respect to growth and instability in the postwar period, it is important to remember the very great difference in starting conditions immediately after the war. In the case of the United States, already around 1948 total output exceeded its prewar peak of 1937 by about two thirds. In Western Europe, GNP at constant prices had only just regained its prewar peak level around 1948, whereas the population was now 8 per cent larger than before the war. Only around 1955 did Western Europe reach the same total and per capita level of production in relation to the prewar peak as the United States had reached in 1948. But of course there existed also great differences between the European countries, as Table 3.5 indicates.

Such observations of postwar levels of activity relative to prewar peak levels can give only a rough indication of short-term growth possibilities as conceived from the *supply side*. In addition to the growth made possible by the correction of the war-induced disorganization of production and trade and the replacement of physically deteriorated and destroyed capital, a big improvement in the production functions, due to the technological advances made during the war, had sharply raised the potential per capita levels of output. Much of this discrepancy between actual and potential levels of output remained in the beginning of the 1950s, the start of the period studied. But the positions of the countries in this respect varied immensely. Compare, for instance, the cases of Germany and Sweden. The former experienced during the 1950s a rate of growth of industrial production that was three times the rate of the latter (1950–60: Germany 10 per cent, Sweden 3.5 per cent per year). The striking difference can be partly explained as being the result of the very much higher growth possibilities of German industry, which had experienced extreme wartime destruction and disruption, and in addition had a very rapidly growing supply of labor due to the influx of refugees, a very high percentage of whom were young. In 1950 the index of industrial production (1937=100) was standing at 90 and 150 for Western Germany and Sweden respectively. Seen from this angle, the very rapid rise of production in Germany relative to Sweden is largely the result of the successive reduction of the large deficiency of actual production with respect to potential production. This type of discrepancy in base-year conditions is certainly important when assessing differences in the trends, and may also be relevant for explaining differences in cyclical instability.

This type of argument, referring to potential growth possibilities viewed from the supply side, certainly is not intended to reveal a sufficient cause for the realization of high rates of actual growth during a recovery period after the war. For the realization of rapid growth, it is necessary that the growth of aggregate demand is sufficiently strong. The development after 1920 may be taken as a good illustration of the point that a large *supply potential* in this sense is not enough for rapid and relatively stable growth. (See Chapter 2.) Table 3.5 indicates the output levels of the industrial sector in 1920 as a percentage of the prewar peak levels of 1913, as compared

TABLE 3.5

Relative Levels of Industrial Production after the Two World Wars

	1920 in per cent of 1913	1947 in per cent of 1937-38 average
Austria	—	18%
Belgium	18%	106%
Denmark	138%	118%
France	69%	88%
Germany (F.R.)	59%	35%
Italy	91%	93%
Netherlands	—	102%
Norway	109%	120%
Sweden	95%	140%
United Kingdom	100%	114%
Canada	—	179%
United States	136%	190%
Japan	—	34%

Source: OEEC, *Industrial Statistics, 1900-1957*.

with the corresponding conditions in 1947. Although these percentages are even lower than the comparable figures after the Second World War, the growth of industrial production after 1920 was in general neither as rapid nor as stable and prolonged as after the Second World War.

Within the limits of potential growth, the actual developments of output during the postwar period was determined by factors of *demand*. The low level of real expenditure on non-military consumption and investment during the war had created backlogs of demand which under the given policy conditions tended to put strong pressure on the available resources. These backlogs referred in general to all kinds of deficiencies with producers as well as with consumers: inventories of goods in production lines, in trade, and in households; the previous lack of adequate replacement of worn-out or technically deficient durable assets in industry, trade, and households as well as the insufficiency of capital accumulation with regard to the growth of population, and new products. Actually, some of the war-related backlogs were added to previous backlogs which were consequences of the depression in the 1930s. There were similar backlogs with regard to civil government. In addition, the reawakening of international tensions a few years after World War II added new "autonomous" government spending for defense. During the first decade after the war, the issue was usually formulated as a situation of *excess demand* or *inflationary* gap. At the then-prevailing full-employment levels of output, the sum of the private and public monetary demand for consumption and investment purposes tended to exceed the actual short-term supply of goods and services at the given prices.[16]

The general existence of strong and persistent demand pressure may be considered as part of an explanation for the absence of any significant setbacks in most Western European countries. The elastic supply conditions discussed above, which implied a rapid response of total production to a real increase of demand, did not necessarily contribute to a quick reduction of the demand pressure, since additional income created by the rise in production and prices tended to add new fuel to the inflation fire.

The tendency toward continued generally strong demand pressure in Western Europe as a direct or indirect consequence of the above-mentioned backlogs manifested itself in a high and usually rising share of government in total GNP and a

16. This concept of "excess demand" can be used as a general vague expression for prevailing inflationary conditions. "By excess demand we mean a volume of aggregate monetary demand that cannot be met at existing prices without exerting undue pressure on productive resources." (OEEC, *The Problem of Rising Prices,* p. 33.) Or we might try, under the precise conditions of an explicit model, to define the "inflationary gap" and even measure it. For the formulation of more exact and abstract definitions of the concepts of inflationary gap ("commodity gap" and "factor gap") see Bent Hansen, *A Study in the Theory of Inflation* (Uppsala, 1951).

high and often rising investment ratio. The postwar restoration and expansion of production facilities furthermore led in a number of countries to a pronounced shift in the foreign balance from a situation of large current account deficit during the first Marshall plan years to a balanced or even a surplus position in the early 1950s. For example, Austria, Germany, and the Netherlands moved from current account deficits amounting respectively to 8, 2, and 10 per cent of GNP in 1948 to surpluses representing 2, 3, and 8 per cent of GNP in 1953. In fact, this shift absorbed from one tenth (in the case of Germany) to three quarters (in the case of the Netherlands) of the rise of real GNP during those years.

Thus the growth of exports, government expenditures on goods and services, and private gross fixed investment during a considerable part of the postwar period can be considered as mainly a reflection of such autonomous "push factors."

It can be seen in the country tables in the Appendix that the pattern of development of these "push factors" from the beginning of 1950 on varied significantly between the countries of North America on one side and the majority of Western European countries on the other. Excepting France and the United Kingdom, the European countries showed much faster and more stable growth in the sum of these demand components than the United States and Canada. In Europe, the above-mentioned backlogs reenforced by ambitious targets with regard to government activity and housing needs were generally much more important and longer lasting than in North America. On the other hand, the impact of autonomous changes with regard to military expenditures (particularly in connection with the Korean war) was much stronger in the United States. They did actually contribute to the higher instability experienced there during the 1950s. As will be shown in Chapter 8, federal military expenditures in particular have on more than one occasion actively created or strongly contributed to cyclical reversals. It is apparent that the mildness of the European setbacks in overall activity are largely a reflection of both the strength and the persistence of these push factors, which on the other hand resulted in problems of excess demand in most European countries.

The autonomous character of a large part of total spending is likely to have successively disappeared between the late 1940s and the mid-1950s. The expansionary effect of an export drive, for example, is likely to have changed character once the original balance of payments disequilibriums have been solved; from then on, following a liberalization of import controls, increasing exports will be more or less matched by parallel developments on the import side. Of course, a balanced rise of exports and imports will still have expansionary effects along the lines demonstrated by the theory of the balanced budget multiplier, but the multiplier effects will be lower than when import reactions were regulated. The growth of the export volume in terms of GNP almost matched the rate of growth of the volume of GNP itself in the case of Norway, and more than matched it in the case of the Netherlands (see the country tables in the Appendix). If we approximately adjust exports (as well as investment) for their content of imported goods and services, then the rate of growth of GNP accounted for by rising exports (or investment) will no longer be quite as high, although still remarkable. However, the pattern of export variations, especially around 1951–52 and 1957–58, reveals that this element of demand was in the case of most European countries the most unstable among the demand-push factors, and contributed heavily to the sharp reductions in the growth rates of GNP which then occurred.

Various parts of the investment sector must have successively lost their autonomous "push" character and become increasingly susceptible to the state of current demand. This, of course, actually happened first with respect to inventory investment. At the end of the war, most branches of industry and trade had very insufficient stocks of raw materials and finished goods. Thus, the early postwar years experienced an extra push from this side. During the 1950s and 1960s inventory investment did not contribute any sustantial amount to growth; as mentioned above, however, as a factor of instability it has maintained a dominating position for various branches of industry and trade as well as for the economy as a whole.

A continued boom in private fixed investment may finally tend to create overcapacity situations in a growing number of sectors in the economy. Already, before any serious deficiencies of capacity utilization occur, new investments in various fields of activity tend to an increasing degree to be influenced by current demand and financial conditions, thus getting more easily involved in cyclical developments. There are indications that a number of branches such as iron and steel, shipbuilding, and wood products had reached this stage around 1957 in Western European countries. The tendency toward increased sensitivity of investment activity to the current demand and profits situation had become even more evident by 1961. It could perhaps be said that European private industry had reached a stage of cyclical sensitivity similar to the stage the United States had reached about a decade earlier. This type of difference seems perhaps still more apparent with regard to housebuilding. In the United States an equilibrium on the market for new or old dwellings was more or less attained in the beginning of the fifties after a long housebuilding boom and a marked adjustment of the rent levels (after rent controls had been abolished in most cities). After that the volume of housebuilding activity became closely related to current overall demand and financial factors, and thereby a variable with relatively high cyclical sensitivity. The contrast in these respects to the conditions in Western European countries is striking. Here there is a domination of excess demand situations on the markets for flats and houses, and a building boom prevailing with the volume of activity mainly determined from the supply side (modified by financial controls and other forms of government regulations).

The conjunctural sensitivity of an economy cannot be understood of course only from the point of view of demand-supply relations of the type discussed. There are interrelations over a period of time manifested in accumulated experiences that must be kept in mind. In this respect it might be suggested that, in the European countries which during the first part of the postwar period had realized rapid and continued growth, there has occurred a buildup of *strong expectations* of continued substantial and essentially uninterrupted growth in markets and incomes. Such confidence in the future would imply relatively strong overall resistance of fixed business and consumer investment expenditures in the face of short-run downward disturbances in some part of total demand (for instance in exports). Thus, downward disturbances in some part of the economy would be dampened not only by the automatic stabilizers built into the fiscal system (plus stabilizing discretionary policy measures) but also by the acquired growth habit of the private sector of the economy. This kind of stability in growth expectations within the private sector would, of course, have been intermixed with anticipations of continued inflation. Generally prevailing expectations of a long-run steady rise of unit wage costs and prices were probably intermingled in an unaccountable manner with the anticipations of expanding markets. Under the conditions that prevailed in most European countries, a setback in some category of final demand would therefore in the short run have been prevented from effectively spreading to other parts of the economy, so that total demand would have tended to go on rising. A setback would be likely to be reflected only in a slowing down of the rate of growth of real GNP rather than in a truly recessionary interruption of growth.

In a "high pressure" economy as compared to a "low pressure" one, certain parts of private investment expenditures may even be automatically accelerated during periods of slack due to quicker deliveries and a more elastic labor supply; investment costs may be lower than during the past boom, and still more so as compared with conditions during an expected new boom. As discussed especially in Chapter 5, that type of reaction may have been quite pronounced in the business sector of the Swedish economy during the 1958 recession and its reversal. Such stabilizing business behavior may be suspected among progressive corporations with reliable growth prospects. But since total investment in plant and equipment at constant prices usually has shown some decline during periods of slack, it appears that any such stabilizing effects have usually not been sufficient to compensate fully for the destabilizing tendencies arising from difficulties of financing investment in periods when profit margins are squeezed, markets are dull, and inventory levels relatively high.

In brief, we have suggested that strong autonomous demand forces in the private sectors supported by similar factors with regard to the public sector have after the war and probably up to the mid-fifties tended to push the economies toward excess demand and have thereby greatly strengthened their resistance against recessionary forces originating from external shocks (including restrictive policy changes). The resulting stable development in turn helped to generate attitudes and behavior which had largely similar stabilizing effects even after the original sources of excess demand had largely become exhausted. To what extent, however, government policy factors have contributed to the favorable result in general and to the short setbacks in particular is a difficult problem that we cannot answer in any definite way.

CONJUNCTURES AND GOVERNMENT ECONOMIC POLICY

The previously presented simplified interpretation of the relationship between trend and conjunctural factors must be considered in the context of government economic policy. Besides the development of government expenditures on goods and services, which only to a limited extent can be taken as evidence of economic policy measures in the sense discussed here, the conditions created by monetary and fiscal policy, as well as by more direct controls over investment and foreign trade, help to determine the actual pattern of economic growth. However, as repeatedly argued in this study, the policy factors generally cannot be isolated from the events in the rest of the economy. In order to understand the short- and long-term developments in the economies in question, we should not only assess the probable effects of the policies that were actually carried out but also try to understand why and how the policy measures came about.

In some of the countries, policy changes can to a large extent be explained by reference to the varying foreign exchange situations. The basic possibilities for fast and stable growth have in several instances been delimited by balance of payments problems. This applies particularly to the United Kingdom, Japan, the Netherlands, Denmark, and Italy. In the United Kingdom, foreign exchange crises, or the serious threat of such crises, have been the basis of restrictive policy measures in 1947, 1949, 1951, 1955, 1957, 1960, 1961, and 1964–65. The restrictive actions were mainly directed at government expenditures, fixed investment, and durable goods purchases. The economic policy restrictions may not only have affected the development of aggregate demand, but may also have reduced the rate of growth of potential aggregate supply via effects on the growth of productivity and capacity. The key to the low rate of growth of productivity and potential output in the United Kingdom may thus lie in the relatively low investment ratio, import restrictions on complementary materials and equipment, and a certain lack of competitiveness following protectionist policies. (See Chapter 4.)

It is interesting to compare the economic progress of a number of countries, all of which had to live through intermittent periods of exchange difficulties with concomitant restrictive policy actions. Up to 1957 the experiences of the United Kingdom and Denmark are rather similar, with frequent periods of foreign exchange difficulties and with interrupted and slow growth of per capita real GNP. From 1957 on Denmark's situation has developed much more favorably than the United Kingdom's with respect to growth. Significantly enough, this change was accompanied by a rapid rise of industrial exports, which represented a strong demand-push factor and for the time being reduced the risk of exchange difficulties at given rates of growth. But a new exchange crisis occurred instead in 1962–63. In the United Kingdom, on the other hand, there was no comparably strong increase in export growth during the same period.

The Netherlands, which in 1950–51 and 1956–57 experienced foreign exchange problems and therefore adopted restrictive policy measures, was nevertheless able to match the rapid per capita growth of real GNP of Switzerland, a country whose ample foreign exchange reserves had never been threatened. A major proximate reason for the much better performance of the Dutch economy compared to the British may lie in the fact that the former had rapidly and continuously expanding exports whereas the latter did not. In the case of France, persistent foreign exchange problems were (up to 1958) dealt with not primarily via restrictions on internal demand, as in the case of the United Kingdom, Denmark, and the Netherlands, but rather via direct import restrictions and devaluations. Part of the difference between the French and the British growth rate might be related to the fact that in France economic policy apparently did not act as a brake on both aggregate demand and supply to the same extent as in Britain. Large government-sponsored investments and rapidly rising productivity promoted a fast rate of growth of French aggregate supply at full-employment levels of production. Italy provides still another case of a serious growth disturbance caused by policy restrictions due to balance of payments disequilibrium. Up to the beginning of the 1960s Italy's growth achievement belonged to the marvels. However by the end of 1961 the boom finally gave way to serious inflation which gathered momentum in 1962–63. The restrictive monetary policy that was introduced from the summer of 1963 on was quite effective in eliminating the balance of payments deficit by the summer of 1964, but the dampening effects on investment and growth became surprisingly prolonged.

Angus Maddison,[17] concluded in his admirable portrait of the postwar business cycle in Western Europe that the European economy no longer operates as it did in prewar years. He related the essential difference not to a really greater inherent stability of the private forces of the economy but to government intervention which succeeded not only in limiting the range of fluctuations but also in ensuring that the fluctuations take place at higher levels of output and employment. However, he also concluded that the fluctuations in output and employment that did occur within that limited range were largely induced by specific government policy measures. Whereas the first part of this statement, referring to government's stabilizing influence in general, is more important, the second part, relating actual instability to particular government intervention, is more challenging.

Milton Gilbert[18] also adopted the view that in most countries of Western Europe growth should, or at least could, have proceeded without the small recessions around 1951–52 and 1957–58 *if* no significant impediments from the policy side had been introduced. In most countries, the prevailing trends of the demand factors were strong, in some countries even so strong as to cause a more or less permanent tendency toward demand inflation. Therefore, the assertion goes, the setbacks that actually occurred were mainly due to the introduction of restrictive government measures. Changes in economic policy were induced not only by the necessity of meeting actual or apprehended foreign exchange difficulties but also by serious concern about inflationary developments. Whereas in the United Kingdom and the Netherlands, for example, the basic

17. Angus Maddison, "The Postwar Business Cycle in Western Europe and the Role of Government Policy," *Banca Nazionale del Lavoro Quarterly Review* (June 1960), particularly pp. 114–25.

18. Milton Gilbert, "The Postwar Business Cycle in Western Europe," *American Economic Review, Papers and Proceedings* (May 1962).

anxiety related to the external position, in other countries, like Sweden, the concern was primarily about the internal situation. Similarly, the widespread manifestations of excess demand in 1955 and 1956 as well as 1960 and 1961 may be brought into relation with the previous government policies aimed at speeding up recovery and accelerating growth. In fact, an account of all the postwar economic policy measures carried out to correct foreign exchange difficulties and to combat either inflationary or recessionary tendencies may look so impressive that little room may seem to have remained for the free play of cyclical behavior patterns characteristic of economic development in earlier periods.[19]

Before we attempt to assess further the relevance and implications of the *theory of policy-induced instability,* it should be mentioned that such an interpretation of events is not restricted to the set of postwar economic experiences. As shown in Chapter 2, the international economic instability of the 1920s cannot be explained without strongly emphasizing the gold and foreign exchange policies of the central banks, which, in conjunction with monetary policy, had a deflationary impact in various countries. If the severity of the American downturn in 1929 can be attributed to the collapse of the financial system brought about by the sudden and violent reversal of the stock market boom, then substantial blame must go to Federal Reserve policy which had permitted the development of a speculative orgy. The sad history of large-scale unemployment, deflation, and reduction of world trade in the 1930s can only be understood by paying attention to the economic policy measures accompanying the debacle.

Policy decisions are taken at discrete intervals for reasons that can be specified to a considerable extent. We are concerned

19. For chronological accounts of short-term as well as long-term policy measures from 1949 to 1961 in Belgium, France, Italy, the Netherlands, Norway, the United States, and Western Germany, see E. S. Kirschen and Associates, *Economic Policy in Our Time,* Vols. 2 and 3.

with the effects of economic policy measures, and thus need a model which will help us to assess the direct and indirect effects on economic development of policy measures as well as of other specifiable disturbances. We therefore need a model giving the essential characteristics of the response mechanism, as well as the major impulses originating outside the economic policy field, in order to determine the system's reactions to the actual policy changes. Of course, the results of such an analysis must be taken with a grain of salt in view of the rather simple hypotheses on which such models usually have to be based.

There are some thorny problems in the way of regarding policy changes as causal factors in the cyclical development of an economic system of this type. It may be unclear how to understand the word "cause," and it is not self-evident how we should interpret the concept of changes in policy.

It is possible, of course, to imagine a stabilization policy so effective that no fluctuations in total activity appear. For example, the 1951–52 and 1957–58 recessions in the various countries could have been prevented by means of a sufficiently inflationary policy before and during 1952 and 1958 respectively; or we could imagine a specific policy with taxes and subsidies, licenses, and directives interfering with those branches where activity was considered too high or too low. Since such effective policy measures were obviously not carried out, economic policy might be blamed for the occurrence of those recessions. It may be said that the experiences with the recessionary tendencies in Europe during 1961–62 in some cases came rather close to this policy perfection. Whether this is a relevant statement or not will be discussed in some of the country studies (especially Chapters 5 and 6).

Our first task is to search for the probable effects of specific policy changes on economic development. For example, we may try to answer questions of the following type: If in the United Kingdom during 1951–52 (and again during 1955–57) none or fewer of the restraining policy measures had been introduced, would the country consequently have experienced a longer expansion period and a shorter recession, or even no recessionary setback at all? Further, to what extent would such a course of events have implied larger imports to the United Kingdom and thus prevented the recessionary impact on other countries' exports to the United Kingdom that actually occurred? Would not a stronger and longer lasting inflationary boom accompanying an easier policy have been followed either by an earlier, or by a later and more severe, exchange crisis for the pound compared with the actual crises of, for example, 1951 and 1957? Would, in the case of a less restrictive policy, inventory accumulation have proceeded much more rapidly with the consequence of more severe readjustments than the ones that actually took place? Should we therefore imagine that a much more restrictive set of policy measures with more serious instability effects would have become necessary during a postponed crisis, or should we adopt the view that a sufficient coordination of expansionary policies between the various governments could have prevented the possibility of serious balance of payments disequilibriums? In the first case, we should apparently conclude that it was not primarily government policy but longer-run weaknesses in the balance of payments that caused the instability. In the second case, however, we could again maintain that the actual recessions were a consequence of faulty and internationally uncoordinated economic policy measures.

Similarly, we might ask questions about the possible effects of introducing less of directly stimulating policy changes during the recession. Would then the setback have been deeper and more prolonged, or would the following period of expansion have developed instead along a lower path and in a less inflationary manner, with less risk to the country's foreign exchange position? (Why do such questions sound ironical?)

It would be very useful in a comparative study of policy effects to have a systematic presentation of the major policy measures which the various countries applied during the period under review. It should be observed, however, that there is no clear line of demarcation between active policy changes and more or less automatic responses of certain policy parameters. A change in tax schedules, for example, can clearly be regarded as a causal factor, and we may therefore try to assess its effects. A change in tax revenue or in the outcome of the government budget, on the other hand, has to be considered as a response of the economic system to the extent that there has been no change in either discretionary expenditures or in the schedule of rates of taxation and rates of unemployment compensation. A change in government investment expenditures may be the consequence of active policy efforts, but it may also be a passive response to changes in the availability of labor and materials when business conditions take a turn. The same kind of considerations apply also with regard to monetary policy. To what extent should the stringency of the money market following a balance of payments deficit be viewed as an automatic response of the central bank's selling of foreign exchange? We usually may also be in doubt to what extent a change in, say, long-term rates of interest is due to a deliberate change in monetary policy and to what extent it is due to automatic changes in market conditions.

In all such cases we have to distinguish between more or less automatic responses to changes in the economic system and deliberate policy actions. An active policy measure will always contain an element of automatic response to economic changes. Thus we cannot without careful analysis of the circumstances compare, for example, the "degree of activeness" of stabilization policy among different countries, since, besides differences in "policy needs" due to different degrees of "autonomous" instability, there is also the difficulty of distinguishing between active policy changes and passive responses.

It would be interesting to characterize and, if possible, to explain the preference of individual countries for stabilization measures of a particular type—as, for example, the French emphasis on government investment planning with active sponsorship of subsidies for and licensing of investment projects as well as on import controls and devaluations; the German and Belgian emphasis on monetary policy; the Dutch stress on econometric forecasting and "monetary planning"; the utilization of discount policy, purchase tax, investment allowance, and installment credit regulations in the United Kingdom; and the strong reliance on fiscal and labor market policies in Norway and Sweden. However, our prime task remains to assess the anticyclical effectiveness of various types of policy measures. How is it possible to verify statements of the following kind: "The effectiveness of monetary policy has been biggest as an anticyclical weapon in Germany where the range of measures used has been large, and where business relies heavily on the banks for finance and has *usually* been less liquid than in other countries"?[20] In all such cases we have to deal with rough distinctions between responses of the economic system as such and deliberate policy actions.

THE NEED FOR COUNTRY STUDIES

Let us conclude this chapter by presenting a brief, preliminary survey of some generally or at least widely accepted notions about the postwar cyclical characteristics of the advanced economies of the Western world. We shall have to study the effects of policy changes against this background. In this connection, it is important for us to return to the question, discussed in Chapter 2, of in what respect the business cycle mechanism has changed since the interwar period.

One basic problem is how the different national economies would have behaved during the postwar period if none or fewer of the policy changes had occurred. If we could show that the economies of some countries would have followed a more

20. Maddison, *Economic Growth in the West,* p. 134, italics added. Also see the same source on p. 138.

stable growth pattern without stabilization policy interference, then it would be established that policy measures were one cause of the instability that actually occurred. But even if we could make such a proposition plausible in the case of some countries (like Germany, Sweden, and Italy, for example, during some part of the postwar period), in the case of other countries (such, for example, as the United Kingdom, the Netherlands, and Denmark) it may instead be possible to show that a "free development" under given conditions—including fixed exchange rates—would have led to more serious exchange difficulties than the ones that actually occurred. Under such conditions, restrictive policy measures may be considered stabilizing because of their ability to prevent, or at least to mitigate, inflation, to keep imports down, and to avoid still more serious exchange difficulties. But, of course, it remains an open question if the necessary measures had to be of such a character that other instability effects, such as growth retardation and recession, were inevitable. If these measures also had restrictive effects on other countries' exports, then recessionary impulses were transmitted to those exporting nations. Of course more steady expansion in combination with devaluation would have been an alternative.

In fact, the *transmission of cyclical disturbances* among countries via repercussions on international trade and capital movements is still an important feature of the development pattern in the Western world, although the disturbances at the source of the transmission process have fortunately been of more moderate size in the postwar period than in the interwar period. In order to analyze this aspect of economic instability, we would have to look at the variations in the volume and value of total exports, and compare the experiences of the interwar and postwar period. Studies of how these export changes are created from import reactions in the major trading nations would have to be followed by a discussion of their connection with policy changes. Such reactions followed, for example, the British policy restrictions of 1951 and 1957; case studies might enable us to discover the influence of British import reductions on other countries' exports. The recessions after 1951 and 1957 were followed by declines of raw material prices affecting the export earnings of a large number of underdeveloped countries; their exchange difficulties might, after varying time lags, have had effects on their demand for imports from developed countries. Observations of total trade could be complemented by corresponding studies referring to some individual branches of activity (in particular textiles, iron and steel, shipbuilding).

Recurrent inflationary tendencies are another characteristic feature of postwar economic development. Periods of strong excess demand are for some countries also periods of rising import surpluses and growing balance of payments problems. The balance of payments consequences of excess demand depend very much on the *relative degree* of internal disequilibrium as compared with corresponding conditions in other countries. Rising prices and unit wage costs are parts of the inflation problem, again varying in degree and as to effects on the balance of payments positions of the various countries. These inflation phenomena are closely related to current policy measures. Starting from 1949 (after the devaluations), 1954, and 1959 respectively, it would be easy to show that in most countries a "free" development with fiscal and monetary parameters at given 1949, 1954, and 1959 levels respectively would have led to more serious excess demand for goods and labor than actually was the case. Note, however, that this hypothetical statement should imply given rates of growth of government expenditures. Inflationary tendencies have been a long-established feature of the boom phases of business cycles; postwar development has differed from previous experiences only insofar as the postwar upturns started much closer to the full-employment ceiling of activity than during earlier periods. As pointed out before, excess aggregate demand is just as much a deviation from some kind of general equilibrium trend as deficient aggregate demand, although the deviations may be weighted differently. There is therefore no reason why fluctuations in demand above a full-employment trend should not be considered as cyclical instability in the same way as fluctuations below the full-employment trend, even if the measurement will be more of a problem.

The interwar upper turning points usually occurred at a time when restrictive policy measures were at a maximum, and the same feature appears in the postwar period. There may be a positive spurious correlation between the frequency of policy changes and the variability of the instrument in question, on the one hand, and cyclical instability on the other. This, of course, will not lead us necessarily to the conclusion that active stabilization policy tends to create instability. But such a possibility may be stimulating for more systematic comparative research. The problems of isolating the effect of policy measures from the endogenous working of the "pure" business cycle are still troubling us in trying to analyze postwar experiences of various countries; the difference compared with earlier experiences is really one of degree only. The postwar booms have mostly been stronger and more prolonged at the same time as the restrictive measures introduced have been more numerous, more varied, and more ambitious. But it would be a difficult task to prove that these measures have been more restrictive in relation to the "expansionary forces" at work in the postwar booms than, for example, in 1920 or 1929.

The difficulty of determining the effects of anti-inflationary measures refers in part to the tendency toward a slowdown of the pace of expansion as the boom proceeds. On the demand side, the high rate of growth of inventory investment—which usually is a characteristic feature in the early development of a boom—cannot be maintained for many years; the rate of accumulation will slow down by necessity and thereby tend to weaken the expansionary forces. A more or less automatic decline in the growth of inventory investment may occur or there will at least be a high vulnerability of inventory investment to negative shocks, possibly but not necessarily originating in tightening monetary policy measures.

Considerable timing conformity of the inventory movements in various sectors of an economy is, of course, necessary for inventories to have a general impact on the cycle in total economic activity. The outbreak of the Korean war initiated a highly synchronous upward shift in the demand for a wide range of commodities in a large number of countries, and the synchronization of the boom was further accentuated by the unusually rapid rise in the world prices and speculative buying that consequently developed. The ensuing setback was therefore—not surprisingly—characterized by large inventory readjustment. Again, during the 1954–57 period, rapidly rising total demand, prices, and wages created an international atmosphere favorable to an inventory boom comprising important sectors of all economies. However, the less synchronized and more gradual start of this expansion period contributed in general to a more balanced development with regard to inventories, so that inventory readjustments in general were not so pronounced when the boom came to an end. In 1961–62, recessionary tendencies due to inventory investment behavior affected some branches of activity—in particular wood pulp and paper, iron ore, iron and steel—but the majority of other branches did not conform with these developments.

The analysis of economic policy measures may give us a better understanding of the pattern of inventory investment in the various countries. Since, however, inventory booms may break down due to the working of their own endogenous mechanism and without assistance from the policy side being necessary, it will in most cases be rather difficult to decide if and how economic policy measures have affected the rate of inventory investment. When trying to determine, for example, whether restrictive monetary action has either precipitated a downturn or reduced the intensity of a boom and thereby possibly prolonged the expansion, we usually have great difficulties in finding convincing evidence. Even if we should find that in a given case economic policy has had little to do directly with the rate of inventory investment, there still remains the possibility of an indirect impact of policy via effects on the size and composition of final purchases as well as on the general state of demand and the conditions of supply.

As pointed out earlier, cyclical reactions of total fixed investment have been comparatively small in the postwar period: stagnation rather than decline has been the characteristic feature during recessions. Residential construction, which in most countries is susceptible to close government control via the high degree of government financing and via licensing, has in many cases been a stabilizing influence during periods of recession in general economic activity. In the case of the Belgian 1958 recession, however, it contributed heavily to the considerable drop in total output. Declines of investment in plant and equipment have characterized especially the recessions in the Netherlands, the United States, and Canada, whereas in most remaining countries no significant declines can be observed for recession years. Some individual branches of activity ran into considerable overcapacity problems in the periods 1956–58 and 1961–63 after high prices and profits during the earlier boom periods had promoted a rate of investment that turned out to be excessive even under generally good economic conditions. Nevertheless, overcapacity features have been rather rare in Western Europe during the postwar period, in marked contrast to the interwar experience. The role of government economic policy for the development of private fixed investment in booms and recessions will again be a difficult problem. How much higher would these investment expenditures have risen without restrictive policies, and what reactions would have occurred in a later recession? There will be much room for subjective views in such matters since, as will be discussed in some of the country studies, the evidence tends to be inconclusive particularly because of the lack of sufficient knowledge on relevant quantitative relationships.

It is usually taken for granted that private consumption expenditure has become a much more stable element of total demand. This is certainly true to the extent that the percentage variations around the trend of the total level of private consumption expenditure are smaller than the percentage variations around the trend of the level of any other major demand category. However, the considerable variability in the relation between consumption expenditures and GNP in some countries—as discussed above—may in part be the result of policy changes (with regard to purchase taxes, income taxes, and hire purchase regulations), as will be shown in some country cases.

It seems that the stability in private income formation, in the downward direction, is the most important factor responsible for the absence of cumulative depressions. But such a statement is just question-begging; we are apparently referring back to the whole mechanism of income determination, including all the factors we have been discussing, not least the automatic stabilizers and the policy measures. And again we should remember that this "downward" stability is "purchased" at the cost of an inflationary bias. It is a common experience of our countries, although in varying degree, that wages and prices tend to rise too rapidly in situations at or close to full employment.

What has been said in this survey of conjunctures experiences in Western Europe, North America, and Japan is rather general and thus tends to blur many important, more specific problems. In order to focus on the latter we have to take account of relevant conditions and circumstances in the individual countries. But instead of a more intensive investigation of all individual countries in question, which is beyond the means of the present study and would in any case be likely to become unnecessarily repetitive, we limit ourselves in the following to half a dozen countries. Even with regard to these countries there is no ambition toward complete coverage of events and problems. As stated in Chapter 1, we have tried to choose among the countries as well as among their specific experiences and problems in such a way that the various conjunctural and stabilization policy problems that have been mentioned here are illuminated from different angles. Efforts are thereby made to understand the reasons for and the effects of stabilization policies introduced. Although the results of this analysis are of limited general validity, only comparisons of the country experiences could in any event be helpful in eliminating or at least casting doubt upon various assertions in this field.

4 GROWTH INTERRUPTIONS AND BALANCE OF PAYMENTS RESTRICTIONS IN THE UNITED KINGDOM

GENERAL VIEW ON INTERRELATIONS BETWEEN GROWTH AND CYCLES

There are some remarkable features of the United Kingdom's postwar development which offer convenient starting points for the discussion. These are: the slow rate of growth of GNP (on average 2.6 per cent per year), in fact the lowest rate of all countries compared; the relatively rapid rise in the GNP price deflator (on average some 3.8 per cent per year); the low variation of the GNP growth rate as compared with most other Western European countries (but which took the form of stagnation periods, interrupted by short spurts of rapid growth). There is, however, high instability in the growth of the volume of exports and imports (only Canada and the United States show a higher degree of variability in this respect) and in the growth of real expenditure for durable consumption goods. On the other hand, total fixed domestic investment has shown relatively high stability (highest of all countries), but a remarkably low ratio to GNP.

These experiences have to be studied against the background of quite ambitious efforts to carry out monetary and fiscal policies aimed at stabilizing the economy. During the period 1950–64, the British authorities repeatedly tried out a series of policy measures in order to check the expansion of demand, on the one hand, and to stimulate demand during periods of recession and stagnation, on the other. In particular, the introduction and continuation of restrictive policy measures has been closely connected with balance of payments strains—such as occurred in 1949, 1951, 1955, 1957, 1960–61, and 1964–65—which implied narrow constraints for the development of the economy.

A number of central issues open up when we try to understand the instability experience of the United Kingdom. There is a wealth of material, and a still greater wealth of high-class economic analysis and a continuing stimulating discussion among economists, regarding the development problems and the policy issues involved.[1] One trouble is that there are so many sensible alternative interpretations of the causes and mechanisms of the conjuncture as well as of the role of the policy changes. The statistical material does not give clear answers to pertinent questions, and the theories simply open up wide areas for possible interpretations and further research.

Let us start by putting down the main problems that are of interest for our discussion of stability problems.

There may exist interrelations between the slow rate of growth and the instability of total demand as given by the development of real GNP. Mathematically such a relation can be taken as self-evident or trivial: if total real demand had increased at an even rate of 4 to 4.5 per cent per year—as in the "best" periods—then the average growth rate would have

1. This survey depends heavily on the excellent analysis presented in J. C. R. Dow, *The Management of the British Economy 1945–60* (Cambridge, 1964). Other books that have been of value are: G. D. N. Worswick and P. H. Ady, eds., *The British Economy in the 1950's* (Oxford, 1962), especially the chapters by I. M. D. Little on fiscal policy and Charles Kennedy on monetary policy; F. W. Paish, *Studies in an Inflationary Economy* (London, 1962): A. Lamfalussy, *The United Kingdom and the Six* (London, 1963). Current issues of the *National Institute Economic Review* provided a further important source of information.

been two thirds higher than the average rate actually experienced and just about equal to the Western European average. This calculation implies among other things the elimination not only of the recession years but also of *the stagnation periods* of relatively slow growth (1951, 1955–57, and 1961) that seem to be characteristic for the postwar development in the United Kingdom.

However, it is clear that such a method of calculation cannot be taken seriously, since these few years of a good growth rate must be regarded as partly conditioned by the "space for expansion" existing after a recession (or a stagnation period) in the form of reserves of labor and capital capacity. As the utilization of capacity during the boom periods seems to have reached close to the ceiling of available manpower, and probably also of physical capital, the instability of demand as such need not imply any retardation of long-term growth—*on the condition* that this instability has not unfavorably affected the growth of the supply factors, that is the labor force and particularly output per man. The low unemployment and high vacancy rates reached during 1950–51, 1955, 1960–61, as well as 1964, indicated that these periods were characterized by full or possibly overfull employment.

In fact, these intervals have been characterized as periods of excess demand for labor and commodities.[2] This implies that an extra push of demand would not have accelerated growth significantly—unless it was specifically directed to areas of unemployment or sectors of excess capacity. The excess demand started declining from the beginning of 1956; the figures for the percentage of unemployment started to rise and unfilled vacancies to decline. This development can be taken as a sign of declining demand pressure. But how do we then know if the stagnation of production growth after 1955 was mainly determined by capacity limitations or by insufficient demand expansion? Unemployment and vacancies were very unevenly

2. See Dow, Chap. 13, sect. 2.

distributed, and there were indications of some excess capacity arising even before the 1958 and 1962 recessions. According to the measurements of the National Institute of Economic and Social Research, the stock of fixed capital in manufacturing industry increased by about 15 per cent from the beginning of 1955 to the beginning of 1958, while manufacturing output increased only a few percentage points from 1955 to 1957 (and came down to the 1955 level in 1958).[3] The situation seemed to be similar after the end of the 1959–61 investment boom. At the end of 1961 there was, according to reports from firms,[4] a margin of unused capacity of around 15 per cent in manufacturing.

Here we thus meet the usual problem of interpretation. During the boom periods there was full employment (according to reasonable definitions) and excess demand for skilled labor combined with indications of excess plant capacity in a number of firms and branches of industry, but with quite an uneven distribution. This situation implied the simultaneous existence of excess demand in some sectors and deficient demand in others, with a consequent, maldistribution of resources. We may therefore maintain that the causes of the low rate of production and productivity expansion during the later parts of the boom period should be sought as much in low flexibility of labor and capital as in a general deficiency of demand.

A calculation of the "growth loss" from unstable development must aim at finding out how the supply of capital, labor, and entrepreneurial initiative and activity may have been impaired by demand instability. The gross (fixed) investment ratio has been relatively low (16 per cent on the average for our period as compared with rates varying between 20 to 30 per cent for most other Western European countries). To what

3. See the *National Institute Economic Review* (January 1959). Cf. the United Nations publication, *Some Factors in Economic Growth in Europe during the 1950's* (Geneva, 1964), Chap. 4, Table 10, p. 21. See also Chapter 3 above (p. 130).

4. *National Institute Economic Review* (February 1962).

extent can this low investment ratio be explained by the instability of demand in the various sectors and the interruptions of general growth? This question has also to do with the problem as to what extent entrepreneurial activity (with regard to the introduction of technical innovations, sales efforts in exploring new internal as well as foreign markets, the training of workers, and so on) in the United Kingdom were disturbed and checked by this type of demand development. Plausible hypotheses in this direction are easy to come by. The unfortunate thing is, however, that such important questions cannot be answered satisfactorily: only assertions that may seem reasonable can be given that there might be some truth in the type of hypothesis in question.

One important observation to be made in this connection is that the problem discussed cannot and should not be put in simple causal terms. There are complicated interrelations and feedback effects that have to be kept in mind. It is thus quite possible that the slow growth rate existing as such for a number of reasons works as a direct cause of the low investment ratio and as a check on other entrepreneurial activities. Experiences of slow and unstable expansion tend to create anticipations of narrowly limited future markets and a consciousness of the existence of considerable risks of setbacks, factors that give a sort of partial explanation of why the actual growth rate has been kept so low.

This problem of interrelation should be discussed more thoroughly. Relatively low rates of expansion in the different markets at home and abroad will mean small "acceleration" effects on investment; the investment propensities in the private sector may also be held back by pessimistic profit expectations, as well as by relatively high profit aspirations, because of the risk associated with uncertain market prospects. The low rate of gross capital formation will, on the other hand, imply a slow rate of capital accumulation, since a relatively large part of the total refers to replacement demand. From this point of view the rate of growth of the capital stock will have been relatively slow during our period—and even slower than a first comparison of gross investment ratios might suggest. Looking at the problem from another side, we may say that the effects on growth of the low investment ratio seems to have been aggravated by a low rate of "productivity of capital" as measured by the marginal capital to output ratio. On average during the 1950s (1949–59), the gross investment ratio in the United Kingdom was 16.3 per cent and the GDP trend 2.4 per cent a year, implying a gross marginal capital to output ratio of 6.7. This figure is high compared with most other countries during the same period.[5]

However, here we must again be careful with regard to the causal interpretation of a complex phenomenon. We cannot simply say that one reason for the slow growth is the high gross marginal capital to output ratio: by saying, for instance, that if this ratio had been as low as in Germany (that is 3.3 instead of 6.7), then the rate of output growth would have been 5 per cent per year instead of the less than 3 per cent realized. The high gross marginal capital to output ratio of the United Kingdom is of course as much *a result* of the slow growth rate as the reverse. There are a lot of factors and interrelations influencing the gross marginal capital to output ratio that have to be analyzed within the framework of a complete growth theory. This is, however, not our task. Here we have only pointed at some factors related to the instability of demand that might explain the low effects on growth of a given amount of gross investment.

Of all causal connections that may be important in explaining the low growth in the United Kingdom, the interrelations with foreign trade and balance of payments developments seem especially strategic. Here again there are no simple causal relations. One possible but perhaps too simplified way of arguing would be the following. The total export volume index has shown a slow and unstable growth pattern: the rate of expansion was only half of the Western European average, and in

5. *Some Factors in Economic Growth in Europe During the 1950s,* Chap. 2, Table 6.

TABLE 4.1

Growth Rates, Investment Ratios, and Incremental Capital to Output Ratios (ICOR), 1949–59

	Norway	United Kingdom	Western Germany	Italy	Holland	France	Sweden	United States
1). GDP trend (per cent)	3.4	2.4	7.4	5.9	4.8	4.5	3.4	3.3
2). Gross investment as percentage of GDP	32.6	16.1	24.2	21.9	25.0	20.6	21.4	18.1
3). ICOR (2:1)	9.5	6.7	3.3	3.7	5.2	4.6	6.3	5.5

Source: U.N., *Some Factors in Economic Growth in Europe During the 1950s* (Geneva, 1964).

fact its average rate of growth was no higher than the rate of growth of industrial production. Taking exports as an exogenous factor, we can therefore say that the United Kingdom, in contrast to most other industrialized countries, has had very little of export-propelled growth. Exports have not been leading in revivals and have shown a clear tendency toward retardation of expansion during the boom periods.

It is plausible that a higher average rate of export expansion, taken as an exogenous factor, would have had indirect repercussions on strategic growth factors: on productivity, profits, and investment. Higher and more stable export demand could, as in other countries, have implied larger profits and better profitability in the export industries, giving rise to stronger investment incentives as well as greater supply of savings out of profits.[6]

There is no doubt about the relevance of export-propelled growth; a number of the other country cases give examples of it. There is therefore some truth in the talk about the "vicious circle" of the United Kingdom economy along the following lines. The competitive disadvantage in world markets, has been implying relatively high costs, depressed investment demand directly as well as indirectly via the supply of savings out of profits. Productivity has thus tended to rise at a slower rate than in competing countries, which in the absence of correspondingly lower wage increases has tended to reinforce the competitive disadvantage.

An important issue is to what extent export development can be taken as an exogenous factor about which we can make alternative assumptions in order to explore its effects on growth and stability. There certainly are many intricate interrelations between export and other growth factors. We should expect not only that exports affect internal demand and supply conditions but also the other way around. One argument refers

6. See the arguments along this line in Lamfalussy, Chap. 9: "The Meaning and Implication of Export-led Growth."

to the possible effects on the export volume of the slow growth of the home market demand and production. A sharp increase of internal demand for investment and consumption may hold back the supply of export goods and therefore check export development in the short run. This possibility has been a recurrent theme of the government "Blue Books," in which the negative effects from high private machinery investment on exports of engineering products are especially feared. Even if this substitution effect between supplying home and export markets may have been important for specific goods during certain periods, the overall impression gained from the tables in the Appendix is, rather, the dominance of a positive correlation between export and GNP changes. During the years of rapid rise of total demand (up to 1950, 1953, 1954, 1955, and 1960), the export volume also showed expansions above average, and during most years when GNP increased slowly (1951, 1952, 1957, 1958, and 1962), the export volume either declined or retarded.

We have to expect crosscurrents of impulses that may be of quite varying strength during different periods. On the one hand, there are multiplier effects on GNP-demand coming from autonomous export-changes, implying—with a varying time lag—positive correlations between export- and GNP-changes. On the other hand, there may be substitution effects in certain branches at certain times, when a rapid rise in home demand orders may have negative effects on the elasticity of export supply. This was the case with regard to the supply elasticity of the engineering industries at times of high defense-expenditures, especially in connection with the Korean war. But in order to test such a hypothesis we have to make a detailed study of the conditions in the specific export branches. There is obviously no such simple systematic negative relationship between changes in GNP and exports that would support a policy conclusion that less demand pressure in the years of rapid expansion mentioned would have been rewarded by a better export performance. Surplus capacity in branches of manufacturing was apparently not automatically followed by increased export sales.

It might be relevant also to look for the longer-term results of slow expansion and recurring conditions of full employment and excess demand instead of observing year-to-year changes. It may be suggested that in the longer run a rapidly expanding home market may very well tend to give space and stimulus to technical innovations and exploitation of new markets outside as well as within the country. The existence of a strong growth mentality in leading branches of industry will naturally mean searching for expanding markets abroad. There is thus a strong positive correlation between the growth trends of GNP and export volume for industrialized countries. Japan and West Germany are the outstanding examples of high rates, whereas the United Kingdom and the United States lie at the other end of the spectrum (see Figure 4.1). However, this comparison does not provide us with a satisfactory interpretation of why the economy of the United Kingdom was exposed to such a slow rate of expansion of both export volume and GNP. We may try to find causal factors in the frequent attainment of full and possibly overfull employment, implying low ceilings and narrow limitations on supply as well as inflationary tendencies. This story is, however, about the same in all Western European countries. It cannot be maintained that the unemployment figures attained in the United Kingdom during the boom periods were exceptionally low in comparison with other countries; the conditions of excess demand do not seem more extreme than in several other countries, although comparisons between countries in these matters are very difficult to make.[7]

The interactions between short-term and longer-term forces are complicated and difficult to analyze in view of the indirect effects. Let us try to give a plausible picture of a model se-

7. There is a rather vague discussion of the comparability between countries of the excess demand situations during the years 1955–57 in OEEC, *The Problem of Rising Prices* (Paris, 1961); see especially Chap. 4.

FIGURE 4.1
Average Annual Rates of Growth of Export Volume and of Real GNP, 1951–64 (percentages)

A-Austria
B-Belgium
CA-Canada
CH-Switzerland
DK-Denmark
F-France
G-Germany
I-Italy
J-Japan
N-Norway
NL-Netherlands
S-Sweden
UK-United Kingdom
US-United States

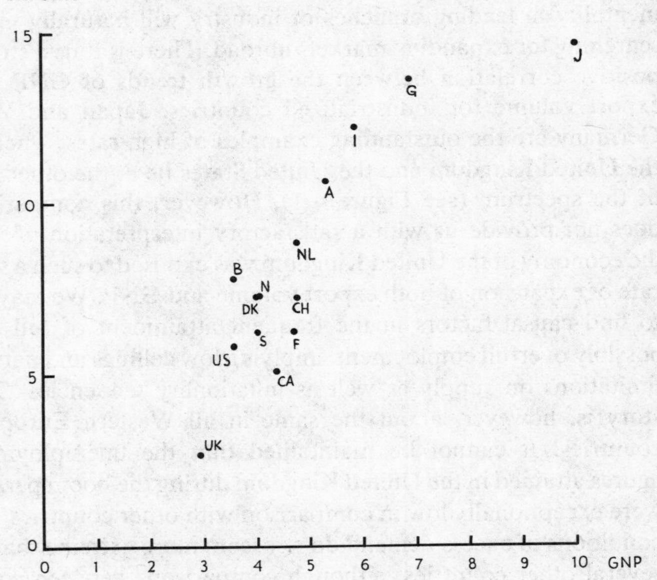

quence of the strategic events.[8] An accelerated increase of total demand—of the kind the United Kingdom experienced in 1950, 1953–54, 1959, and 1963—seems quickly to result in excess demand in various sectors of the labor market, as unemployment is low even in the recession years (around 2 to 3 per cent). The mobility of labor seems to be low, and other forms of rigidity also appear to be strong in the British economic system. Wage rates and earnings will start rising rapidly, and, as there is not sufficient response in the form of increased productivity, wage costs and prices will tend upward. The model implies considerable instability in the rise of labor productivity: a rapid rise in the revival after a recession (during one or two years) and then a marked retardation with hardly any rise during the boom and the year of recession during which hoarding of labor seems to have been common. This pattern comes out clearly in the development of manufacturing productivity (production per man-hour), but of course generalizations are dangerous on the basis of the two cycles, 1952–58 and 1958–62; the pattern of development during 1945–52 is less clear, although it does not contradict the generalization. The rate of wage increase, having got a push during the rapid increase of demand and perhaps support from the space created by the above-normal productivity rise, tends to acquire a momentum far above the retarded productivity rise during the following boom and recession. The consequent increase of wage costs—and prices—is not compensated for by developments during the following recession, as reduced rates of wage increase are more than matched by a low productivity rise, resulting in a larger rise in wage costs (per unit of product) than in the boom. It is thus not only the combination of relatively slow average rate of productivity increase in the United Kingdom and high rate of employment (with a consequent too-rapid average rise of wage rates) that should be blamed for the high rate of price

8. In his book *Studies in an Inflationary Economy* (London, 1962), F. W. Paish has presented a very persuasive picture of the interrelations between uneven growth and inflation in the United Kindom economy.

inflation. There are reasons to believe, according to the suggested model of the process, that the uneven development in the rate of increase of demand and productivity—in the way these factors are interrelated—has given an extra push to the process of rising wages and prices.

A relatively rapid rise in wage costs and prices may not have had independent retardation effects on home demand and production, but the effects on export demand and supply may be important. Here we must again be aware of interdependent relations. Rising wage costs and prices within the economy could be balanced by a more rapid productivity rise in the export sector. This seems to have been the case to an important extent in countries where the export volume has been expanding considerably more rapidly than production for the home market; there is in fact a high positive correlation between the rise in productivity and the rate of increase in production.[9] Since in these countries the most expansive and progressive firms seem to have been directing their efforts especially to the export markets, the rise of export prices has been much lower than the rise of home market prices. The high degree of competition in the international markets for manufactured goods that has been the rule since the Korean inflation period has apparently been a part of these tendencies. We find an indicator of the inability of the British export industries to follow these tendencies in the development of the United Kingdom price and cost indices in comparison with those of most other countries. (See Table 4.2.)

9. A good illustration of this relation is to be found in W. E. G. Salter, *Productivity and Technical Change* (Cambridge, 1960). The conclusions are drawn from statistics on development of about thirty United Kingdom industries over the period 1924–50 (the conclusions are corroborated by a parallel investigation of United States industries). The overall pattern reads (p. 124): "Industries which have achieved substantial increases in output per head have, in general, been successful in other respects: their costs have risen the least, the relative prices of their products has fallen, output has expanded greatly, and in most cases employment has increased by more than the average."

TABLE 4.2

Export Price Development and Share in World Trade

	Percentage Change in Export Unit Price Index 1953–61	Share in World Trade of manufactures 1953	1961
United Kingdom	+11	20.9	15.2
United States[a]	+10	26.2	19.9
France[b]	+ 2	9.1	9.2
Germany (F.R.)[c]	+ 2	13.4	20.1
Italy	−16	3.3	6.1
Japan	− 8	3.8	7.5
Sweden	+ 3	2.3	3.2

a. Excluding "special category" exports.
b. Allowing for a 29 per cent devaluation in 1957 and 1958.
c. Allowing for a 5 per cent appreciation in 1961.

We should, of course, be very skeptical as to the comparability of the export price indices of the various countries; the differences in unit price changes are partly effects of the varying composition of exports. However, the temptation is great to believe that the figures given above point at an important causal connection between export price developments and changes in the different countries' shares of world trade. The exception of Sweden could be explained by its good choice both of export composition and markets. (See Chapter 5.)

British export goods have since 1950 been becoming less competitive in price-sensitive world markets. Of course, the development of British exports is influenced also by a number of other factors, for example the composition and structure of British trade, particularly the relatively large share going to slow-growing markets in the primary producing countries. But the fact that the United Kingdom in the postwar period has been losing ground in all important markets may be taken as a clear indicator of a lack of competitiveness.[10] Another factor

10. For an analysis of the various factors determining the declining share of the United Kingdom exports on the international markets

has been the rather unhappy composition of exports, with a greater share of products (like textiles, clothing, and coal) subject to low-income elasticity and overcapacity tendencies than in other Western countries. This composition of exports has, however, been changing, with engineering products taking a rapidly increasing share.

The slow growth of exports has implied a relatively small rate of increase in export volume during the expansion and boom periods. Looked at from the demand side, there will be less stimulus (multiplier effects) to total demand from the side of exports than in other countries. This influence may, however, be secondary to the retarding effect on expansion coming from balance of payments restrictions or the *"lack of international space"* that also follows from too slow export expansion. In the United Kingdom as in other countries the import volume will tend to grow more rapidly than GNP. During the first one or two years of revivals, the volume of imports has expanded by 10 to 15 per cent per year, that is much more rapidly than GNP and the export volume, partly in connection with a rapid increase of inventories. The relative rise of British costs and prices may imply an extra push on imports. If now at the "given" slow GNP growth rate and under the general conditions suggested above, the rate of increase of the export volume will not more than reach up to the GNP growth rate, then the balance of payments apparently must tend to become a growth constraint, unless, which is unlikely in the longer run, changes in the terms of trade offset the unfavorable volume changes.

When, during years of rapid demand expansion—1950–51, 1953–55, 1959–60, 1963–64—the volume of imports is rising much more rapidly than the volume of exports, and changes in the terms of trade either do not help or even aggravate the situation, then the balance of payments will begin to deteriorate. The current account surplus has even during the "best"

---

see Chapter 5 in Lamfalussy. His conclusion is that the weakening of Britain's competitive position is the main factor.

postwar years (like 1958) not left anything to spare after covering capital exports. The variations in the current account, surplus or deficit, have however been surprisingly moderate over the postwar period. The average year-to-year swing, up or down, of the current account balance between 1949 and 1963 was around £250 million, which corresponds only to about 5 per cent of total turnover. In fact the total balance of payments accounts over the whole period have resulted in quite stable total exchange reserves. However, this development may simply show that a further deterioration of the balance of payments position in the years of crisis was prevented by government policy measures (see below); potentially the deficits would have become much higher *if,* at fixed exchange rates, the expansion of GNP and imports had been "allowed" to continue unrestrained. In fact, the rate of expansion was purposely held back in connection with the balance of payments difficulties arising during 1951, 1955, 1957, 1960–61, and 1964–65. Why and how were such minor balance of payments disturbances allowed to provoke such large repercussions on the general growth process? We find similar and ever larger relative changes in other countries without such unfavorable consequences on growth. An important part of the explanation of the sensitivity of the British economy to balance of payments disturbances must be sought in the vulnerable position of the pound sterling as a world currency. The British exchange reserves—complicated by the existence of large and varying sterling area accounts—have apparently been too low to provide a reasonably secure buffer against the variations in the current balance. As the pound sterling is a world currency, with big amounts of sterling debits and credits floating about in the world's foreign exchange markets, the *confidence factor* plays a strategic though largely stochastic role. Capital flights have tended to aggravate the deterioration of the foreign exchange position that had appeared as a result of a negative current balance.

There may be a considerable number of random elements

influencing the exchange situation, implying disturbances given the vulnerable position of the pound sterling.[11] An important question that Dow raises is to what extent the apparently big fluctuations in the stocks of imported commodities are partly of this character. Such increases had a considerable impact on the foreign balance in the years of rapid expansion such as 1955, 1959, and 1960, probably accounting for the major part of the deterioration of the current balance.[12] Nobody can tell what share of this investment in inventories should be considered as closely determined by the current expansion of demand and the rise in prices, and what part might be connected with other factors of more undefinable and erratic nature. But the existence of an inventory cycle for a number of branches (for instance steel and textiles) cannot be denied, and it is very likely that these cycles are to some extent synchronized by the general rhythm of the United Kingdom economy as partly affected by the policy cycle.

There have been years when a confidence crisis in the pound appeared without apparent weakness in the current balance (as in connection with the Suez crisis in 1956). There has also been a relatively big current account deficit without speculation against the pound (as in 1960, when there was a speculative flight from the dollar). But the general rule has been that a rising current account deficit was bound sooner or later to be followed by a confidence crisis and an outflow of capital from London. The consequent strong pressure on the pound has made necessary strong restrictive measures—regularly announced by raising the discount rate to high levels (6 and 7 per cent).

The repeated balance of payment disturbances in combination with restrictive government policies and the consequent retardation of business activity must have had an impact on the long-term growth rate—with feedback effects, along lines discussed above, on the short-term developments of private

11. See Dow, pp. 384–91.
12. See Dow, Table 15.1 on p. 386.

investment, exports, and productivity. Already the general awareness of a *low balance of payments ceiling,* coming from repeated experience of how the beginning of a strong expansion has generated exchange difficulties and been followed by a setback in activity, is likely to have had strong effects on growth expectations, influencing the activities of entrepreneurs as well as of government authorities. The formation of stabilization policy in the United Kingdom has necessarily been deeply marked by apprehensions of a coming balance of payments crisis, but also by relief after a more-or-less successful solution of a crisis just passed. We find therefore a succession of *policy waves,* each consisting of a period of restrictive measures instituted during the boom to dampen excess demand and price rises and to counteract a menacing exchange crisis, followed by a subsequent period of relaxation of these measures and the introduction of policies aimed at stimulating the economy. These waves of changing policy measures cannot possibly have had negligible influences on developments; in fact, the fiscal and monetary policies have been carried out with remarkable intensity, often having the character of a shock treatment of the economy.

The unfortunate situation is—as discussed in Chapters 1 and 3—that we have to expect poor or uncertain success in our efforts to isolate the effects of policy changes in order to find out what would have happened if those parameter changes had not occurred. Direct and indirect effects of policy changes are embedded in the observed statistical series, and we cannot know what belongs to the working of the British economic system "as such" and what belongs to policy reactions. A systematic isolation of these categories can only be accomplished by means of some type of heroic model-building in which the very assumptions underlying the structural equations to an unknown extent contain the policy effects. The developments have so often and so quickly been broken or at least seriously disturbed by package deals of policy measures such as tax changes, hire-purchase restrictions and relaxations, introduction and abolishment of investment allowances, all kinds of credit policy measures, and so forth, that such effects can be imputed only with great uncertainty.[13]

THE POLICY CYCLES

A rather general pattern of stabilization policies and interrelations with the conjuncture can be seen in many countries. Too bold relaxations of economic policy, such as occurred around 1953–54, 1958–59, and 1962, have stimulated such a rapid rise in demand and production that the boom led to excess demand situations that made necessary the introduction of new restrictive measures—breaking the boom (or helping it to break itself), which in turn led to new expansionary policy measures and a new cycle of interactions. We cannot hope to answer the fundamental question as to whether these policy waves of restriction and relaxation have had dampening effects on the variation of activity around the trend or whether they have worked as extra disturbances, aggravating the deviations. It is, useful however, to have this issue in mind when looking more closely at some of the British policy experiences.

The succession of restriction and relaxation periods has the following general outline. (Only the main policy changes are mentioned.) It should be observed that the periods marked out refer merely to relevant changes in policy decisions working in the one or the other direction; the effects of the policy changes will of course be felt over longer but indeterminable periods.

1. *Period of restriction* from the fall of 1951 to the spring of 1952: increase of bank rate from 2½ per cent to 4 per cent; funding operations pushing down the liquidity ratio of the com-

13. No serious effort has been made to build a policy-planning model along the Dutch line. Interesting pieces of a model have been constructed—as for instance the Dow and Dicks-Mireaux analysis of the working of the price-wage spiral.

mercial banks; hire-purchase restrictions; restraint of bank advances; initial allowances withdrawn; increased company taxes.[14]

2. *Period of relaxation* from the spring of 1953 to the summer of 1954: initial allowances restored; tax rates reduced; bank rate lowered to 3 per cent; hire-purchase restrictions removed (July 1954); investment allowances introduced (1954).

3. *Period of restriction* from the beginning of 1955 to the spring of 1958: increase of bank rate (4½ per cent February 1955, 5½ per cent February 1956, 7 per cent September 1957); hire-purchase restrictions (from February 1955, tightened in the middle of 1955 and again in the beginning of 1956); quantitative control of bank advances introduced; investment allowances withdrawn; cuts in public investments.

4. *Period of relaxation* from the spring of 1958 to the beginning of 1960: reduction of bank rate (successively to 4 per cent), removal of the control of bank advances; hire-purchase restrictions first relaxed and then removed; reduction of tax rates.

5. *Period of restriction* from the beginning of 1960 to the autumn of the same year: increase of bank rate (from 4 to 6 per cent); call for special deposits; hire-purchase restrictions. New and sharper restrictive policy from the middle of 1961: a 10 per cent increase in most indirect tax rates; and increase in the bank rate from 5 to 7 per cent; and a new increase in special deposits.

6. *Period of relaxation* from the autumn of 1962 and again

14. The method of "initial allowances" (introduced for the first time in 1945) is a scheme of accelerated depreciation, implying an unchanged aggregate depreciation over the whole lifetime of machinery or a building. "Investment allowances" (introduced in 1954) mean a permanent exemption from taxation, that is an extra depreciation or an investment subsidy; the rate of the allowances was (1954) 20 per cent of expenditure on plant and machinery and 10 per cent on building (thus at 50 per cent tax rates implying subsidies of 10 and 5 per cent respectively).

with greater force from the spring of 1963: reduction of bank rate (successively to 3½ per cent); release of special deposits; restrictions on bank lending removed; extensive tax reductions (including higher investment allowances); and increased budget expenditures.

7. *Period of restriction* starting in the beginning of 1964 with the bank rate being raised from 4 to 5 per cent. The restrictive policy was successively sharpened during the year.

This is an impressive cycle of policy changes. During each period of restriction and relaxation a number of different instruments were used (package deals), and usually the different types of policy measures were introduced in changed combinations of time sequences. Nevertheless, certain regularities in the pattern of these policy waves can be observed.

Reversals in the Bank of England discount rate have during the whole period served as the signal of the recognition by the policy authorities of a new policy phase: a rise of bank rate following earlier declines signaling a period of restraint, and a decrease of bank rate following earlier increases introducing a period of relaxation. It is also possible to generalize as to a kind of division of labor between monetary and fiscal policy. Measures of restrictive monetary policy—in the form of higher interest rates, various forms of credit restraint, and hire-purchase restrictions—have been applied with the purpose of checking a boom considered to be or soon expected to be characterized by a too-rapid rise of demand and by too rapidly rising wages and prices, and of alleviating the menace of an approaching balance of payments crisis. In fact, it seems that the introduction of severe monetary restraint signaled by a rise of the bank rate has regularly been called forth by falling exchange reserves due to a too-rapid rise of imports in relation to exports and, at the end, by a rising lack of confidence in the pound sterling taking the form of short-term capital exports (a flight from the pound). On the other hand, various fiscal policy measures have been applied as the main stimulus in case of slack in the economy. These fiscal measures have taken the form of lowered tax rates, more generous depreciation allowances for investment, and, to some extent after a long time lag, acceleration of public investments.

This interpretation of a division of labor between fiscal and monetary policy over the cycle should not be taken too literally, however. In a period of relaxation, when fiscal stimulus is given to the economy, it is of course a precondition that the restraining monetary measures applied in the previous phase have been abolished. And when a boom has to be checked, it is also natural that some of the stimulating fiscal measures are eliminated, as for example the investment allowances. In spite of such interrelations, it seems in the main to be a correct characterization that monetary instruments have carried the main burden for stopping a boom and saving the country from or alleviating an exchange crisis, while the main policy push stimulus to the economy during a recession or recovery has come from the application of fiscal instruments.

In this general characterization of the British policy cycles it is implied that the fiscal and monetary policy changes included are planned and introduced with mainly short-term stabilization purposes in view. But this can never be fully true. Tax reductions that have been made since 1950 have this character only to a limited extent; the government has had the political ambition to reduce successively the high postwar tax rates, but the reduction seems accidentally or intentionally to have been fairly well timed to the recession periods. It was largely a political accident (a pledge from an election campaign) that direct-tax rates were reduced in April 1955, when there was a general tendency to excess demand, and exchange difficulties were clearly discernible. Monetary restraint had therefore at that time to carry the extra burden of compensating the effects of an expansionary fiscal measure which from a stabilization point of view was misplaced. This conflict of policies was eliminated by the autumn of 1955, when higher tax rates and restrictions on public expenditures were adopted.

We have not emphasized public expenditure variations as a special policy instrument because such changes seem to have had importance as a consciously applied short-term stabilization instrument only to a limited extent and partly accidentally.[15] But, of course, the declining rate of increase in public expenditures during the years 1953–57, as well as the pause in tax reductions during the years 1956–58, had disinflationary effects—at least as compared with more expansionary budget policies that could be imagined.

To some extent we can also regard some part of the monetary policy carried out since 1951 as being aimed at long-term rather than short-term goals. The successive rise of the level of long-term interest rates (long-term government bonds) from 3 to 3½ per cent in the beginning of the 1950s to 5½ to 6 per cent in the beginning of the 1960s can be put in relation to the simultaneous decline in tax rates. (Central government taxes as a share of GNP fell from around 35 to 25 per cent over the period 1946–59.) A long-term substitution of high interest rates for high tax rates had thus occurred. If tax rates are reduced—for political reasons—then under given conditions (including given propensities of government expenditures) interest rates may have to be higher (in order to attain economic balance) than in a comparable situation in which the high tax rates were kept constant.

However, we can certainly not explain the increase in interest rates and still less the decline of tax rates with the help of a model of policy planning of this simple kind. Instead, we have here an interesting example of interaction between short-term *monetary* policy and short-term and long-term *fiscal* policies. The expansionary fiscal policies inaugurated in the recessions and continued at least during a part of the phases of rapid expansion—partly being the result of long-term tax reduction decisions—have "prevented" interest rates from declining back to the previous minimum level before new monetary restraints

15. See Dow, Chap. 8.

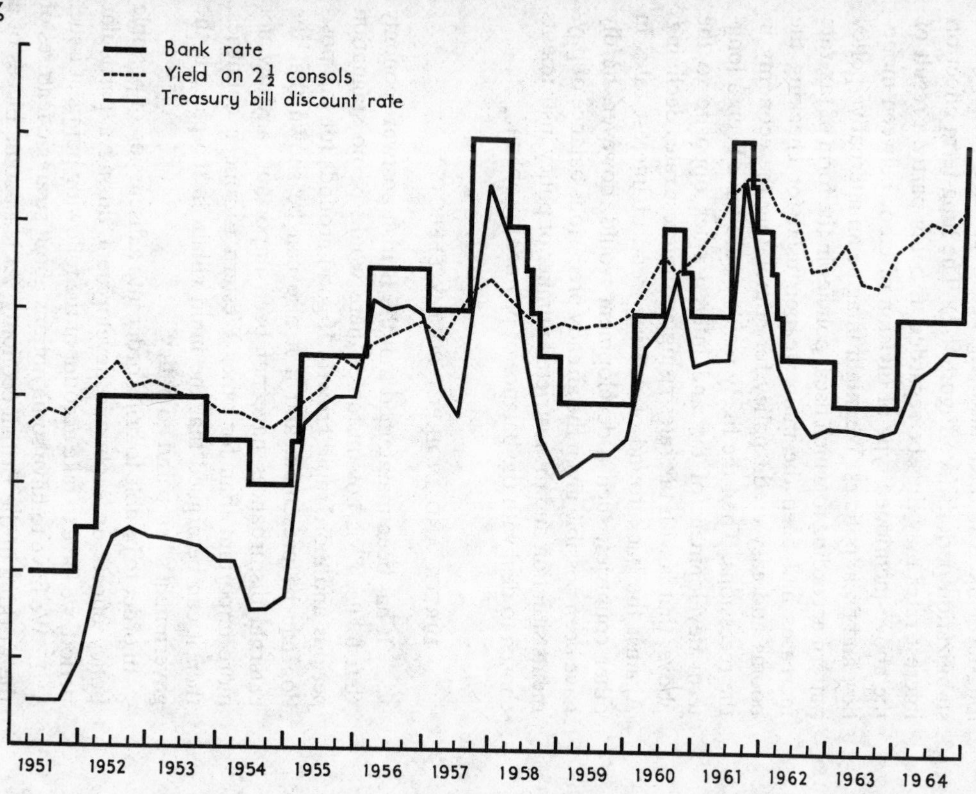

Development of Interest Rates in the United Kingdom, 1951–64

have become necessary. In this ratchetlike way, both short- and long-term interest rates have zigzagged upward through the stabilization periods (see Figure 4.2). The long-term effect on interest rates may thus be regarded as being partly a result of the above-mentioned type of division of labor between monetary and fiscal policies. We might imagine an alternative policy pattern according to which fiscal policies in the form of tax-rate increases had been the main weapon used for checking the booms and easy credit policy for stimulating the economy in the recessions. Then the likely result would have been a long-term development of tax and interest rates opposite to the above, that is with tax rates rising and interest rates declining. Against the background of a rising trend of interest rates in other countries, such a development would, however, hardly have been possible given the already precarious balance of payments situation and the restricted number of policy instruments chosen to deal with the balance of payment problem.

DIRECT AND INDIRECT POLICY EFFECTS

It has been maintained that the British postwar economy "left to itself" is not unstable: there would be no stagnation periods and more rapid growth. If good grounds for this position can be presented, and if it also can be shown that the external disturbances have not been important, anyhow not more important than for other Western European countries, then it can be argued that the main villain in the piece is the government's "stop and go policy."

In order to be able to bring order into a discussion of possible policy effects on economic development during a particular period, we have to take account of the following points at issue.

1. We have to have some notions about strategic features of the working of the British economy. At least some pieces of a model are necessary for this purpose. We must ask to what extent multiplier and acceleration effects seem to exist; how changes in exports appear to be influenced by, and work back

on, developments inside the economy; how price and wage movements are determined and how they interact.

2. What kind of *external disturbances* have affected the British economy, and therefore implied shocks to the economy, that can be considered independent of policy changes? We know that the definition of external or exogenous factors depends on our choice of model, yet because we have no accepted model to work with there are no clear demarcations. It seems defensible, however, to regard in particular large parts of the export variations, of the changes in terms of trade as well as of the variations in capital account, as external disturbances. It therefore seems reasonable to regard a considerable part of the changes in the balance of payments position as random or uncontrollable factors disturbing the economy.

3. In order to judge the possible effects of government policy on the actual economic development as it is registered in the current statistics, the first necessary step is to ascertain the *primary or direct impact* on demand of the various measures. The second step should refer to an analysis of the indirect effects taking account of the reaction mechanism of the economy.

This way of dividing up the problem at the same time shows the close interrelation between these steps. The effects on the economy of external disturbances cannot be studied in isolation as they—if sufficiently important—have been followed by policy reactions. But these reactions are also responses to the internal endogenous working of the economy, implying for instance a wage-price spiral. These interconnections also mean that policy measures must be considered as partly reactions to earlier policies that may have had undesired and belated indirect effects, i.e. the problem of overshooting.

When we study the primary impact of the policy measures, the timing of the effects is an essential element. There is and must be much uncertainty about the various lags involved. It seems that in 1953–54, in 1959, and in 1963 the British authorities were late in responding to the tendencies of a too rapidly expanding demand and the coming of a boom. During these years the government authorities apparently underestimated the current and prospective rate of demand expansion, which meant that expansive policies were continued too long—at least from the point of view of the balance of payments. The restrictive policies in the following year can be considered as having come too late. Stabilization policies during the booms were, as already mentioned, mainly oriented toward impending balance of payments strains which were observed at a late stage and apt to be underestimated.

At this point it is important to make a distinction between two kinds of "excess demand." Total demand may be in excess with reference to production capacity and the supply of labor at various sensitive points of the economy. We may as an alternative define an excessive increase of demand with regard to balance of payments restrictions, implying another kind of ceiling for expansion. In the British case the balance of payments ceiling seems to be lower than the production capacity ceiling; in the Swedish case (see Chapter 5) we find the opposite relation of the ceilings.

One reason for the underestimation of the strength of the rise of demand during the revival may be found in a short-term disinvestment in stocks that regularly occurred during that stage (but was not observed until later) and tended to have a dampening effect on the development of production and imports. Though it was less pronounced, there was also a lag in the observation of a recession, and a lag in the introduction of expansive measures. The inventory recession of 1952, after the very rapid accumulation of 1951, was not foreseen, and the revival in that year of monetary policy was if anything rather misplaced in time. Expansive measures in the recession year 1958 came late and became vigorous first with the April budget in 1959. The development during 1962 seemed especially difficult to judge, the signs of a revival during the first part of the year giving false reasons for postponing the introduction of more expansive policies.

The difficulties with the response lag are aggravated by the lagged effects of the policy measures working on an economy with rather quickly changing "conjuncture moods." The boom and recession periods have been rather short,[16] and therefore a large part of the stimulation effects may have had their main impact during a late phase of the expansion. This may have been the case with fiscal and credit policies affecting fixed investment. There is more clear evidence as to the timing of policy effects on private consumption. The changes in expenditures on consumption seem to follow closely the changes in tax rates and in hire-purchase conditions. Changes in consumer credit conditions can be expected to have quite immediate effects on consumers' purchases of durable goods, although there is a reaction lag between changes in credit terms and credits extended. But the impact of tax changes—affecting disposable real income—on consumption seems to have a longer time lag. The full impact may be delayed six to eighteen months.[17]

The timing of policy effects can of course not be ascertained without having some notion of the relative size of the direct impact during the relevant time periods. Dow has made a pioneering effort in this direction.[18] His estimates—necessarily based on a number of assumptions, which he explicitly mentions—ought to give some conception of the order of size as well as of the timing of the direct effects. Dow attempts only to quantify the *direct effects* of a part of the measures, namely changes in tax rates, subsidies, grants, and insurance contributions as

16. There are no officially recognized periods of the cycle as in the United States. The National Institute of Economic and Social Research has, however, made an inquiry of the cyclical pattern of leading indicators. "Leading Indicators for the British Economy," *National Institute Economic Review* (May 1963).

17. Dow, p. 297.

18. See Dow, Chap. 15. The estimates of policy impact refer to the contributions to year-to-year changes in final expenditure (in 1954 prices). Assumptions are made as to the time lag and as to the share of policy-determined changes in real disposable income that is consumed.

well as hire-purchase controls that influence consumers' disposable income and "purchasing power." The direct impact of fiscal policy on investment is assessed very hypothetically only.[19] The results of Dow's analysis seems to be that the sum of the analyzed policy measures had a considerable impact on the year-to-year changes of expenditures, especially in the years of revival. During such years the direct impact on consumption expenditures are calculated to reach around one half of the actual changes.[20] The direct restrictive effects on consumption are estimated to amount to up to 1 per cent of actual expenditures. This same order of importance also results from very rough estimates of the effects on total final expenditures of policy measures directly affecting consumption as well as private investment. Thus the policy measures in question had a direct impact on total final demand which was at least in some years of about the same order of size as the average yearly increase of real GNP. The direct stimulus of the expansive measures taken during the second half of 1962 and with the April budget of 1963 should amount to about 2 per cent of consumer demand.[21]

It is important to remember that the account given above is only a part of the story of policy effects on the short-run development of the United Kingdom economy. We must pay attention to the impact of monetary policy and to the indirect effects of the measures. In both these respects there are few possibilities of reaching quantitative estimates without introducing such heroic assumptions that the answers will seem uninteresting.

The debate in the United Kingdom regarding the actual effects of monetary policy after 1952, as well as regarding its

19. The direct effects of changes in profit taxes and depreciation allowances are just *assumed* to amount to one third of the change in tax payments. This method means, of course, assuming away all intricate problems of the investment function.

20. See diagram on p. 382 in Dow.

21. OECD, *Economic Survey: United Kingdom* (Paris, June 1965).

potential possibilities, is highly interesting. Here we can only touch on some of the main points that are of importance for our subject.

Using the usual criteria, it seems that monetary policy has been quite restrictive during the boom periods. Since the activation of monetary policy at the end of 1951, a number of tools have been applied in varying proportions: changes in the discount rate (a variation latitude between 2 and 7 per cent); open market operations; requirements of special deposits by the banks with the Bank of England (since 1958); indirect controls of the development of bank advances;[22] and direct regulation of hire-purchase conditions.

There are widely differing views as to the effective *impact* of monetary policy in the United Kingdom. Partly it is a question of belief in the value of acts to create confidence—not least in the international financial community during periods of balance of payments strains.[23] There can hardly be any doubt about the effectiveness of the high discount rates in turning the tide of short-term capital movements, partly because of favorable interest-rate differentials, partly as a result of the demonstration to the world of "good" (that is orthodox) behavior and the willingness to carry out a "sound" (that is restrictive) policy. The main question is, however, to what extent the restrictive monetary policy has had dampening effects with regard to the development of the price level and demand.

The end of the policy of cheap money and the introduction of an active monetary policy from 1952 on occurred at the same time as the economy was successively liberated from physical controls (rationing of consumption and licensing of imports and building activity). In a way it was convenient for the British government to have great confidence in the revived monetary policy, since from a political point of view it was

22. Partly as effects on bank liquidity, partly as the result of exhortations and requirement by the Bank of England (or the Treasury).

23. See Sir Robert Hall, "Reflections on the Practical Application of Economics," *Economic Journal* (December 1959).

difficult to increase tax rates or cut down public expenditures during the booms. The Radcliffe Report, after having scrutinized an impressive volume of statistical evidence (from expert research and hearings) came, however, to rather devastating conclusions as to the actual working of monetary policy in the United Kingdom since 1951.[24] According to the report, monetary policy was a failure, especially during the period 1955–57. Changes of interest rates over the cycle, capital issues control, regulation of credit and money supply, all of these devices were in general judged to have been very ineffective as means of controlling investment in private business. Not least, the evidence from businessmen confirmed the view that the actual changes in interest rates and in the availability of credit should have had little influence on current investment in fixed capital as well as in stocks. Effects via changes in the money supply were ridiculed with reference to a more or less complete flexibility of income velocity. However, the report did not deny the existence of certain effects from changes in the "general state of liquidity" of the economy that among other things was connected with the structure and inflexibility of interest rates. These effects were, however, of a rather uncertain and unreliable nature. Only in one respect did the Radcliffe Report give evidence of high efficiency of credit policy, namely with regard to the hire-purchase controls.

Against the background of this very schematic account of some conclusions of the Radcliffe Report, let us consider some pertinent questions with regard to British experience with monetary policy that seem to be of general interest for our survey of country experiences. The part of British monetary policy that seems to have been most original, and in a way also most successful, has been the control of consumer credit, with effects on the demand for durable goods (cars, furniture, radio sets, and so forth). Undoubtedly there is a close connection between

24. The Radcliffe Report was published in August 1959 under the title *Report of the Committee on the Working of the Monetary System,* Cmnd. 827.

changes in consumer debt (including personal bank loans) and expenditures on durables.[25] The covariation was especially clear during the wave of rapid credit extension during the last quarter of 1958 and during 1959, followed by a rapid decline during the second half of 1960. The rate of spending on durables followed this pattern very closely, apparently without a noticeable time lag but on a somewhat smaller scale. Dow estimates the maximum effect within a year on total consumer demand to be of the order of size of 1 per cent following the transition from tight to very easy credit.[26]

There are a number of interesting issues connected with the British experience with this type of credit control.

1. The amount of change in outstanding consumers' credit in response to changes in hire-purchase and other credit regulations is the first problem. The time lags and the primary effects on new credits may vary a great deal with the business situation and the position of the banks and the hire-purchase institutions.

2. The question of reaction of consumers to consumer-credit restrictions raises interesting problems as to the personal savings function. It is conceivable that the restrictions will act as a *stimulus to savings:* that the money that otherwise would have been used for downpayments and installments for credit purchases of durable goods is now saved, the expenditure postponed, and savings thus increased. Alternatively, the credit restrictions may function more like increased relative prices for durables, with a resulting *substitution effect* implying a diversion of demand to nondurables and services. As Dow points out, there is also a third possibility. The demand for durables might be quite inelastic with regard to credit conditions, so that changes in the supply of credit will imply corresponding changes in disposable purchasing power set free (or drawn in) for buying other goods and services. In reality there will probably be a combination of these possibilities for differ-

25. See Dow, Diagrams 11.2 and 11.3, pp. 280–81.
26. Dow, p. 279.

ent consumer groups, and there are also likely to be disturbances of various kinds. The series in Table 4.3 are presented to help the reader in finding the most realistic hypothesis.[27]

TABLE 4.3

Fluctuations in the Savings Ratio and Changes in Consumer Debt

	1 Including effect of changes in consumer debt	2 Excluding the effect of changes in consumer debt
1957	5.8	
1958	4.7	6.4
1959	5.5	9.8
1960	8.2	9.4
1961	10.0	9.8
1962	8.9	9.0

The table shows that changes in consumer debt seem to account for a large part of the fluctuations in the total savings ratio (the latter, as presented in column 1, being the usual national accounts definition of savings as the difference between disposable income and current consumption expenditures). In 1958–59 and 1962—the years of easy credit conditions—there was a decline in the total personal savings ratio implying a stimulus to total consumption demand.

3. The wide fluctuations in the demand for durables resulting from a successful credit policy of this directional type raises an important issue for stabilization policy. The share of

27. *National Institute Economic Review* (May 1963), p. 12. It should be observed that the savings figures in column 1 as residuals in the national accounts are apt to be very unreliable. There is, in fact, a systematic bias of overestimation, this bias being greater the earlier the estimate. To illustrate: the 1957 estimate of the personal savings ratio for 1956 was 10.1 per cent and the 1962 estimate 6.2 per cent.

durable goods in total consumption outlay was only about 8 per cent around 1960. It is evident that the concentration of credit policy effects on consumer durables must be quite disturbing to production and trade in this field. For reasons discussed earlier in this chapter, the resulting instability may imply long-term losses in potential productivity increases.

How about the general effects on investment during the periods of restrictive monetary policy? Dow is about as skeptical as the Radcliffe committee about its efficiency. He is certain that there is some significant impact from the squeeze of credit availability only in the case of private house construction. The similarity with conditions in the United States is quite apparent. It is the stickiness of building-society interest rates that during a period of rising rates (as during 1955–57) reduces the supply of building-society finance; the reverse happens during the recessions. We therefore find big fluctuations in the rate of growth of private housebuilding. The stagnation during 1955–57 and again during 1961–63, as well as the rapid spurts during the periods of high credit availability, seem to confirm the importance of credit policy in this field.

It is certainly very debatable what effects restrictive monetary policy during the boom periods may have had in other directions. No clear evidence exists, only the varying opinions and attitudes of economists, businessmen, and government officials.[28] We may observe that, as in other countries, monetary policy became restrictive with a time lag and was kept restrictive too long in the recession. As a general consideration —not least for a comparison with the experiences of other countries—we should also note that in fact the degree of restrictiveness of British monetary policy has been relatively great. Let us take the period 1954–57 for example. Bank

28. As presented in the Radcliffe report. See also the large amount of literature quoted in Dow, Chap. 12, and in H. G. Johnson, "Monetary Theory and Policy," and G. L. S. Shackle, "Recent Theories Concerning the Nature and Role of Interest Rates," in *Survey of Economic Theory* (New York, 1965), Vol. 1.

deposits and advances of the London clearing banks stagnated or declined at the same time that nominal GNP expanded by about 25 per cent. Short-term interest rates (on treasury bills) went up from below 2 per cent to about 5 per cent, and long-term rates from below 4 per cent to around 5.5 per cent. These changes indicate quite impressive monetary restrictions that may have implied—in other countries as well as in Britain—serious difficulties in getting outside finance for firms in vulnerable positions, for instance because of commitments to carry through current investment programs. The statistical fact that industrial investment in plant, machinery, and buildings continued to expand rapidly up to 1957 need not be interpreted as evidence against this hypothesis; an indicator of the existence of restraining influence may be found in the downturn of factory building starts as early as in the fall of 1955.[29] Against this background it is natural to raise the question whether the main impact on private business of the credit restrictions during 1955–57 did not fall on inventory investments.

The Radcliffe Report denies this type of influence. In order to assess the validity of the hypothesis we have to study the pattern in the movements of inventory investment. Leaving out the special conditions during the Korean boom (with a record rise of inventories during 1951), it seems as if the changes in inventory investment have either been low or negative during the first phase of rapid demand expansion in a recovery, to be followed (in 1955 and 1960) by a very rapid rise implying a strong stimulus to the boom. This can be regarded as an international pattern, not deviating much from the National Bureau description for the United States. When total demand rises very rapidly, "involuntary" decumulation of inventories may occur. But this phase will be followed by planned investment in inventories stimulated by rising sales and prices. Our problem here is why there was such an abrupt break in the develop-

29. *National Institute Economic Review* (August 1963), diagram on p. 8.

ment of inventory investment as early as 1956. There is a corresponding slowing down also in most of the other countries, but the United Kingdom experience seems more extreme. This turn in inventory investment may be interpreted as being the result of the dynamic mechanism of work in the economy, being a result of the general retardation of growth (acceleration principle) combined with a certain amount of perhaps involuntary overstocking in various fields during the 1955 boom—just as in 1951. This might mean that these inventory booms tend to break their own necks, and that the restrictive policies in 1951 and 1955 had only a minor influence.[30] Comparing British developments during these years with other countries' experiences, we should be inclined to maintain, however, that restrictive policy may have played an important role both via total demand and directly via credit restrictions. Credit restrictions and the elimination of fiscal support of fixed investment must have implied financing difficulties for a number of firms with heavy investment programs under way. Cutting down and keeping down inventories is a natural reaction as a method of overcoming financial difficulties in such situations.

In this section we have so far discussed only the direct impact of policy changes on consumption and investment expenditures. The indirect effects via multiplier relations and acceleration effects on investment cannot be ascertained without a complete econometric model that may give a false sense of precision. For our purposes it is sufficient to observe that cumulative processes of expanding production and incomes start quickly after the initial impulse to revival, and that fixed private investment begins rising with a short time lag. It would be hard to tell to what extent we are here dealing with lagged acceleration effects, with a stimulus from rising or high profits, or with the lagged results of easy credit policies and investment allowance measures. Time-series studies cannot help us much in allotting responsibilities, as the policy measures occurred about

30. This is the view of Little, but no convincing evidence is presented.

simultaneously with the stimulus from rising exports and consumption (the system of investment allowances introduced in 1954 must have implied an extra stimulus).[31] In the same way, we cannot judge to what extent the following retardation of fixed nonhousing investment (with a yearly rate of expansion falling successively from 16 per cent in 1955 to 0.5 per cent in 1957) was a direct result of the policy restrictions or was determined mainly indirectly via the retardation of growth in GNP.

As discussed above, a central issue in ascertaining indirect effects of the policy changes involves the working of the price-wage mechanism. The expansive policies in recessions seem to have been quite effective according to the evidence presented above. But indirect effects in the form of rising wages and prices have created problems of inflation as well as more or less related balance of payments strains. The restrictive policies during the booms do not seem to have been effective in dampening concurrent inflationary tendencies.

It is possible to "explain" from the cost side the 4 per cent annual rate of increase of the GNP price level over the postwar period by adding up weighted influences of the rise of import costs, the average rate of increase of wage and salary earnings (6.5 per cent per year), and then correcting for the rate of increase of labor productivity (2¼ per cent per year). The fit to the actual course of prices will be quite close because average profit margins seem to have kept fairly stable over the longer run. This is, however, not an explanatory model, especially for the short periods in which we are interested. Changes in import costs may be taken as exogenously determined, but we have to treat changes in earnings and productivity as determined endogenously to a large extent. As pointed out above, the rate of rise of labor productivity varies considerably over the phases of expansion and stagnation; being high during periods of rapid

31. A 20 per cent investment allowance for expenditure on equipment (with an expected life of five years) means about 10 per cent subsidy on the investment and would—from a cost point of view—be about as good as a zero rate of interest (Little, p. 248).

demand expansion (3 to 4 per cent per year during 1949–50, 1952–55, 1958–60, and 1962–64) and low or negative during periods of relative demand stagnation (1.5 to –1 per cent in 1950–52, 1955–58, and 1960–62). Dow makes the interesting point that the rate of increase of productivity is a function of the rate of change of total demand (in real terms), whereas there is no significant relation with the general *level* or pressure of demand. This would mean that there may be as much productivity rise at a level of general demand corresponding to full employment as at a lower level with some excess unemployment.[32]

There has been considerable variability in the yearly changes in wages and salaries per employed (referring to agreed rates as well as to wage drift). Following periods of high demand pressure (excess demand for labor) the average rate of change has amounted to 8 to 10 per cent per year, and to 3 to 4 per cent following recession periods. We find a corresponding, though dampened and lagged, rhythm of the price level. The interrelations between the variations in demand pressure, productivity development, and the rates of wage and price rise are of central importance for the working of the British economic system. In a loose way the mechanism seems to function along the following lines. Rapid demand expansion, as after 1952, 1958, and 1962, is accompanied by relatively large increases in labor productivity that neutralize a part of the current rise in wages and earnings per hour. Prices seem to be marked up with some time lag, so that during the early part of the expansion real wage and salary incomes will rise more rapidly than later, when wage costs rise more quickly due to a retardation of the productivity rise and lagged effects on prices. The rapid increase in real wages and in hours worked are parts of the explanation of the high rate of increase of consumption demand during the revival. Rising import costs may be added as cost-push factors at the same time as wage rates tend to be

32. See Dow, pp. 361–62 and Chap. 16, sect. 1.

increasingly influenced by demands for compensating cost-of-living adjustments.

This pattern of wage-price interactions has been given quantitative precision in some interesting research contributions.[33] According to the presented regression equations that are intended to give a model of the short-term response mechanism, a rise in the demand pressure, corresponding to one percentage point decline in unemployment, is associated with an increase of wages and salaries per employed of about 3 per cent. A productivity rise working as a cost-reducing factor should according to the results have immediate effects on prices and only indirect effects on wage development. It should be observed that the regression model contains important constant terms implying an "automatic" process of rising wages and prices.[34]

From the point of view of stabilization policy, the strategic relation concerns how changes in the pressure of demand affect productivity. There is no equation for this relation but, as mentioned above, the short-term connection that seems to exist puts great difficulties in the way of controlling inflation.

33. For references see Dow, Chap. 13, sect. 4. The best-known contributions have come from Phillips and Dicks-Mireaux: D. W. Phillips, "The Relation between Unemployment and the Rate of Change of Money Wages in the UK 1861–1957," *Economica* (November 1958); L. A. Dicks-Mireaux, "The Interrelationship between Cost and Price Changes, 1946–1959," *Oxford Economic Papers* (October 1961). See, for another interpretation, H. A. Turner, "Wages, Productivity and the Level of Employment: More on the Wage Drift," *Manchester School* (January 1960), p. 94.

34. Dicks-Mireaux' regression equations (p. 272; also quoted and discussed in Dow, pp. 357–60) look as follows:

$$L_t = 3.90 + 0.30\,P_t + 0.16\,P_{t-1} + 2.78\,D_{t-1/4}$$

$$P_t = 2.47 + 0.27\,L_t + 0.21\,I_{t-1/4} - 0.54\,X_t$$

where L = annual percentage change in wage and salary bill per person
P = annual percentage change in final prices
I = annual percentage change in import prices
X = annual percentage change in output per head
D = index of demand for labor

The transition from high to low pressure as a result of a "successful" restrictive policy will according to this hypothesis be followed in the short run by a dampening of productivity growth and a corresponding rise in costs per unit of output without restraining effect on the rise of wages—before the recession. However, we cannot be sure that this account gives more than a part of the story. It may not only have been the dampening of real demand expansion that has mattered. The retardation might partly in some sectors of the economy have been determined by ceilings on capacity; to this extent the slowing down of production and productivity growth during the last one or two years of the boom would not have been determined by effects of policy restrictions on demand. In general, however, it seems to us more plausible that the main influence has come from the demand side via restrictive policy measures; we have above referred to some evidence that full-capacity growth of around 3 per cent per year during the whole phase of the boom could have been possible. However, we meet here very complicated problems of interaction between demand and supply factors that leave room for various interpretations. There will always be an uneven impact of demand changes, so that relatively inflexible supply conditions, which seem characteristic of the British economy, will imply low short-term elasticity of total production. The introduction of restrictive policies of the types discussed above will mean uneven development of demand and with inelastic response of supply factors there will be inflationary tendencies. More research directed to the detailed functioning of the economy within various branches of activity may help us to understand why the British economy apparently has not had as high a degree of flexibility in responding to uneven demand pressure as there seems to have been in other countries.

A SKETCH OF A MODEL WITH POLICY ALTERNATIVES

One fundamental property of the United Kingdom's cycle mechanism over the period 1950–64 seems to have been the narrow room permitted by the balance of payments ceiling. An expansion of real demand starting from a year of recession with 2 to 3 per cent unemployment hits this ceiling rather soon. The ceiling is, however, not a simple one à la Hicks, against which the demand development curves are reflected.

In schematic form the disequilibrating forces in the British mechanism may be presented as follows. The expansion gets off to a flying start—stimulated not so much by an increase of exports as by a rise in consumption following expansive policy measures—and at first is characterized by rising productivity, relatively stable prices, and rapidly rising real wages. There will be acceleration effects on, and high profit stimulus to, industrial investment that with a short time lag will add to the fast expansion of consumption at the same time as house construction also rises rapidly, thanks to easy credit conditions. The process looks most satisfactory, but disequilibrium tendencies are already built into this development. The expansion is too rapid and cannot be maintained. More rapidly rising wage rates (and wage drift) will follow upon lower unemployment rates, and excess demand for labor will arise at various points. There are no automatic equilibrating tendencies arising out of spiraling wages, prices, and nominal demand—except via balance of payments restrictions. Rapidly rising imports and retarding exports will tend to result in balance of payments deficits. We have seen above how stabilization policy reactions appear in the second phase—as a response both to the inflationary tendencies and menacing balance of payments difficulties. In this stage of rapidly increasing prices and demand, mildly restraining measures will not be effective. And it seems that only shock methods help, and perhaps even these only after the boom has for various reasons lost a large part of its momentum.

An interesting problem—the same issue that we in fact meet in all countries—is why the policy response comes so late. According to this sketch of a model, the disequilibrium tendencies had already started during the first phase of rapid demand expansion without much inflation. One could argue that a restrictive policy—with less of stimulating measures—should have been initiated so early that the expansion from the beginning would have been kept down close to a rate that could be maintained, with a rate of employment somewhere between the recession level and the boom level. That would mean less stimulating fiscal policy during the recession, or still better, less recession or stagnation after the previous boom.

The central policy issues we have raised are just a way of pointing out a series of interrelated problems of the working of the economic mechanism and policy changes. The most fundamental problem is perhaps why the ceiling of expansion has to be kept so low for the British economy. There are many problems involved in the issue as to the precise interrelations between a relatively slow long-term growth trend and the United Kingdom's special kind of cyclical instability. The slow growth trend will affect the ceiling and therefore have a determining influence on cyclical instability, and this in turn has feedback effects on the trend. Feedback effects arise—as argued above—when the series of short-term cost and price inflations influence the competitiveness of British exports, at the same time as the cycle of restrictive policies tends to keep the investment ratio low, again contributing to the low productivity trend. We may ask the question: If the long-term rate of productivity growth had been twice as high (4.5 per cent instead of 2¼ per cent) could then the demand expansion have gone on longer? It could be maintained that there would be more room for wage increases as determined by declining unemployment rates; balance of payments difficulties would be postponed or less likely or frequent since the export volume under these conditions would rise more rapidly and export retardation would be postponed. Certainly these conclusions do not necessarily follow. They are only possibilities that might be inferred from experiences of other countries with higher ceilings and less balance of payments constraints. It could, on the contrary, very well be asserted that more "space" of this kind for the British economy would rather call forth so much more of rapid demand expansion—with correspondingly higher wage and price inflation—that the same type of convulsive policy restrictions would have to be introduced with perhaps rather unchanged consequences as to instability. The experience after the 1949 devaluation might be quoted as supporting evidence of this view: space was created (with respect to the balance of payments constraint) but rapid inflation in the United Kingdom did away with this space in two years' time.

Instead of *assuming* more rapid growth we should like to find the policy mix that would mean an approach to *both* targets: greater stability (including absence of stagnation periods) and a more rapid growth rate. These aims seem to be closely related. Perhaps the suggestion to brake the expansion at an early stage of the revival (or provide more moderate doses of stimulation), and thereby prevent expansion from surpassing significantly the longer-term growth rate, would imply longer expansion periods, less inflation, and higher ceilings—but also on the average a lower rate of full employment.[35] The success of such a policy might ultimately mean a higher rate of growth of exports and GNP than has resulted from the "go-stop" policy pattern so far followed. We should not forget, however, that such policies of restraint, to be carried out before a crisis is discernible, may be politically naïve, especially as the results must be uncertain. There is a "learning process" in stabilization policy, implying that the sequence of measures (and mistakes) are not exactly repeated;

35. Dow, in Chap. 13, sect. 5, draws the following conclusions from his analysis of the price-wage mechanism: "My own belief is that if the pressure of demand had been somewhat lower, and the margin of unused capacity somewhat larger, than in most of the postwar years, there could have been steady expansion of expenditure, output and output per head as rapid as that which in fact occurred. Since *alternations* of policy were probably to some extent disrupting, the preservation of a steady but lower pressure of demand might even have resulted in faster growth" (p. 361). "But whatever qualifications are made, the results appear to me to justify the belief that with a lower pressure of demand, the rise of prices would have been considerably less" (p. 363).

we find some evidence of this process in some holding back of expansive policy measures during 1962. The extreme alternative—a policy of consistent inflationary pressure without breaks—might in a way be easier to carry out, in any event from a political point of view. Instead of avoiding the cycle of too-restrictive policies by preventing demand at an early stage from increasing too rapidly, the balance of payments constraints might be neutralized by repeated devaluations or successive schemes of import controls. The positive argument for this type of policy would also be that inflation should imply higher profits and savings out of profits, thereby helping to bring up the investment ratio and ultimately the growth rate of productivity.[36] However, the international repercussions of such a policy—including the position of the pound sterling—would make this alternative very unrealistic.

There is not much scientific basis to support the one or the other alternative policy strategy as being the best solution. The reason is not only that there are too many uncertainties about how the British economy really works and will work in the future. Evidence from the experiences in other countries is in this respect of limited value (see Chapter 3). There are also questions of conflicting targets, not least between the degree of full employment and the rate of inflation. Last but not least, in considering the British economy we must remember that the perspective of short-term stability here mainly applied can give only a very incomplete understanding of the whole set of deep-seated structural problems that seem to be most relevant.

36. N. Kaldor, in *Essays on Economy Policy* (London, 1964) Vol. 1, Chap. 8, exposes his theory of how the "marginal efficiency of capital" and the "money rate of return" are closely determined by how fast an economy is growing and by the rate of inflation. The underlying assumptions are very demanding (for example as to the level of aggregation and the stability of savings propensities), but the conclusions are quite general, for instance: "Hence a slow and steady rate of inflation provides a most powerful aid to the attainment of a steady rate of economic progress" (p. 188).

5 STABILIZATION POLICY EXPERIENCES IN SWEDEN

THE POLICY MILIEU

The general appearance of Swedish postwar cycles does not look especially interesting. As can be seen from tables and graphs in Chapter 3 and in the Appendix, Sweden seems to show a low degree of cyclical variation. There are no very pronounced yearly variations in real terms. The periods of retarded growth (1951–52, 1958, and 1961) fit into the general Western European pattern. As to the rate of growth in GNP, Sweden is about medium, with a characteristic acceleration of the growth rate from around 1959; only in the rate of general price rise does Sweden seem to be a little more outstanding.

However, these very general features of development conceal some rather interesting characteristics relating to specific stability problems that will be discussed in this chapter. Let us examine the main points of interest in a short introductory survey.

As a general background to an understanding of Sweden's postwar development it should first be remembered that Sweden, as one of the few exceptions in Europe, started out on a relatively high level of production and standard of living. There was not as much of a process of catching up as in most other European countries. In 1945 real GNP was about 10 per cent above the level of 1938–39, real wages per hour were about unchanged, the consumption price level was 40 per cent above the prewar level. But the total supply of money was about 70 per cent above the level of 1938–39. On the other hand, foreign trade was restricted. In the third quarter of 1945 the export volume was about 25 per cent below the prewar level, and the import volume as much as 70 per cent below. The reason why exports kept up better than imports was the high level of foreign aid and credits given by Sweden during the first postwar period.

The main point of interest with regard to the Swedish postwar experiences refers rather directly to the issues of stabilization policy, not so much because of clear successes or failures, but rather because of a highly intensive experimentation with old and new tools of policy. In fact, Sweden represents a case in which the possibilities for successful stabilization results seem especially favorable in several respects. The following reasons may be mentioned:

1. During the whole postwar period in Sweden there has been a stability and continuity in government power that can hardly be matched by any other democratic Western country. The Socialist party has all the time (really since 1932) been the dominant party in parliament and government, and except for a few years of coalition, the Socialists have formed the government. This fact has, of course, not excluded political difficulties, risks of losing the dominant position, and the consequent need to make political compromises with nonsocialist groups. But on the whole, and in comparison with governments in most other Western countries, the Swedish government has had better opportunities to carry out consistent policies according to its own beliefs and preferences and also to harvest the fruits of a "learning process." It has not been "compelled" to change policies and to make new mistakes just because of some shift in political power. Instead, it has been allowed to "enjoy" its own mistakes and then to search for improved lines of policy. The political strength of the government has certainly been an important favorable condition for successful stabilization policy.

2. Of course, a strong government is not necessarily a favorable condition for good policy results. The government may be too reactionary (from the point of view of experimentation), or too radical, or too silly, too badly informed, or too dogmatic to reach good results. On these scores the Swedish government has—according to our view—been on the progressive side. There has been very little dogmatism: no superstition as to budget balancing, no ceilings on government debt, hardly any limits to tax rates or what the state can tax, and a very open mind as to the acceptance of new policy parameters. Associated with these attitudes is a ready acceptance of economists both as civil servants and as advisers to the government. This is an old tradition in Sweden from the days of Cassel and Wicksell as well as later on of Hammarskjöld, Lindahl, Myrdal, and so on, all of whom had a strong influence on policy formation.

3. That the government should continuously be strong and enlightened (as to economics) and well informed is not a sufficient condition for successful policy. If a government following advice given by sophisticated economists comes into serious conflict with a business community of the American type (pre-1961), then advanced policy measures may appear to be very misplaced and meet devastating reactions, for example along the lines of the New Deal measures in the United States (1933) or the Blum experiments in France (1936). It seems as if in Sweden the business community has to a large extent understood and accepted in a positive way the policy experiments of the socialist government. Partly this attitude is a function of a type of relative confidence in the government authorities, depending on the fact that the government has not been socialist in any aggressive sense. There have hardly been any manifest socialist ambitions (in the sense of socialization) during the postwar period.[1] On the contrary, the government's attitude has been to accept the existence and position of the private business sector and to aim at making it work efficiently. From

1. There are two important reservations: with regard to housing policy and to the pension fund policy (see below).

this point of view, the government has received much praise from private business, especially for its liberal business taxation policies and for its efficient labor market policy. To this area also belongs the government's strong belief in effective competition supported by free trade and low tariffs. Of course, there have been minor clashes on this point, because in Sweden as well as in other countries industries hurt by foreign competition will apply for increased protection. But on the whole there has been a common view, strongly supported not only by the government and the business community but also by the trade union movement, concerning the need for competition and free trade within a predominantly private enterprise sector.[2]

The general acceptance by the business community of the government's policies also very much depends on a kind of cautious confidence. It is assumed that the government's full-employment policy will in general imply stable and expanding demand for most branches of activity, as well as relatively high profits. There does not exist the American horror of government budget deficits; on the contrary, the opposition parties as well as the business community tend to be highly alarmed when the finance minister tries to overbalance the total budget and thereby create "forced savings."[3] Of course, people are certain that any other government would have to carry out about the same type of policies with results that would probably be quite similar. From this point of view it may be considered just as well to have a strong and steady socialist government. In any event, the success of the government in carrying out a full-employment policy and the fact that private business has thrived in this climate are the strongest reasons for the relatively good relations between government and business in Sweden.

To this picture of a friendly policy climate belongs an ac-

2. Ninety-five per cent of industry and 85 per cent of banking are in private hands.

3. It should be noted that the attitudes of American business have changed significantly since the proved success of the tax reductions in 1964.

count of the role of economists. There are in Sweden scarcely any "ivory tower" economists of the sophisticated American campus type who build models and carry out research on such high levels that only a few colleagues on the same level can appreciate their masterpieces. Most Swedish economists are "practical" in the sense that they have a high preference for positions in business, labor and employers' organizations, government departments, and committees. There is a tradition of using them in this capacity, and it occurs at the cost of teaching and high-level research. We believe, however, that the economists sitting in strategic advisory and research positions all over the field—not only in government offices but also in banks, trade organizations, and in employer and trade union organizations—do a lot to create an understanding of targets and methods of government policies. There is in fact a community of outlook, created and maintained by economists sitting in the opposing camps of interest, that should not be underestimated.

4. A very important reason for the favorable policy conditions derives from the simple fact that it must be much easier to control the economy of Sweden than that of the United States or Canada or France. Sweden is a small, rather homogenous country that is easy to survey. The government authorities can get a quick and useful grasp of the fundamental economic tendencies in a given situation by calling on a limited number of some ten to twenty men sitting in strategic positions (the big export industries, the leading men in the central trade union and employer organizations, leaders of the important central cooperative organization). This type of contact is important for the government in order to find out about the attitudes that play a strategic role for policy success. The Swedish economic statistics are reasonably good in most fields and are currently used by a great number of research institutes in order to assess the economic situation. There is a lively economic debate, and a good deal of information is transmitted by newspapers and economic periodicals.

However, a fairly high level of general economic enlightenment and a certain community in outlook are clearly not sufficient conditions for efficient stabilization policy. The following account will show that there are also plenty of reasons for policy failures.

THE INSTABILITY PROBLEMS

There is a considerable variability in the yearly growth rate of GNP (in real terms) and industrial production; the GNP rate varying between —0.4 and +7.2 per cent, industrial production between —1.5 and +8.5 per cent. There is some regular cyclical pattern in common with most West European countries, with boom conditions during the years 1946–47, 1950–51, 1954–56, 1959–61, and 1963–64 and various signs of slackening in production and employment during the years 1948–49, 1952–53, 1958–59, and "potentially" in 1962. This rhythm in development appears clearly in the conditions on the labor market. Demand and supply on the labor market and unemployment have varied in a significant cyclical pattern.

The variability of the components of GNP is summarized in the table on Sweden in the Appendix. The Swedish pattern of instability is characterized by rather high contributions from the side of exports and inventory investment. Private consumption tends to vary in a stabilizing manner. According to the studies by the government Economic Research Institute (Konjunkturinstitutet), the marginal propensity to save (from private income takers) tends to increase during boom periods and to decline when the rate of income increase is below normal. Figure 5.1, presenting the relative changes of disposable incomes and private consumption (in constant prices), shows how consumption tends to rise by around 3 to 4 per cent per year rather independently of the relatively wide variation of real disposable income (between 1 and 7 per cent).[4] It can be

4. See Börje Kragh, *Konjunkturbedömning* (Stockholm, 1964), p. 89. It should be observed that the points for 1957 and 1960 fall far

FIGURE 5.1
Annual Percentage Changes of Private Consumption and of Private Disposable Income (both at constant prices), 1952–64

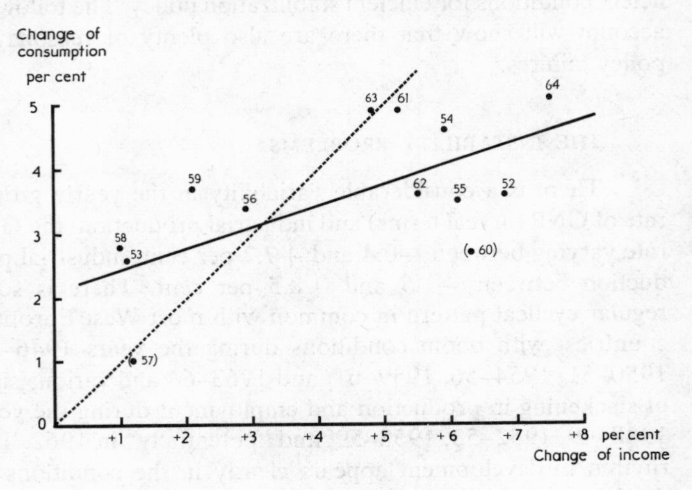

argued that the variation of the growth of the production indices and the employment rate tend to underestimate the true instability on the demand side. Characteristic of the Swedish instability problems, as in most other countries, are the repeated tendencies toward serious excess demand situations. These tendencies, in both the commodity and labor market, were pronounced during the years 1947, 1950–51, 1955, 1960, and 1963. Figure 5.2 on the relation between vacancies and applicants in the labor market illustrates this point. The actual course of production need not and will not usually be significantly influenced by excess demand tendencies. Production may get an extra push (as in 1960) but it may also be retarded because of bottlenecks and disorganization tendencies as was

---

outside the pattern because of special reasons (the Suez crisis and the general sales tax introduced January 1, 1960).

the case in 1947, when, among other factors, overmobility of labor had bad effects on productivity. One symptom of these excess demand situations is the big price and wage increases that can be observed during the years characterized by strong excess demand. In connection with the Korean war boom there was a price and wage explosion of exceptional magnitude (hourly rates rising by some 20 per cent in 1951 and 1952), but also in the other boom situations wages and prices have risen rapidly. There is a rather close relation between the state of demand on the labor market and the general rate of wage increase. During the boom years with considerable excess demand for labor—as in 1955, 1960, and 1961—wages per hour in industry have risen by 8 to 9 per cent; in more quiet years—as in 1953, 1954, and 1958—the rise has been limited to around 4 to 5 per cent. (The average rise of hourly wages over the period 1953–63 was 7 per cent.)

There has been no effort by the Swedish government to carry out an "income policy" or interfere with the bargaining process on the labor market. The strong labor market organizations (on both sides) have had a very determined view on government neutrality in this respect. On the other hand the government seems to have been relying on "responsible" wage-policy reactions. But this is certainly a relative concept, depending among other things on current economic policies. Under inflationary conditions, with high profits and excess demand for labor, the government cannot and should not expect a holding back of claims for wage increases as a method to dampen the rise in prices. From the point of view of responsible trade unions, the rise in wages claimed should at least be so large that the *expected* increase in cost of living will be covered and room granted for a full share in the growth of productivity. This attitude has repeatedly been expressed by leading trade union economists in Sweden and accepted as a target for the wage policy. But such a "reasonable and responsible" attitude to wage policy will under existing postwar conditions imply an inflationary rise of wage rates. Assume, for

FIGURE 5.2
Annual Changes of Wages per Hour in Relation to the Percentage of Vacancies Filled (Manufacturing Industry), 1950–63

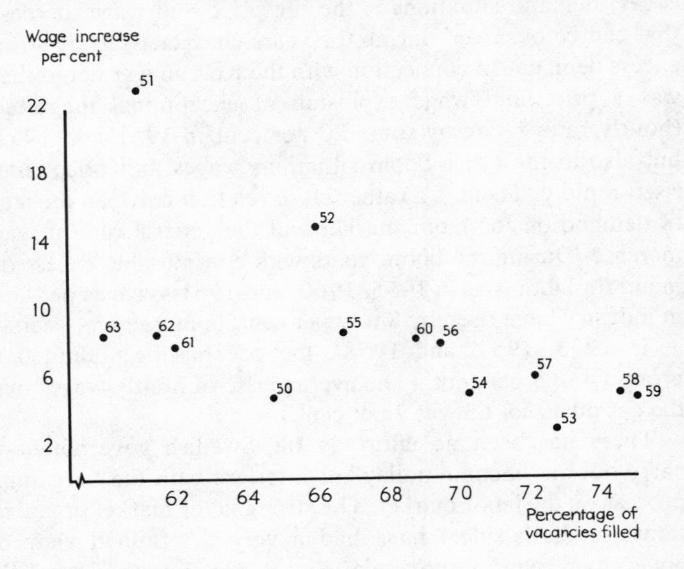

example, that the trade unions anticipate a rise of 5 per cent in the cost of living in the course of the coming year, or that they want to recover an unexpected increase of the same size which has occurred during the current year; then the need for a wage increase to offset the effect on the standard of living of this price rise must lead to a minimum claim for wage increases substantially exceeding 5 per cent. It is here assumed that wage earners wish to maintain their accustomed standards of consumption, and accordingly require full compensation in their wages after the deduction of income taxes. If one assumes, using the approximate present-day Swedish figures, a marginal income tax of about 40 per cent for workers, and an average tax of about 20 per cent, and an expected rise in the cost of living as a result of the rise of the general level of wages corresponding to 25 per cent of the wage rise over the course of the year, the required general increase of wages becomes nearly 10 per cent.[5] The wage multiplier in this example would thus be 2. With a rise of money wages of less than 10 per cent, the increase in disposal income (after deduction of taxes), reckoned as a percentage, would be less than the rise of the cost of living index.

An arithmetical model for rational (or responsible) wage demands as indicated above (and in the footnote) is certainly of

5. This is the theory of the "wage multiplier" (see Lundberg, *Business Cycles and Economic Policy,* pp. 241–43). Designate the workers' average wage by w, the wage increase by Δw, the marginal tax rate by t_m, the average tax rate by t_s, the price level for consumer goods by p, and the consequential price rise by Δp. The induced rise of the cost of living from a rise in the wage level—expressed by the coefficient k—is defined in the following equation:

$$\frac{\Delta p}{p} = k\frac{\Delta w}{w}$$

If the workers' disposable income (after taxation) has been reduced or is expected to be reduced by a price rise of a per cent, the workers will seek compensation for the amount $a(1-t_s)\cdot w$ through a rise of their money wages (Δw). This target of wage policy is expressed in the equation:

$$(1-t_m)\cdot\Delta w = (1-t_s)w \cdot (a + k\frac{\Delta w}{w})$$

$$\frac{\Delta w}{w} = a\frac{1-t_s}{1-t_m-k(1-t_s)} = a\frac{1}{\frac{1-t_m}{1-t_s} - k}$$

The factor $\frac{1}{\frac{1-t_m}{1-t_s} - k}$, the wage multiplier, thus indicates how much larger than the given price rise the percentage wage rise must be in order to provide full compensation in the sense indicated. On the example given in the text, k was assumed to be 25 per cent, $t_m = 40$ per cent and $t_s = 20$ per cent, and the multiplier then becomes exactly 2.

only limited value for explaining actual wage development during the postwar period. However, the model gives a rationalization of an existing trade union attitude that is part of the background to the wage claim process. In fact the seemingly very high wage claims in 1951 and 1952 had the motivation that they were necessary for after-tax compensation for current cost of living increases and such expected cost of living increases as were forecasted as consequences of the wage rise demanded.

It should be observed that a considerable part of the wage rise has consisted of the so-called "wage drift" which is defined (and measured) as the wage increase in excess of that recorded in the collective agreements. This part of the yearly wage rise has determined half or more of the total increase in industrial wages during years of high demand, the share being especially high when (as for instance in 1960–61) efforts were made to check the inflation by means of restrictive collective agreements.

On the whole, the Swedish government has had greater difficulty in preventing expansions from developing into inflationary boom conditions than in stopping contractions or counteracting recession tendencies. The strong expansions of demand that got under way in 1946, 1954, 1959, and 1963 were not well controlled and were followed by pronounced boom situations signifying serious disequilibria. Of course, it is a matter of political valuation whether such disequilibria are "worse" and therefore more important to manage than the recession periods, when monthly unemployment has reached 3 per cent (compared with around 1 per cent in booms). The deflationary gaps, measured as the difference between annual potential GNP and actual GNP during the recession years, hardly ever exceeded 2 per cent (as compared with around 10 per cent for the United States in 1958 and 1960–61). It is partly a question of the relative emphasis placed on the various policy targets and the political valuation attached to the deviations from these targets. From the point of view of

Swedish politics, an increase in unemployment even to the moderate rates mentioned is apparently considered much worse than the inflationary tendencies of a boom; anyhow, this conclusion may be taken as an interpretation of actual economic policy efforts. These have without doubt been both more ambitious and more successful in counteracting recessionary tendencies than in controlling inflationary booms.[6]

A broad and generalized picture of the policy cycle looks very much the same as in the United Kingdom and several other countries. Starting with the results of a relatively successful antirecession policy at the end of a period of slow growth and dampened activity, favorable conditions for rapid expansion have in fact been created. An expansive fiscal and monetary policy during the past period will have resulted in a substantial amount of surplus liquidity. Large budget deficits will have created high liquidity reserves in the banking system at the same time as private business is well equipped with cash. During the recession, decisions have been made to expand public investment of various kinds and to increase housebuilding. Decisions on such expansive measures will necessarily have been made with a certain time lag. As the period of recessionary tendencies is short (say one year), it easily occurs that the maximum rates of public and housing investment coincide with an acceleration of export and private investment coming with a new expansion phase of the cycle. This is what apparently occurred in 1953–54, 1958–59, and to some extent also in 1962–63. As even at the "bottom" of the recession there is not much distance from the ceiling of full employment and full use of production capacity, there is not enough time for reversing the expansionary policy before inflationary tendencies appear. The stepping up of government expenditures and government-controlled housing expenditures continues of its own momentum. There are, how-

6. However, we may note a trend in the distribution of emphasis in government documents, not least in the public speeches of the Finance Minister. There is much less emphasis on the target of price stabilization after 1958 than during the first part of the postwar period.

ever, specific features of the Swedish cycles that have to be observed.

An increase of export demand is regularly an important stimulus to the Swedish conjuncture at the beginning of a revival. An 8 to 10 per cent increase in volume from one year to the next is not unusual and will imply up to 1.5 to 2 per cent of GNP. Allowance must be made for the average import content of exports—which amounts to some 25 per cent—and especially to the fact that a considerable proportion of the export increase may be taken out of inventories of unsold export goods accumulated during the recession. This moderator especially refers to wood products and iron ore. Private investment in industry and trade, a leading series in the revivals, tends to give a further push to the economy. It is easy to see how the Swedish economy tends to receive a flying start after a short period of dampened activity: accelerated expenditures for housebuilding and government investment resulting from the recession tend to be reinforced by strong increases of exports and private investment, while private consumption goes on rising at a rather stable rate of 3 to 3.5 per cent per year.

The space left before the ceiling of full-employment production is reached will be quite narrow, this ceiling being determined by existing capacity reserves and by the current increase of productive resources and of productivity. There has been a low rate of natural growth of the labor force (around 0 to 0.5 per cent per year) and a relatively low rate of immigration into Sweden. Hence there are limited reserves of manpower in addition to the unemployment that exists during the recession. There will be some limited response to the increased demand for labor from the side of some underutilized manpower (to some extent hoarded by management over a period of slack demand for fear of losing labor in a full-employment economy), a higher rate of female labor force participation, and possibly some extra exodus from agriculture and forestry. The increased rate of utilization of capital and labor will imply an acceleration in productivity that, although it cannot last, will match the rise in demand during the first part of revival. The relatively low ceiling will imply that just about one year's expansion of total demand at the rate determined by the mentioned factors of revival will bring the economy close to the full-employment ceiling (see Figure 3.2 in Chapter 3). The approach to a full-employment ceiling will not "automatically" imply a check on demand. On the contrary there are forces working in the direction of demand acceleration. These forces are very pertinent to the Swedish economy and operate on all fronts. Thus investment demand, public and private, surges upward due to narrow or no margins to full use of capacity in most sectors and strong "secular" forces. And public consumption as well as private consumption demand will be influenced by the rapid wage increases at high and rising rates of full employment.

It is important not to apply a too-mechanical approach when using the concept of a ceiling. It has many dimensions. Expansion will be unevenly distributed in relation to available resources. As these are mobile, although far from perfectly so, there is always a flexibility in the ceiling. This flexibility will partly be a function of the mobility of labor and of current labor market policies (see the last section of this chapter). Anyhow, in an economy of the Swedish type working with narrow margins, the rapid rise of demand after a recession will very quickly create scarcity in strategic sectors of the labor market: for example, skilled workers, building workers, and labor in special geographical areas of rapid expansion. Such situations were reached already in the fall of 1954 and 1959 after not much more than one year of revival; after the nearly invisible slowdown of activity in 1961–62, an excess demand situation started right away.

The reaction mechanism of the Swedish economy is certainly not unique. We have in the case of the United Kingdom discussed the problems of controlling an expansion that, from a balance of payments point of view in particular, starts out in too high a gear and thus cannot persist. The Swedish experience is interesting from the point of view of illustrating how another setup of stabilization policy measures has tended to generate inflationary tendencies.

The most important difference from the United Kingdom developments is the absence of disturbing balance of payments difficulties. Since 1947 and up to 1965 foreign exchange conditions have not—or at most only to a negligible extent as a potential factor—worked as a restriction on demand and costs, and have therefore not necessitated restraining policies. It is in fact quite remarkable both in the shorter and longer run how parallel export and import volume as well as value indices have been moving. (See Figure 5.3.) After the liberalization of imports in 1950 (more or less completely effectuated by 1954),

FIGURE 5.3
Annual Changes of the Volume of Exports and Imports; Surplus or Deficit of Current Account of Balance of Payments

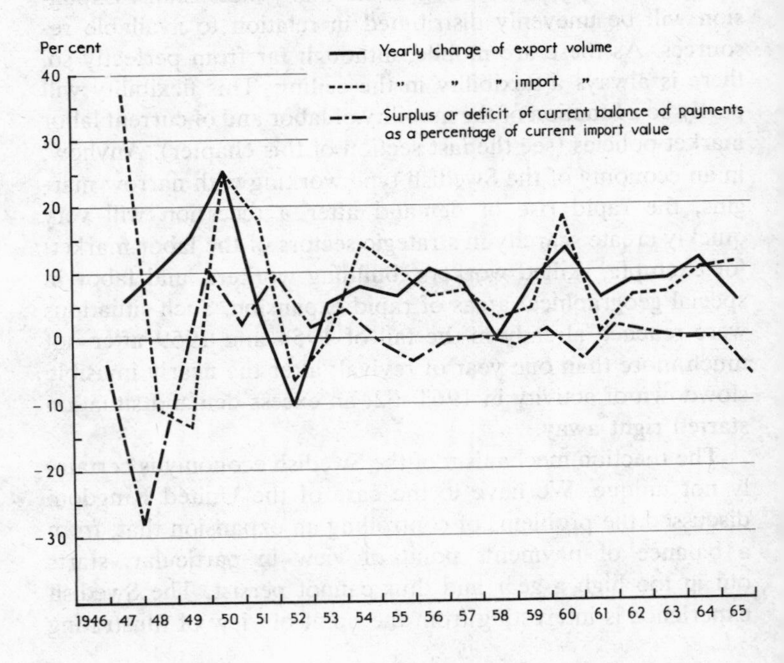

there have been no controls of any relevance on imports, and Swedish tariffs have been kept on a relatively very low level. According to rough measurements, the income elasticity of imports (in real terms) has been of the order of 1.8, implying that the import volume during the postwar period has tended to grow nearly twice as rapidly as real GNP, although with large short-term variability mainly due to inventory fluctuations. On the other hand there is also a high elasticity of demand for Swedish export products, at the same time as the direction of exports (with 60 per cent to Western Europe) is favorable from an expansion point of view. During the spurts of demand expansion, imports—as shown in the diagram—tend to rise very rapidly, a rate partly determined by the high marginal import content of inventory investment. But as mentioned above, this demand acceleration is to a considerable extent propelled by a boom in exports. It is in fact remarkable how little the import surplus varies over the cycle; during the period 1948–64 the deficits in the current balance of payments never reached higher values than corresponding to 3 per cent of the current import value (to be compared with values above 10 per cent for Holland and the United Kingdom). Figure 5.3 demonstrates this remarkable stability quite clearly.[7] The terms of trade—except for the extreme variations during and after the Korean war boom—do not usually create extra instability; the relative high raw material content (including fuels) both on the import and export side explain the relatively small amplitude.

Another important condition for the stable balance of payments development is the behavior of capital movements. Sweden is fortunate enough, compared to the United Kingdom,

7. The year 1965, with a deficit corresponding to 6 per cent of imports, may indicate the beginning of a new era. Such factors as rapidly rising labor costs (11 per cent per hour in manufacturing industry in 1964–65) and excess demand conditions have together with cyclical weakness in some export branches (pulp, steel, iron ore) contributed to a more serious weakening of the balance of payments conditions than ever since 1947.

not to have a world currency with attached confidence problems. The regular longer-term capital import and export movements are controlled by the government and are of small importance. Short-term capital movements have so far not been disturbing. On the contrary, in times of strong inflationary tendencies, combined with restrictive credit policy, there has been an extra high amount of "unaccountable capital imports" in the balance of payments account, signifying increased foreign credits to a large extent coming from more rapid export and slower import payments. It should be emphasized that Sweden has during the whole period kept a certain amount of exchange regulation, mainly implying control of long-term capital movements, thereby also giving more free space for independent monetary policy than is possible in countries with internationally highly integrated money markets.

It should be added that this absence of balance of payments troubles in Sweden since 1947 does not mean that such problems have played no role in policy decisions. There have been repeated warnings that the relatively high and rapidly rising labor costs in Sweden, especially when combined with excess demand situations during the boom years, must sooner or later be causing serious pressure on the balance of payments. However, as these warnings—coming not only from export associations but also from the government's Konjunkturinstitut—had up to 1965 turned out as exaggerated or misplaced, the influence of this consideration has been secondary. On the other side, the resistance to high wage claims has been growing stronger under the impact of a potential and actual squeeze of the profit margins of the main export industries. Figure 5.4 shows the quite remarkable development of the export price index in relation to wages and consumer-goods prices. This kind of restriction on the strong tendencies toward rising wages at full employment has been at work intermittently since 1952 but cannot very well be observed or be given any precise form.

As described above, the acceleration of the growth of total

FIGURE 5.4
Development of Wages, Productivity in Manufacturing, and Prices (annually)

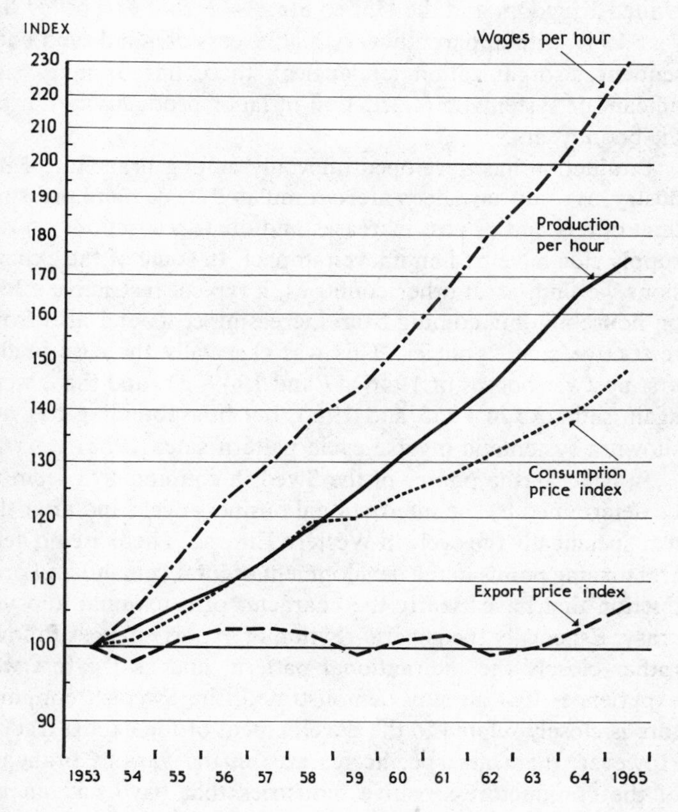

demand during the first one or two years of expansion after a recession will take the form of increasing production and sales followed by rapidly rising wages and upward movements of prices. What forces are there which tend to create *imbalances* during the boom? As said above, increasing scarcity of labor, especially of the more skilled types, will under all conditions imply a restriction on *real* growth after the small reserves of open and concealed unemployment have been absorbed. One remarkable fact—as compared with the experience of the United Kingdom and the United States—is that except for the year 1947 with apparently very high excess demand (and consequent disorganization tendencies), there has been no significant or systematic retardation of labor productivity during the boom years.[8]

Production has developed unevenly among branches of industry, as some have been more stimulated by demand pressure than others and as cost increases and other restrictions on the supply side have had an uneven impact. In some of the expansions we find, as in other countries, a typical restrictive effect on housebuilding coming from increasing costs and also from restrictive credit policies. This was especially the case in the first postwar booms of 1946–47 and 1949–51, and there were again setbacks in 1955 and 1960, but housebuilding has not shown a systematic inverse cycle pattern since 1951.

In general, the phases of the Swedish conjunctures seem to be determined by the international business cycle and after the war specifically the cycle in Western Europe. There are no general turning points in the development of total demand and production that have clearly the character of a national idiosyncrasy. Especially the general rhythm of export changes follows rather closely the international pattern, and as the interwar experiences had already demonstrated, the Swedish conjuncture is closely related to the development of the export trade.[9] However, there are specific features in the various branches of the conjuncture-sensitive industries that have had an influence on the general pattern. As in other countries the varia-

8. Only during 1951 of the Korean boom did there occur a decline in real GNP at full employment that seems strange and probably refers to deficient calculations. There was no decline in industrial production. Probably there is something wrong with the price deflating procedure during the period of very rapid price rise, especially with regard to the valuation of the relatively big inventory fluctuations.

9. Lundberg, Chap. 2.

tion in inventories plays an important role as a factor making for instability. This is especially so with respect to the big export industries: pulp, iron ore, and iron and steel. There are inventory cycles especially in pulp (and other forest products) that follow a specific pattern that has not been well synchronized with developments in the other fields, and this creates policy problems especially as to employment in forest work in northern Sweden. The specific cycles in pulp, iron and steel, iron ore, and textiles tend to offset each other to a considerable extent. The pattern of the setbacks in the volume of production and exports seems to have been quite consistent during the three recessions (1951–52, 1957–58, 1961–62): the wood and pulp industries have led, followed closely by iron ore and the iron and steel industries, and with a consistent lag by the engineering industries (textiles have shown a very irregular pattern). This development has, for instance, implied that production indexes of the wood industries have been recovering when the recession has hit engineering. This incomplete synchronization of the downward reactions has of course partly been a function of the relatively light recessionary impacts from outside the Swedish economy, but it has also been a result of independent cross movements of production in other sectors.

The recessionary impulses have not been strong enough to start a cumulative process of decline in investment and income. On the other hand, in expansions there is certainly enough of synchronization of developments in the various sectors to create definite inflationary tendencies, but there is no evidence of a development of cyclical disequilibria tending toward a built-in break of the boom.[10]

The problem in Sweden's case mainly refers to a general policy issue: why the Swedish policy authorities have "allowed" so much instability in the inflationary direction. Why and how

10. Neither was that the case with the interwar expansions—not even in 1929–30. See Lundberg, Chap. 2, pp. 42–54.

have the restrictive policy measures that have been applied tended to come too late or been too ineffective with regard to the strong expansionary forces? And what impact have these measures eventually had on the recessionary tendencies that followed? One can always raise the question—but not answer it—as to whether the restrictive policy measures applied during the boom (to be described below) may not have aggravated the recession. It is easy to show that the shift in policy direction from restriction to stimulation has occurred with a time lag, although shorter than in the expansion phase. Destabilizing effects from a lagging policy cycle have to be weighted against the restrictive and expansive impacts that do occur during the right phases of the conjunctures. One of our recurrent problems of analysis refers precisely to the difficulty of isolating policy effects from other exogenous disturbances as well as from the working of the whole conjuncture mechanism.

METHODS OF FORECASTING

Before taking up some of the policy issues, it is necessary to add some notes on the methods of judging current trends in the economy that the government and its authorities use as guidance and background to policy decisions. The above discussion of the general postwar conjuncture experience is colored by a rather humble attitude as to the possibilities of good forecasting. There is so far in Sweden very little of Dutch econometric courage in finding a system of responses, a model, to be used for forecasting purposes. Instead of econometric relations that have been applied only to a small although increasing extent, the government has been relying on surveys of expenditure plans in various sectors of the economy in order just to get a notion of the direction and if possible the strength of current and expected changes in demand.

For the overall surveys, methods of interpretation corresponding to the usual forms of inflationary (or deflationary) gap calculations are found to be quite useful. The starting points are found in the preliminary national accounts for the passing year, complemented by surveys of the current situation on the labor and commodity markets. The expected changes in demand to the next year are to a considerable extent based on surveys of expenditure plans—referring to private investment (mainly in industry, electric power, some parts of trade, and housebuilding) and the expenditures by the government and the communes. The results of the investment surveys in Swedish industry have proved to be rather reliable as to tendencies. The surveys made in the fall for the coming year's investment tend to underestimate the rise in machinery and building investment; the surveys made in the spring of the year of forecast turn out much better. In any case, the big actual or potential changes in investment plans—for the years 1947, 1955, 1959, 1962, and 1965—signifying decisive changes in the prospective situation have come out clearly in the surveys. These surveys have in fact served as a rather reliable alarm bell.

As discussed above, changes in foreign trade have had very important impacts on the Swedish conjunctures, and great efforts are therefore made to ascertain the expected changes in this field. Surveys of the probable export developments in the main fields during the coming year are made with the main exporters and export associations. The results of such surveys have during recent years been complemented by simple forecasting methods using existing forecasts of production developments in the most important export countries (within the OECD). Simple relations (income and production elasticities) are applied to ascertain the trends of the main Swedish exports in the various markets. The great difficulties in reaching reliable forecasts as to the changes from year to year of total export volume come out clearly in Figure 5.5). The mistakes especially seem to refer to the turning-point years (1952, 1954, 1959).

In estimating expected import changes, very rough methods are used, applying rather stable import elasticities to expected production increases with some allowance for expected changes in national expenditure composition, especially with regard to

FIGURE 5.5
Forecasts and Results with Regard to the Annual Changes in the Volume of Exports, 1950–64

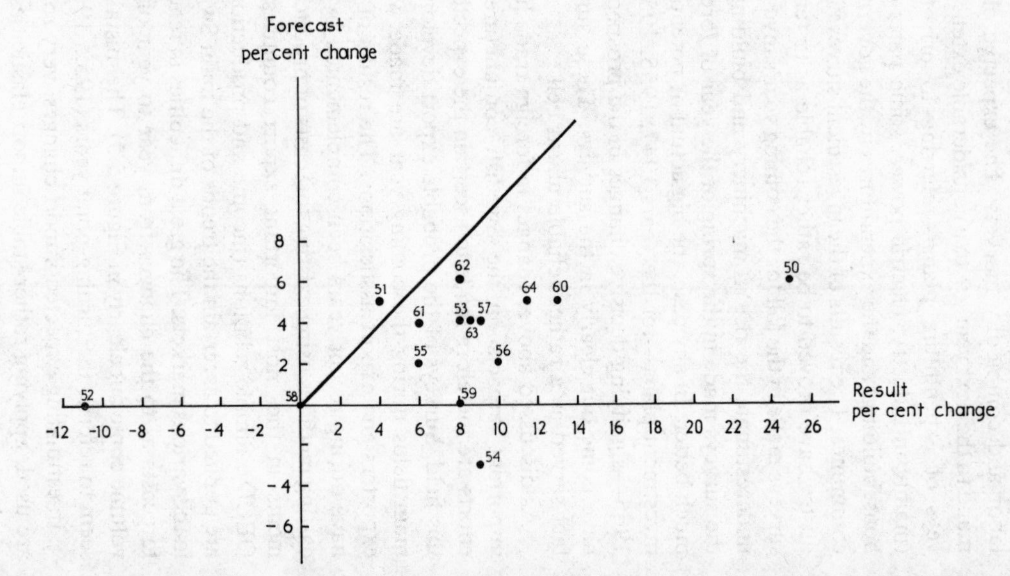

the inventory situation. However, the forecasts on inventory changes are the weakest part of the estimating procedure; they are not much more than pure guesswork, although some attention is paid to existing stocks and apparent tendencies. Some guidance is coming from "Munich tests" among a sample of producers and importers answering questions about their inventories (for example, if they are too big, too small, or just satisfactory). Lastly, the biggest item, private consumption expenditures, is calculated on the basis of estimated private income change, with deductions for marginal direct taxes followed by application of a simple consumption function with an estimated marginal propensity of about 85 per cent.

The estimated demand change is then compared with a forecast of the probable addition to total supply (at given prices). This is mainly done in a rather simple way: the estimated change in the available labor supply is added to the expected rate of productivity increase (usually around 3 to 4 per cent). The estimate is sometimes modified after consideration of the capacity effects of investments and a more detailed account of likely production changes in the main branches of activity.

That is the main outline. As usual, the actual application of a given forecasting technique is less mechanical and more intelligent than appears from a simple account of this type. There is at each point of the forecasting process a rather big range of arbitrariness, opening up possibilities of more or less subjective choice of modifications that can be guided by special insight based on various grounds of judgment (from, for example, Munich type barometer tests, which have been used quarterly in Sweden since 1954). The close contacts of the local Labor Market Board offices with employment tendencies in various branches of industry play an increasing role in forming the judgments. There are certainly great possibilities—and dangers—of fitting personal or eventually politically colored judgments into this type of rather loose projections. On the other hand, such flexible forecasting may, if well managed, turn out better than a more mechanistic and objective approach based on a systematic econometric model. A comparison of the Dutch and the Swedish forecasting results over the period 1952–59 does not seem to demonstrate any significant superiority as to either approach. (See Chapter 6, page 305.)

The estimates from the demand and the supply sides have usually been adjusted to each other in order to form a national budget, presented as an appendix to the government budget at the beginning of the year in question. (Later, in May of the same year when the definite government budget is presented, there will be a revised national budget.) The national budget is as a result of such adjustment a curious mixture of forecast and plan. It might be called "compensatory" planning. In a way it is a forecast of a development that is accepted and acknowledged by the government.[11] However, there are several difficult problems of interpretation that make the Swedish concept of national budget rather obscure. The same questions, plus some extra ones, may be raised with reference to the gap measurements when an "ex ante" difference between the changes in total demand and supply is left open. This was done during the first postwar years (1946–50) and also in some later years (1958, 1959), when there seemed to be an open disparity between supply and demand tendencies.

Here we can take up for discussion only some of the most relevant problems of interpretation that are of importance for understanding recent Swedish policy issues. One very important point refers to the question as to how and to what extent current and expected government policy measures are considered in the projections. The general rule has been that the estimates are based on given policy parameters as they are fixed at the time of the calculations. One justification of the gap estimates is to find out if policy changes are needed in order to combat eventual disequilibrating tendencies, and, if they are, how strong they should be. If an inflationary gap results from the

11. Ingvar Olsson, *On National Accounting* (Stockholm, 1953). See especially Chap. 8, "Swedish National Budget Work."

calculations, the analysis may be followed up by a projection of probable outcomes of the disequilibrium, of how the gap will be closed, for example, by a rise of prices (pressing down consumption and inflating profits) or an increased import surplus (as was the rather successful forecast from the gap estimate for 1947). The deflationary gap analysis may suggest an increase of unemployment or/and an increased export surplus (as discussed for 1959). If such results cannot be approved by the government, the projections will not be "glorified" as national budgets. Policy changes will be introduced—and eventually the revised forecasts will have the character of a national budget.

The important thing to remember, however, is that the national budget projections taken as conditional forecasts do not aim to include the results of coming policy changes that may partly be motivated by the projections themselves. This was the case, for instance, with the projection for 1959 when the analysis resulted in a deflationary gap of 2 per cent, implying a rise in unemployment above the too-high level already reached in the base year 1958. Expansionary measures that were motivated by the deficiency of demand contributed to a development that deviated considerably from the conditional forecast. This means that one has to be careful when comparing the relative success of conditional forecasting in different countries.[12]

Another important difficulty with the Swedish projection method refers to the treatment of expected wage and price changes. As mentioned above, the main policy problems have referred to the inflationary tendencies. When excess demand situations are developing, wage increases will tend to accelerate. New wage negotiations are often (each or every other year) going on at the time that the projections are being made. There has been much anxiety that any assumed or expected wage

12. H. Theil's comparison in Chap. 3 of his *Economic Forecasting and Policy* (Amsterdam, 1958) seems to suffer from a neglect of such considerations.

increase entered into the gap calculations might have some prejudicing or irritating influence on the bargaining process. Therefore the estimates are made on the basis of given prices and wage costs as existing in the past year.

This method apparently excludes an important part of the issue, namely, how rising wages and prices have feedback effects on demand and supply factors. Instead, the effects of higher wage rates plus the wage drift on price development are analyzed separately.

The weaknesses of the Swedish national budget analysis stand out clearly. The interrelations within the economic system are largely neglected. The emphasis is laid on the primary changes, the direct pushes on demand coming from changes in exports, government expenditures, and private investments. Attention is paid to the absorption of the shocks by leakages from consequent import changes and tax payments having direct repercussions on disposable income and consumption expenditure. But typically the changes in income (and consumption) are not derived out of a complete multiplier process, nor are repercussions on private investments from changes in demand or profits considered explicitly. Changes in consumption usually refer to production changes at given rates of employment and changes in productivity. It is evident that an analysis of primary tendencies that, as a first approximation, are considered independently of each other, may result in big errors if we are studying periods of development involving considerable deviations from full employment or if changes in prices and money income have to be analyzed. The primary purpose is, however, only to find out *direction and relative strength* of the disturbances from last year's trend in order to set the problems for policy discussions.

It should be emphasized that the national budget estimates are not to be considered as some kind of fundamental basis for policy planning and decisions. These budgets are important for bringing the government budget into the framework of the whole economy. From this point of view the exercise in constructing national budgets (as well as corresponding gap calculations) has had great educative value during the long time since the inauguration of this type of technique in Sweden in 1943. It may be mentioned in this connection that the limitation in time perspective of the national budget surveys (just to cover the coming year) is to some extent corrected, since they are also related to the current long-term projections (covering five years at a time) that have been presented since 1947. However, the current need to forecast business trends—for instance, with regard to the quick changes in monetary policy—have mainly been satisfied by inferring from the usual types of information: changes in orders in the main export and investment industries, investment plans, current and expected conditions in sensitive sectors of the labor market. There is nothing remarkable in Swedish experience with respect to the uncertainty in forecasting and the lags in policy decisions. As in other countries a learning process seems to be going on also in this respect—with the lags in policy changes getting shorter. The most remarkable observation is the "negative" lag in 1962, when expansionary policies were applied mainly on account of an *expected* decline of employment and investment during the coming winter without significant changes in the business situation yet having occurred.

THE INSTRUMENTS OF STABILIZATION POLICY

The Swedish government (including the Central Bank) has during the postwar period had access to and used a large number of policy parameters for achieving stabilization targets. In this survey of policy experiences, emphasis is laid on instruments that seem to imply specific Swedish issues.

Physical Controls—During the postwar years up to about 1949, direct controls of investment and imports (by permits and licenses) as well as general price control played a substantial role. Swedish experience has been similar to that of other countries, namely, that such controls tend to be managed with increasing inefficiency as supply conditions become more normal. We shall not discuss the specific problems of physical controls here, as they are of minor general interest. It should be mentioned, however, that one type of physical control has remained in Sweden, acting at some times as an important complement to general monetary and fiscal policy measures, namely, control of building starts by means of licenses and permits issued by the Labor Market Board or its local offices. This technique is useful for timing house and factory construction with regard to variations in local supplies of manpower, especially with regard to seasonal variations. But on various occasions this permit control has also had some general stabilization effects.

Fiscal Policies—Budget policy in Sweden had already in the 1930s a reputation for being relatively sophisticated. A cyclical aspect within the framework of the balancing principle was introduced in the 1933 budget according to which the current budget (as well as the total budget) could be underbalanced in depressions, with corresponding overbalancing to occur during boom periods. The argument was simple and straightforward and was accepted by leading politicians. Even though not much came out as to actual effects of expansionary fiscal policy during the 1930s, at least dogmatism and superstition as to the importance of the annual budget balance had disappeared in Sweden well before the new policy problems of the postwar period became actual.

It is well known that budget surpluses and deficits as such tell rather little about the stimulating and restraining effects, respectively, of fiscal policy. The surpluses and deficits are largely built-in results of economic developments and can only with reservations be taken as approximate indicators of the directions and order of size of budgetary policy effects in different years. Nevertheless, the development of the actual budget balance during the postwar period is such that fiscal policy cannot be considered to have been strongly stabilizing. Big deficits have occurred frequently during inflationary years, and even when comparing consecutive years one does not get a conclusive impression that growing inflationary tendencies are counteracted by increasing fiscal restraints. As examples of the difficulties in managing budget policy, we can take the years 1952–54. The overbalancing of the current budget of 1952–53 was decided upon before the setback of 1951–52 became evident, and the very "weak" budget of 1953–54 was decided in the low conjuncture in the beginning of 1953. The liquidity created by the big budget deficit became "inflation dynamite" during the strong beginning of the investment boom in 1954. Again the big budget deficits of 1959 were very untimely—as well as the relatively more restrictive budget during 1962. There is no impression of tendencies toward dampening effects on the booms coming from the government budget. (Compare the United States experiences of increasing budget surpluses during expansion periods; see Chapter 8.) In fact the budget deficits during the 1955–57 boom and the small surplus during the 1960–61 (and again in the 1964–65) boom signified rather stable fiscal push, because of multiplier effects of the parallel expansion of government incomes and expenditures.

This general impression of a rather badly timed budget policy has to be more closely scrutinized before we can reach any defensible view on stabilization effects. The first distinction we must try to make refers to the difference between built-in effects and results of autonomous policy changes.

The government has been using a great number of fiscal parameters of action for stabilization purposes. Some of them may be briefly mentioned. The first line of defense in recession has been various kinds of public works. The problem has been to get them started quickly at an early stage of a recession when unemployment begins to increase, and also to have the means to cut down the expenditures as soon as a significant revival implies an increased demand for labor. In short the Swedish system works as follows. A reserve of projects is continuously prepared and under preparation with local and central government authorities. The national Labor Market Board elaborates proposals for a public project reserve for submission to the government. Appropriations for such projects are voted in a *General Emergency Budget,* and financial powers are delegated annually by parliament. The main idea is that projects should be important and generally of such character that they can be expected to be realized during the next few years. The advance planning of such projects (such as roadbuilding, forestry works, construction of dwellings) thus aims at making it possible in a recession to carry out important central and local government projects somewhat earlier than would normally have been intended. (Grants are made to cover extra costs of advance planning.)

During the 1958–59 recession, experiments were made with extra government orders to Swedish industry. They were made on a small scale but indicated possibilities of an acceleration of activity in not only building but also in sectors of the engineering industry that are sensitive to recessions. Along the same line of thought the government has during boom periods made efforts to dampen investment by the slowing up of ordering and by urging the authorities to postpone investment projects.

The main control powers actually applied on the expenditure side refer to emergency public works, expenditures for vocational training and geographical mobility, and government control of house construction. The starting and cutting off of emergency works (to a large extent roadbuilding) has been a major method to take care of unemployment, especially during the winter seasons of recession years. Even during such years summer unemployment has been quite low (1.2 per cent in 1958 and 0.6 per cent in 1962 to be compared with the averages over the corresponding years of 2.5 and 1.3 per cent.[13] It should be observed, however, that persons employed on

13. These unemployment rates refer to the unemployment insurance statistics.

public works or transferred to vocational training are not counted as unemployed. The importance of this type of policy can be judged by the fact that men on emergency public works covered about 60 per cent of the gross number of unemployed during the winter season 1958–59. The number of these men was then radically reduced in the fall of 1959 when the strong revival of the economy was on the way. In 1962 and 1963 the gross number of unemployed was about twice as high as the official unemployment rate. The gross figure also includes labor withheld from the market by means of vocational training courses embracing around one third of the gross figure in 1962–63. In fact the modern setup of active labor-market policy in a full-employment economy makes the concept of unemployment more blurred than ever.

When looking at Table A11 (in the Appendix) showing the annual growth of various expenditure items of GNP, one gets the impression that government expenditures belong to the more stable items of total demand. One sees only limited evidence of efforts to countercyclically vary the growth of this component of total demand. The Swedish government has however, by means of its control of long-term financing of new houses, a strong hold on the volume of construction. The government decides on the total frame of subsidized financing for the coming year, and this can be, and is actually, adjusted to the state of the conjuncture. In the earlier years 1947–51, the government actively as well as passively (rising building costs) allowed a considerable decline in house construction (by 25 per cent from 1946–51) as a counterbalancing factor in the general excess demand situation, thereby giving space to the growth of industrial and other private investment. However, this type of policy very must disturbed the long-term housing program and was after this episode not considered to be a desired part of stabilization policy. House construction was allowed to continue to increase, although in a retarded tempo, during the later boom periods (1954–57 and in 1961), the retardation of building starts mainly coming from partly unplanned disturbances in short-term financing due to the restraints on bank advances (see below). The main emphasis in the control of house construction as a part of general stabilization policy has instead fallen on stimulus to more building activity during periods of recession. The government has been increasingly effective in stimulating housebuilding; during the recessions of 1952 and 1958 there was a considerable lag, so that the big push in this field largely came when the economy was already on the way to starting a new boom. There was more success in the very slight recession tendency after 1961; the number of dwellings under construction increased by about 20 per cent during 1962.

One result over a longer period of the type of conjuncture flexibility of government expenditures (including housing loans) discussed above is a kind of ratchet effect. There has been success in expanding expenditures during the recessions—with some time lag—but the reduction in the following boom periods has not been impressive even if regarded in a relative way. The more or less normal rate of expansion of government expenditures during the boom periods has each time started from an "abnormally" high level determined by acceleration efforts during the previous recession period. The main villain in the piece on the side of public expenditures has been the communes; their expenditures on goods and services have been expanding at about twice the GNP rate.

There have also been changes in income tax rates and indirect taxes that have had considerable impacts on the budget results. These changes have been only partly applied for stabilization purposes and need not be discussed here. It may be of interest to note, however, that a general purchase tax that was introduced during the war was abolished at the beginning of 1947 (for political reasons), when strong inflationary tendencies were evident, and was reintroduced at the beginning of 1960 (and increased at the beginning of 1962 and again in the middle of 1965). The tax policy instruments of special interest are the investment tax and the tax allowance system through investment reserve funds. The actual application and working of these devices will be discussed in the next section. Here we shall only give an account of the principles underlying these measures and the form that they have taken.

An *investment tax* has been applied during some of the periods of inflation (1951–53 and 1955–57). The tax base was the actual investment expenditures for machinery and construction incurred (excluding dwellings) during the year, and the rate has been around 10 to 12 per cent. This is certainly quite a high extra investment cost; how high it is considered to be and what effects it will have very much depend on the *anticipation* of how long the period of the tax will last. It is clear that if the tax when introduced is expected to last over a long period or to be permanent, then the tax will tend to act just as a cost-push factor and will tend to be incorporated in the price system. The inflationary conditions ruling when the tax is introduced will imply a favorable condition for transmitting the higher cost on to prices of finished goods. But if it is generally anticipated that the extra charge on investments will last only for one or two years, then the tax will tend to have a strong postponing effect. To the entrepreneurs the tax will mean an additional capital or interest cost of 12 per cent for one year and about 6 per cent (per year) for two years, and thus will be a very high short-term additional cost (although deductible like interest payments for tax purposes). In a way we have here an example of the application of a type of flexible relation between short- and long-term "interest costs" that are necessary for a successful management of anticipations. In most countries, and especially in Sweden, short- and long-term rates of interest have moved over the conjuncture in a rather parallel fashion: the short-term rates have for various reasons not been allowed to move high enough in relation to long-term rates during boom times to demonstrate the short perspective of the rate changes and thereby induce a postponement effect on investment. It is a natural consequence of a successful handling of this technique that the elimination of the tax will quickly be followed by a rapid increase of postponed investment expenditure. (See the next section.) However, there are important technical difficulties in handling such an investment tax instrument. The control measures are also rather demanding. The introduction and abolition have to be announced in advance, and there will therefore be large possibilities for manipulating the dates of payments around the point in time when the tax is introduced or abolished. It was apparently just good luck that the investment tax was abolished at such an excellent point of time as January 1, 1958. (The decision was made in May 1957.)

The *investment funds* scheme is a specifically Swedish invention, designed to level out fluctuations in private investment (exclusive of house construction). The principles involved in this type of investment stabilization were already established during the 1930s—the first law was introduced in 1938—but the actual application came about first after the 1955 revision of the legislation. Here we meet a typical product of the Swedish line of thinking of the 1930s about how to even out the business cycle. As with an active budget policy, the issue was that of changing the timing of private investment expenditures, that is of shifting some part of these expenditures from the boom to the recession periods without necessarily affecting the total volume over the whole cycle.

In order to reach this effect the government authorities must introduce well-timed and sufficient doses of stimulus and repression, having a high degree of flexibility with regard to the changes in the conjuncture. The taxation incentives applied have their effect both on profitability of the investment projects selected and on liquidity of the firms for financing the corresponding expenditures. The main principles of the scheme are the following. A company may set aside a certain share of a year's profits (up to a maximum of 40 per cent of net profits) into an investment fund; a part of this allocation (46 per cent, corresponding to a little less than the sum of taxes that otherwise would have been paid) has to be paid into a blocked account in the Central Bank. The rest of the investment fund is "kept" within the company.[14]

These investment funds, mainly built up during boom periods, are to be released during a recession period. Then, after the announcement by the government, the construction and machinery investments allowed under the system are immediately written down by the amount of funds released. The stimulus to use these funds also comes from an extra depreciation corresponding to 10 per cent of the funds used and from the drawing on the Central Bank account in the given proportion. The period of release is announced by the government (or the Labor Market Board), implying that only investment expenditures made during that period can be financed by investment fund appropriations. It should be noticed that so far the use of investment funds has been voluntary from the side of the corporations, the initiative to use the opportunity coming from them. However, the authorities have the power of compulsion—so far not used—in the sense that they can prescribe that investment funds not used in a period of release have to be transferred back to the income account for taxation.

The statistics on investment funds created (and released) clearly show the positive interest of corporations in this system, especially within industry. The total stock of investment funds at the end of 1962 corresponded to nearly 50 per cent of the sum of annual fixed investment within manufacturing industry; the maximum new addition to the funds (in 1960) amounted to nearly 20 per cent of current industrial investment, and during the periods of release (1958–59 and 1962–63) the actual release of funds had the order of size of 15 to 20 per cent of

14. According to special complementary legislation covering the years 1960 and 1961, companies were stimulated to pay 100 per cent of the investment fund allocation into the Central Bank account by means of an extra income deduction of 12 per cent of the investment fund appropriation (during the following taxation year). This was an effective device to absorb liquidity from the market.

industrial investment expenditure per year. This comparison with investment in manufacturing industry is relevant inasmuch as the overwhelming majority of firms having investment funds belong to this branch.

It is not difficult to understand that corporations accept the system of investment funds as quite a generous method of control, implying welcome possibilities of tax rebate and increased supply of liquidity in times of need. The possibilities of immediate depreciation of investments by the use of the funds is especially important with regard to construction (where the Swedish depreciation rules are as bad as in other countries). It is difficult to estimate the size of the net tax advantage of using investment funds for writing off construction expenditures in comparison with not having this privilege. A number of assumptions have to be introduced as to the discount rate, the pattern of future profits, and other means of tax deduction (for example, a write-off of inventory values). According to certain calculations, the size of the comparative tax rebate may reach about 20 per cent of the expenditure. For machinery and equipment expenditure, the corresponding subsidy is less than 10 per cent owing to the existing generous write-off possibilities for taxation purposes. The incentive to create and add to the investment funds will of course be determined by these possibilities of tax rebates on investments during periods of release. During the years 1960–61 there was, as mentioned above in footnote 14, an additional incentive referring to the extra part (above 46 per cent) paid into the Central Bank account; the extra tax rebate implied about 8 to 10 per cent annual yield on this amount.

Compared with various forms of investment allowance systems used, for instance, in the United Kingdom, the Swedish method of providing for investment funds has certain clear advantages from the point of view of stabilization policy:

1. The period of effective stimulus can be made quite short, as the experience of the 1962 application showed. The decision in May 1962 to release these funds beginning in July apparently

had measurable effects on investment expenditures and employment as early as September, and reached maximum effect in the following February–March.

2. In principle the investment fund system works in a *symmetric* way over the cycle; the system automatically combines ways of stimulating private investment during a recession with ways of dampening investment during the boom. The possibility for a company to set off funds for writing off the value of future investment means that there should be less incentive to invest in fixed capital just in order to create writing-off objects (for keeping down taxes on company profits during boom periods). This type of tax incentive to invest refers to the relatively favorable writing-off possibilities in Sweden on machinery and inventories.

As the part of investment fund allocations to be paid into the Central Bank account is a little less than the the tax rate (46 instead of 49 per cent at the rates around 1960–63), there is a stimulus to use the device when other depreciation possibilities have been fully utilized. When the government—as in 1960 and 1961—is tempting the companies to put the whole of their investment fund allocation into a blocked account at the Central Bank, this results in a kind of very effective open market operation by absorbing liquidity from firms and banks without creating a substitute kind of liquidity (as easily is the case when the Central Bank sells bonds). In a comparable way the use of investment funds created during previous boom periods has stimulating effects on investment. Again there is a strong tax stimulus to finance investment expenditure by means of the investment fund, using the generous writing-off possibilities and on top of this a liquidity effect coming from withdrawing funds from the Central Bank accounts.

3. The investment fund technique involves considerable possibilities of *controlling the time shape* of the use of funds released for financing investments. The achievements in this respect have partly been an effect of the less favorable experiences of the 1958–59 application—that is, a learning process.

During the recession the release came too late so that the main stimulus occurred when, in the autumn of 1959, the rate of demand expansion was on the way to becoming excessive. We again find a model example in the policy during 1962. The investment surveys during the fall of 1961 and spring of 1962 had revealed a clear tendency toward declining industrial investment. A limited recession in construction activity and machinery production concentrated in the winter half year 1962–63 was foreseen. On the other hand, it was this time clearly recognized that the economy was still close to over-full employment. As early as May the Labor Market Board announced the release of investment funds for construction to last from July 1962 to the end of April 1963. Construction had to be started before the first of November, and funds were generally not available after April 1963 (certain exceptions were made under condition that activity was kept low during the summer). Release of funds for investment in machinery was also controlled as to timing by specifying what orders had to be given during the period November 1962 to April 1963 and investment funds would be released only on the condition that delivery was finished before the end of the year. This type of controlling the time shape of the use of funds is certainly quite a specific attribute of this policy parameter. To what extent it also means control of the actual time path of real expenditures—what really matters—is another problem that will be discussed below.

4. An important quality of the investment fund technique refers to the positive and general acceptance of this type of investment control by the business community and the consequent *close cooperation* between the corporations and the policy authorities with regard to the selection of projects in question. This cooperation has become an important aspect of the technique and has meant possibilities both of adjustment to labor supply conditions and of supervision and control.

5. So far the investment fund technique has mainly been applied as a *general* policy parameter. All corporations (and

other eligible units) have been allowed to use their funds during the periods of release (although a system of application for individual projects has been the rule). There are exceptions where fund allowances have been applied for local developments, but these exceptions as a rule do not belong to stabilization policy. However, there are possibilities of systematically using the technique in order to direct the investment injections into regions of existing or expected unemployment, or into branches where a recession is concentrated.

These possibilities have been made use of to an increasing extent during 1964–65 when a very uneven development with a combination of inflationary and recessionary tendencies made it dangerous to apply more general expansion stimuli to demand.

6. One more doubtful merit of the investment fund instrument is ascribed to its quality of implying some kind of minimum disturbance to investment allocation. This type of statement is always more or less unclear. The comparison in mind is usually with a system of varying degrees of credit rationing or a fiscal policy implying relief works. The investment-fund system as such aims only at changing the time distribution of investments over the cycle without disarranging the priority scales. The corporations should in principle be persuaded only to accelerate certain types of investments during a recession and conversely postpone investments during a boom. The selection of investment projects is left to the management of the corporations, which should mean that the projects selected are well prepared, useful, and profitable, for instance in comparison with an extra expansion of public works.

There is certainly some truth in statements of this kind. From the point of view of a good allocation of investment resources, it may be advisable to rely not merely on expansion of public works during recessions, and as a result to attain a ratchet effect of an increasing share of government investment. But it must be observed that the investment fund technique is not free from having "non-neutral" or discriminatory effects. The results achieved by means of the investment fund system will imply substantial tax rebates (subsidies) and higher profits after taxes and thus a marginal change in income and wealth distribution that should have permanent effects also on both the amount and distribution of investment. It is especially the allocation of investment among corporations of different size (the big firms clearly being favored) as well as firms with differing profit rates (and probably growth rates); the firms with the highest profits probably gain most from the tax rebates.

Monetary Policy—As discussed in Chapter 1, it is impossible to draw clear lines of distinction between fiscal and monetary policies. Changes in the budget surplus or deficit as well as manipulation of the investment fund reserves will have important effects on money supply and credit conditions. But there are also specific instruments that clearly belong to monetary policy, such as the discount rate, open market operations, and cash reserve controls. In this survey, we shall give a short account of some specific techniques of monetary control used in Sweden; the actual operation and the results are discussed in the following section.

In the same way as we have been trying to summarize the impact of fiscal policy looking at changes in the budget surplus or deficit, we also may try—with the same type of reservations—to concentrate attention on variations in total money and credit supply when studying the possible influence of monetary policy. The same type of difficulties exist with regard to the distinction between autonomous (exogenous) and endogenous changes in the supply of money and credit as with regard to the budget balance. Figure 5.6 showing changes in the total money supply, bank liquidity, and the development of bank advances can nevertheless, in the absence of more appropriate indicators, be expected to provide some impression of the problems.

One can observe an interesting regular rhythm in the movements of money supply in relation to GNP. In fact, it is rather similar to the experience of many other countries. There is an accumulation of liquidity and an increase in liquidity ratios of the banks during the recession periods. The excess liquidity is worked down (relatively) during the revivals as a result of rapid wage and price increases and rise of production. It looks as if the accumulation of liquidity in the banks and also outside the banking system during such periods as 1945–46, 1953–54, 1958–59, and 1962–63 made possible the following rapid expansion and hampered the possibilities of dampening the boom.

FIGURE 5.6
Changes in Money Supply and Bank Lending, Actual and Recommended Liquidity of Commercial Banks, 1953–64

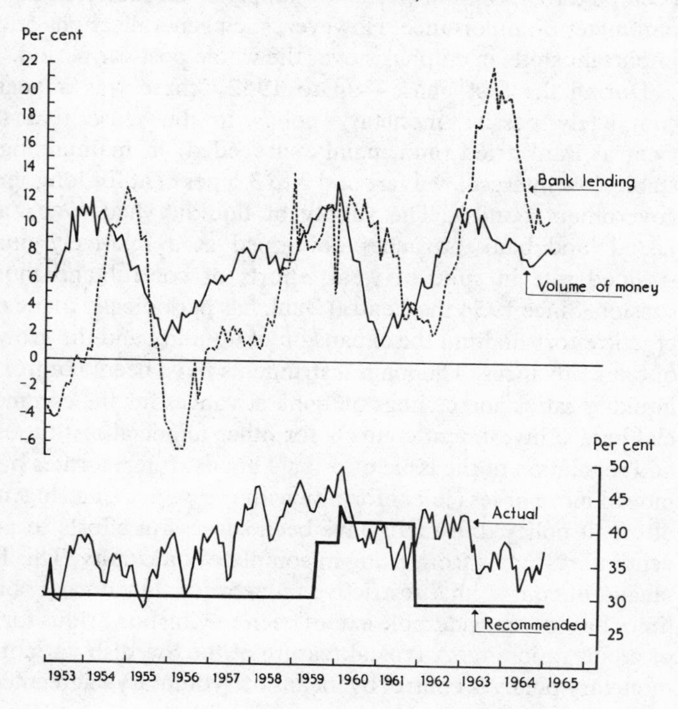

It may, on the other hand, be maintained (along the lines of Milton Friedman) that the strong relative decline of liquidity (rise of income velocity of money) during the last phases of the boom may have contributed to making the booms less excessive than otherwise would be the case. However, such assertions have not much value—other than in formulating the problems of research. We have to study the actual application of the instruments of monetary policy.

The chief emphasis has been directed at controlling bank liquidity and, directly or indirectly, the advances made by the commercial banks. There has been, at least officially, little confidence in changes of the discount rate and of long-term rates (by open market operations). Hardly any attention has been paid to variations in money supply as an indirect control parameter of importance. However, such generalizations cover important shifts in emphasis over the whole postwar period.

During the first phase—up to 1952—there was a nearly completely passive monetary policy in the sense that the Central Bank tried (and mainly succeeded) in maintaining a stable, low interest level (around 3 to 3.5 per cent for long-term government bonds). The supply of liquidity had to be adjusted, and bank advances developed at a relatively unrestrained rate in spite of weak efforts of control and moral suasion. Since 1954 the Central Bank has periodically made energetic efforts to limit the expansion of liquidity and the growth of bank advances. The main instruments have been: control of liquidity ratios and ceilings on bank advances for the commercial banks, investment controls for other financial institutions, and regulation of the issue of private bonds. Interest rates have moved more or less in conformity with the degree of stringency of credit policy, but there have been successful efforts to prevent interest rates from rising in complete conformity. This has meant, of course, that restrictive monetary policy during boom times has to a considerable extent been relying on various forms of credit rationing. A typical feature of the Swedish variant of monetary policy is control by means of "voluntary" agreements between the Central Bank and the commerical banks. With a law of cash and liquidity reserves in the background that at any time can be applied to prescribe the holding of cash or liquidity reserves in a variable proportion to deposits, both parties have preferred the more flexible procedure of agreements as to certain liquidity ratios to be attained during or within certain time periods. The Central Bank puts pressure on the commercial banks to attain the targets, the intention being to compel the banks to restrict their granting of new loans. The efficiency of this technique depends both on the Central Bank's power to control the supply of liquidity to the banking system as well as on the banks' skill in outwitting the Central Bank. The first condition has of course much to do with the current budget policy and the financing of an eventual budget deficit.

The difficulty of effecting a sufficiently prompt impact on bank advances (especially under conditions of budget deficits) compelled the Central Bank in the summer of 1955 to introduce ceilings on outstanding loans (excepting building credits), implying a reduction of 1 per cent within a quarter and 5 per cent within a year. This type of "credit-stop" policy seemed effective as far as one can gather from the statistics of credits; evasions by means of an increasing volume of bank guarantees and other indications of credit markets outside the banks were encouraged, however. Otherwise the method of liquidity ratio control has worked relatively slowly on money supply and still more on bank advances. (See Figure 5.6.) The rate of change in total loans started to decelerate at a late stage in the 1959–61 boom and again with a long lag after 1962. The contrast to the effective "ceiling"-policy of 1955 is apparent.

There is another important shift in policy to be observed. During the boom of 1954–57 government budget policy was badly coordinated with credit policy. Large budget deficits created liquidity that had to be "sterilized" by means of "prescriptions" of liquidity ratios and putting ceilings on bank advances. During the next period of inflationary boom (1959–61) there was a relatively successful coordination of policies. The government succeeded by such measures as overbalancing the budget (the new sales tax), including rapidly growing payments to the newly created government pension fund, absorption of liquidity in investment fund accounts at the Central Bank, and sales of government bonds outside the banks to reduce bank liquidity drastically.

Looking at the general picture of the direct or visible results of monetary policy as they appear in the form of the development of liquidity ratios, bank advances, and money supply, a number of problems come up, in particular the problem of time lags. It tends to take some time for the Central Bank to start a desired change in policy, with lagging effect on liquidity ratios, and still more time to attain results on bank advances and money supply. This was clearly the case during 1959–61 and again in 1963-64, when bank advances continued to rise seemingly unimpeded about six months after significant effects had been reached on bank liquidity. On the other hand, there was an essential improvement in the adjustment rate of monetary policy after the downward turns of the cycle. In 1951–52, and more clearly after the turn in 1957, there was a considerable time lag until the Central Bank gave the signal of monetary ease (by reduction of the discount rate). In 1962, on the other hand, monetary policy reacted very quickly in an expansive direction.

DISCUSSION OF DIRECT POLICY EFFECTS

We have in the first section of this chapter ascertained that the Swedish economy has shown a relatively high stability in volume terms. The deviations from the average growth rate of GNP have been small, and the same is true of the deviations from full employment. We have noticed that the various components of GNP (as well as different branches of activity) have shown considerable fluctuation of a cyclical nature, but these have averaged out quite effectively in the totals. On the other hand, we have observed the strong bias toward inflation during the booms, with excess demand in the labor market and a permanent inflationary rise of wages and prices. Our task in this section is to discuss to what extent these results are determined by the stabilization policies carried out. As usual we cannot give conclusive and satisfactory answers to these questions; the only possibility is to discuss some partial answers of general interest that also may clarify our view that clear-cut answers are impossible.

As a continuation of the account of the policy applications in the previous section, we shall discuss the plausible direct or impact effects of automatic and discretionary policy adjustments, the question being whether these policies, in their direct effects, seem to have contributed to dampening the booms and mitigating the recessions.[15]

The first question is whether and to what extent the government budget as such has had an automatic effect as a *built-in stabilizer*. The relatively high direct tax rates (highly progressive income taxes) plus the relatively high degree of automatic reactions on the expenditure side (including generous compensation to unemployed) should imply a considerable built-in stability factor. On the expenditure side, the distinction between automatic responses and active changes is partly very arbitrary. A considerable part of government expenditures will more or less automatically rise when recessionary tendencies set free labor and capacity for government orders, so that deliveries and planned expenditures occur more rapidly. In the same way certain government expenditures will be retarded to some extent automatically when in an inflationary boom work has to be postponed and delivery times tend to become longer. There are also more or less automatic long-run tendencies for government expenditures to increase independently of short-term changes in GNP, for example because of the yearly

15. The significance of an analysis in terms of direct (or impact) effects of changes in fiscal or monetary policy has been discussed by Assar Lindbeck, *A Study in Monetary Analysis* (Stockholm, 1963), Chap. 5.

increase in the number of pensioners, school children, and so forth, who can be included in this estimate of "built-in effects." We even may take the trend rate of rise of government expenditures for goods and services as the best simple measure of automatism on the expenditure side: this rate has on average been about one quarter higher than the GNP growth rate.

Take the following very simple calculation just to illustrate the possible stabilizing effects built into the Swedish economic system through the automatic behavior of the income and expenditure side of the government budget. Assume that real GNP tends to decline or rather retard from one year to the next because of a decrease in exports and private investment. The order of magnitude of this disturbance measured as a direct impulse may be given as corresponding to 4 per cent of GNP (at annual rates). A neutral budget policy would just permit a 4 per cent primary retardation in GNP (of course only referring to this rate of change per unit of time, but not implying any type of time localization). Let us assume that this development of GNP would correspond to an increase in unemployment by 2 percentage points. We include a 6 per cent automatic growth in government expenditures for goods and services in the measure of built-in stability, implying an automatic acceleration from a normal increase of 5 per cent to 6 per cent.

The example indicates that over 50 per cent of the "primary" GNP recession impulse may be neutralized by built-in budget reactions, if we use a relatively wide concept of primary automatic budget response. The automatic stabilizing effect includes an arbitrary figure to indicate the fact that the government will more or less "automatically" start relief works (instead of paying unemployment compensation) and expand public investment, postponed during the previous boom, without necessarily making new decisions. In addition, we could have included a primary effect of the automatic tax reduction compared with a state where the sum of taxes is fixed.[16]

16. It need not be stressed that we have used an extremely simple static method in order to illustrate the possible order of size of the

TABLE 5.1

An Illustration of the Primary Effect of Built-in Fiscal Stabilization Features

Assumptions:	
Rise in unemployment as a percentage of the total labor force, due to autonomous decline of activity in export and investment industries (corresponding to 4 per cent of GNP)	2%
Average share of wages in GNP	70%
Compensation per unemployed as a percentage of average wage per employed (free of income tax)	60%
Marginal propensity to consume of unemployed with regard to unemployment compensation	100%
Government expenditure for goods and services as a share of GNP	20%
Automatic rate of increase of government expenditure for goods and services	6%

Results (as percentage of GNP):

Primary effect on consumption due to increased unemployment compensation	Primary effect of automatic rise of government expenditure on goods and services
$0.02 \cdot 0.70 \cdot 0.60 \cdot 1.00 = 0.0084 = 0.84\%$	$0.06 \cdot 0.20 = 0.012 = 1.20\%$

The interesting question is why there are reasons to believe that the automatic dampening effects are much weaker or even nonexistent to expansionary impulses in an inflationary situation. An extra demand push (from exports and private investments) in a boom with full employment (leading to no further decrease in unemployment) will only be dampened (automatically) by an absorption of a part of the extra income via the marginal taxes while the automatic rise of expenditure may continue unabated. This would mean that there will not be a tendency to restrictive effects from the budget during the boom years corresponding to the expansive effects in a recession. This asymmetric position of the government budget during opposite phases of the cycle means an inflationary bias. One indication of this bias is the fact that the "full-employment budget balance" in the boom years of 1955–57 and 1959–60 was a total central government deficit of 1 to 2 billion Swedish crowns. Small surpluses were reached in the boom years 1960–61 to 1964–65, thanks to the introduction of a general sales tax. But looking at the full-employment years of rapid GNP growth during the fifties as well as the sixties, we find no significant tendency of rising surplus or declining deficit with the inflated expansion of GNP. This means that we should have to take account of the expansive effects of a government budget with more or less parallel increases of expenditures and incomes.

It is tempting to compare this situation with the measures of "potential" full-employment federal budget surplus in the

---

government budget forces automatically counteracting a recessionary impulse on GNP. We have not only neglected certain relationships (for example import leakages); the multiplier process over time is assumed away. A more complete analysis should be based on a simplified econometric model (see Chapter 6); then the effects of built-in budget reactions could be given a precise meaning by comparing results (at given time periods) of models working with alternative tax and expenditure parameters.

United States of some 10 to 15 billion dollars (before the 1964 tax reductions). However, it must be remembered that such comparisons are most dangerous, because of great differences as to what is and what is not included in the government accounts. For instance, if the government housing loans financed over the Swedish budget were excluded then the balance would be increased by about one billion Swedish crowns for the years in question.

With respect to short-term changes in government expenditures and tax rates, active fiscal policy measures seem to have had a rather limited impact on stability. There have been some countercyclical movements of government expenditures on goods and services. The introduction of the sales tax from the beginning of 1960 had, however, a clear dampening effect on private consumption during that year. The time lags in the acceleration of expenditure during the 1952 and 1958 recessions may, on the other hand, have had some destabilizing effect on the demand side, contributing to the following inflationary rise of demand. Again the judgment as to stabilization effects cannot be made in isolation. The policy results must not only be related to measures taken during the same phase of the cycle; attention must be paid also to the policies during the previous boom or recession. We must furthermore consider the impact of the *package deal* of fiscal and monetary policy introduced to control the boom—and the following recession. Here we shall pay special attention to the specific Swedish mixture of investment fund (and investment tax) and credit policies during the booms of 1955–57 and 1959–61.

As a matter of fact, the stabilization results during the recessions of 1958–59 and 1962 can be understood only against the background of the very restrictive policies that were carried out during the previous booms. As a positive feature in the economic policy pursued during the boom of 1955–57, it can be pointed out that this policy was not generally too restrictive or so directed as to check the general rate of economic growth, as the case appears to have been in the United States and Great Britain during this period. The total volume of production continued to rise at a high rate during the boom years of 1955–57, corresponding to approximately 3.5 per cent a year. The very restrictive credit policy that was inaugurated in 1955 by means of raising the level of interest rates and introducing various forms of credit control thus does not appear to have checked the actual development of production. Nor did the building and credit controls prevent a high and, in fact, rising total investment ratio from coming into being during these years (there was an increase in the ratio between gross investment expenditure—including inventory investments—and the gross national product from 30.6 per cent in 1954 to 32.4 per cent in 1957). These observations do not exclude the possibility that the restrictive policy had important dampening effects on a boom that *might* have become much more excessive. Perhaps the most striking result of the stabilization policy during the years 1955–59 was that industrial investment expenditure on machines and buildings (calculated in real terms), after remaining at a fairly constant level during the boom—it did not, in fact, expand noticeably above the peak reached in 1951—experienced a powerful increase of 12 per cent during the recession in 1958 and again by nearly 10 per cent in 1959. It could thus be maintained that the stabilization policy over the full course of the business cycle had been so successful in this sector that the increase in investment expenditure was shifted from the upward to the downward phase of the cycle. Surveys carried out among a representative number of industrial enterprises during 1955 and 1956 confirmed the hypothesis that the combination of the investment tax and credit restrictions caused quite heavy reductions and postponements of investments, implying that investment was 14 per cent lower than it otherwise would have been.[17] According

17. Guy Arvidsson, "En enkät rörande verkningarna av investeringsavgiften, kreditåtstramningen och räntehöjningen på den svenska industrins investeringar 1955," *Ekonomisk Tidskrift,* Nr. 1 (1956). The questionnaire study of the direct effects on investment was carried out in

to the results of these surveys, about half of the direct dampening effect on investment during 1955 came from the credit restrictions—and the rest mainly from the investment tax; there was, however, a tendency in the direction of increasing relative impact of the credit policy. When the investment tax was abolished at the beginning of 1958 and there was a simultaneous relaxation of credit policy, the natural consequence was that accumulated investment plans, which had been postponed on account of financing difficulties or excessive cost, were quickly realized during 1958 and 1959.

The investment incentive during 1958–59 was reinforced by virtue of the fact that during the period of May 1958 to September 1959, a considerable number of firms were granted permission to make tax-free use, for investment purposes, of investment funds previously set aside. The national Labor Market Board released funds amounting to one billion Swedish crowns (corresponding to about 30 per cent of industrial investment), this being tied to the condition that investment financed in this way should be undertaken rapidly and preferably in those localities where unemployment prevailed or threatened. There was very great interest in utilizing these possibilities of "tax-free" financing through rapid writing-off

---

1955 and repeated in 1956. It covered a representative number of manufacturing corporations (representing about 80 per cent of the value of manufacturing investment). The questions referred to the *direct* effects during the year, implying how much higher investment (of various kinds) would have been *if* the measures had not been introduced. It is evident that the answers to such questions must be subjective and uncertain, especially with regard to the relative importance of the three policy measures (rise of interest rates, investment tax, credit restrictions). One indicator as to the significance of the results is perhaps the fact that the order of size of the estimated total restriction effect (14 per cent reduction) agrees with the difference between the investment plans of the fall of 1954 and actual investment in 1955. According to the plans there should have been an increase of about 15 per cent whereas in fact manufacturing investment turned out to be constant.

of investment, especially in buildings. But it is unfortunately impossible to judge from the figures how effective this specific incentive to investment actually was. A considerable proportion of investment specified as being "financed" in this way would probably have been undertaken anyway.

The experience of the period 1955–58 thus seems to give evidence that the rather drastic restrictive policy measures applied (having had something of a shock effect) had powerful stabilization effects on private investment. When we come to the following boom (1959–61) the evidence is less clear. The rise in private investment this time seems to have progressed unhampered by the restrictive credit and budget policy; anyhow there was a long time lag. In fact the state of business confidence (according to barometer tests and investment plan interviews) was toned down beginning in the fall of 1961, first in connection with deteriorating export markets and the ensuing setback in profit expectations.

The failure to dampen the 1960–61 investment boom should be studied in light of the relative success in eliminating the 1962 recession. And here the most interesting feature is related to the successful exploration of the possibilities of the investment-fund technique in this period. As with other policy measures, we would really like to study the *net stabilization effects* of the application of the investment fund system.[18] What has been said in the previous section about the characteristics of the investment fund technique was just an account of its possible merits. Although there is good statistical information both on the number and kind of the investment fund projects as well as on the number of workers employed and the funds expended during the periods of release, this says very little about the size of the *direct net* effects. A considerable part of the construction projects as well as machinery orders would have come about

18. The effects of the application of the investment fund technique during this period have been analyzed by Gunnar Eliason, *Investment Funds in Operation,* Occasional Paper 2 (Stockholm, Konjunkturinstitutet, 1965).

anyhow, that is even if the fund release had not occurred. Some corporations just took advantage of the financial and taxation facilities offered for investments that were planned for the period. It is certainly very difficult to adjust for this error. The government's National Institute of Economic Research (Konjunkturinstitutet) has made a survey study embracing a good sample of the corporations that have utilized investment funds during the 1962–63 period of fund release. A questionnaire study followed up by intensive field surveys of individual projects has given some rather reliable indications of how large a part of the projects may be considered as new, implying a real shifting of investment to the period of release. According to these results, 50 to 60 per cent of the gross value of the investment-fund projects should imply net effects. This should mean a net direct effect over the year 1962–63 corresponding to about 20 per cent of the value of actual industrial construction and 5 to 10 per cent of orders on machinery and equipment. (It should be noticed that 30 per cent of these orders were placed in foreign countries.)

This result as to the size of the direct net effect is not implausible. According to the investment surveys made in October 1961 and March 1962, some decline of construction and investment expenditure was foreseen for 1962 (of the order of 10 per cent). Actually the total volume of industrial investment expenditures was nearly unchanged from 1961 to 1962. It seems reasonable to maintain that the investment fund policy was the main explanation of this stability during the 1962 "recession."

However, there are intricate complications involved in the analysis of the period 1962–63, even if we can rely on the result of the questionnaires, that is, that the firms have given quite correct answers about net effects (in the sense of the questionnaire). There are relations of interdependence between investments that hardly can be accounted for. The addition of projects during the period of release may have absorbed scarce workers and skilled labor, as well as liquid resources, to such an extent that other investment expenditures were slowed down or postponed. Such effects may only very partially have been considered in the survey study. This is of course especially so if this absorption of resources reduced the supply of such resources for other firms. Such negative indirect effects should have been especially common in places of southern and middle Sweden, where skilled labor resources, especially construction workers, were scarce even during the "recession." As the investigation shows, a very considerable share of the utilization of investment funds refers to such regions of scarce labor. Then there are other indirect effects along the line of linkages between factory building and machinery ordering—as well as unknown multiplier effects.

We should remember other possible but nonverifiable effects over a period of time. We have, for instance, to pay attention to a "backwash" effect from the earlier timing of projects during the release period. There should be a negative effect on investment propensities after that period (a slight effect in this direction was found by the survey in the fall of 1963), an effect that should work in a stabilizing direction if the release period was well timed. As mentioned above, this was apparently not the case during the strong revival of 1959–60, when the investment fund stimulus was maintained much too long. The interaction over some time of the stabilization policy measures is certainly a very complicated matter. Let us illustrate. The large build-up of investment funds during 1960 and 1961 combined with sizable payments into the Central Bank accounts (about one billion Swedish crowns from the middle of 1960 to the middle of 1961) implied an impressive squeeze on the liquidity of the banks as well as of the business sector. As mentioned above, this liquidity squeeze during 1960–61 and the accompanying stringent credit and fiscal policies seemed to have no significant effects on the current boom in industrial investment (an increase by 15 to 20 per cent in volume to 1961). Or would investment have been still higher if these restrictive policies had not been carried out to this degree?

But we may have here an example of the rather long time lag between liquidity and credit restrictions and effects on investment expenditures. One hypothesis would then be that the potential decline of industrial investment during 1962 (referred to above) to a large extent should be considered as the lagged result of the very strong combination of investment fund, credit, and fiscal policies during 1960–61. Then the release of investment funds during 1962–63 had just the function to counteract the strong measures taken during the boom. This would then be a part of the story of a sequence of stabilizing and destabilizing policy measures.

INDIRECT EFFECTS OF STABILIZATION POLICY ON THE FUNCTIONING OF THE CREDIT AND LABOR MARKETS

Our main conclusion from the discussion in the last two sections is that the rather vigorous stabilization policy efforts carried out during the period 1953–64 has had some substantial effects on the time pattern of private investment; other direct effects seem to have been less interesting. It seems clear that these results as such have implied considerable stabilization effects: the industrial investment boom in 1955–57 was contained and a considerable part of investment shifted to 1958–59, and furthermore an anticipated decline in industrial investment in 1962–63 was prevented. However, this conclusion only refers to the "visible" primary effects. For a more conclusive judgment with regard to the general consequences for the economy, we have also to pay attention to accompanying changes in the functioning of the economy under heavy "policy disturbances."

It must first be remembered that the primary stabilization results mentioned have been attained by means of large parameter changes. We may in this connection just note the existence of "ratchet" effects. The short-term changes in the level of interest rates as well in government expenditures and tax rates have had a strong upward bias; the raising of interest rates during the boom periods has only very partially been neutralized by declines during the following recessions; the acceleration of government expenditures during recessions has not been compensated for by significant retardations during boom periods; and the raising of indirect tax rates on various occasions has not been followed by later reductions. These results of stabilization policies must have had some long-term impact on the allocation of resources. More interesting from our point of view, however, are the indirect effects of the changes in stabilization policies on the functioning of the credit and labor markets.

A serious criticism of the type of stabilization policy pursued in Sweden is that during most of the time it has involved a combination of inflationary pressure and extensive controls of the credit and capital markets. In a way, the development can be looked upon as a transformation of the kind of combined regulative and inflationary pressure policy that was characteristic of the early postwar years. There was during these first postwar years a case of excess demand on the commodity markets, which the government tried in vain to keep in check by means of various kinds of physical controls (rationing, building controls, and import regulations). Since 1952 the problem has concerned a substantial excess in demand for credit and capital, and attempts have repeatedly been made to solve this problem by means of a combination of credit inflation and credit controls. The lack of balance on the credit and capital market was, practically speaking, just as pronounced—although it assumed different forms—during the inflationary period of 1955–57 as again in 1961–64.

During the years 1955–57 drastic credit restrictions were resorted to in order to hold back the demand for savings from the private business sector—especially industry—and to make room for the rapidly expanding central and local government investments, as well as house construction. The supply of "voluntary" savings did not suffice. The restraining effects on investment demand from increased capital costs (in the form of higher interest rates and the investment tax) was more than compensated for by the expansion of government and housing investment. The result of the great difficulties in financing the government budget deficit was an extensive credit inflation and an alarmingly big increase in liquidity that created new credit control problems during the boom of 1959–61. From 1960 the disequilibrium took other forms. As mentioned above, the government budget became balanced by means of sharply increased taxes, at the same time as accumulation of the Public Pension Fund was started.[19] A considerable shift in the distribution of savings was affected in the same direction by the payments of investment funds into the Central Bank. Table 5.2 gives some approximate notion of the process of transformation.

During the years before 1960 there had been much discussion as to whether and to what extent the creation of the rapidly increasing Public Pension Fund would imply an improved balance on the capital market. The question marks referred especially to two problems: (1) the influence on existing

19. The creation of the Public Pension Fund was combined with the introduction of a general pension reform from 1960. This reform implies that, after a transition period, every Swedish citizen will be guaranteed a pension right that for workers and lower salary groups corresponds to about 60 to 65 per cent of income earned during the "best" years before pension age—with full compensation for a further rise in the cost of living. This very generous pension reform was expected to have considerable negative effects on private savings. Although there was no need for fund accumulation from an "insurance (actuarial) point of view," the need for neutralizing the expected effects of declining private insurance savings motivated the creation of "forced savings" from the fees levied on wage and salary payments and paid into the Pension Fund. This fund had already during 1965 reached about 10 billion Swedish crowns (corresponding to about 10 per cent of GNP) and will attain about 25 per cent of GNP in 1970. The yearly rise of the fund as part of total savings had by 1964 reached 2.7 per cent of GNP and will amount to more than 4 per cent in 1970, then approaching the order of size of household savings.

TABLE 5.2

Investments and Savings as Percentages of GNP[a]

	Public sector	Housing sector	Public pension fund	Private insurance sector	Enterprise sector	House-holds	Sum
A. *Savings*							
1955–59	9.7	2.8		2.0	11.7	4.3	30.5
1960–64	11.7	2.2	1.8	1.5	9.8	5.6	32.6
1964	11.4	1.9	2.7	1.5	9.3	6.3	33.1
B. *Investments*							
1955–59	11.9	6.2			12.8		30.8
1960–64	12.1	6.3			14.4		32.8
1964	12.6	6.7			13.9		33.2
C. *Financial savings*[b] (A-B)							
1955–59	−2.1	−3.4		2.0	−1.1	4.3	−0.3
1960–64	−0.4	−4.1	1.8	1.5	−4.6	5.6	−0.2
1964	−1.2	−4.8	2.7	1.5	−4.6	6.3	−0.1

a. Figures from Börje Kragh, *Finansiella Långtidsperspektiv* (Stockholm 1967), p. 28. Later revisions of the national accounts give lower figures for household savings and higher ones for the enterprise sector.

b. The sum differs from zero owing to transactions with foreign sector.

private insurance savings when a large part of the savings-motivation was eliminated by the radical pension reform; and (2) how the supply of savings out of business profits would be affected, the question being if profit margins would be squeezed between the extra increase in labor costs (due to the pension fees) and prices largely given by international competition. The actual tendencies—no complete verification seems possible at this stage—seem to show that private life insurance and pension insurance have been affected to a surprisingly small extent (after the first year of downward adjustment). The squeeze of profit margins that has occurred since 1959 is of course not only or even primarily a result of the increasing pension fees; the sharper competitive conditions on the export and home markets (under import competition) have implied less than full compensation for the rapid rise in total wage costs. The result can be read off from the significantly lower degree of self-financing of industrial corporations: from about 100 per cent in the second half of the 1950s to 80 to 85 per cent in the years 1961–63.[20]

Table 5.2 should give a general impression of the significant shifts in savings supply in relation to investment expenditures of the main sectors in the economy. The figures for "Financial Savings," defined as the difference between savings and investments for the sectors in question, illustrate how the stronger self-financing position of the public sector (including the Public Pension Fund) has implied a substantial weakening of the financial position of the private enterprise sector, when comparing the periods 1955–59 and 1960–64. This shift proves how the strengthening of fiscal policy (by means of higher tax rates and pension fees) has implied a greater average dependence on outside financing for the private enterprise sector,

20. Degree of self-financing is here defined as the relation between business savings (gross profits after taxes and dividends and total investments made (including change in the volume of inventories). See J. Järv and E. Lundberg, "Business Investment and Corporate Savings," *Quarterly Review of Skandinaviska Banken,* No. 1 (1964).

and should therefore also mean greater potentials for the effectiveness of credit policy. However, this table can only give a very rough picture of the relevant changes. Within the big aggregates there may be considerable shifts in the distributions of savings supplies and investment demand between branches and firms, having significant effects on the demand for credits and other sources of outside finance. In any case as mentioned above, monetary policy has not turned out to be as effective even under the improved conditions of the 1960s; the increased demand for bank credit has taken the form both of higher interest rates and accelerated credit expansion.

We can say that the rise in the supply of savings from the Public Pension Fund has been offset by the relative decline in business savings. The resulting increase in the total gross savings ratio (see the table) has, however, not implied any significant improvement in the balance on the credit and capital markets. Investment, especially in housing and for the public sector, has expanded so rapidly that the pressure from excess investment demand seems to be about the same—with a further rise in interest rates as a consequence. The disequilibrium has taken other forms, however, because of the changed distribution of savings funds and the improved control over the supply of liquidity. The regulation of bond issues and bank credits have therefore been preserved under the new conditions.

One problem is how disrupted credit and capital markets affect the economy. One point of great importance when judging the effects of severe credit rationing and control of new issues (criticism has often been leveled against this type of monetary policy on this score) refers to the fact that liquidity and financing difficulties must strike unevenly in other ways than a rise of interest rates. It seems that particularly sensitive points are firms that have undertaken extensive investment programs and which, in an unstable phase of the boom, suffer a contraction in their profit margins (due to increased costs) or a temporary decline in sales, thus finding themselves in an embarrassing liquidity situation and in need of greater credit. All depending on how the credit market is organized, it would normally be such a credit-dependent sector as housebuilding that is first hit by a contraction in credit availability. In Sweden, however, such tendencies have largely been eliminated, thanks to regulatory measures which since 1952 have protected the housing sector from most of such disturbances in the supply of credit. Small firms may more often than large corporations (which frequently have intimate banking connections) find themselves in a troublesome situation on account of difficulties in obtaining credit when liquidity becomes scarce. A survey dealing with the effects of the 1955–56 restrictive economic policy indicated that the small firms were to a relatively large extent forced to shelve investment projects in consequence of credit difficulties. In general the uncertainties of credit availability—during the current period as well as in the future—will imply high dependence on internal resources (and share issues) with corresponding distorting effects on the size and distribution of investment.

One important feature refers to the rather deficient *policy norms* of this type of monetary policy, where the control of credit expansion is the main point. The demand for credit during an investment boom rises not only in consequence of an expansion of production, sales, investment, and the rise of wages and prices, but also because of a growing need for credit funds to be transferred from sectors and firms with a surplus to those with a deficit of savings funds. Because of this transfer process, it would appear that the marked attention paid by the Central Bank to the behavior of the credit volume of the commercial banks involves placing its trust in a very deficient indicator of the state of the credit market.

At this point it may be useful to illustrate an important problem concerning two alternative "ideal types" of restrictive monetary policy that may be called the "Swedish" and the

"American" type. Monetary policy may aim at creating—through a system of prescribed liquidity ratios, a ceiling on loans, and bond issue controls—a number of obstacles to credit transfers and to the general functioning of the capital market. In this way the Central Bank is indirectly also holding back the rise in the velocity of circulation that is threatening to reduce the dampening effect of a relative contraction in the supply of money. Controls, rationing, and priorities for the controllable sectors of the credit market are measures that belong to the type of policy which we may call the "Swedish line" of monetary policy. Results are thus attained through strengthening the imperfections of the credit and capital markets, making it impossible for a sufficient number of firms in various situations to rely on outside finance. Narrow limits to the flexibility of interest rates will be a necessary condition for this kind of monetary policy—as well as the underdevelopment of gray and black credit markets.

The alternative form, which may be called the "American line," aims at avoiding public control of the credit market as an instrument of economic policy, instead allowing a contraction of the supply of money to have free play over the whole of the credit system via the functioning of the capital and credit markets. The "bills only" doctrine, applied by the Federal Reserve authorities up to 1960, went so far that the authorities did not even want to disturb the free operation of the long-term capital market through the purchase and sale of long-term government bonds; the money needed had to be pumped into and sucked out of the system via operations in the short end of the market and by means of changes in bank reserve requirements. But certainly even the American credit and capital markets do not live up to the economist's dream of perfect markets; there is a marked sluggishness in the banks' fixing of interest rates, and there is also an increasing degree of credit rationing during tight-money periods. The difference as compared with the Swedish policy pattern lies in the absence of active attempts to utilize measures that are designed to put the credit market partially out of function—to make it operate especially badly during periods of inflationary booms.

The American line of monetary policy is open to the criticism of being relatively inefficient. The rise in interest rates that takes place during a period of restriction is coupled with an increase in the velocity of circulation. It is natural that reasonably well-functioning credit markets, that are not disturbed by government interference, must imply a high elasticity in the supply of credit and resiliency in the financial system. Instead—referring to the "ideal type"—it is the rise in interest rates that has to do the work of checking the demand for credit and investment activity. But there are strong reasons to doubt that moderate interest-rate fluctuations within tolerated margins will have significant effects on business investment. In fact there has also in the United States been increased emphasis on the "credit availability doctrine" by those who defend the effectiveness of monetary policy.

In a strong, inflationary upswing—such as that in Sweden and many other countries around the middle of the 1950s and again in 1959–60, and 1964, when excess demand situations appeared quickly with abundant investment opportunities and high and rising profits—significant dampening effects could probably only be achieved through a shock therapy with drastic tightening of policy and much market disruption. But we may raise the same question as in the case of the United Kingdom: could not the desired dampening effects have been achieved at an earlier stage with less of disruptive measures?

There are many complicated problems associated with the desideratum that a smoother monetary policy should be pursued. It is easy to say that a gentle braking could be applied at an early stage so that the policy should not need to assume the more drastic forms along the Swedish line in a later phase of an "overheated" boom. We have lots of experience with difficulties in forecasting, and all the time lags that make a "too late" and drastic policy natural. Furthermore, a smooth and slow rise of interest rates will, anyhow under Swedish conditions, have insignificant effects; they may even be adverse, if small adjustments are anticipated to be followed by more drastic measures.

An appraisal of the actual and possible efficacy of monetary policy should take into consideration targets of economic policy other than the stabilization of business fluctuations. A repetition of periods with a drastic sharpening of monetary policy or prolonged periods of credit rationing may give rise to a permanent reduction of the investment ratio in the private sector of the economy, which in the long run can have a negative effect on the rate of growth. Investment plans may be seriously disrupted by a "jerky" policy, with accompanying risks of efficiency losses. Here we have an obvious dilemma. Economic development is jerky by nature—this is part of the business cycle rhythm in a relatively free economic system. An economic policy that aims at ironing out these fluctuations, and —for the reasons discussed above—tends to be put into operation at a relatively late stage, must also be jerky if it is to be effective.

One conclusion from this discussion of the monetary and fiscal policy efforts in Sweden since around 1953 is that there has been only a limited success in reaching stabilization aims. The rather continuous and rapid rise in the price level and in wage rates is one indication of this. It is, however, primarily the deficient control of the excess demand conditions—especially on the labor market—during the sustained boom periods that may be taken as signs of policy failures. There has been more success in counteracting the recessionary tendencies. But as argued above, this success has been relatively easy to achieve, as the recessionary disturbances have been small, the built-in stability of the Swedish economy to downward disturbances probably has been relatively high, and policy restrictions on account of balance of payments considerations have been absent.

The achievements of stabilization policy in Sweden must, however, be judged against the background of very high ambitions as to the "degree of full employment." The "revealed preference" of the responsible government authorities seems to be a permanent excess demand pressure on the labor market; there should be more jobs than men. This disequilibrium on the labor market should not only be taken as a welfare criterion and a good thing in itself for the majority of people, but can under certain policy conditions also be a favorable growth factor. The excess demand for labor in most skills and regions will imply good job opportunities, working in the direction of an adaptation of jobs to applicants that will minimize obstacles to the entrance into the active labor force (one visible result is a rapid rise in the participation rates of married women). The big question refers to the effects on productivity from excess demand for labor. As mentioned above, Swedish experience since 1953 gives no evidence of negative effects during the boom years; rather on the contrary, the higher demand pressure on the average during the 1960s as compared with the 1950s has been accompanied by an acceleration of productivity growth; the growth rate of total productivity (GNP per man hour) has increased from 3 per cent in the 1950s to 4.5 per cent in the first half of the 1960s. The negative effects with regard to excessive turnover of labor and supply bottlenecks for rapidly expanding firms seem to have been outweighed by such tendencies as fuller utilization of capacity and efficiency drives, necessitated because of foreign competition on export and home markets. The longer-term danger from a more permanent excess pressure situation arises from wage inflation and negative effects on productivity due to distorted allocation of resources in the direction of protected activities—such as building and services.

One of the most interesting policy problems of an economy with "overfull employment" refers to labor mobility. It is self-evident that the excess demand for labor will be very unevenly distributed, concentrated in the rapidly growing firms, sections, and regions, at the same time as there will be actual or potential deficit demand in other firms, sectors, and regions.

In the same way there will tend to be a concentration of excess demand for various types of skilled labor. The problem of mobility is accentuated by the fact that the total labor supply in Sweden is growing very slowly—taking into account the shortening of the work week and longer vacations, hardly at all. The rapidly growing branches of activity and firms have therefore to recruit their needs of skilled and unskilled labor to a large extent from the stagnating and declining sectors of the economy. An *active labor market policy* of the type mentioned above has, especially since 1959, been the main complement to the general stabilization policy. Rapidly increasing amounts have been paid out by the Labor Market Board in order to make the labor force more mobile geographically as well as between skills. The retraining of workers has during the last years continuously embraced about 1 per cent of the labor force.

There is a well-known type of policy theory—sponsored by some progressive labor union economists ever since the late 1940s[21]—that stabilization policies in an economy with very high ambitions as to full employment will have to take other forms than the old-fashioned Keynesian approach. In slight recessions the policy approach should not mainly be to start a general expansion of demand, with the risks of strong cumulative processes that are so difficult to control, but rather to give differentiated "point injections" of credits and subsidies, and to combine such measures with intensified efforts to move labor to expanding regions and branches of activity. In this way policy is directed toward creating an improved functioning of the labor market. Higher mobility of resources should help prevent inflationary developments in the rapidly expanding branches and regions. The formulation of a "solidaric wage policy" fits into this picture: the less progressive branches should not be subsidized by lower wage rates. On

21. For a survey of the issues of active labor market policy in Sweden, see Gösta Rehn and Erik Lundberg, "Employment and Welfare: Some Swedish Issues," *Industrial Relations* (February 1963).

the contrary the pressure from sufficiently rapidly rising wage costs should squeeze the profit margins of marginal firms and compel them to release labor for the benefit of firms with good growth prospects.

This type of policy thinking, which can only very incompletely be presented and discussed here, has without doubt had a considerable influence on the actual labor market policy in Sweden, especially since 1958. However, again the success has so far been very partial. The achievements with regard to training and mobility have been impressive, there have been efforts in differentiation and localization of policy stimuli during the 1962 "recession" as discussed above, but the strong expansion stimulus from other sources has again quickly brought along the usual problems of controlling excessive inflationary tendencies by means of drastic credit restrictions.

It is a Swedish policy paradox that the admirable efforts to bring about a more perfectly functioning labor market are combined with disruptive policy measures with regard to the functioning of the credit and capital markets. There is one specific, very important "cause" of this paradox that must be mentioned. The efforts to create higher mobility, that is to move labor to the centers of rapidly growing sectors of excess demand, have been effectively obstructed by adverse housing conditions. The big deficiencies in the supply of houses in the growth centers (with big and increasing queues of applicants) have implied great obstacles to making the active labor market policy effective. One could perhaps say that this restriction on policy effectiveness takes the place of balance of payments restrictions in other countries. The big difference is, however, that this Swedish type of restriction does not necessitate a "stop-go-policy"; on the contrary, the disequilibrium situation on the building markets tends to accelerate an inflationary boom. Rent control, badly distributed housing supply, queues, excess demand for building workers and materials, these phenomena are closely interwoven and imply the nucleus of inflation in the Swedish economy. There is in fact another paradox of Swedish economic policy, namely that Swedish economists, who have succeeded so well in making the politicians as well as the public accept modern stabilization and growth policies and abandon old superstitious beliefs, have not at all been able to persuade the politicians and the pressure groups of residents to understand the simplest theory of supply and demand.

6 ECONOMETRIC FORECASTING AND POLICY PLANNING IN THE NETHERLANDS

SOME BACKGROUND CONDITIONS

The Netherlands' long-term growth rate between the beginning of 1950 and the end of 1964 amounted to 4.8 per cent per year, which was about average for Western Europe. Since the rate of growth of real GNP was accompanied by a relatively rapid growth of the labor force of some 1.3 per cent per year, output per man-year rose at a rate slightly below the Western European average.

The long-run rate of growth of real GNP is composed of annual rates which, at least according to the GNP-variation index, shows a relatively high degree of instability in comparison with most countries in Western Europe. (See Table 3.1 and also Figure 3.2.) The years with the lowest rates of growth, 1951–52 and 1958, coincided with the widespread experiences of recessionary tendencies in the other European countries.

Among the expenditure components of the growth of GNP in the Netherlands, exports and imports are of particular interest. The growth of exports, which on average matched the growth of GNP in absolute terms and thus potentially was a prime source of demand instability, continued at a remarkably stable rate during the recession years. The major shortfalls of demand growth came from the side of private fixed and inventory investment which declined even more strongly than in the case of the more serious recessions in the United States.

The apparent paradox, which this comparison could be considered to imply, is easily resolved by a look at the very strong stabilizing variations in the growth of Dutch imports during those years. This is, of course, largely a reflection of the very high import content of Dutch production for the home market and for export. Except for very small countries such as Luxemburg, the Netherlands are by far the most open industrialized economy in the world. The ratio of total imports of goods and services to GNP, both at constant prices, was some 46 per cent in 1950 and grew to some 63 per cent in 1964. This increase implied a marginal import to GNP ratio of almost 100 per cent for the fifteen-year span. Changes in autonomous expenditure therefore had in general very low multiplier effects.[1] The already strong stabilizing tendency resulting from the high marginal import share was further strengthened, particularly in recession years, by the positive cyclical variation of the average import ratio around its trend.

Since the marginal import content is very high not only in

1. The multiplier effect of a sustained change in autonomous expenditure is, under the usual assumptions,

$$\frac{\Delta Y}{\Delta A} = \frac{(1-m_A)}{1-c(1-m_c)(1-t)}$$

where

ΔY: change in GNP

ΔA: change in autonomous expenditure, presumed to include all changes in private investment, government expenditure on goods and services, and exports

m_A: marginal import content of autonomous expenditure

m_c: marginal import content of consumption

c: marginal propensity to consume disposable income

t: marginal tax rate in relation to GNP

If, for example, the following numerical values are inserted, then the marginal ratio of imports to GNP will be equal to 1, and the multiplier as low as 0.66:

$$m_A = m_c = 0.5$$
$$c = 0.8$$
$$t = 0.4$$

Dutch products for the home market but also in Dutch exports, the growth of exports, which on average was equivalent to some 4.7 per cent of GNP per year and thus by far exceeded the corresponding figures for other countries, strongly exaggerates the magnitude of the growth of the foreign demand for Dutch products per se. Adjustment of exports for their marginal import content of approximately three fifths, reduces the direct stimulus to Dutch production activity, which is due to the growth of exports, to about 1.9 per cent of GNP per year on average. Although it still suggests a very strong external stimulus to demand, this roughly adjusted figure is much more in line with the experience of some other widely open economies. For example, Sweden's exports, before adjustment for their marginal import content, grew at an average annual rate of 1.9 per cent of GNP, which is only two fifths of the comparable Dutch figure. But since Sweden's exports are much more strongly based on the country's natural resources (forests and iron ore) and thus have a much smaller marginal import content of perhaps one quarter, the direct export stimulus to Swedish production activity was still some 1.4 per cent of GNP per year on average, which is three quarters of the corresponding Dutch figure.

A degree of openness as in the Dutch economy has, of course, implications for the state of economic activity not only via the direct demand effects of changes in foreign trade but also via changes in the balance of payments. The state of the latter, unless neutralized, affects the internal liquidity situation relatively strongly. Furthermore policy decisions are to a high degree formed with a view of their implications for the external liquidity situation. The high marginal import content of domestic demand, in particular of equipment and inventory investment, is likely to induce large current account deficits in boom periods, even if the boom is primarily export-induced. In fact, during the period covered, the Netherlands have had two periods of substantial current account deficits: in 1950–51 and in 1956–57. The government authorities had to be alert most of the time to the development of the external liquidity situation. The restrictive actions aimed at safeguarding the balance of payments situation were a major factor behind the recessions of 1952 and 1958. But in contrast to the experience of the United Kingdom, the balance of payments constraints have not prevented the achievement of a rapid long-term rate of growth in the Netherlands.

The economic policy authorities of the Netherlands have a reputation for applying more sophisticated methods of short-term forecasting and more refined ways of planning policy measures than the methods used in other Western countries. The short-term econometric models of the economy set up by the Central Planning Bureau (CPB) make possible a systematic quantitative approach to the determination of short-term policy needs and the evaluation of the results to be expected from alternative policy measures. The analytic framework implied in the succession of models has had great educational value and apparently has also given a certain precision to the general debate on policy questions.[2] At the same time the policy makers in the Netherlands had a rich choice of parameters of action for stabilization purposes. The fiscal policy parameters used during the postwar period include changes in direct and indirect tax rates, public utility rates, changes in depreciation allowances and other investment subsidies, government expenditure changes, and changes in the supply of government loans for residential construction. Monetary policy measures used include not only general liquidity control and frequent discount rate changes, but also cash reserve prescriptions, requirements on special deposits related to changes in bank advances above certain prescribed limits, restrictions on hire purchase loans, and also controls of capital imports and exports, especially in the form of regulation of issues of foreign bonds on the coun-

2. However, in spite of efforts at econometric precision, even the Dutch are human and sensitive to political temptations. An example: there were elections in 1956, and direct taxes were lowered in the boom of 1955–56.

try's capital market. Building investments have been regulated also by means of direct physical controls (licensing). Important parts of policy changes have been carried out through gentlemen's agreements and by means of moral suasion, especially from the central bank. This way of operating is possible in a small country with strong organizations. In this respect the Social and Economic Council, a tripartite organization with the respective groups appointed by the federation of trade unions, employers' organizations, and government, apparently has played an important role in creating mutual understanding and making possible political consensus in difficult situations.[3] In this connection it should be emphasized that the Netherlands are the only example of a country having consistently tried to carry out during the postwar period a centrally directed general wage policy, at times combined with some measure of price control. The wage policy should without doubt be considered as an important part of the Dutch stabilization policy.

Against the background of these favorable conditions for successful stabilization policy, that is, the application of systematic forecasting and policy-planning methods, and a rich setup of policy instruments, the actual record of relatively high output instability raises a number of problems.

Having by far the most open economy of the countries compared, the Netherlands might have had more difficult stability problems to contend with than many of the other countries. The particular difficulties in this connection could refer to the size and the importance of exogenous disturbances from abroad and to the narrow limits of policy autonomy due to the sensitivity of the current and capital account of the balance of payments to the state of economic activity. But we have already pointed out that the growth of Dutch exports has been remarkably steady even in connection with the 1952 and 1958 reces-

3. The experts of the Council are appointed by the government (but are completely independent from it) and are expected to take care of the "general interest." The meetings of the council are attended by government representatives, but only as observers.

sions. Short-term exogenous disturbances from abroad seem thus to have been rather moderate, especially if it is remembered that the very high marginal import content of exports (and domestic demand components) results in very low multiplier effects, in any case if, as is customary, the more uncertain induced investment responses are neglected. The very high marginal import propensity implies furthermore that the current account will respond strongly to successful restrictions on the state of economic activity, so that it should have been (almost) as easy to come out of balance of payments difficulties as to enter into them.

It seems, therefore, that internal rather than external factors have acted as the main source of instability. The sources of instability may, at least in principle, be divided into the working of the economy's mechanism with given policy parameters and changes in the latter which may reinforce or counteract the former. We should try to determine to what extent changes in the policy parameters have brought the economy more closely in line with the policy targets. But which welfare or target function should be utilized as the standard of comparison if the individual targets in part conflict with each other? The Dutch seem, for instance, to have put more emphasis on price stability as a target than some of the other countries compared. At least the Central Bank (De Nederlandsche Bank), which seems to have had considerable influence on current policy affairs, has at times come out very strongly in favor of price stability, though primarily for the sake of a satisfactory balance of payments.[4] Thus restrictive monetary policy in the interest of price stability and balance of payments equilibirum has repeatedly come in conflict with the full employment and growth targets. By the time inflationary demand conditions in 1950–51 and 1955–56 were recognized as a major problem, the accompanying serious deterioration of the balance of payments seemed to justify measures so restrictive that quick results with

4. See the yearly reports issued by this bank.

regard to the latter could be expected. The consequent slow-down of the rate of growth of output and the increase of the unemployment rate, at least to the extent that it was due to the package of restrictive measures introduced, could be considered as a social cost of restoring a satisfactory balance of payments. On the other hand, alternative policy approaches might have helped to avoid part of that social cost.

In practice we are usually not able to isolate clearly the policy-change reactions from the operation of the economic mechanism that would have occurred with unchanged policy parameters or with alternative policy changes, so that questions of the above type cannot be answered in a definite way. Nevertheless, we should in general at least be able to point to specific factors or relations that primarily do or do not seem to belong to the policy sphere. In fact, in the case of the Netherlands we are able to assess the sources of stable or unstable overall economic performance much more thoroughly than in most other countries, since there exists a widely accepted econometric model—or rather a set of successive models—with a convenient choice of exogenous and endogenous variables for assessing in particular the short-run effects of fiscal policy changes. Such a model permits us to avoid, or at least to reduce the undeterminacy in a numerical sense of more general but mostly only qualitative methods of analysis. On the other hand, a critical attitude may be appropriate. We must avoid falling in love with other men's models (which is *their* irresistible temptation). Even if the econometric models constructed by the skillful economists and statisticians of the Dutch CPB were the best possible under given conditions, for example as to the availability of data for estimation purposes, there may still exist other possible interpretations of causal factors and interrelations that seem more realistic than the interpretations implied in the CPB models. Since, however, it is hardly possible for us as outsiders with a very limited knowledge of the Dutch economy to contribute new insights, we intend here only to describe some of the lines of thought and to raise for discussion some of the problems involved in the Dutch type of forecasting and policy analysis.

ON THE COUNTRY'S SHORT-TERM REACTION MECHANISM[5]

The Central Planning Bureau's 1961 version of an econometric model of the Netherlands' economy shall serve in the following to illustrate some of the major lines of thought which provided the basis of Dutch short-term forecasting and policy planning since the end of the 1950s. In the light of new information, new insights, and improved techniques of analysis, the macroeconomic models applied by the Central Planning Bureau during the postwar period have undergone frequent revision which in particular tends to separate the models up to 1957 from the later ones. In general, the models started to loose their strongly comparative static character after that date. In addition the later family of models contains important nonlinearities not found in the previous models.

The short spans of time that can be considered as sufficiently homogeneous with regard to the underlying mechanism generating the annual changes in the economy may result in a serious dilemma by narrowly limiting the number of annual

5. The CPB models in various versions are presented and discussed in a number of publications. Here we refer to the 1961 model as given in Netherlands Central Planning Bureau, *Central Economic Plan 1961* (The Hague, 1961). Reference is also made to the following publications: Netherlands Central Planning Bureau, *Forecasts and Realization,* Monograph No. 10 (The Hague, 1965); C. A. van den Beld, "Short-term Planning Experience in the Netherlands," and Wilhelm Hessel, "Quantitative Planning of Economic Policy in the Netherlands," in Bert G. Hickman, ed., *Quantitative Planning of Economic Policy* (The Brookings Institution, 1964); OECD, *Techniques of Economic Forecasting* (Paris, 1965), Chap. 4 on the Netherlands.

The writing of this chapter has been greatly improved thanks to observations and remarks by the director of the CPB, P. de Wolff, who also provided some unpublished material that has been of help in understanding the working of the model.

observations available for parameter estimation. Furthermore, with regard to the postwar period, the information contained in the available annual observations must be considered as limited to a rather narrow range of variation around full employment. The Central Planning Bureau has in connection with its 1961 model tried to solve both problems by (courageously) including the interwar years 1923–38 in the sample together with postwar data from 1949 on, although the interwar figures were given only half the weight of the postwar figures in view of the smaller number and better quality of the postwar data. This procedure implies a strong assumption of structural stability of the economy over a relatively long period of time covering subperiods of such varied experience that they are often referred to as fundamentally different from each other. According to the CPB approach these differences would have been generated by (largely) the same short-term reaction mechanism and, accordingly, the much greater stability reached during the postwar period would be due mainly to the absence of important external disturbances of a deflationary nature and presumably to more competent economic policy.

The 1961 version of the model, like previous and subsequent versions, is intended to explain and forecast short-term economic changes, mainly over one year. In view of this short-term emphasis, demand changes are in a Keynesian fashion put in the foreground as the determinants of variations in output growth; capacity and productivity effects of variations in the growth of investment are neglected. On the other hand, in contrast to the pre-1958 models, the 1961 model is no longer a pure demand model. A curvilinear transformation of the unemployment rate inserted in the investment and export equations purports to take account of changes in the degree of domestic supply restrictions. Most of the endogenous variables of the model as well as most exogenous variables are expressed as annual percentage rates of change, which means that the coefficients are not to be interpreted as propensities but in general as elasticities.

Given the values of the exogenous and predetermined variables, most of which for actual forecasting purposes have to be assessed or estimated by various separate procedures, the equation system furnishes numerical predictions of the short-run development of the endogenous variables. In a similar manner the model can be used for estimating the short-run impact of policy measures.

The 1961 model consists of a set of eleven reaction equations and twenty-five definitional equations. The former attempt to explain the development of private consumption, private fixed nonresidential investment, inventory investment, and commodity exports; there are, furthermore, equations for commodity imports, employment in enterprises, and registered unemployment; and finally for price indexes of consumption, investment, commodity exports, and autonomous expenditure.

This is not the place to discuss the entire model in detail. We shall limit ourselves in the first place to the presentation and a brief discussion of the reaction equations for exports, investment, and consumption that seem to be of special interest for understanding the CPB interpretation of short-term economic change. In the following discussions we ignore the problem of distortions of the numerical estimates due to collinearity and related characteristics of economic time series.

According to the 1961 model, the annual percentage change of the volume of commodity exports, b, is determined as follows:

$$b = 1.46b_c - 1.71\,(p_b - p_b') - 1.11\,(p_b - p_b')_{-1}$$
$$- 0.64\Delta p_v{}' + 1.42\tilde{w}_1 - 7.52$$

where

b_c refers to the percentage change of the volume of competing world exports (weighted on the basis of the country composition of Dutch exports);

p_b and p_b' refer to the percentage change in the price of Dutch exports and of competing exports, respectively;

p_v' refers to the percentage change in the price of total output (excluding stock changes and net invisibles);

$\tilde{w}_l$ refers to the curvilinear transformation of the unemployment rate as an indicator of available capacity.

The commodity part of the rapid postwar growth of Dutch exports of goods and services finds its major explanation in an almost as rapid growth of the exports of competing countries, that is, in the general growth of demand for imports in the customer countries. The corresponding elasticity coefficient of 1.46 does not really mean that, in the absence of any influence from the side of the price variables in the second, third, and fourth term on the right-hand side of the equation, Dutch commodity exports would rise at about 1.5 times the percentage rate of growth of (weighted) world trade. Taking account also of the mean influence of the capacity indicator at an unemployment rate of 2 per cent and the value of the constant term, exports are expected to rise about 1.5 times the percentage rate of growth of competing exports only when the growth of the latter is in excess of 2.5 per cent. In case of a lower rate of growth of competing exports, Dutch exports would accordingly be expected to decline 1.5 times the difference between 2.5 and the actual (or predicted) growth of competing exports. Thus, Dutch exports would appear to be more sensitive to fluctuations in the growth of world market demand than the competing countries' exports. Other influences given as assumed above, Dutch commodity exports would grow at a rate of some 17 per cent if the weighted volume of world trade grew at the 1960 rate of 14 per cent, and would decline by some 3 per cent if the volume of world trade grew at the 1958 rate of 0.4 per cent. But other influences are not likely to remain unchanged in face of such wide variations in the growth of world demand for exports, particularly in a country as strongly dependent on foreign trade as the Netherlands. To the extent that the country does not succeed in neutralizing the effect on home activity of booming or stagnating world trade, available capacity in particular is likely to vary in a strongly compensating manner. As a result, exports can be expected to grow much more evenly in the boom and recession years than the quoted figures suggest. The combined effect in reality was a higher degree of stability of export growth than in the case of most competing countries—the contrary of what could be expected when no account is taken of the effect of interrelated variations in available capacity.

There is another factor that may have been of importance for the trend as well as for the short-term reactions of the Dutch export volume. The level of wages in Holland in relation to other competing countries seems to have been very low in the beginning of the postwar period. In spite of rapid wage increases, the Dutch wage level was kept relatively low during the postwar period surveyed. (The appreciation of the guilder in 1961 did not matter very much. The wage explosion of 1964 by close to 20 per cent from 1963 may have first effectively reduced the gap.) But the favorable wage-cost position may have had a stimulating impact on the export trend that is not explicitly taken care of in the model. This long-term stimulus may have worked both on the demand and the supply side by keeping Dutch export prices relatively low and at given world market prices by implying relatively high profits in the export industries (thereby having stimulating effects on the supply side, for example with regard to investment and employment).

The export stimulus from the low wage level may have been of secondary importance during years of overfull employment and capacity restrictions (as in 1956 and 1961) and, on the other hand, especially strong during periods of recession (as in 1958, when the export volume rose by 10 per cent although the volume of world trade rose by only 0.4 per cent). An explanation of the rapidly rising export volume during the recession years may to some extent be made in terms of a relatively high downward flexibility of Dutch export prices and the corresponding effect on demand. However, the main influence must have come from the supply side, not only via the easier labor supply in the recession years but also because of the strong stimulus from relatively high export prices. The relative importance of the long- and short-term supply effects discussed above cannot easily be estimated by econometric methods, as it is a question of a rather permanent stimulus. We can only get a vague idea of its importance from the observation of the relatively stable and rapid growth of the Dutch export volume in comparison with most other countries or with the Dutch interwar experience. The variations from year to year in the export volume may, on the other hand, to a large extent be explained by the factors included in the export equation.

The development of the balance of payments during booms and recessions is strategic with regard to short-term stability. The short-term behavior of exports has therefore to be put in relation to that of imports. Since 1951 a high import propensity has not appeared to be in any apparent long-term conflict with the trend of exports, thanks to the rapid growth of Dutch exports. Again the relatively low level of wages (or undervaluation of the guilder) has contributed to the balance of payments stability also on the import side, by making home industries more competitive relative to imports of fabricated goods.

However, in spite of these favorable long-run conditions it is easy to imagine how short-run disequilibrium developments may arise under given structural conditions. When total GNP (in real terms) expands rapidly, as from 1953 at about 8 per cent per year, the result will tend to be a still more rapid increase in imports, a tendency that will be strengthened because of intensified inventory investment and perhaps also because of a rising degree of capacity utilization. With some time lag, these same factors will have dampening effects on exports. To what extent rising inelasticity on the supply side and rising home prices and costs will actually have retarding effects on the volume of exports and accelerating effects on the volume of imports will depend on a number of external factors and conditions not determined in the model, such as price and trade developments in the outside world and policy changes. During the 1950, 1954–56, and 1960–62 booms, the Dutch export volume showed retarded growth rates that fell significantly below the simultaneous import growth rates. The consequence has been quite substantial variations in the current account of the balance of payments. (The surplus has been as high as around 7 per cent in 1952 and 1953 and 4 to 5 per cent in 1958–59, and the deficit as large as 2 per cent of GNP in 1956 and 1957.)

With large foreign exchange reserves or extensive drawing rights in the International Monetary Fund, discrepancies in the growth rates of exports and imports within reasonable margins would not necessarily imply serious disturbances to the internal economy, for example on the demand for labor. There are certain automatic reaction mechanisms built into the economy, tending to rectify a balance of payments disturbance. First and simplest, the slowing up of export growth will imply a retarded expansion of import needs for export production and related inventory accumulation below that of the earlier growth rate. This effect is not neglible in the Dutch economy, where the marginal import content of exports is so high.

There are also important indirect relations that are determined by the working of the internal economic mechanism. Most interesting are the reactions via changes in investment. If we accept the equation for private fixed nonresidential investment as realistic, then such investment is very sensitive to changes in liquidity and profits. The investment equation in the 1961 model reads as follows:

$$I = 0.82(Z_{-1} - T''_{z}) + 0.46\, p_i + 0.80\, c^{r}_{-1} - 7.18\, \Delta\tilde{w}_{1-1/2} - \Psi_i + 29.62$$

where

I refers to the percentage change in the value of private fixed nonresidential investment;

Z_{-1} refers to the lagged percentage change in the value of nonwage income;

T''_z refers to the change in the average rate of direct taxation (on a cash basis) on lagged nonwage income;

p_i refers to the percentage change in the price of investment goods;

c^r_{-1} refers to the percentage change in the volume of time and demand deposits at the end of the previous year;

$\Delta\widetilde{w}_{1-1/2}$ refers to the change in the curvilinear indicator of available capacity lagged half a year;

Ψ_i refers to an autoregressive scheme (defined by a specific equation) according to which a large residual as defined by the other terms in the investment equation, would in the following year lead to a similar residual of opposite sign.

In order to illustrate some of the indirect effects of changes in the growth of exports and imports, we assume an increase in the value of imports or a decrease in the value of exports of 100 million guilder leading to a corresponding loss of foreign exchange. If the Central Bank would carry out a "neutral policy" according to the old gold-standard rules, then total liquidity, as defined by c^r, should decline to the same extent. Such a reduction of liquidity (corresponding to a little less than 1 per cent of the total time and demand deposits around 1960) would according to the investment equation after one year lead to a negative effect on private fixed investment of about 70 million guilders. As the marginal import content of investment is estimated to be around 70 per cent, imports would in due time be reduced by some 50 million guilders on account of the liquidity effect of an increase in imports or a decrease in exports of 100 million guilders.

The investment equation furthermore indicates some of the consequences of a squeeze on the growth of disposable nonwage income. Such a squeeze can be the result of a declining rate of increase in labor productivity and a faster rate of increase of real wages. These tendencies account largely for the change from very rapid growth of nonwage income in 1954 and 1955 to much slower growth in 1956 and 1957. In manufacturing, disposable nonwage income fluctuated even more.[6] The elasticity coefficient of 0.82 with regard to disposable nonwage income suggests that private fixed investment should ceteris paribus fluctuate only slightly less than proportionately in response to fluctuations in disposable nonwage income a year earlier.

Negative changes in the capacity indicator are lagged half a year, that is, decreases in the unemployment percentage are expected to stimulate the growth of investment demand whereas positive changes will depress it. The growth of investment demand thus received a strong stimulus in 1955 and 1956 in connection with the rapid decline of the unemployment rate, whereas in 1957 and particularly in 1958 the influence from this side was negative. The large decline in the value of private fixed investment in 1958 is thus largely explained by the development of lagged disposable nonwage income, lagged liquidity, and lagged changes in available capacity.

The coefficient of 0.46 for the price of investment goods suggests that the growth of the value of private fixed nonresidential investment increases by about half a percentage point for every 1 per cent rise in the price of investment goods.

The equation for the percentage change in the value of inventory investment measured as a percentage of total turnover one year before (the equation is not reproduced here) suggests a technically desired ratio of inventories to final sales of some 30 per cent. This ratio can be modified by anticipation and speculation effects, the determinants of which are changes in profits per unit of product and changes in import prices respectively. Since sales and unit profits tend to grow most rapidly in the first half of an expansion period, the growth of inventory investment can be expected to become negative or in any case to strongly decline in the second half of an ex-

6. See *Central Economic Plan 1961*, p. 41.

pansion period. Since the greater part of inventory investment is expected to be imported goods (the marginal import propensity with regard to inventory investment which is implicit in the import equation lies between 0.8 and 0.9), this means a dampening effect on the rate of import growth in the later phases of an expansion.

Even though we have not aimed at a complete presentation of the 1961 model, we finally cannot avoid considering the model's consumption function

$$C = 0.64L^{B}_{-1/3} + 0.17\,Z^{B}_{-2/3} + 0.46\,\Delta\,p_c$$
$$- 0.16\,\Delta C_{-1} + 0.05\,c^{r}_{-1} - 0.63$$

where

C refers to the percentage change in the value of private consumption;

L^B refers to the percentage change in the value of disposable wage income lagged four months;

Z^B refers to the percentage change in the value of disposable nonwage income lagged eight months;

p_c refers to the percentage change in the price level of consumption; and

c^{r}_{-1} refers to the percentage change in liquidity as previously defined.

The growth of disposable income is obviously the major determinant of the growth of consumption. The elasticity coefficients of the first two terms imply a marginal propensity to consume between 0.8 and 0.9 with regard to wage income and around 0.4 with regard to nonwage income. The increasing strains on the labor market associated with the approach of full and overfull employment in a boom are likely to lead to rapid wage increases which bring about a temporary redistribution of income in favor of wage and salary earners. During recession, in particular its early stages, this redistribution can be expected to be maintained or accentuated mainly because of the rapid decline in the rate of growth of labor productivity. This type of cyclical redistribution of income, which occurred in spite of wage policy efforts to prevent it, stimulated the growth of consumption demand in the boom and helped to maintain the level of consumption demand in recession. However, the effect on consumption growth of the actual cyclical redistribution of income between the low point in 1955 and the high point in 1957–58 does not seem to have exceeded one percentage point. This neutralized in any case part of the dampening effects which the redistribution exerts via the growth of investment. Among the remaining variables of the consumption function only the change in the percentage change of consumer prices seems to have some importance in explaining variations in the growth of consumer demand.

This presentation of the 1961 CPB model is of course far from complete with regard to the number of equations in the model, and even more incomplete with regard to the interactions between the various parts of the model. It is hoped, nevertheless, that the presentation provides a useful impression of some important features of the short-term reaction mechanism of the Dutch economy as seen by the CPB and by analogy of other economies with high ratios of foreign trade to GNP. The parts of the model discussed suggest how a recovery from recession automatically tends to lead to cumulatively higher rates of activity, which in turn may give way to a slowdown in the activity rate that once again will tend to be self-correcting. With the help of the CPB model giving the hypothetical structure of the economy, we have been able to give a general picture of the short-run reaction mechanism of the Dutch economy, of how economic growth tends to produce its own disturbances mainly via balance of payments and private investment reactions. But the actual development has more or less continuously been disturbed and stabilized by exogenous changes and by the introduction of policy measures. The model helps us to understand how and to what extent changes in world demand had destabilizing effects on internal activity and how and to what extent various kinds of fiscal and monetary policy measures affected the economy during the postwar period. But how good these explanations are will also depend on how accurate the model is, a question that will be discussed in the last section of this chapter.

POLICY EFFECTS ON STABILITY

The CPB model has without doubt great pedagogic value, not least with regard to its ability to demonstrate the plausible order of size of the total direct and indirect effects on the economy of changes in policy parameters. This *can* certainly be of great value when, for instance, total demand is expected to increase too much in relation to supply and there are narrow balance of payments constraints. In order to carry out an efficient stabilization policy, it is not enough to know in what direction fiscal and monetary parameters should be changed, although this is certainly a primary condition for a successful stabilization policy. The government authorities should also have some quantitative knowledge about the projected size of the potential disequilibrium as well as about the total expected effects of policy changes considered. It is, however, not simply a matter of putting alternative values of the policy parameters into the model (for example as to government expenditures, tax rates, a change of the exchange rate) and of reading off the results after one and two years, and in this way getting the differences (as to GNP, export and import volume, price level, and so forth) between the situations at the given and at the changed parameter values. The model cannot be used as a mechanical device but must be operated with skill and also with good taste as to choice of exogenous changes and as to plausible assumptions of government and central bank reactions. Let us illustrate the method by taking an example from the Central Economic Plan 1961.[7]

7. Ibid., p. 72

The policy problem refers to a reduction of direct tax rates corresponding to 500 million guilders. It is necessary to distinguish effects from tax reductions separately for wages and for other incomes, as quicker effects are reached in the first category ("pay as you earn system") and because of differing marginal consumption rates. The calculated results are given in the following table:

TABLE 6.1

Consequences of a Tax Reduction of 500 Million Guilders

	Unit	1st year	2nd year
Export value	million guilders	−100	−450
Import value	million guilders	+120	+150
Surplus on current account	million guilders	−220	−600
Consumption price level	%	0	0
Private consumption (value)	%	+1	+1.5
Investment in fixed assets (volume)	%	+1	+3.5

The policy discussion can take a good start from the results derived from the econometric model and presented in this table. The CPB authors were able to deduce the important conclusion that the expected deterioration in the current account of the balance of payments arising from the tax reduction was within a tolerable margin owing to a high expected surplus in 1961 under otherwise given policy parameter values. There are, certainly, a number of interesting issues involved in deriving the table, some of which are discussed in the 1961 Central Economic Plan. The policy measure evaluated will, for instance, have certain primary effects on liquidity owing to the reduced balance of payments surplus and a decrease in the government budget surplus. To what extent such tendencies will have effects on actual liquidity, and therefore in the second

TABLE 6.2

Estimated Consequences

		of a wage increase by 1 percent (=210 million guilders)[a]		of a rise of investment by 1 per cent (+100 million guilders)	
	Unit	1st year	2nd year	1st year	2nd year
Export value	million guilders	−80	−170	−70	−120
Import value	million guilders	+20	+10	+70	−10
Surplus on current account	million guilders	−100	−180	−140	−110
Consumption price level	%	0	0.5	0	0
Private consumption (value)	%	0.5	0.7	0	0
Investment in fixed assets (value)	%	0	0.5	1.5	1

a. At an unchanged level of production per manyear.

year on private investment, will depend on monetary and debt policy (for example, what the government borrows on the capital market). Certain explicit assumptions have to be made in this respect. The same is true as to the development of wages and prices. The insertion of a constant consumption price level is just a working assumption, but certainly not very realistic. In order to take care of possible alternative developments as to wage rates and investment, the expected effect of variations in these variables have been derived from the model.[8]

It is interesting to observe the relatively large effects of wage changes on the balance of payments position. As wage policy was a central issue in government economic policy, this kind of quantitative estimation may have been of great importance for policy formation. It is in fact impressive how the CPB model is and can be used in connection with important policy decisions to compare the outcomes with and without proposed policy changes. A fine example is the application of the model to analyze plausible effects on target variables of a revaluation of the guilder in 1961. The decision had to be taken very quickly (after the appreciation of the German mark in March 1961), and the CPB had to give its advice on the basis of a model calculation of the explicit short-term effects. The outcome is shown on Table 6.3.[9]

According to these calculations the disturbing effects on the balance of payments and on unemployment would be insignificant. Weight was placed on the favorable results as to price developments in view of the prevailing inflationary tendencies. It is plausible, as asserted, that the CPB analysis gave support to the government decision to appreciate the currency. In this case there was little chance that mistakes in the analysis with the model would be observable, as the order of size of these policy effects was drowned in the flow of current changes of the variables from 1960 to 1961.

8. Ibid., p. 74.
9. From van den Beld, p. 156.

TABLE 6.3

Some Short-term Effects of a 5 Per Cent Appreciation of the Guilder

	Initial situation according to 1961 forecast (assuming unchanged policies)	Effects on 1961 outcomes
Surplus of current balance of payments (billions guilders)	1.0	−0.14
Price level of consumption (1960=100)	101.5	−1.20
Volume of investment (billion guilders)	9.4	−0.02
Unemployment (per cent)	1.0	+0.10

In the ways exemplified above, the CPB model represents a systematic *theory of the short-term effects of policy*. It can be and is systematically used for inferring short-term repercussions over the entire economic system of policy changes. Efficient stabilization policy does not, of course, necessarily follow from the availability of such a theory of policy. Even if sophisticated and well-thought out, the model might give outcomes with too-large errors with regard to the target variables both for forecasting purposes and for the assessment of policy effects. These problems will be discussed in the next section. The first question is to find out how well timed and adapted the *actual policy changes* in the Netherlands have been in relation to the needs. The simplest way of doing this is to look at the primary policy impulses on the economy and to study their conformity with the conjuncture movements.

The *primary* or direct effects on GNP of a great number of fiscal policy changes have been summarized in a special investigation carried out by the Central Planning Bureau in 1963.[10] In Table 6.4 some of the budget "impulses" are taken from the memorandum reporting the investigation. The "weighted" sum should give an approximate expression for the total size of the direct budget effect on total demand for goods and services. The impulses are measured as changes in budget expenditures from one year to the next (excluding financial expenditures without direct effect on demand). Effects of tax changes are measured with regard to changes in direct and indirect tax *rates* and calculated on the basis of incomes of the previous year. This means that automatic changes in tax revenues following income variations are *not* considered. The expenditure and tax impulses are weighted on account of effects on demand, so that, for example, the sum for a decrease in direct tax rates is reduced with regard to the assumed marginal saving ratios.

10. C. A. van den Beld, *Conjunctuurpolitiek in en om de Jaren Vijftig* (January 1963). This stenciled memorandum was kindly supplied to the author by Professor de Wolff.

TABLE 6.4

Changes in Value from Previous Year (in million guilders)

Year	Total government expenditures for investment and consumption	Direct and indirect tax changes	Income payments and producers' subsidies	Price control measures	House investment control	Total (unweighted)	Weighted total impulse on GNP in percentages
1952	195	−160	55	−200	50	−60	−0.3
1953	535	145	135	5	180	1,000	3.7
1954	55	440	390	−130	140	895	4.9
1955	255	370	460	5	345	1,435	4.2
1956	435	240	255	−10	410	1,330	4.5
1957	235	−130	310	−135	320	600	2.1
1958	−350	−65	1,040	−155	−40	430	0.5
1959	55	110	−395	−30	205	−55	0.0
1960	355	330	485	−240	220	1,150	3.7
1961	355	0	225	−70	80	590	1.9
1962	410	−300	260	−70	90	405	1.7

Up to 1959 this series is not impressive from the point of view of the timing of stabilization policy. Fiscal policy measures of the various kinds included in the table implied, apparently, a considerable stimulus to economic activity in 1955 and 1956, when there were already strong tendencies toward excess demand. The figure of 4.2 per cent of primary impulses in 1955 (measured in relation to 1954 GNP) is very high indeed when compared to the accompanying increase of real GNP of 7 to 8 per cent. The small rise in the impulse effect to 4.5 per cent in 1956 may be regarded as strongly procyclical, if we pay attention to the smaller space for further increase of demand (the actual increase of real GNP was 4 per cent in 1956) and to the lagged indirect effects of the expansionary fiscal policy of 1955.

An effective anticyclical fiscal program was first seriously considered *after* the too-rapid increase of demand relative to supply already had resulted in a substantial balance of payments deficit during 1956. Apparently the destabilizing tendencies had not been foreseen in the 1955 Economic Plan. The recommendation of a restrictive program by the Social and Economic Council in the fall of 1956 was put into effect by the government in the beginning of 1957. The program, based on CPB model calculations aimed at reducing national expenditure during 1957 by 700 million guilders by means of a combination of measures including a reduction of government expenditures, raised charges by public utilities, higher tax rates for corporations, increases in other direct and indirect taxes, suspension of an investment rebate granted to industrial firms, reduction of consumer subsidies, and, as an important element in controlling private consumption, an agreement to keep wage rates constant except for adjustments in accordance with a cost-of-living clause. The package deal also included a successive rise of the discount rate which had been 2.5 per cent in the beginning of 1956 and reached 5 per cent in August 1957, plus other forms of restrictive monetary policy.

As measured by the direct impulse factor in the table, it is evident that a restrictive effect was attained during 1957, but also that the restrictive impulses were higher in the recession year 1958 and reached a maximum in 1959. If we take account of the time lags of the indirect effects on economic activity, the conclusion must be that the timing of the restrictive policy measures was rather bad. The sharp decline in investment and the small decline in consumption during 1957 and 1958 discussed above, which were considered as being in part automatic effects of the working of the Dutch economic system, were apparently strengthened by these fiscal policy measures. To this extent it can be said that government policy during the conjuncture 1955–59 worked in a procyclical way, strengthening the fluctuations in activity, blowing up excess demand during 1955–56, and pressing down consumption and especially investment demand during 1958. The awkward fact was that the recession was aggravated by restrictive policy after the 1957 balance of payments difficulties had in fact been rectified. Already during 1957 rapidly declining imports and rising exports implied a quick transformation from a balance of payment deficit in 1957 to a big surplus in 1958.

The inadequate timing of fiscal policy during the 1950s may have been a one-time affair belonging to the "learning process." After too much stimulation given in 1960, the direct budget impact in the following years has implied a less expansionary policy than during the 1950s. No balance of payments disturbance or rise of unemployment occurred during the period 1959–64. The very big spurt in production, as well as in investment, consumption, and export demand up to 1960, was followed by a balanced retardation of growth. The sequence after the similar 1954–55 spurt was not repeated, as had been feared, apparently thanks partly to the successful avoidance of the earlier policy mistakes. However, we cannot be too certain about this. In other countries also the 1961–62 development was just a retardation in growth, and no recession, implying less international disturbance and easier policy problems than during the corresponding period of the 1950s.

As mentioned above, the Dutch put considerable emphasis on *monetary conditions*. It should be observed that it is only a liquidity variable (in the form of total bank deposits) that enters the investment equation, but not interest rate changes.[11] In the equations for investment, and to a small extent consumption demand, the supply of liquidity at the beginning of the period is a determining factor. To the extent that monetary policy has control over this variable, the CPB model also supplies a theory for the effects of monetary policy. The Nederlandsche Bank in its reports gives great emphasis to the development of liquidity (in the above sense) in relation to GNP for evaluating the efficacy of monetary policy.[12] The Central Bank's approach is in fact very close to the simplest versions of the quantity theory. Recurrent diagrams showing the relation between liquidity and GNP give emphasis to this aspect. The liquidity requirements normally correspond to 40 per cent of GNP, implying an annual rise of money supply by 1.6 per cent of GNP when the latter is rising by 4 per cent per year. There will be "inflationary impulses" when liquidity is rising more rapidly; but if a certain rise of the price level is accepted as unavoidable (for instance because of higher import prices), then the extra increase of nominal GNP will just mean a canceling of a "deflationary impulse." There is, how-

11. It is an "old tradition" in the Netherlands—since Tinbergen's econometric study of 1939, *Statistical Testing of Business Cycle Theories: Business Cycles of the United States 1919–1932* (Geneva, 1939)—not to consider interest-rate changes as relevant variables in an econometric system. The neglect of these variables is certainly not due to a dogmatic view, but to the fact that neither Tinbergen nor the Central Planning Bureau has been able to find within their systems a significant explanatory effect of the interest-rate variables.

12. The arguments cited here are repeated in the yearly reports of the Nederlandsche Bank. We here especially refer to the reports of 1962 and 1964.

ever, a very important and characteristic reservation to such a passive attitude: "The standard for domestic liquidity creation cannot of course be simply adjusted to the nominal liquidity requirement, since that would mean taking as the standard that the country's own price inflation should be financed without any resistance from domestic resources. The principle must on the contrary be that the source of finance for a rise in domestic prices shall be a surplus on transactions with foreign countries."[13] This statement points at a strategic issue of monetary policy. The relatively favorable cost position of the Netherlands has implied two interrelated and rather persistent pressures on the economy: (1) inflationary impulses on internal prices and wages, (2) balance of payments surpluses in most years. Liquidity creation corresponding to the surpluses could from this point of view be accepted as a necessary and unavoidable adaptation as long as the exchange rate was fixed. But when balance of payments deficits came up, a monetary contraction had to be accepted. All this comes pretty close to the old dream of the working of the gold standard.

From the point of view of timing it seems that monetary policy (ex post) has been somewhat more successful than fiscal policy during the years 1955–58. The following table demonstrates this point.[14]

According to this table and the econometric model, monetary factors (as measured by liquidity changes) should have had a restraining effect in 1956 when the total liquidity ratio was permitted to decline significantly, and an expansive effect should have been quite strong during 1958. However, the table is a dangerous one to use for judging the effectiveness of monetary *policy*. This is so not only because of the unclear implications of global liquidity *effects,* considering the well-known difficulties of finding out anything relevant about de-

13. Report of the Nederlandsche Bank for 1962, p. 19.

14. Ibid., Table 10, p. 36. Liquidity mainly refers to bank deposits. The deficit or surplus in the balance of payments includes capital transactions.

TABLE 6.5

The Creation of Liquidity (per year in per cent of GNP)

Via	1954	1955	1956	1957	1958	1959
Total government	−1.1	−0.5	0.4	2.2	0.6	−2.8
Banking system	1.8	2.0	1.2	0.6	−0.9	1.6
Balance of payments	2.2	1.5	−3.1	−0.9	6.3	3.6
Total sum	2.9	3.0	−1.5	1.9	6.0	2.4

mand and supply conditions for liquidity as a stock that is significant for the determination of demand flows. From Table 6.5 we cannot find out much about actual changes in monetary policy, in fact much less than about fiscal policy in the previous table. What we really see in the table are ex post changes of liquidity, largely coming out of changes of endogenous variables. We note that the most effective parts of the total liquidity changes have arisen from the shifts in the balance of payments position. It is thanks to the deficit in 1956 that liquidity (according to the above definition) was reduced in agreement with the largely automatic working of the economic system implying a sort of built-in stability. This restrictive effect was to a certain extent neutralized by total government deficits and liquidity effects coming from increased bank lending. Although there was in 1956 a significant dampening of liquidity creation by the banking system, we cannot a priori determine to what extent the corresponding retardation in bank lending was an effect of monetary policy restraint, or simply a passive result of the slowing down of GNP growth having effects on demand for credit and liquidity. The current monetary policies, that is the changes in parameters of action, refer to the changes in discount rates, cash requirements, controls of government financing, and so forth that in interaction with other variables determine the results given in the table.

A word should also be said about the working of the Dutch

wage policy.[15] If we look at the average rate of wage increases in the Netherlands, we get no convincing notion of the effective functioning of a control machinery. The Dutch wage level has risen by 7 to 8 per cent per year on average over the period 1952–63.[16] The remarkable achievement is, however, that in connection with the balance of payments crises in 1951 and 1957 the government could enforce, with the help of the Board of Government Mediators and the Labor Foundation, agreements that actually implied and were intended to imply reductions in real wages. (Compare for a contrast the wage multiplier in Sweden discussed in Chapter 5.) Only partial compensation was given for increases in the cost of living (determined by rises in indirect taxes, higher rents, and so on). The growth of real consumption in 1951–52 and 1957–58 was negative or very low. But it is easy to point out that these wage-policy achievements came too late from a stabilization point of view. During 1955 and especially 1956, excess demand for labor had created a substantial wage drift and had also caused a new wage round with increases in rates that reached a record level of 11 per cent in 1957. The wage inflation in 1955–57 may have contributed to the balance of payments deficit discussed above. It is natural that the atmosphere for a very restrictive wage policy should first occur *after* the tensions had become strong and a crisis was imminent. When activity in 1952 and 1958 had turned down, and unemployment was high, then it was relatively easy to bring about restricted wage increases of about 3 to 5 per cent per year.

15. The institutional framework and sociopolitical conditions of this policy have been presented in many publications. See especially OEEC, *The Problem of Rising Prices* (Paris, 1961).

16. This development must again largely be regarded as a consequence of the fact that Holland started out with relatively very low wages and an undervalued currency. In 1953 the government seriously considered an appreciation of the guilder, but that occurred first in 1961, after a 3 per cent yearly deterioration of the value of money had on average occurred in the meantime.

The norms of wage policy have been shifting over the post-war period. Prior to 1953 they were closely related to changes in the cost of living index; after that, up to 1959, the criteria were based on the labor share in national income. After 1959 the criteria became less rigid and more differentiation in wage developments was allowed with regard to changes in labor productivity in the various branches of activity; in 1962 this type of criterion was abandoned, and very general guidelines as to the desirable development of the wage level were introduced (given in reports of the Social Economic Council).

The most interesting aspect of the Dutch wage policy experience seems to have been the overwhelming strength of the market forces which broke through the guidelines of wage policy in situations of strong demand. The following figure gives an impression of the considerable variations in the relation between the supply and the demand for labor.

Were the actual wage changes just a consequence of these changing conditions in the labor market, or did the wage policy efforts significantly affect the results? The following

FIGURE 6.1
Labor Reserve and Unfilled Vacancies

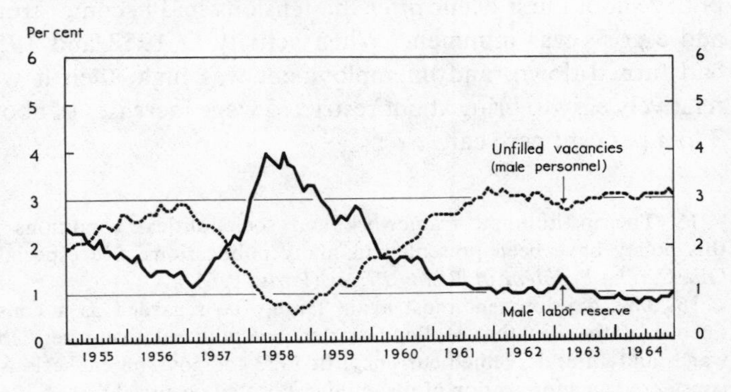

wage change equation for moving averages of quarterly figures from 1950 to 1962 does not provide us with a satisfactory answer, but it does furnish us with some interesting clues:[17]

$$l = \frac{11.8}{\breve{\hat{w}}_t + 2.8} + 0.5p_{c\ -1} - 1.0\Delta\left(\frac{\breve{L}}{\breve{\hat{Y}}}\right)_{-3} - 1.0h - 1.0$$

Here

l stands for the percentage change of the level of industrial wages;

$\breve{\hat{w}}_t$ for the unemployment percentage;

p_{c-1} for the percentage change in the price of consumption lagged one period;

$\Delta\left(\frac{\breve{L}}{\breve{\hat{Y}}}\right)_{-3}$ for the change in the share of wages in national income lagged three periods;

and h for the percentage change in the standard number of working hours.

The first term on the right-hand side of the equation is expected to reflect the effect of the labor market situation on wage changes. The second term, which enters only during 1951–53, is to account for cost-of-living increases which were then used as the criterion for controlled nationwide wage increases. The coefficient of this variable presumably reflects the half compensation for the major cost of living increase in 1951. The third term enters only during 1954–58 when the traditional share of wages was actually used as the criterion for controlled wage increases. After that, weighted averages of sectoral and national productivity increases were used as guidelines up to 1963, when a yearly fixed target for the national average wage increase was introduced as a strategy. There is no specific term

17. See van den Beld, "Short-term Planning Experiences," pp. 151–54.

in the equation to reflect wage policy after 1958. The effect of the reduction in the standard number of working hours in 1961 and 1962 was according to the fourth term a lower increase in money wage rates. The equation accounts for three fifths of the variation of wage rate changes during the postwar period.

The first (curvilinear) term and the last (constant) term on the right-hand side of the equation were determined separately on the basis of annual wage changes and unemployment percentages for 1923–38 and 1949–62. This curvilinear relationship is, as mentioned above, expected to reflect the influence of the general labor market situation. Postwar departures from the pattern of association established in the interwar period might be interpreted as evidence of the influence of postwar wage policy. Unfortunately, but not unexpectedly, this "Phillips curve" for the Netherlands hardly allows any such inferences, since the range of the low postwar unemployment rates was almost entirely detached from the range of interwar unemployment rates. Furthermore, the unexplained variance of this curvilinear relationship is so large in either period that relatively subtle differences on account of postwar wage policy cannot be considered significant.

On the other hand, the clear tendency for wage changes to be relatively low in years of recession (1952 and 1958) and revival (1953 and 1959) and high in boom years (1955, 1960, 1964) means that wage policy has in any case not eliminated the cyclical pattern of wage changes. Actually, it has even been suggested that Dutch wage policy has to a certain extent accentuated the normal cyclical pattern.[18] According to that view, the procyclical effect of wage policy resulted from the tendency to underestimate the increases in exports and productivity in the first phase of an expansion. This tendency implied a too pessimistic outlook with regard to tolerable wage increases.

18. See for instance, Wilhelm Hessel, "Quantitative Planning," p. 175.

Consequently wage rates lagged and unit profits rose rapidly during the revival. This pattern then presumably reinforced the customary tendency of wage rates to rise rapidly in the later stages of the expansion. In fact, the differences during the cycle between the lowest and the highest annual wage changes in the Netherlands seem to have been among the largest in the groups of countries compared. This high degree of cyclical variation, however, is not so much due to relatively smaller Dutch wage increases in recession and revival as to generally larger Dutch increases in the later phases of expansion. As a result, the average rate of wage increase in the Netherlands has been among the most rapid of the countries compared, in particular during the decade after 1953. As in many other countries the uncontrolled part of the postwar wage rate increases in the Netherlands, largely wage drift, amounted on average to about one half of the total increases and varied in conformity with the labor market situation. Only during 1950–53 may wage policy be credited with some restraining effect. However, as the comparison with several other countries suggests, the total rise during those four years might have been no larger in the absence of wage policy efforts.

APPLICATIONS OF THE ECONOMETRIC MODEL FOR POLICY PLANNING

It is relatively easy, and generally gives an unsympathetic air of misplaced ex post wisdom, to point out errors in actual policy decisions and to analyze them against the perspective of what afterward really happened. Economic policy decisions are usually made under great uncertainty as to future possibilities and under more or less awkward pressures from political bodies and organizations. From this view the Dutch seem to have achieved a better milieu of economic rationality and mutual political understanding in economic policy matters than any other country.

There is no doubt that the research work done by the CPB

and presented in a series of projections of the short-term trends of the economy has been an important basis for the good policy atmosphere in the Netherlands. It seems that the econometric models of the economy presented and continuously revised have created common notions of how the Dutch economy works in *aggregate* terms. From this point of view it is certainly a great responsibility of the CPB to present a model embodying these ambitions and to apply it for projections and policy planning. There are considerable risks, however, that mistakes will be made, and these risks may be greater than if the analysis and conclusions were less precise, more modest, and the results were presented in more qualitative and vague terms.

The advantage of the Dutch way of basing projections and policy analysis on a specified system of equations and explicit assumptions as to the changes in exogenous factors is the generally accepted basis of understanding thereby created, including the belief that the model gives sensible indications also in quantitative terms. General consensus with regard to the basis of interpretation does not exclude the possibility in a given situation of paying attention to uncertainties and to relevant exogenous factors that are not included in the model. In other words, knowledge from other sources can be used to qualify the conclusions. In this spirit the picture the CPB presents annually of the trends and prospects of the economy is complemented by other sources of information.

Nevertheless the econometric model is essential as the basis for the forecasts. So much work would not be put into this type of analysis if the results were not taken seriously and if these results were not considered to be of great use in understanding the working of the economy. Two main questions must therefore be raised: (1) How close to reality have the Dutch projections actually been; that is, how large have the deviations between forecasts and results been over the years? (2) How good is the model in really explaining the working of the Dutch economy?

Even if the deviations in the first sense turn out to be reasonably small, there might still be reasons, intuitive or theoretical, for being skeptical that parts of the model make sense. On the other hand large deviations may not be proof of the unrealism of the model as describing the working of the economy; unexplained and badly projected external factors and disturbances might be responsible for the deviations.

As a matter of fact the CPB itself has made interesting critical studies of its own predictions over the years.[19] In Table 6.6 comparisons between forecasts and realized results are given. The forecasts are the final ones presented by the CPB in the central economic plan, usually at the beginning of the year the prediction refers to. Earlier versions of the forecasts, worked out in connection with the government budget proposal in September of the previous year, will be touched upon only very briefly. The model predictions refer primarily to the mutually dependent endogenous variables of the equation system, which are usually expressed as annual percentage changes. But the predictive accuracy of the predetermined variables deserves attention, too, since it helps to locate a major source of prediction errors regarding the endogenous variables for which the model in its narrow sense should not be blamed.[20]

19. The results presented here are taken from *Forecasts and Realization.*

20. The following definitions are used in the table: if R_t is the observed percentage change of a variable (ex post) and F_t is the corresponding forecast, then the forecasting error is equal to: $(F_t - R_t)$.

The root-mean-square error (u) over the period of n years in question then is: $u = \sqrt{\frac{1}{n} \Sigma (F_t - R_t)^2}$

This measure of error is standardized by dividing by the root-mean-square of the observed changes, s being the *normal rate of change:*

$$s = \sqrt{\frac{1}{n} \Sigma R^2}$$

The inequality coefficient is thus u/s.

TABLE 6.6

Normal Rates of Change and Indicators of Forecasting Errors, 1953–63

	Normal rate of change (s)	Root-mean-square error of forecast (u)	Inequality coefficient (u/s): Unconditional	Inequality coefficient (u/s): Conditional (On the basis of the 1962 model and under the condition of perfect exogenous prediction)
Predetermined variables				
a. Controlled				
Wage level in industries	7.7	2.2	0.29	
Government wage bill	10.9	2.8	0.25	
Public investment	12.4	11.3	0.91	
Total government budget impulse (as a percentage of GNP)	3.1	1.2	0.40	
b. Noncontrolled				
Volume of world trade	8.7	5.3	0.61	
Competitive price level of foreign trade	2.7	1.5	0.57	
Endogenous variables				
a. Policy targets				
Unemployment	0.9	0.5	0.58	0.20
Volume of fixed business investment	14.1	11.0	0.78	0.49
Current account of balance of payments (as a percentage of GNP)	2.9	2.2	0.74	—
Price level of consumption	2.7	1.2	0.44	0.56
b. Other endogenous variables				
Volume of industrial production	5.9	2.7	0.45	—
Volume of private consumption	5.7	2.1	0.38	0.23
Volume of commodity exports	9.6	5.4	0.56	0.23
Volume of commodity imports	13.3	5.6	0.42	0.31
Inventory investment (as a percentage of GNP)	2.0	2.0	1.01	—
Nonwage income	8.7	6.6	0.81	0.34

An inequality coefficient of zero would mean that all predictions were perfect. A coefficient of one, on the other hand, would mean that the forecasting errors are on average as large as the normal rates of change, that is predictions no better than "naïve" no-change projections. Finally, an inequality coefficient in excess of one would indicate that no-change projections would have led to smaller prediction errors. Among the results presented, the unconditional inequality coefficients of the policy targets are of course the most relevant in the present context. The size of the respective inequality coefficients lies between 0.44 and 1.01, which can hardly be called a brilliant record.[21] Among the other endogenous variables mentioned in the table, the percentage change in the consumption volume was on average predicted most accurately. However, its inequality coefficient of 0.38 shows that considerable unexploited potential for improvement remains even in this case. Predictive accuracy with regard to the changes in nonwage income and in inventory investment is clearly lacking.

The predetermined variables, which are assessed with the help of different, in general less formalized methods, have inequality coefficients that range from 0.25 for the changes in the government wage bill to 0.91 for public investment.

The graphs in Figure 6.2 show the individual forecasting errors of a number of variables, including predetermined as well as endogenous ones.

What strikes the eye is a systematic tendency toward underestimation. This tendency, which is characteristic of nearly all series, reflects a bias against "bold estimates" with regard to the predetermined variables. In fact we find such a bias in all "responsible" predictions also in other countries. It is in a way quite natural that a government institution especially tends to guard its predictions in this manner. It is usually considered better to err on the prudent side than the contrary, in particular

21. It should be observed, however, that a large part of the results (in particular for the earlier years) are derived from models widely differing from those in use during the 1960s.

FIGURE 6.2
Forecast (F) and Realization (R)

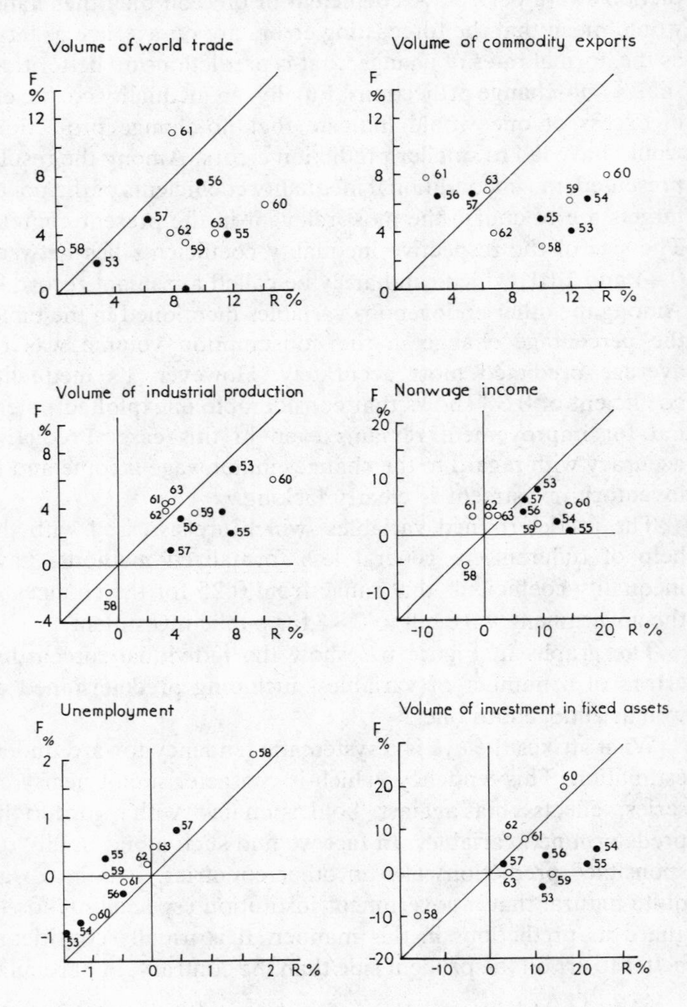

Source: *Forecasts and Realization*, pp. 21–27.

when the latter may provoke or justify too-expansive government policies or too-large wage increases. We can in fact observe how underestimation tends to be especially large in the case of exceptionally big actual increases. In the case of changes of less than average size the errors tend to be smaller and may be underestimations or overestimations.

Most prominent among the exceptions to this tendency of underestimation are unemployment and the current account of balance of payment, which are both target variables. Underestimation of changes in effective labor demand relative to supply up to 1958, and greater systematic overestimation of changes in labor supply than in labor demand thereafter, led to overestimation of increases and underestimation of decreases in unemployment. This resulted in the predicted level of unemployment always being too high. The accuracy in predicting the net changes in the current account of the balance of payments is very low, the instability coefficient being 0.74. This is not surprising, since the variable is a marginal difference between quite uncertain aggregates. The errors in prediction of balance of payments and unemployment changes may become especially serious when they take the form of *turning-point errors* (the points in the graphs are then placed in the second and fourth quadrants). The graphs show, for instance, that an increase of unemployment was projected for 1955 whereas unemployment actually declined considerably. A deterioriation of the balance of payments position was predicted for 1959, but actually there was an improvement. In particular the first of these turning-point errors may have had some share in the shaping of destabilizing policies. It seems likely that the misdirected policy of budget stimulus in 1955 had something to do with a fear of increasing unemployment that both the September version and the final version of the Central Planning Bureau prediction made plausible.

To what extent are the errors in the prediction of the endogenous variables due to errors in the prediction of the exogenous variables? A large part of the errors in the unconditional prediction of the endogenous variables depends on the great difficulties in projecting the changes of the controlled and uncontrolled exogenous variables, such as the volume of world trade, the price level of imports and government expenditures. The predictions of the rather crucial changes in world trade are in fact very unsatisfactory, as the high inequality coefficient shows.[22] The errors in the export predictions are to a large extent explained by the unsuccessful projections of changes in world trade. If the correct actual changes in world trade are put into the export equations, the resulting conditional forecasts represent a substantial improvement in accuracy.[23] The last column of Table 6.6 informs about the accuracy of conditional forecasts. The systematic declines of the inequality coefficients are, however, due only in part to the hypothetical elimination of errors in the projection of exogenous variables; the other part results from using the superior 1962 model in calculating the conditional forecasts for the entire period. That these conditional forecasts do not show any systematic underestimation comes hardly as a surprise, since the methods for estimating the equations automatically lead to a symmetric distribution of the errors.

However, even after correction for errors in predicting the exogenous variables, the forecasting efficiency of the model is still not too convincing. The average prediction error for ten variables and ten years is still about 40 per cent of the normal rate of change. The conditional forecasting efficiency is lowest (around 50 per cent) for fixed investment, industrial employment, the consumption price level, and for export goods. The general improvement in the accuracy of the unconditional forecasts after 1957 is a result of better information and improved models. Undetermined parts of the improvement are, however, due to circumstances that have little to do with the models as

22. *Forecasts and Realization,* p. 20.

23. Note that the conditional forecasts obtained by eliminating the errors in the prediction of exogenous variables are all based on the 1962 model.

such. In fact there are several reasons for believing that it became easier to forecast the changes after 1958 than before. The variations and intensities of the actual changes have been less than in the previous years, and this should mean an improvement in the forecasts. Furthermore there is a learning process going on, successively embodied in the coefficients of the model, but also implying corrections of the solutions of the equation system in the light of useful extraneous information. The lower conditional inequality coefficients for the period after 1958 may be as much the result of skillful adjustments of the outcomes of the model as of improvements of the model itself.

The investment plan surveys made by the CPB in October and November are an important source of extraneous information. The superior forecasting efficiency, compared to the investment equation of the model, is quite telling.[24]

TABLE 6.7

Comparison Between Investment Survey and Model Forecast (in percentages)

	anufacturing investment		Business fixed investment	
	Investment survey forecast	Actual change	Unconditional model forecast	Actual change
58	−21.4	−20.4	−10.1	−15.6
59	7.1	9.8	−1.0	13.7
60	25.7	20.2	19.0	17.4
61	17.5	21.2	7.1	8.2
62	6.3	5.0	7.9	3.8

urce: Forecasts and Realization, pp. 43, 57.

The partly disappointing experiences during the 1950s of using the CPB model seem to call for some concluding considerations of the technique of planning and evaluating policy measures by means of an econometric model. It is self-evident that an outsider can take up only some very general considerations.

With regard to forecasting future tensions in the economy, it seems that the Dutch technique of analysis was not efficient

24. *Forecasts and Realization*, p. 43.

enough when it mattered most, namely in 1950–51 and in 1954–56. In both instances the dangers of the situation were apparently not discovered before serious disequilibria had developed. The pertinent policy decisions were therefore made at too late a stage. Experiences of the type represented by the Korean boom will probably remain a hard challenge to any forecasting model for a long time to come. An annual model like the Dutch one will hardly ever have much of a chance in a case of that nature. A quarterly model would at least offer the possibility of coming more quickly in contact with such a brush-fire type of phenomenon. A forecasting and policy planning setup built around a quarterly model would also be less likely to lose touch with the actual situation in more normal experiences of the 1954–56 type. There is furthermore some risk that the formalized CPB type of approach can create a kind of blindness with regard to relevant other information which, particularly in connection with oversimplified models of the pre-1958 type, is apt to lead to major misjudgments. As an illustration of this possibility it is interesting to note the significant difference as to success in forecasting and government policies related to the actual course of events in the Netherlands and in Sweden during the period 1955–58.

The Dutch model apparently gave quite misleading predictions for the years 1954–56. The increases in exports, investment, and private consumption were greatly underestimated (see the graphs in Figure 6.2); the model gave no clear signals of the tendencies in the direction of overheating of the economy. On the contrary, it predicted rising unemployment in 1955. In the models applied before 1958, no attention was paid to bottlenecks in production, and this failure contributed to the underestimation of the pressure on the balance of payments during 1956. The expansionary impulse from the government budget was very high in the years 1954–56 and must have contributed strongly to the excess demand conditions during these years.

As pointed out above, the causal relations between the CPB

forecasts and government policies can hardly ever be clarified. Nevertheless, it is worthwhile quoting the CPB's own view on this matter: "It would be wrong to suggest a very close connection between policy measures and forecasting (errors), but the fact remains that in 1955 when underestimation of domestic expenditures was high, the government policy was far from anticyclical."[25] Anyhow, as already mentioned, the movement of the economy during 1957–58 in the recessionary direction (with a big decline in industrial investment) was reinforced by restrictive monetary and fiscal policy; the main impact from reduced government expenditures came with an unfortunate time lag first in 1958–59. The careful conclusion made by the CPB reads: "Generally, therefore, the forecasting errors were reflected to some extent in government policy actions."[26]

The corresponding Swedish experiences during the same years appear in sharp contrast. (See Chapter 5, page 242) The danger of a coming boom with excess demand conditions was perceived in the fall of 1954 by means of surveys of investment plans within industry and observations of trends in the labor market. Restrictive fiscal and monetary policies were introduced from the beginning of 1955 and were on the whole maintained up to the end of 1957. The most conspicuous difference in experiences following from the respective policies refers to the cycle in business investment: in the Netherlands very big increases in the volume index in 1955 and 1956 were followed by a sharp contraction in 1958; in Sweden there was a more-or-less constant volume of fixed private investments followed by a sharp rise in 1958. There were no balance of payments strains in Sweden during this period.

Of course no general conclusions, for instance as to the dangers of using econometric forecasting models, can be drawn from this comparison. As shown in Chapter 5, the Swedish experiences were quite special in several respects, and the partly successful outcome apparently very much depended on

25. Ibid., p. 49.
26. Ibid., p. 50.

good luck. It is too bad in a way that no equally interesting comparisons of Dutch and Swedish experiences can be made for later years. The economic developments of the first half of the 1960s have in both countries turned out to be less interesting from a conjuncture point of view than the 1950s, and the methods of forecasting have come much closer to each other. The Dutch model has been improved in important respects, by having been made dynamic to a certain extent and by the introduction of a variable reflecting changing supply conditions. The Swedes have been applying econometric techniques of analysis to an increasing extent at the same time that the Dutch have been paying more and more attention in their predictions to surveys of entrepreneurial investment and sales plans.

HOW GOOD IS THE CPB MODEL IN DESCRIBING REALITY?

Although the CPB econometric model even in its revised versions of 1961 and later does not give very accurate short-term predictions, it might be accurate enough in a general and more fundamental sense. The model may give a good and realistic picture of the main short-term interrelations in the economy, headlighting the strategic variables and parameters and demonstrating how they are interrelated. It is claimed, and we think rightly, that the Dutch model has had a high educative value and a favorable influence for common understanding of the issues. But how do we know that the CPB model gives an essentially correct picture of the short-term mechanism of the Dutch economy? In order to be able to answer such a question it would be necessary to study the theories incorporated in each part of the model and the theory of economic change implicit in the system taken as a whole. Unfortunately, economic reality as given by the actual statistical time series furnishing the material for the determination of the coefficients of the equation is such that, given almost any reasonable specification of the model, we are bound to get a reasonably good "average" description of the facts. There must be a great number of differently specified equations that would give about equally good statistical descriptions. Little or no attention is and can be paid to the *potentialities* of other outcomes than those given by the actual statistical series.

Let us illustrate what we have in mind by some examples from the model. The price equations, determining relative changes in the price levels of consumption, investment, and export goods, are mainly based on price-cost relations (including wage-rate changes, productivity changes, and import cost changes). Demand changes seem to play a subordinate role.[27] If, for example, during the boom prices had been given the function of clearing the markets, developing in the *short run* independently of unit costs and in turn influencing these costs (for example via changes in wages and profit margins), then profits might not be squeezed during the boom (not so quickly anyhow), and investment could go on rising for a longer time, being less vulnerable to liquidity changes. Taking care of such a potentiality would change the model considerably. It is possible that such potentialities have been excluded by specific policy measures carried out. Price control efforts during 1956 and some other years of the postwar period might have made this conception of cost-determined price formation more plausible. We are back to the question of the interdependent play of forces operating within the time unit of one year used by the CPB, which may make it impossible to unravel the economic forces at work. (See also the remark with regard to credit and liquidity policy above.) Price changes have effects on wage costs and other costs during a year of strong demand forces which are not explicitly considered in the model and which *might* have been dominating in certain situations, for ex-

27. In the price equation for consumption (p_c) there is, however, at the side of the cost variables (labor, import, and interest-rate costs), a term expressing how p_c will experience an upward pressure when, because of capacity limitations, demand shifts from internal to external sources.

ample in 1950–51 and 1955–56, not to speak of the deflation spiral of the 1930s. The fact that regression analysis gives an acceptable fit even in these cases is no proof that the price index changes are not in certain periods mainly demand-determined, with costs being pulled up ex post.

From another point of view the export equation seems to be of questionable economic significance. As noted above, according to this equation the export volume is quite sensitive to changes in the relation between Dutch export prices and prices of competing countries. What is really measured? Under conditions of a relatively competitive world market, conditions that have anyhow ruled for considerable parts of the period and for a sizable portion of Dutch exports, there may be just one single world market price (except for differences in qualities). Not much economic significance can then be attached to changes in price relations that may appear partly as a result of deficient index numbers. The CPB export equation should perhaps be partly interpreted as containing an expression for a relation between the *supply cost* of Dutch export goods and (demand) prices on the world market. This should mean an interpretation of how changes in Dutch exports are affected other than the one implied in the model. The sad fact is that probably nobody really knows whether the statistical material used makes the one or the other interpretation nearer the truth. The fact that the regression analysis is statistically significant according to conventional criteria again does not help us here to understand if in a given period it is low relative costs and high profits that affect Dutch exports from the supply side or if it is relatively low prices that stimulate foreign demand.

As mentioned above, the economic significance of the investment function is strategic for understanding the fluctuations of economic activity. Relative changes in profits after taxes and in liquidity are the main determining factors. One difficulty of interpretation must be that changes in profits and liquidity may be related as firms build up their liquidity by means of current profits (in order to finance later investments). Therefore the relative importance of these factors in influencing changes in investment may be uncertain within wide limits. Liquidity can be influenced by changes in the availability of bank credit, but strangely enough this factor does not enter directly into the investment equation, not even in the form of changes in the rate of interest. Restrictions on the availability of bank credit, which at times have been an important part of monetary policy, may have affected investment plans directly (as in Sweden) rather than via the consequent changes of liquidity (in the form of bank deposits).

There are other uncertainties about the investment function in the model that should be taken up in this conection. The method of introducing supply conditions as a nonlinear function of unemployment is just one of many alternatives. This very special capacity impact curve will have a pronounced effect on business investment when full employment is reached: for instance a decrease of unemployment from 1 to 0.5 per cent will, all other things being equal, according to the equation, be followed by a rise of the value of investment by 6 per cent. Situations will appear, however, and the conditions will vary as between branches of activity, when changing scarcity of labor is *not* closely related to the utilization of plant capacity and demand for new investment. The accumulation of new capital during years of high investment intensity can, for example, result in specific over-capacity tendencies in individual branches and in this way modify the relationship describing total investment over a period of time. In the CPB model eventual developments of this type are in part taken care of in an indirect way via the nonwage-income or profit variable. But obviously, to the extent that the mechanism in such instances is really working via, say, an acceleration or capital stock adjustment process modified by related profit and liquidity changes, then the CPB investment function used will be doubtful from the "fundamentalist point of view" of how the economy "really" works.

An acceptable statistical closeness of fit concerning each

equation in a system is not a sufficiently discriminating criterion. Different sets of equations would imply different theories of change being embodied in the equations considered as a system. Such a critical view is perhaps not very useful from the pragmatic point of view. However, the intention here is only to point to the *need* for specifying an explicit theory of change incorporating our understanding of the economic interrelationships during the cycle in order to reach a critical evaluation of the validity of an econometric model. Therefore an evaluation with the help of careful theoretical reasoning will always be in place as a "productive disturbance" to counteract any tendency toward complacency in the minds of model builders and model users.

As discussed above, the CPB model offers policy authorities the possibility of making stimulating exercises in the analysis of multiplier effects over the whole economy. This raises the question as to how stable the various coefficients are, both during the various phases of a cycle and over longer periods of time. To an outsider it would be most surprising if the multiplier effects of, for instance, an export decline in the depression year of 1931 would be about the same as the consequences of an expenditure increase in the full employment boom of 1956 or 1960. We have in mind not only problems of changing structure and reaction patterns for firms and consumers over such a long time span. The interesting problem from a stabilization point of view refers to the short-term variability of the coefficients over the different phases of the cycle. Except for the curvilinear factor mentioned, the multiplier effects are derived from the demand side. But there must be complex interrelations between demand and supply during most of the expansion periods, and predominantly demand-governed developments during the downturn. In short, there may not be much of stable reversibility in some of the relations: the entrepreneurial reactions especially must be expected to be quite different in response to increases of demand and liquidity during the expansion phase as compared with declines during a contraction period. As discussed in Chapter 3, variability in time lags may also be a serious complication that is not considered in the CPB econometric system, and this possibility may be of strategic importance with regard to any discussion about the effects of policy changes.

Behind much of the skepticism expressed here as to the explanatory efficiency of the CPB econometric model lies also the crucial question referring to the *large aggregates* being used. How much of the relatively small variations in activity during the postwar period refer to specific cycles of a few branches of industry? Do we not neglect a lot of essential information by utilizing the big aggregates of the model? The theoretical shortcomings of the system and the possibly consequent high inequality coefficients may be traced to the neglect of the varying contributions to cyclical change of different branches of activity. If efforts were made to disaggregate and catch the varying contents of the big aggregates, then there would be room for intensive application of truly dynamic short-term systems of explanation in each activity, by following more or less complete *sequences* of events, for instance between orders to deliveries.[28] However, such an approach would mean introducing a number of complications, and most important it would mean making the model much less straightforward in its direct application to policy analysis and planning. The great ad-

28. Much new ground in the directions indicated has been broken in a recent contribution: Jean-Claude Schoenman, *An Analog of Short-Period Economic Change* (Stockholm, 1966). In this book the theoretical mechanism of short-period change is developed basically at the micro level. This consists of a fully explicit demand and supply system permitting adjustments between the two sides. These adjustments take place via changes in all types of current stocks (liquidity, goods, labor, unfilled orders, etc.). This means that regard is paid to changes of lags in the relations between the flows attached to these stocks, and in that context also to price and wage variables. This type of mechanism is then transferred to a set of sectors covering the economy. The conceptual system has been applied in the form of an econometric model of the postwar French economy.

vantage of simplicity and direct adaptability to policy questions would be lost.

It is clear that the economists responsible for the handling of the CPB model are very aware of these and other weaknesses of their system of analysis. Some of these weaknesses are unavoidable because of the limited supply of statistical information, determined for instance by the need to have a sufficient number of years for the regression analysis. Other weaknesses are being continuously repaired by means of a steady improvement process.

7 "EXPLOSIVE" GROWTH AND GROWTH INTERRUPTIONS IN JAPAN

THE STATISTICAL PICTURE

A look at Japan's table of annual changes in GNP and its components (in the Appendix) immediately gives the impression of some specific features of postwar economic development in Japan:

1. The very rapid pace of economic growth; from 1950 to 1964 GNP (in real terms) advanced on average by nearly 10 per cent per year. During the boom period 1959–61 real GNP rose by 15 per cent.
2. The relatively high share of fixed domestic investment and the relatively low share of private consumption in the growth of total output.
3. The wide amplitude of fluctuations in inventory investment and in imports.
4. The steady but relatively slow expansion of private consumption.

The overwhelming impression, of course, is of the swift pace of Japan's economic development. Since we are not directly interested in the immediate postwar reconstruction and reorganization, we shall in general take as starting points 1950, or rather 1952–53 when prewar per capita standards were reattained and the economy was relieved from the inflationary Korean boom which exerted a strong upward push to the Japanese economy.[1]

1. For an excellent account of the radical reorganization of the economic and social structure of Japan during the early postwar period,

The instability in Japan's GNP growth rate is relatively high, at least in comparison with some other countries with high growth rates (Germany, Italy). The yearly growth rate has varied between a little over 3 per cent in 1954 and 1958 and a maximum of over 17 per cent in 1959. The impression of cyclical instability becomes even stronger if we measure the variations of real GNP with the help of seasonally adjusted quarterly data between turning points.

TABLE 7.1

Variations of Seasonally Adjusted Quarterly Real GNP
Change in per cent

Trough to peak		Peak to trough	
1951–53	+31	1953–54	−8
1954–57	+37	1957–58	−4
1958–61	+60	1961–62	+2

The immense strength of the expansion periods stands in impressive contrast to the short setbacks. The recession periods are very short, the declines lasting between one and four quarters. The following revival very quickly gathers momentum and breeds an "explosive" rate of expansion. There is not much sign of retardation of growth before the upward surge suddenly breaks. One gets the impression of some kind of exogenous disturbance putting a sudden stop to the growth "explosion." (See Japan's case in Figure 3.2.)

We get a first insight into the growth process and its cyclical deviations by looking at the aggregate composition of GNP changes. Table 7.2 shows the average contribution of each GNP component to the mean rate of growth in total GNP dur-

---

including the deflationary "Dodge episode" of 1949–50, see G. C. Allen, *Japan's Economic Recovery* (London, 1958).

ing 1950–64 according to Japan's table in the Appendix. In Table 7.3 we put this growth pattern in contrast to the cyclical composition of the GNP changes during years of boom and recession.

TABLE 7.2

Long-term Growth Composition, 1950-64

	Average annual growth rate related to GNP	Share in growth (as a percentage)
Private consumption	4.7	46
Government expenditures	1.9	19
Private fixed investment	2.7	27
Inventory investment	0.6	6
Exports	2.0	20
Imports	−1.8	−18
GNP	10.1	100

Source: Table on Japan in the Appendix.

TABLE 7.3

Cyclical Percentage Composition of GNP Changes

	Boom years 1950–52, 1955–56, 1959–61, 1963–64 (average annual growth rate 12.6 per cent)	Recession years 1954, 1958, 1962 (average annual growth rate 3.6 per cent)
Private consumption	41	80
Government expenditures	15	52
Private fixed investment	27	9
Inventory investment	18	−94
Exports	18	33
Imports	−19	20
GNP	100	100

Source: Table on Japan in the Appendix.

There are a number of interesting features appearing in this table. In the years of very rapid expansion, the main propelling force was apparently private fixed investments, and in this category mainly expenditures for equipment and machinery. The stimulus from investment in inventories was strongly concentrated in some of the boom years (1955 and 1959), when its marginal share was over 40 per cent of the GNP increase. Total private investment expenditures accounted for up to two thirds of the GNP increase during some of the expansion years.

We find the patterns reversed during the recession years. The reversal of stock investment seems to explain most of the recession (that is the retardation of growth). If the yearly rise of inventories had been kept up during the recession years at

FIGURE 7.1
Industrial Production and Value of Imports

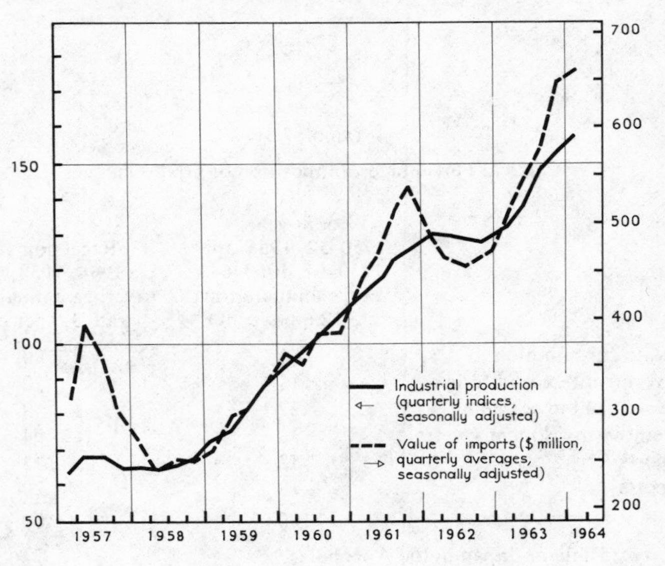

its average rate (corresponding to about 0.6 per cent of GNP), then also GNP growth would have been close to its average rate (that is around 10 per cent per year). This is of course only "mechanical arithmetic" and tells nothing about causal relations. But the calculation gives a notion of the order of

FIGURE 7.2
Quarterly Development of Private Fixed Investment and Inventory Investment, 1953–64

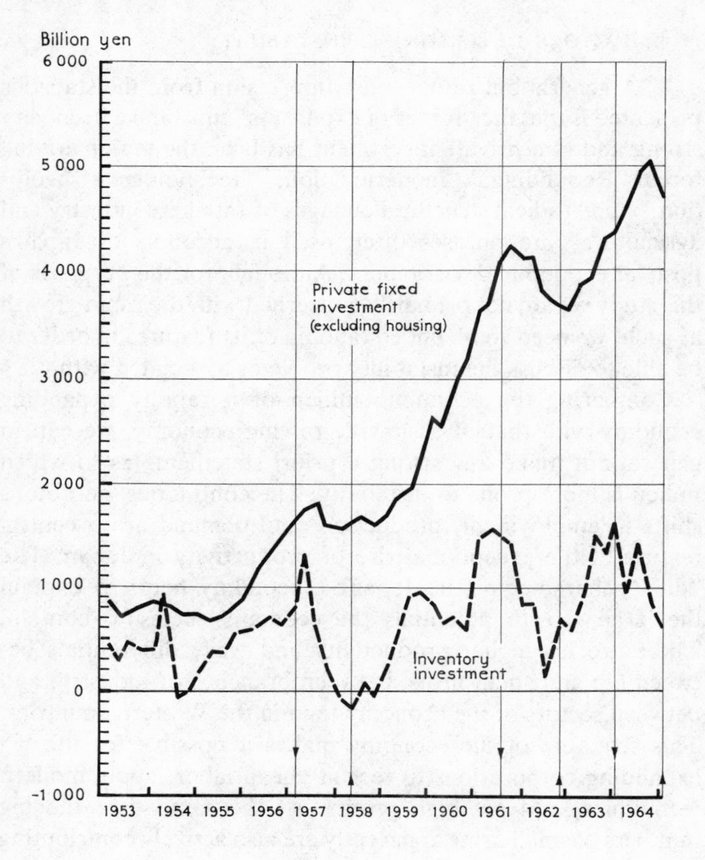

importance of the fluctuations of inventory investment. Table 7.3 also indicates the reversed order of importance of the other components: the much higher marginal importance of private consumption, government expenditures, and also exports in the retarded growth rate during the recession years.

Figures 7.1 and 7.2 give some impression of the statistical characteristics of the cyclical movements of private fixed investment, inventory investment, imports, and industrial production.

FACTORS DETERMINING INSTABILITY

A general but rather loose impression from the statistics presented is that the "forces of expansion" must have been very strong and that private investment has been the major driving force. "Rebuilding," "modernization," "technological revolution," and "radical structural changes of Japanese industry and agriculture" are phrases often used in accounts of Japan's postwar economic development. Although, for the purposes of this study we are not primarily concerned with the rapid growth as such, we need some understanding of its features in order to be able to discuss the instability problems associated with it.

Comparing the economic milieu of a rapidly expanding economy with that of a slowly growing economy, we can in general not make any strong a priori statements as to which milieu is more prone to instability. The continuous, enormous shifts in employment, production, and demand are a central feature of the exceptional rise of productivity in Japan. The "dual" character of the Japanese economy helps to explain the large growth potentials the economy seems to contain. There are far higher productivity and wage differentials between big and small firms, between branches of industry, and between sectors of the economy than in the Western countries. This structure of the economy makes it possible for the big expanding corporations to recruit cheap labor, apply modern techniques, and get high profits. At the same time the big numbers of small firms apparently are also actively contributing to the general growth process, stimulated by subcontracts from the large corporations, subsidized by low wage rates, and satisfying their capital needs on well-developed markets for secondhand machines. The annual issues of the *Economic Survey of Japan*[2] give an impressive account of how rapidly labor is moving from agriculture to industry, what a surprisingly large part of the increase in manufacturing production is accounted for by special growth industries with high and rapidly rising productivity,[3] what a large proportion of the rise in output consists of new products, and so on. There are, of course, also correspondingly rapid changes in the demand for productive resources and finished products.

Is it not reasonable to suspect that an economy in process of exceptional structural change might be rather susceptible to shocks? The concentration of the growth results in certain branches of activity may imply special risks of backfiring on home and export markets. On the other hand, these risks should be mitigated by the fact that Japanese economic growth largely consists of a catching-up process in relation to the more advanced Western countries, rather than of a pioneering into new fields of technology and demand. The existence of big differences in the pace at which this lag is reduced in different sectors, together with the flexibility of the production factors, would seem to permit a quick redirection of the latter to previously neglected fields in case of saturation or overshooting in some fields.

2. Published by the Economic Planning Agency (EPA) of the Japanese government. See, in particular, the 1960–61 issue. The mass of facts elaborated in tables and diagrams in these voluminous annual reports is impressive.

3. Referring especially to various branches of the machinery industry, the chemical, synthetic fibers, steel, construction, and oil refining industries. In EPA, *Economic Survey of Japan 1963–64*, p. 47, there is an account of the high rate of transformation of the Japanese industrial structure as compared to other countries (using coefficients of structural change).

FIGURE 7.3
Postwar Growth of GNP and Extrapolation of Interwar Trend

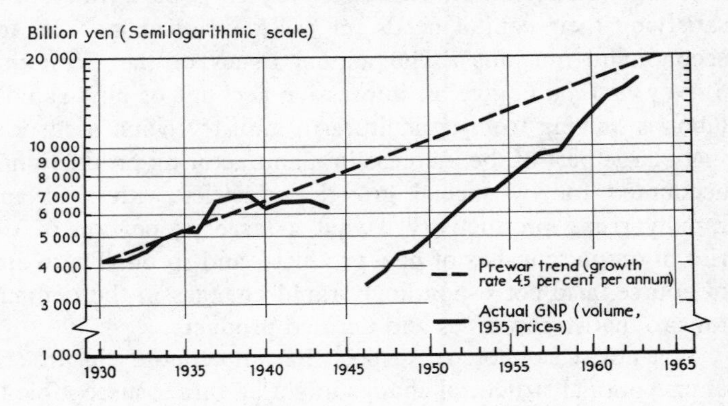

We may get a notion of the extent of the catching-up process in Japanese growth from Figure 7.3. In 1953 GNP had about reached the maximum prewar level. But with regard to an extrapolation of the interwar trend of 4.6 per cent per year, the actual 1953 figure was about 50 per cent below the trend level. The graph gives a strong impression of the tremendous "room for expansion," or a gap that in some mysterious way seems to be pulling up the GNP curve to its explosive postwar growth rate. Such a mechanical way of looking at the catching-up process certainly does not offer much explanatory evidence. However—as argued above—the picture of "room for growth" should imply the conception of a big potential for rapid rise of productivity that can be realized, if *demand conditions* are sufficiently favorable.

The very rapid development of Japanese aggregate demand has been associated with the danger of an overheating of the economy, manifesting itself in excess demand for goods and services. In fact, this problem became acute repeatedly, in 1950–51, 1956–57, 1960–61, and 1963, but given the magnitude of the increases in total demand (reaching above 20 per cent per year) the open inflation has been surprisingly modest since the end of the Korean war boom and up to 1960. During the period 1952–60, the GNP price deflator has on average not risen more than about 2 per cent per year. In manufacturing, wage rates did advance three to four times as rapidly, but thanks to the phenomenal rise of productivity (10 per cent per year in manufacturing industry), labor costs per unit of output actually declined. It is interesting in this connection to observe the big variability of wage increases in manufacturing industry over the cycle.[4]

Apparently, the high flexibility of the economy permitting continuous large shifts of labor out of agriculture and other low productivity fields must be given considerable credit for the price stability. But as the boom periods have shown, these flexibilities, although very considerable, do have their limits. This has more clearly become the case after 1960, when rising labor shortages and consequent rapid wage increases (especially in low-wage sectors) are paralled by an acceleration of the increase in the consumers' price level to around 6 per cent per year.

As shown in the first section, private gross fixed investment has risen by almost 30 per cent per year in the period 1953–61, whereas private consumption has shown a much smaller annual increase (of 7 per cent). This tremendous rate of investment increase—implying an average investment ratio of 40 per cent in 1962 (including government investment)—has been the main propulsion force of the rapid rise of total demand. Business cycle theory demonstrates the instability risks involved in a rapidly *rising and high investment ratio:*

1. There are problems of financing—depending on the sufficiency and distribution of savings, as well as on the functioning of the credit system.

4. For example, in 1956 and in 1961 wages per employed in manufacturing rose by 11 to 13 per cent, whereas in 1954–55 and 1957–58 the rise in earnings was negligible. This flexibility of wage rates is to a considerable extent determined by the unique payment system with sizable bonuses to employees during prosperity.

2. There are questions with regard to cumulative increases of capacity and the productivity effects of investment. To what extent will there be markets for the enlarged supplies, and what implications arise for the utilization of capacity?

3. The investment data quoted above point to an unstable situation with respect to investment acceleration; investments are apparently to an unusually large extent made for expanding the production capacity of the investment and construction industries. Japanese input-output studies for this period show that more than 40 per cent of the output of the investment goods industries were directed to that purpose. According to these estimates, a 100 billion yen increase of investment in plant and equipment will, via enlarged needs for steel, other metals, machinery, electricity, and so forth, require additional investment of 200 billion yen.[5] Due to a higher frequency of bottlenecks in the 1955–57 boom, this type of inter-investment acceleration was considerably weaker at that time than in 1958–60.

Table 7.4[6] gives an impression of the spectacular rise in the gross investment ratio since 1953. The comparisons with the GNP growth rate show how exceptionally low the marginal capital-output ratio seems to be. These low ratios are partly explained by the fact that the increase in cooperating manpower has been relatively high. The main explanation must, however, be the unusual domination of relatively short-term investment in machinery and equipment—and the extremely low share of residential and also public infrastructure investments. Table 7.4 gives evidence both of the acceleration effects of the rapid increase of demand (GNP) and of the high productivity of investment.

For a very rapidly growing economy, the development of the balance of payments is particularly important. Imports are

5. *Economic Survey of Japan, 1960–61,* p. 204.

6. The table is taken from OECD, *Economic Surveys: Japan,* (Paris, 1965), p. 40.

TABLE 7.4

Growth of Investment and GNP

	Annual rate of increase in GNP		Total fixed investment as a percentage of GNP	Private fixed investment as a percentage of GNP[a]	Apparent gross marginal capital output ratios	
	1.		2.	3.	2:1	3:1
1954–56	7.4	1953–55	21.1	11.0	2.9	1.5
1957–60	10.3	1956–59	26.2	15.9	2.5	1.5
1961–64	10.8	1960–63	35.2	21.0	3.3	1.9

a. Excluding residential construction.

likely to expand with the growth of output in general, and in boom periods this tendency becomes even stronger. If exports of goods and services and other sources of foreign exchange do not keep pace with the rise of imports, growth is likely to become retarded because of the restrictions necessary to lessen the drain on the country's gold and foreign exchange reserves. There are, as we know (see Chapter 1), two stability issues involved here. It may be that the longer-term developments of foreign trade at a given GNP growth rate tend toward disequilibrium, implying restraints on growth. This is largely the case in the United Kingdom. The other alternative refers to short-term disequilibria in the expansion of foreign trade and the balance of payments, being the more usual case. Such short-term balance of payments disturbances apply to the case of Japan.

Japan's longer-term dependence on imports seems to have remained rather stable in value terms since its rapid recovery from the extremely low levels of the first postwar years. The ratio of import value to GNP has fluctuated around 11 to 13 per cent. However, this relative stability has been the result of a substantial decline of import prices in later years, offsetting the rising tendency of the ratio of import volume to GNP (from 12½ per cent to 15½ per cent). The rise in the latter ratio is a consequence of the increasing importance of manufacturing output in total production, compensated only partly by a fall in import requirements per unit of output in most industries and a reduction in the dependence on food imports. But in boom years, the marginal import-GNP ratio (the marginal propensity to import) has been as high as two thirds. As shown above, this has been largely due to the behavior of inventory investment and its relationship to the import of raw materials and fuels. It even seems likely that the existence of import controls during certain periods has tended to raise import requirements, since the uncertainty about receiving a quota, especially in boom times, with rising expectations of balance of payments restrictions, may have induced higher inventory holdings. However, on the whole, the existence of import controls, especially on motor cars, must have kept the average propensity to import lower than it would have been in the absence of such restrictions. After 1960 Japanese import policies have become freer; at the end of 1963 about 90 per cent of imports were liberalized (against 40 per cent in 1960).

The average annual increase of the volume of exports has apparently been sufficient over the longer run to cover the import needs associated with the very rapid rate of growth during most of this period. This advance of exports doubled Japan's share in world exports between 1951 and 1960. Japan's export market shares have been increasing markedly in the United States and in the primary producing countries. However, as the pre-World War II peak level of the volume of exports was not passed until 1959, Japan's share of 3.6 per cent in 1963 is still considerably below the share it had attained once.

The postwar rise of exports has certainly been a principal condition for allowing the country's growth potential to be realized to such an unusual extent. It is interesting to look at some of the factors behind the rise of exports, which may also be relevant for a study of cyclical disturbances. From the point of view of country distribution, Japan's export trade has not been especially favored. On the contrary, during the period in question the main export countries have been the United States (taking about one third of the value of Japan's exports) and underdeveloped countries in Asia, Africa, and South America (taking about one half). These are country groups with relatively low general growth rates as compared with Western Europe as a region. It is the high competitiveness and aggressiveness of Japanese export industries that have been important. Japan has not only been able to maintain the export advantages of its exchange rate as fixed in 1949 but has become even more competitive by a reduction of its export prices in relation to other countries, where the rise in wage costs has not been so amply matched by the advance of productivity.[7] Here we have an interesting case with what is hypothetically an undervalued currency—according to price and cost comparisons and to judge from the rate of export expansion—that has not manifested itself in a balance of payments surplus. On the contrary the rapid growth of national income (that to some part may be regarded as a multiplier result of the rising exports) has tended to create such a rapid rise of imports that balance of payments restrictions have repeatedly become actual. This expansion process has, up to the beginning of the 1960s, not created much of the European type of cost inflation that would eliminate the undervaluation. The rapid rise of productivity associated with the growth process, together with an elastic supply of labor at relatively slowly rising wage rates, has tended to imply a conservation of Japan's export cost advantage position. The tremendously high rate of investment in the growth industries has not only boosted productivity but also expanded Japan's capacity for producing goods particularly favored by the trends in world demand. The relative concentration of growth in these branches characterized by a high income elasticity of domestic and foreign demand has on the other hand raised Japan's sensitivity to declines in economic activity at home or abroad.

It appears that the continued rapid expansion of the home market for consumption and investment goods has strongly promoted Japan's success in entering foreign markets with new and high quality products. This proposition is supported especially by the experience in various branches of the machinery industry, where there is a clear positive correlation between

7. See EPA, *Economic Survey of Japan 1961–62,* p. 361. Miyohei Shinohara, *Growth and Cycles in the Japanese Economy,* (Tokyo, 1962) has tried to estimate the degree of undervaluation of the Japanese yen. He reaches very high values and argues that this is an important factor of explanation (p. 33).

the growth of domestic and export sales.[8] However, we can never be quite certain as to the causal relations here. There occurred an acceleration of Japanese exports during the recessions of 1958 and 1961–62 that very well can be attributed to increased export capacity following lower pressure from home demand. In the same way it could also be argued, on the line of the debate in the United Kingdom (see Chapter 4), that exports from Japan would have expanded still more with less pressure from home demand. The slower increases of export receipts in 1953, 1956–57, and 1960–61 might partly be taken as an indication of the unfavorable effects of a drastic short-term rise of domestic demand.

The coincidence of these periods of export sluggishness with the start of recessions in Japan's major customer country, the United States, should not be overlooked. Actually, after adjusting for unequal trends, a considerable degree of conformity between Japanese exports to the United States and industrial production in the United States is apparent.[9] The growth trend of Japan's exports to the United States has been so strong that no actual declines from one year to the next have occurred —only retardations in growth. However, if we compare quarters, there have been declines in exports to the United States both in 1953–54 and 1959–60.[10] In fact there has been more instability in Japanese exports to underdeveloped countries in Asia, Africa, and South America (taking about 50 per cent of Japanese exports), with rather sharp export downturns in 1952–53, 1954–55, and 1957–58 that are closely connected with export setbacks and exchange difficulties of these regions. These difficulties can again be regarded as partly secondary effects of American recessions. But the total of Japan's volume of exports shows an unbroken growth line over the whole

8. See Chart 28 on p. 29 of EPA, *Economic Survey of Japan 1960–61*.

9. Exports to the United States accounted for one third of Japan's exports in 1960.

10. Ibid., pp. 209–11.

period, although with pronounced retardation in 1958, when the index rose by 3 per cent only, and again in 1960–61.

SOME FEATURES OF THE JAPANESE BUSINESS CYCLE

As pictured in Figure 7.2 above the cycles come out clearly in inventory investment and private fixed investment in equipment and machinery. The growth line for GNP does not seem equally interesting from that point of view, although the variations in the growth rate are quite evident. The actual disturbances in Japan's economic growth process have instead so far been dominated by the interconnections between variations in inventory investment, the balance of payments, and economic policy. Nevertheless, the dynamics of a high growth rate have had considerable influence on the actual course of the cyclical movements. We shall return to this problem at the end of the chapter. In the context of rapid long-term growth, Japan's business cycles have manifested themselves primarily in the rates of change of demand and output variables rather than in the interruption of growth by absolute declines. Total final demand, that is GNP minus inventory investment, has either held or advanced its level during most of the recession quarters.

The instability of inventory investment has been closely related to economic policy changes, which in turn are mainly a reaction to fluctuations in the balance of payments. During boom periods with rapidly rising profits and investment the value of imports of goods and services has tended to rise much more rapidly than the corresponding value of exports. This tendency, together with budget surpluses arising out of rapidly rising tax returns, has had the usual automatic effects on liquidity conditions. On top of this, the deterioration of the foreign exchange position has forced the authorities into restrictive action, reversing the trend in inventory investment and slowing down the rate of growth. Due to the fast and strong impact of such measures in Japan, it has been possible to relax the brakes on the economy rather quickly and so to enable a return to the spectacular overall growth. In the recessions, imports showed large declines relative to exports. So, for example, in 1957–58—apparently largely as a consequence of the restrictive policy measures introduced at the beginning of 1957—the quarterly volume of imports of goods and services declined by 14 per cent whereas the corresponding export figure still rose by 1 per cent. Due to a coinciding decline in the prices of Japan's imports not matched on the export side, the improvement of the current account balance was even greater.

THE FINANCING OF INVESTMENT AND THE ROLE OF MONETARY POLICY

The stabilization policy measures carried out during the boom periods must be regarded as an important part of the reaction mechanism of the Japanese economy, responding to endogenous and exogenous deviations from a balanced growth pattern. There are some peculiarities in the Japanese policy setting which point to some interesting new aspects of the potential possibilities of monetary policy.

As mentioned above, one of the central issues regarding the stability of economic growth in Japan refers to the financing of the rapidly increasing private investment. A total gross investment ratio reaching almost 40 per cent in 1960 (including government investment) and, still more, the tremendous pace of private investment during cyclical expansions, imply the need for a high and rising supply of savings as well as a considerable flexibility in the credit system.

It is easy to imagine several reasons for the tendency to high savings ratios in a setting of rapid economic growth. Government revenues tend to increase more rapidly than expected owing to high tax yields on increased private income. The tendencies toward rapidly increasing tax yields and rising budget surpluses during the boom periods have, however, been partly offset by cuts in tax rates and increases of government expenditures. In fact the fiscal policy measures have largely been procyclical, partly due to bad timing of the measures.[11] The Japanese authorities have adhered strongly to the principles of the balanced budget or a "neutral budget" and have not systematically applied fiscal policy as an anticyclical instrument.[12] We can therefore concentrate attention on monetary policy.

The same tendency toward rising surpluses during the booms works with much greater impact on private profits. The advance of total wage payments tends to lag behind the rapid rise of total revenues. As pointed out above, between 1952 and 1961 the continued increase of labor productivity has on average been larger than the rise in hourly wage rates at the same time as the price level has been rising slowly. It is, as usual, difficult to get reliable direct information about the development of profit rates and total profits. According to available statistics, during the period 1955–60 an increase of GNP by 70 per cent was accompanied by a rise of corporate profits four times as rapid. It is interesting to note in this connection that this rise in profits was very much concentrated in the growth industries (such as motor cars, industrial machinery, electric equipment, plastics, aluminum) where net profits in relation to very rapidly growing sales rose steadily with hardly any retardation in 1958, in contrast to the more "stagnant" branches (such as shipbuilding, coal, paper, pulp, textiles) where the profit rate has tended to decline and showed quite wide cyclical fluctuations.[13] In considering the total of Japanese savings, we must look also at the savings habits of the numerous smaller firms as well as the savings habits of wage earners. The intense

11. See Hugh T. Patrick, "Cyclical Instability and Fiscal-Monetary Policy in Postwar Japan," mimeographed paper, September 1963.

12. See OECD, *Economic Surveys: Japan* (Paris, December 1965), p. 28.

13. EPA, *Economic Survey of Japan 1960–61*, p. 97.

growth and investment ambitions of the small firms seem to compel them to do their utmost to save—not least in recession times when a credit squeeze tends to fall on them particularly heavily. The high savings propensity of the Japanese wage earner seems to result from traditional thriftiness, a peculiar wage system with large bonus payments, and an inadequate social security system with relatively little protection in case of unemployment and old age. The latter factor is even more important, as the age composition of the population contains an unusually small percentage of people in the high age bracket who tend to be "dissavers." In any case, the official statistics show a savings propensity of households completely out of line with the usual figures of Western countries.[14]

The factors mentioned above thus make it plausible that the high total savings ratio in Japan has been positively influenced by the rapid growth rate, this influence being especially effective via the savings propensities of firms and corporations. One central feature of Japanese development is, however, that investment is highly concentrated in the industrial sector; it is interesting to note that house construction represents only about 10 per cent of total fixed private investment, while the corresponding rate in Sweden, for example, is about 40 per cent. In spite of high average rates of retained profits, Japanese firms have in the postwar period been self-financing their investment only to a very limited extent. In the boom years of 1956–57 and 1960–61, savings out of corporation profits covered on average only about 30 per cent of total investment expenditures. This means that the high and rising profits were far from sufficient to finance current investment expenditures. The main explanation for the low average degree of self-financ-

14. Japan's ratio of personal savings to disposable income of 14.4 per cent compares with ratios varying between 4.4 per cent for the United Kingdom and 9.6 for the Netherlands. (United Nations Yearbook of National Accounts.) Shinohara refers to budget studies according to which workers' households have average savings ratios of 16 per cent (p. 238).

ing of Japanese enterprises is of course the tremendously high rate of fixed and inventory investment during the booms. But we must also pay attention to the usual maldistribution among enterprises of savings out of profits compared with their current investment expenditures; the demand for credit is partly a function of this distribution.

Out of the external funds for covering the deficit in savings the major part (around 75 per cent) consisted of bank loans.[15] The strategic role of bank financing is in fact a remarkable characteristic of postwar Japanese investment financing. During boom years, the advances of commercial banks have been increasing up to 50 per cent per year, making possible the tremendous expansion of investment in plant, equipment, and inventories. Without this credit creation such record investment booms would not have been feasible.

Following some older lines of argument in the savings-investment controversies during the 1930s,[16] it could be maintained that "planned" savings, or rather savings out of "last year's" income, are quite insufficient for such rapidly rising investment as in postwar Japan. The gap had to be covered by new bank credits, implying "forced savings" which, ex post, at the increased national income corresponded to saving out of increased profits, household incomes, and government surpluses. In fact this is a rather good interpretation of the process of "financing" the investment boom in Japan. The tremendous increase of private investment apparently necessitated some kind of "Vorfinanzierung," as the liquidity situation of the

15. For a discussion of this problem, see Hubert F. Schiffer, *The Modern Japanese Banking System* (New York, 1962). As described in the EPA *Economic Survey of Japan 1961–62,* there was less dependence on bank credit and more financing by means of stocks and bonds during the 1961 boom. However, indirectly as well as directly, there was still heavy dependence on bank financing and rapid increase of bank credit.

16. See for example the discussion of the place of planned savings in a "model sequence" in E. Lundberg, *Studies in the Theory of Economic Expansion* (Stockholm, 1937), Chap. 9.

"pushing" corporations was predominantly very weak with liquidity very unevenly distributed. The economic mechanism "saw to it" that incomes, consumption, and savings increased in such a way that the savings-investment identities were satisfied, also eventually implying some relatively stable relationships as to marginal savings and import propensities.

There are some necessary conditions to be fulfilled for such an expansion process to go on. The banks should be able and willing to expand credit at the required very rapid rate, implying among other things that the Bank of Japan would be willing to supply them and the community with desired cash. The corporations and other firms should also be willing to finance investment by means of bank loans (stock and bond issues to a limited extent) to a degree far above the limits usual in European countries. There exists in Japan a tradition of very high dependence on bank credit financing; however, this tendency seems to have become even more pronounced during the postwar period. As in other countries, enterprises seeking funds to finance investment have also had other potential sources. There is, for instance, some government lending (from special funds and institutions) to certain industries, but the scale is not important from a global point of view. There is also a certain volume of industrial bond issues (controlled by the Bank of Japan) and possibilities of raising funds by means of stock issues. However, these sources of financing have so far been of limited importance in comparison to bank loans. It is characteristic of the Japanese system of investment financing that the city banks (which directly and indirectly dominate the lending business) seem to concentrate their lending on big business, favoring the large enterprises and their investment projects, and this is especially so during boom periods with credit restrictions. Small firms have chances of bank borrowing in the short recession periods, when the banks have surplus funds; otherwise they must to a large extent rely on trade credits.

The incentives for new investment, especially in the growth

industries, have apparently been so strong during these years that there has been no reluctance to finance investment by borrowing at the high effective bank rates prevailing (10 to 12 per cent, including cost of compensating balance holding). The rising revenues and profits seem to have justified the expansion of bank loans. The commercial banks have in their turn been willing to engage themselves heavily in rapidly expanding industrial loans, partly of a long-term nature, and to take big risks involved in low cash ratios, "operating at levels of illiquidity that would drive an English or American banker into a state of permanent neurosis."[17] The tremendously rapid expansion of bank lending during the boom periods has implied that the banks have had to operate with substantial short-term funds from the call market and with credits from the Bank of Japan. This is the so-called "growth money." In the late stages of the boom, city bank borrowing from the central bank has risen above 10 per cent of their own loans and investments. This means that the position of the banks tended to become very vulnerable to the supply of outside funds as the boom proceeded—and the same holds true for the rapidly expanding enterprises.

There is no apparent automatic balancing mechanism in this engine of expansion, checking a too-rapid development of credits and investments. It is the repeated experience of Japanese postwar development that an expansion of the sort described gets out of hand, so that the economy becomes "overheated" with serious consequences for the balance of payments. It is possible that *if* serious exchange reserve losses had *not* occurred in 1953, 1957, 1961, and (although more doubtful) in 1963, the expansion could have continued until "too much" inflation would have come about, and restrictive policy would have had to follow, or until the investment boom, especially in inventories but perhaps ultimately also in machines, had broken its own back. Anyhow, on those four oc-

17. *The Economist* (September 1, 1962).

casions restrictive monetary policies had to be introduced rather soon due to the foreign exchange situation *before* such other factors had created disturbances.

The lag structure is of considerable interest when discussing this range of policy issues. The decline of foreign exchange reserves is in Japan the important signal of the need for restrictive measures. However, as usual, there is a rather long *decision lag*. The strong desire to maintain and stimulate economic growth may be one factor. Anyhow we can observe a lag of about half a year between the peak in exchange reserves and the introduction of restrictive policies. On the other hand we may notice a very quick reaction of the economy to these restrictive policies, particularly with regard to inventory investment and imports. There is thus an unusually short *effect lag;* each time the balance of payments situation has very quickly improved substantially. Another interesting aspect of the policy lags refers to the observation that the actual decline of foreign exchange reserves has lagged in relation to the deficit in the current balance of payments because of the inflow of short-term capital that has been closely related to the rise of imports. But again the balance of payments deficits can in turn be regarded as lagged effects of the too-rapid rise of demand and demand inflation that started much earlier during the expansion. We may in this way explain how and why the restrictive policies in Japan have come about at a very late stage of the boom.

The policy restrictions have, as already mentioned, mainly referred to monetary measures. In the 1953–54 crisis, a certain amount of fiscal restraint was also introduced, but in 1957–58 and 1960–61 the government, in fact, carried on an expansionary budget policy, lowering tax rates on the first occasion and increasing expenditures on both occasions. The most interesting part of the Japanese case refers to the high efficiency of monetary policy in breaking the boom, and, as this appears most clearly in the period 1957–58, we shall concentrate our attention on this case.

It is evident that monetary policy should have particularly

good possibilities to become effective under the conditions of investment financing described above. The very high dependence on bank credit financing must make the investment propensity sensitive to changes in the credit supply. And as the commercial banks are very heavily dependent on the Bank of Japan for their supply of liquidity, this represents the best possible case for effective monetary policy. The discount rate of the Bank of Japan was raised in May 1957; the bank also introduced a strong credit squeeze, as well as "moral suasion," especially as to certain forms of credit (for example for import financing). High penalty rates were used to prevent borrowing at the central bank from being profitable. The rise of the call money rate to 22 per cent around midyear may be indicative of the degree of monetary restraint. As is often the case when we try to read off the degree of credit squeeze, the behavior of loans and advances from the commercial banks gives no clear evidence of the degree of restraint. The sum of outstanding loans continued to rise during 1957 and 1958, although at a retarded rate. But this retarded increase of supply apparently implied a severe disturbance to the expanded demand that had been made vulnerable because of lower profits or actual losses, as well as surplus inventory stocks.

The most interesting observation to make about the consequences of the monetary restraint is its very quick effects. Within a few months there were noticeable symptoms of reduced purchases and efforts to cut down inventories.[18] Apparently, wholesale and import firms were most vulnerable to the reduced credit supply and were reached most quickly. They had to restrict purchases, especially of imported goods, in order to bring down inventories. This tendency applied a little later to manufacturing firms and corporations. A drastic cut in the supply of funds—especially to firms in weak positions—had to be met by a quick reduction in purchases, a reaction that in

18. There is an interesting account of the effects of the tight money policy in the *Economic Survey of Japan 1957–58,* pp. 213–32.

most cases became effective more rapidly than a reduction of fixed investment. Smaller firms were hit first. According to bank statistics the increments in loans to small firms had already reached a peak in 1956, but for big corporations the peak occurred first during 1957.[19] The big corporations, being very dependent on bank credits, were also hit by the restraint, partly in the form of a refusal of new loans.[20] When they tried to meet the shortage of funds by reducing purchases, by stepping up collection of trade credits, and by postponing payments to (often small) supplying firms, the effects of the credit squeeze became transmitted throughout the economy. A number of small firms felt the pinch especially hard. Many went into bankruptcy, and their stocks were sold out—with falling prices as a consequence.

The real effects of the tight monetary policy appeared quickly. The quarterly value of imports went down by about 30 per cent from the peak level in the first quarter of 1957, and the index of import volume was reduced by over 20 per cent between 1957 and 1958. This reduction to a large extent resulted from the decline in inventory investment that had already started in the second quarter of 1957. As there was also some reduction in fixed investment from 1957 to 1958, industrial production declined for a short period. A most important result of the policy was a quick reversal of the balance of payments, following the rapidly declining imports and the rising exports. (As mentioned above, the rise was probably partly an effect of the weaker home demand.) Already at the end of 1957 exchange reserves started to rise. In the middle of 1958, the discount rates were lowered and the credit squeeze eliminated, and after that a new wave of rapid expansion started.

An interesting aspect of this successful case of monetary policy is that the results were achieved quickly, and, partly because of this, there were no longer-term dampening effects

19. See Shinohara, p. 188.

20. See the interesting graph on p. 232 of the *Economic Survey of Japan 1958–59,* showing "the rate of sufficiency in long-term funds."

on fixed investment and growth. This stands in strong contrast to the British experience, where the efforts to cure balance of payments difficulties had dampening effects on total demand as well as on the rate of growth. (See Chapter 4.) The Japanese case demonstrates the possibility of checking a very strong investment boom by means of sufficiently strong monetary restraint without creating a tendency in the direction of a downward spiral and without killing off the strong forces of growth. It shows how the adoption of restrictive monetary policy can have quick and sharp effects especially on inventory investment (with high import content) and how again the elimination of the restrictive measures could give room for a new, apparently undisturbed, expansion.

This account of the experience with restrictive monetary policies in 1957–58 may be considered as rather typical; we find the same main patterns, with some variations, in the other postwar restriction periods.[21] One interesting feature of Japanese monetary policy is a strong reliance on the control of the supply of funds by means of credit rationing. The level of official interest rates is kept relatively inflexible (moving only one or two percentage points over the cycle), and the structure of rates therefore tends to become quite distorted. The Bank of Japan is able not only to ration its own supply of funds to the banking system but also by other means to have a strong influence on the expansion of loans and on credit rationing carried out by the individual banks. In addition to moral suasion, a number of specific devices are used such as reserve requirements, import deposit requirements, a complicated discount rate structure (with penalty rates partly dependent on the amount of borrowing of the individual bank), limits set on loans and investments of each bank. How these various mea-

21. One such variation that seems important is the positive effect on short-term capital imports that in 1961–62 and 1964 became a function of the internal credit stringency. This extra supply of foreign exchange implied a higher "ceiling for expansion" than was the case in 1957.

sures are applied in varying proportions is, however, a secondary question for explaining the effectiveness of Japanese monetary policy. The chief explanation refers to the very specific conditions prevailing in Japan, in particular with regard to the high importance of bank credit in the financing of investment. The strategic position of the Bank of Japan has no counterpart in the other countries.

As a final point, we might ask whether, under the given conditions, the Japanese stabilization policy since the beginning of the 1950s could not have been more effective. One error of policy that has already been mentioned is the long lag in the application of restraints. The booms were allowed to develop in ways that implied inflation, overinvestment, and overimportation. The brakes in the 1954–58 cycle should perhaps have been applied in 1955 in a series of steps, thereby perhaps minimizing disturbances to the economy. To a very limited extent we can observe an example of this latter possibility of handling the stabilization problem in the 1959–60 expansion. Monetary brakes were applied from the end of 1959 to the middle of 1960 in order to counteract the development of a deficit in the current balance of payments and tendencies toward overinvestment in inventories. It looked as if the policy had been effective: inventory investment was reduced, the rise of imports was dampened, and this time no effects on fixed investment could be noticed. The restrictive policy was relaxed in the autumn of 1960, the liquidity of enterprises increased, and the supply of funds for investment looked ample (with a decline of interest rates). But again the Japanese economy demonstrated its high instability in the upward direction: the rate of increase of equipment investment reached 40 per cent per year during 1961, and the annual rise of industrial production in the first half of 1961 was as high as 22 per cent at the same time as inventory investment and imports started rising rapidly. Since exports kept rather stable during the year from September 1960, foreign exchange reserves started to decline rapidly from the spring of 1961. The stabilization policies taken by the government from July 1961 on (in the form of increased discount rates and higher rates on Bank of Japan loans, increased claims on liquidity reserves, plus some restriction on fiscal expenditures) did not need to be so restrictive as in 1957, partly because the ceiling of expansion had been elevated. It seemed as if the marginal import propensity had become lower, thanks to the enlarged production capacities and higher supply elasticities, at the same time as higher interest rates tempted a considerable short-term capital flow into Japan.

The 1962 "recession" was relatively mild. The GNP growth rate was still 5 per cent (which was, however, no more than one third of the rate achieved in the three preceding years). But again the main achievement of the restrictive policy was attained: the rate of inventory accumulation was radically reduced and imports fell, while exports showed an accelerated growth, so that foreign exchange reserves could rise substantially during the year. Then a new boom developed with total demand again rising so rapidly during 1963 that a new substantial deterioration in the balance of payments developed, followed by the introduction of restrictive policies from the end of 1963. The sequence of demand explosions and balance of payments restrictions has thus once again been repeated, but it seems that there has appeared a new interesting variation of the theme that will be discussed in the next section.

THE CONJUNCTURE MECHANISM AND ITS CHANGES

The main impression from the account of Japanese conjuncture experiences given above is the extremely high propensity for investment demand to expand too rapidly. This implies a tendency toward instability in the upward direction—toward excess demand and overheating of the economy. This excess demand bias is matched by interrelated downward reactions.

Compared with Western industrialized countries, Japan has had much more space for expansion, thanks to such factors as an elastic labor supply (employment in industry rising by 8 to 12 per cent per year) and vast possibilities of transferring resources from low to high productivity firms, and application of new techniques. Very high savings ratios among wage earners and family firms plus rapidly rising profits during the expansions have implied a relatively high and swiftly increasing supply of savings for capital formation. As pictured above, this elasticity of finance has been effectively complemented by an elastic supply of bank credit. To this account of elastic supply factors also belongs the opportunity for rapidly expanding imports (of raw materials, fuels, machinery, and so forth) that was a necessary condition for Japanese economic expansion. This international space was provided by the high rate of growth of Japanese exports (about 20 per cent per year in volume terms). These elastic supply conditions have permitted a rate of long-term growth of GNP of 10 per cent per year. How is it, then, that the Japanese economy seems to come into such excess demand conditions that reactions are apparently unavoidable?

The very mechanism of rapid growth seems to be what creates exaggerations. The tremendous growth rate of equipment investment apparently tends to create acceleration effects, for example in the form of capital expansion needs for producing new investment goods. In a developing boom there seems to arise a big rush to push ahead: a competitive fever to keep and conquer increasing shares of old and new markets, of applying the new techniques. The "growth mentality" seems to create rising anticipations of expected growth possibilities. Under such conditions there will be a large acceleration effect through an increasing demand for inventories—goods-in-process as well as anticipatory buying of raw materials and half-finished goods—creating an extra push on total demand corresponding to up to 10 per cent of GNP.

It is interesting to note that this growth optimism has not lived on speculation in rapidly increasing prices. Elastic supplies of import goods at given prices and mostly declining labor costs up to 1961 (thanks to the rapid rise in productivity neutralizing the increasing wage rates) have in the main prevented the appearance of significant cost inflation. It is also interesting to note that private consumption expenditures have rather tended to dampen the process, thanks to the cyclical sensitivity of the marginal share of profits in income and high marginal savings rates of households. Rapidly increasing profits during the expansion have preserved the "growth optimism" and also played an essential role in financing the investment process. The supply of elastic bank credit has, however, been a necessary condition for the very high investment ratio, vastly surpassing the average self-financing resources of the rapidly expanding corporations and firms.

It is thus not difficult to understand how a rapid growth process under the Japanese elastic supply conditions more or less automatically accelerated into a state of overheating. The important problem is how checks and balances belonging to the mechanism tend to break such a process. The essence seems to lie in the reactions to the demand acceleration. In the short term there were inelasticities or bottlenecks at various points with regard to internal supply conditions just because of the very high rate of increase in demand. The two types of reactions were: (1) quick rise of imports of the scarce goods (machinery, steel, raw materials); (2) rapid increase of investment in equipment and machinery when capacity limits were reached or were expected to be reached in the near future. These two types of reactions were complementary and more or less simultaneous. As pointed out above, the increase of investment demand had acceleration effects inside the economy, implying acceleration effects on fixed investment. The same may be true to a considerable extent of the sharp increases of inventory investment; speculation due to expected balance of payments restrictions may on occasion have reenforced this tendency.

As we pointed out in the first section, two types of limits to the boom (or ceilings on the expansion) are conceivable: (1) the investment boom may be broken by difficulties of financing the expansion of private investments; (2) the investment acceleration may break its own back because of insufficient rise of demand due to the appearance of overcapacity in various branches. These two types of "causes of crisis" belong to rather old-fashioned versions of business-cycle theory, but we may still find some use for this dichotomy.

From the account given in this chapter, the first type of interpretation is the one that, in the first instance, seems applicable. There is no direct, automatic limitation of the "supply of savings"—for instance by way of reduced profit margins—that leads to the financial restrictions. The origin is to be found in the balance of payments disequilibrium that arises from the too-rapid increase of imports. But we can maintain that this is just one form of insufficient supply of savings; if the savings propensity had been higher, or profits had been increasing still more rapidly during the boom, then also the rate of import rise should have slowed down.

The main part of the reaction mechanism thus refers to the too-rapid rise of imports during the boom and the consequent deficit in the balance of payments. The resulting effects on liquidity and availability of funds are partly automatic, partly consequences of restrictive policy measures by government authorities introduced to protect the exchange reserves. The response mechanism of the economy has shown a high sensitivity at the margin to a limited credit restraint. This phenomenon is a natural outcome of the investment excesses during the boom, when financially weak firms, especially in wholesale and import trade as well as in industry, have become vulnerable to even small changes in credit and liquidity conditions. The characteristic response has therefore been a rather quick turndown in imports. The result has been a rapid improvement in the balance of payments situation without much of a disturbance to the growth process: this is verified by the fact that when liquidity and bank credit conditions have again become normalized, the rapid growth process has quickly been regained and followed by a new acceleration.

The "downward" instability element—the check on unlimited expansion— that seems to be built into the Japanese economic system can in these ways be said to be determined by a belated response to the excessive demand expansion that the government has allowed to develop. However, such a conclusion would not be indisputable.

In Japan, as in other countries, there are economists who regard the actual application of restrictive policies as a mistake, creating instability and repressing growth. According to this view the retardation of economic growth, for instance after 1957–58, was mainly due to the tight monetary policy that had the effect of keeping production below capacity growth. This view implies that rapid rises of inventories and imports during the boom should be regarded as temporary, and thus would correct themselves during an undisturbed growth process.[22] It is quite sobering to observe that, even in the case of Japan with its record growth rate, this antipolicy view can be held and defended by responsible economists.

The old question, as to whether the breaking of a boom has been caused mainly by unintelligent and mistaken policy restrictions, has an interesting bearing on the Japanese experience. The question is how much longer the booms would or could have lasted if the restrictive monetary policy had not disturbed financial supply conditions and in that way repeatedly put an end to the investment booms. We have to imagine the use of policy measures such that the balance of payments restrictions would not have appeared or would have been solved by other means (for instance implying more of foreign borrowing or import controls).

As to the postwar cycles up to 1962 we can only conjecture regarding the issue of equilibrium growth not restrained by exchange crises. There are, however, indications that during the 1963 boom other factors—belonging to business cycle theory of

22. This is especially Osamu Shimomura's view. Reference to literature and an account of the debate are found in Chapter 5 of Shinohara's book, quoted above.

the second type—would have entered the picture and weakened the forces of expansion. As mentioned above, the extremely high rate of inventory investment noted cannot go on for any great length of time; at the end of the boom part of the stimulus has apparently come from the expectation of coming exchange and financial difficulties. It is of special interest to note that there were some signs of weakening of the incentives to private fixed investment *before* the monetary restrictions were introduced at the end of 1963. One indication of a changed reaction pattern refers to the more elastic response of output to the rise of demand than had been usual in similar stages of the earlier cycles; inventory-delivery ratios had already started rising half a year after the beginning of the boom.[23] Domestic machine orders were reduced before credit restrictions were introduced when some excess capacity conditions had appeared in various branches of heavy industry (in machinery and iron and steel). An indication of such lower pressure for increased capacity in equipment and machinery also appears from the inertia in the revival of private investment after easy monetary policy had been reestablished in 1964.[24] This is in contrast to the usual response to the elimination of restrictive policies in Japan, which has been a quick expansion of private investment thanks to the strong pressure of demand on existing capacity. During 1964–65, demand was apparently not increasing rapidly enough to absorb as quickly as in earlier recessions surplus inventories and machine capacity.

There are other signs of a changing conjuncture pattern. Import trade has been liberalized at the same time as capital imports are playing an increasing role. As has also been mentioned above, labor has become more scarce, and wages have been rising much more rapidly than during the 1950s. We can also observe that the share of investment in the 1963 GNP

23. OECD, *Economic Surveys: Japan* (Paris, 1965), p. 39.

24. See the interesting discussion of this new phase of Japanese conjunctures in ibid.

increase was lower than in the previous expansion periods. The demand for capital has apparently become less concentrated on the enlargement of production capacity (with regard to the acceleration of demand) and to a larger extent is now taking the form of substitution for labor and enlargement of various types of infracapital.[25] These tendencies would imply an increase in the relatively low marginal capital-output ratio in Japan.

These remarks on recent trends are based on very preliminary observations of the possibility of a changing business cycle mechanism in Japan. Before drawing conclusions as to the relevance of the observations, we have to remember certain other peculiarities of the Japanese economy. One peculiar feature in the Japanese development is the extremely low share of housebuilding in total investment. This also refers to public investment in social infrastructure. From the point of view of Western countries, there seems to be considerable disequilibrium in the nation's capital structure, with too much of private production capacity in relation to the supply of housing, roads, schools, harbors, and so forth. This consideration can be used either to imagine that there could have been much more of excess demand and inflation during the past period, if these needs had been allowed to be active to a higher degree, *or* to forecast a future transfer of resources from private investment in order to satisfy the social needs. This latter alternative may be taken as a part of an eventual equilibrating process that has to come when the extreme growth rate of private equipment investment cannot continue. A shift of resources from private equipment investment toward long-term construction of houses, roads, hospitals, and so forth, would probably involve a slowing up of the GNP growth rate. Such a change in the distribution of investment would imply raising the exceptionally low average and marginal capital-output relations in Japan.

25. There is an interesting discussion of this problem in the EPA *Economic Survey of Japan 1963–64*, pp. 11–22.

One conclusion of this schematic survey of possible new adjustment problems in the Japanese economy may be that more policy parameters will be needed. The relatively simple overheating version of instability that so far has predominated could be managed relatively easily by means of monetary policy—by restricting and expanding the supply of liquidity in a general sense. The policy issue tends to become more complicated when balance of payments and investment problems of growth and stability become more diversified, and "growth energy" cannot just be tapped from a bottle of "unlimited" growth potential. A flexible fiscal policy with a number of policy instruments will come into the foreground, at the same time that rapidly increasing public expenditures and investment in housing will imply changing conditions for long-term growth.

8 POSTWAR STABILITY PROBLEMS IN THE UNITED STATES AND CANADA

DIFFERENCES BETWEEN AMERICAN AND EUROPEAN EXPERIENCES

This chapter contains a short survey of the postwar instability experience in North America, referring both to the United States and Canada. It will not be necessary to offer a systematic and thorough account of the conjunctural patterns and the policy issues in these countries, as there already is an overwhelmingly rich literature available. The principal task we are here setting ourselves is to discuss some aspects of the American experiences against the background of and in comparison with those of other countries taken up in this book. Such an approach, it is hoped, will give a perspective that is somewhat different from the one gained by the more usual comparisons of American interwar and postwar cyclical experiences. Furthermore, certain similarities and dissimilarities between the postwar and interwar patterns were already described in Chapters 2 and 3.

Which are the most important features of postwar economic instability in the United States and Canada; and to what extent are they different from, or similar to, the postwar experience of other countries? Both the variation and the variability of the GNP growth rate (as referred to in Chapter 3) has been higher in the United States and Canada than in any of the European countries considered. (See Tables 3.2 to 3.4.)

The characteristic of higher American instability does not, however, extend to the growth rates of the major expenditure categories within GNP. The higher coefficients of variation and variability of the GNP growth rate in Canada and the United States are thus the result of a relatively lower degree of mutual offsetting among the various GNP components; in other words, in America there was a higher degree of synchronization among the growth rates of the major components of aggregate demand.

In general, the term "business cycle" is more clearly applicable in the case of the postwar instability experience, particularly in the United States but also in Canada, since the wave-like movements of the growth of total production and employment tended to be more distinct, and, in relation to at least some European countries, also more frequent. Aside from the first postwar readjustment, upper turning points or peaks of economic activity occurred in both countries in 1948, 1953, 1957, and 1960; they were in each case followed by lower turning points or troughs during the subsequent calendar year. Of these experiences only the 1957–58 setback was shared rather widely—though to a milder degree—by the European countries. These were in general subject to a recessionary setback only on one more occasion, namely around 1951–52.

Perhaps the most prominent feature of postwar economic instability in the United States and Canada refers to the persistent deficiency of actual output with regard to potential output from about the middle of the 1950s onward up to 1965.[1] Actually, on the basis of our own estimate, which defines full employment as a 98 per cent utilization rate of the labor force,

1. For the United States, see for example the Council of Economic Advisers' estimate of the gaps in the *Economic Report of the President* (Washington, January 1965), p. 82, which assumes a 96 per cent utilization rate of the labor force as representing full employment. For Canada, see G. J. Drabble, *Potential Output 1946 to 1970,* Staff Study No. 2, Economic Council of Canada (December 1964), p. 39, which is based on the assumption of a 97 per cent potential utilization rate of the labor force.

the economies of Canada and the United States were already operating below their potential in the first half of the 1950s. (See Figure 3.2.) European countries, on the other hand, have in general been operating much closer to their potential output paths. Application of the 96 per cent full-employment norm to the European countries would imply persistent excess demand throughout the period 1950–65 for most of the countries. The tendency toward excess demand and overfull employment predominates in most of these countries even according to the 98 per cent norm. Only Belgium, Denmark, Germany, and Italy were operating considerably below their potential during the 1950s, but by 1960 they had more or less closed the gap even according to the 98 per cent full-employment norm.

The difference between Europe and America as to the pressure of demand is not only manifested in, on average, much smaller gaps between actual and potential output in Europe, but also in generally larger price rises than in America. Excess demand and rapid inflation are of course also manifestations of economic instability, though of a different type. The American economies have not gone free entirely from spells of rapid inflation. This happened in the beginning of the 1950s in connection with the Korean war boom, and before that in 1947–48. But since the passing of the Korean boom, American price rises have been very moderate by European standards. Instead, the tendency toward persistent underutilization of available labor and capital increased so much that it became the major American instability problem. Unemployment remained considerably above the level compatible with any reasonable definition of full employment even during periods of cyclical peak.

We are here apparently confronted with a type of issue discussed in Chapter 1. Should the deceleration of economic growth in the United States after 1953 and in Canada after 1956, and the consequent substantial gaps between actual and potential output, be regarded mainly as a problem of short-term instability or as a problem of long-term growth?

The first type of interpretation would suggest that the forces of cyclical expansion have been too weak in relation to the position reached during recession to bring about full recovery close to the path of full-employment output. A closer approach to the full-employment path has been checked prematurely by short-term recessionary forces. According to this interpretation, short-term cyclical forces would be the proximate causes not only of a variable gap between potential and actual production, but also of a slowdown of actual and potential long-term growth. In particular, net fixed investment over the cycle is likely to be lower if there is persistent, though variable, slack in the economy than if output attains or exceeds at least periodically the full-employment path; considerations of the supply of investment funds and of the incentive to invest in these alternative circumstances would tend to support the conclusion.

The approach discussed above thus implies that the slowdown of economic growth in the United States and Canada from around the mid-1950s and up to the beginning of the 1960s should largely be regarded as a consequence of cyclical instability, just as the rapid rise of prices and unit wage costs in Europe and Japan could largely be regarded as a consequence of cyclical instability with an excess-demand bias. The alternative interpretation, that the trend forces represent the primary phenomena whereas the cyclical developments are secondary variations around the "given" growth trends, implies that these "trend forces" are largely cycle-independent. Alternative formulations of this type easily take on a metaphysical flavor and cannot as such be clearly verified. They are mentioned mainly because they have often, in one form or another, appeared in the discussion of the somewhat disappointing performance of the American economies since the mid-1950s.

However, this setting of the issues as given by these alternative interpretations does throw some light on a fundamental difference between European and American instability experiences. In Europe, and also in Japan, the setbacks in the growth of production as well as the inflationary booms can more easily be interpreted as deviations from "normal" growth patterns.

The long-term trends of GNP seem to have moved relatively independently of the demand-determined short-run instabilities (a considerable part of which was of the excess demand variety). In the case of the American economies, the development of aggregate demand seems to have been the decisive factor not only for the cyclical movements but also to a considerable extent for the actual growth trend. However, the lines of distinction cannot be drawn quite clearly. The growth of potential GNP under the predominant full-employment conditions of Western Europe and Japan cannot be considered as entirely independent of the strength and variability of aggregate demand. We have, for instance, pointed out that the slow rate of growth of actual and potential output in the United Kingdom may partly be a result of the slack in demand during the periods of stagnation. Similarly, the acceleration of growth in Sweden from the 1950s to the first half of the 1960s seems to have been influenced by the increased and steadier demand pressure promoting a faster rise of the supply of capital, and partly also of labor during the later period. Here relatively small variations in the degree and steadiness of demand pressure can plausibly be argued to have affected to some extent the growth of potential output, and therefore also the growth of actual output (since potential GNP was reached, and even exceeded, at least at the top of the boom periods). In the United States and Canada, on the other hand, the reduction in the rate of growth of full-employment output on account of the general slack in demand should not *as such* have any relevance for the actual growth rate as long as economic activity was inadequate to reach and exceed the full-employment path even during the most favorable periods.

THE INSTABILITY OF THE U.S. GNP DURING RECESSION AND RECOVERY

The comparatively high average variation and variability of the (annual) rate of growth of GNP in the United States has been noted repeatedly. The high degree of instability is of course closely associated with the stronger relative decline of the growth rate in the United States in connection with recession and the consequent relative rise of the growth rate in connection with recovery. The United States table in the Appendix shows the GNP changes and their expenditure composition during years of recession and recovery.

Personal consumption expenditures (on nondurables) were affected relatively little by the recessions, whereas inventory investment may have accounted for more than half of the GNP decline if measured on a quarterly basis. This was the case in the 1957–58 recession. These features are largely in line with both European experience and United States experience in other recessions. Business fixed investment accounted for another third of the quarterly decline during the same recession. Although this expenditure category is relatively unstable in the United States, we find that in the Netherlands and Belgium there have been bigger declines during some of the recessions. With the exception of the first inflationary booms after the war (during 1947 and 1950) the United States economy—in contrast to the majority of Western European countries—has not had much of a problem preventing fixed business investment from reaching too-high levels, so that excess demand conditions have become actual. On the contrary—up to 1965—the main preoccupation has been with the retardation or insufficient rise of business fixed investment during the later phases of expansion, this being one of the main factors accounting for the unfinished expansions and the gaps between actual and potential production at the peaks in 1957 and 1960 as well as also during 1962–64. (Total unemployment remained above 5 per cent during the whole period 1960–64.) Plant and equipment expenditures (in constant prices) did not surpass the boom level of 1956 until 1964.

The higher average variation and variability of the growth of residential construction in the United States than in the other countries compared cannot simply be taken as a factor contributing to the explanation of the greater general cyclical instability. In fact, it seems as if the variations in residential construction have had more of a stabilizing effect on the development of GNP in the United States than in most other countries. Residential construction has turned down rather early in the expansion periods, leaving space for expansion in other types of investment and in consumption, and has turned up rather early during the contractions. This timing pattern has implied a certain compensatory effect on the cyclical variability of actual GNP growth. On the other hand, however, a continuation of the more rapid pace of residential construction growth into the late stages of expansions would have meant a slower widening of the gap between actual and potential GNP.

In the United States, expenditure on durable consumption goods as a share of GNP is somewhat higher than in other countries. The relatively high variation and variability of the growth of this expenditure category might have to be considered partially as an independent factor of explanation of the cyclical instability of GNP growth and partially as a rather responsive reaction pattern. Furthermore, due to the relatively sensitive inventory and fixed investment reactions in branches related to the production of consumer durables, the instability of durable consumption goods purchases reflects only part of the GNP variability that is closely related to this variable.

High instability in the above-mentioned GNP components does not necessarily mean high overall instability. The variations in the different components of total demand—including nondurable consumption goods and services, federal, state, and local government expenditures, and transactions with foreign countries—might to a considerable extent offset the variations in expenditures on investment and consumer durables. For instance, a rise or decline of the growth of expenditure on durable goods might be compensated for by opposite movements in the growth of the other five sixths of private consumption (only relatively small movements would be needed), so that total consumption expenditures would keep on a rather stable growth path. It is also conceivable that variations in the rate of growth of investment expenditures might be more or less automatically compensated for by opposite variations in other expenditures. This type of problem has been discussed in Chapter 3, when it was suggested that there was less of such mutual offsetting among GNP components in the two American economies than in those of Western Europe. How and why this should be so is a question regarding the respective mechanisms both of the business sectors and of government policy reactions.

EX ANTE SAVING AND INVESTMENT AT POTENTIAL GNP

Clarification of some of the issues raised in the previous paragraph would actually make desirable a careful analysis of the operating characteristics of the economies that we like to compare. We would need to determine if and to what extent differences in the patterns of instability are due to differences in the cyclical mechanism, in the size and type of the disturbances, or in policy reactions. A careful analysis of this type could be attempted on the basis of comparable, more-or-less complete econometric models of short-term economic change. But such an attempt will have to be a task of the future since the presently available econometric models of short-term economic change are neither sufficiently comparable and complete nor sufficiently precise to make an international comparison of this nature possible and worthwhile.

We shall instead concentrate on the more manageable and more modest task of considering a set of simple saving-investment relationships which seem to determine some basic conditions for the operation of the intricate mechanism of short-term economic change.

As pointed out above, the United States economy (together with the Canadian economy) has, since about the middle of the 1950s and up to around 1964, shown a persistent tendency of inadequate demand even by the only moderately ambitious 96 per cent full-employment norm. The other countries, in contrast, showed generally clear tendencies toward excess demand during the same decade if also judged by the 96 per cent norm. It is self-evident that these contrasting tendencies can be interpreted as a result of an excess of ex ante saving over ex ante investment at (hypothetical) full employment in the case of the United States and Canada, and as results of an excess of ex ante investment over ex ante saving at full employment in the case of most of the other countries. The question is how fruitful an interpretation in such simple terms can be made. The possibility of putting the issue in this way will be illustrated in the example of the United States; the contrasting tendencies in the other countries compared can easily be visualized with the help of the studies of those countries (especially in the chapter on Sweden).

It appears that the ratio of annual gross private saving to GNP in the United States is rather stable.[2] During years of expansion and cyclical peak, as well as during the years of postwar recession, the sum of household and business saving has remained rather close to 15 per cent of GNP. It is plausible that this ratio would have been practically the same if actual GNP had fully matched potential GNP. To this private supply of saving we have to add the excess saving by the public sector, that is the difference between public saving and public investment. The ratio of excess public saving to GNP—in contrast to the gross savings ratio in the private sector—is very sensitive to the degree to which potential output is utilized, particularly on account of the federal part of the public revenue. This makes it necessary to take explicit account of the relationship between actual and potential GNP when the behavior of the ratio of public—and total—saving to GNP is being considered. Considerations of this nature have in recent years led to the develop-

2. See especially Edward F. Denison, *The Sources of Economic Growth in the United States and the Alternatives before Us* (New York, 1962), pp. 121–24; and "A Note on Private Saving," *Review of Economics and Statistics* (August 1958), pp. 261–67.

ment of the concept of implicit full-employment surplus or deficit of the public sector. This concept attempts to show what the respective budget surplus or deficit on a national-income-accounts basis would be at potential full-employment output. Given the structure of the tax rates and expenditure patterns that prevailed during the decade prior to the 1964 tax reform, the potential full-employment budget surplus of the federal government has been estimated to correspond to between about 1 per cent and 2.5 per cent of GNP for the years in question.[3]

These calculations, which were based on the presumption of a 96 per cent utilization of the labor force representing potential full employment, would imply a ratio of total private and public excess saving to potential GNP of some 16 to 17.5 per cent. According to the more ambitious 98 per cent norm, which we have favored particularly in view of the postwar experience of the non-American countries, the estimates of the ratio of the potential full-employment savings to GNP of the federal government of the United States would be still larger.

Provided that gross private investment—including business fixed investment, residential construction, inventory investment, and net foreign investment (defined as the excess of total exports over imports)—would attain and retain a corresponding 16 to 17.5 per cent ratio to GNP as actual output successively approached potential output during expansion, then gaps between actual output and potential output according to the 96 per cent norm would not appear.

Given the savings propensity of the private household and business sectors (including the distribution of income between profits and other incomes) around the positions of full employment as well as the structure of public incomes and expenditures, there has, since the large cutback in defense expenditures

3. For the development and elaboration of this concept see Chapter 6 in Michael E. Levy, *Fiscal Policy, Cycles and Growth,* Studies in Business Economics, No. 81 (National Industrial Conference Board, 1963). The Council of Economic Advisers has discussed the concept in its 1962 Annual Report.

after the end of the Korean war up to 1964, been a lack of investment demand to offset the sum of private and public saving at potential GNP. According to this interpretation, potential excess saving was the "cause" of why potential GNP was not reached after 1955 even during the most prosperous phases of the business cycle. In these "comparative static" terms we have reached an oversimplified kind of explanation of why expansion has tended to stop before full employment was attained. At full employment, ex ante saving would have been higher than the sum of the items providing an offset to ex ante saving, and this implies that total demand expanded insufficiently to eliminate fully the gap between actual and potential production. However, such an interpretation will be interesting only if we are able to explain why investment demand does not or cannot rise sufficiently.

Let us therefore take a closer look at the behavior of total gross private investment and its major components. The GNP share of actual gross private investment in prosperous years tended to decline from the middle of the 1950s. At current prices it barely approached 15 per cent during the first half of the 1960s, to be compared with the 16 to 17 per cent potential savings ratio. Since the share of residential construction has tended to rise and the shares of inventory investment and of net exports, both of which are very variable in the short run, do not seem to have undergone any relevant longer-run change during these years, the main source of the declining investment share was business fixed investment. One might easily be tempted to blame this declining share on the appearance and persistence of general slack in the United States economy. However, Bert Hickman has tried to show that the share of business fixed investment would have decreased substantially even under conditions of continuous full-employment growth.[4] His calculations are based on an econometric capital stock adjustment

4. Bert G. Hickman, *Investment Demand and U.S. Economic Growth* (The Brookings Institution, Washington, D.C., 1965), in particular Chap. 7.

model for the business sector of the United States economy according to which the desired stock of fixed capital—which presumably would minimize total unit costs and thus represent long-term equilibrium under the prevailing conditions—is a positive function of the level of production and a negative function of time.[5]

Net investment, then, is specified as a function of the gap between the desired and the actual stock of fixed capital. Replacement investment is assumed to correspond to depreciation and is determined on the basis of the size and composition of the existing capital stock. Utilizing instead of actual production data the Council of Economic Advisers' estimates of potential production, which is based on the previously mentioned 96 per cent norm and indicates that real potential GNP was equal to actual GNP in 1955 and increased at 3.5 per cent thereafter, Hickman arrived at estimates of potential real gross fixed investment in the business economy. The estimates show an annual rate of increase of only 1.2 per cent, which is about one third of the above 3.5 per cent rate of growth of potential GNP. This implies that the investment share would have fallen substantially even if actual GNP had followed the path of potential GNP. The downtrend largely remains even after taking account of the differential price trends of investment goods and GNP; on a current-price basis, which also underlies the previously mentioned savings ratios, the estimated GNP share of potential gross business fixed investment would decline from 10.7 per cent in 1956 to 10.1 per cent in 1960, and 9.7 per cent in 1965. Given the longer-run tendencies of the shares of residential construction, inventory investment, and net exports that would be likely to add up to some 5 to 5.5 per cent at potential output, this implies a deficiency of potential total private investment of some 1 to 2 per cent of GNP when comparing with the previously mentioned potential savings ratio of some 16 to 17 per cent. Figure 8.1 illustrates the consequence of such a deficiency.

5. Attempts with a model containing also a relative price variable were not successful at the aggregate level.

FIGURE 8.1
Ratio of Actual to Potential GNP Related to the Ex Ante Savings Ratio and Investment Ratio

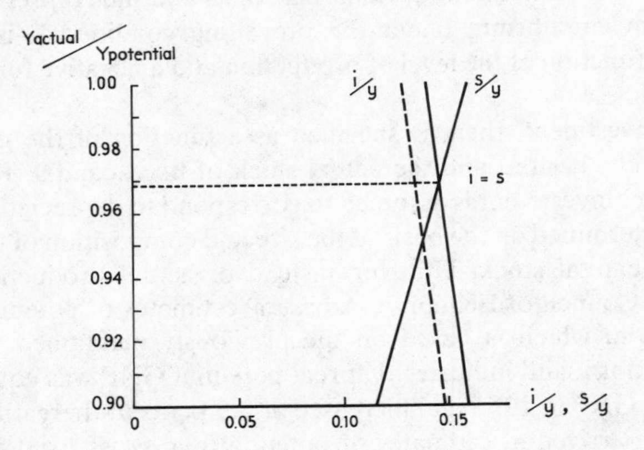

The diagram shows the ratio to GNP of ex ante private and excess public saving and of ex ante gross private investment on one axis and the ratio of actual to potential GNP on the other axis.[6] The intersection of the two schedules indicates the gener-

6. The schedule for the savings ratio can be expressed as the result of three empirical relationships:

a. Denison's observation of a relatively stable private gross savings ratio of 15 per cent. See footnote 2 above.

b. Levy's regression equation for the surplus of the federal government expressed as a percentage of GNP and specified as a function of the unemployment rate. It has to be added to (a) above. See Michael E. Levy, *Fiscal Policy*, p. 37.

c. "Okun's law" which expresses potential GNP as a function of actual GNP and the unemployment rate. Rearrangement of this relationship provides estimates of the unemployment rate as functions of the ratio of potential to actual GNP. Substitution of this function for the unemployment rate in (b) finally yields the savings ratio as a function of the ratio of actual to potential GNP. For "Okun's law," see Arthur M. Okun, "Potential GNP: Its Measurement and Significance," *Pro-*

al tendency with regard to the utilization of the steadily growing potential output.

According to the diagram, the economy would "tend" to operate some 3.5 per cent below the potential output path (generated by a 4 per cent unemployment rate). This GNP gap would imply roughly an additional percentage point of unemployment. The broken investment line in the diagram indicates the reduction of the investment ratio over a period of time on account of the downward trend of the capital-output ratio in the business sector of the economy. Hickman's results suggest a decline of the desired capital-output ratio of 1.8 per cent per year, or about 20 per cent per decade. The decline is assumed to reflect the increasing efficiency of newer capital goods and represents a tendency that can be traced back to the time before World War I. Offsetting increases within the aggregate investment ratio are of course possible, but they are not likely to be either permanent or fully compensating. They can occur because of shifts in the composition of business output in favor of industries with above-average unit capital requirements, or because of an increase in the share of residential construction and net exports primarily for exogenous reasons. A sufficient rate of investment demand may also appear because of an unusually large initial gap between desired and actual capital stock as a consequence of a major war. However, sooner or later the full-employment operation of the economy would, according to the interpretation implied in the diagram, necessitate a decline in the aggregate savings ratio (that is, a shift of the s/y line to the left). Changes in the fiscal structure—reduction in tax rates or an upward shift in the trend of public expenditures—will be able to achieve this.

The above types of offsets to the demand effects of the

---

ceedings of the Business and Economic Statistics Section, American Statistical Association, 1962.

Similarly, most of the components of the investment ratio can be expressed as functions of the ratio of actual to potential GNP.

declining trend of the capital-output ratio in the business economy played a role during the postwar period. But after the end of the Korean war, their combined offsetting power greatly diminished, primarily because of the downward shift of the trend of public expenditures in connection with the defense cutback which was not accompanied by a sufficient reduction in taxation. Factors of an accidental or passing cyclical nature propped up aggregate demand temporarily even after that, particularly in 1955, but also in 1956 and the first half of 1957. By the beginning of the 1960s the trend toward increased slack in the economy even during relatively prosperous years started to gain wide recognition. But it was not really before 1964 that a major tax cut was permitted to alleviate the problem. The reduction implied a decline of the ex ante savings ratio by some 1.5 per cent, which according to the above diagram should by itself have raised the utilization of potential output by some 3 per cent and reduced the unemployment rate by about 1 percentage point. Further stimulation after that occurred because of the rapid rise in federal military expenditures in connection with the increased engagement in the war in Vietnam. The combined effect of these fiscal changes seems to have been adequate to return the United States economy to a 4 per cent unemployment rate and the associated potential output path. This would still leave a GNP gap according to the more ambitious utilization norms in Europe, the achievement of which would require further fiscal stimulation and would be likely to involve more rapid inflation than in the longer run is likely to be considered tolerable in the United States.

The above sketch of the structure of ex ante saving and investment refers mainly to the longer-run tendencies apart from cyclical and brief accidental variations in the various components of the two schedules. Our analysis—within a comparative-static framework—has demonstrated why with the long-term savings and investment propensities as given before 1964 it would be impossible for the United States economy to attain and then follow a full-employment growth path. This result thus helps us to understand how the approach to full employment during an expansion would involve increasing instability. Short-term cyclical forces may, however, counterbalance the longer-term tendencies and create boom conditions that will not last very long—how long will of course partly depend on government policy measures. Let us therefore take a look at the short-term variations of the main categories of investment demand.

The main problem refers to the disequilibrating effects of the accumulation of capital stock during peak levels of activity, implying rising excess production capacity, as long as the growth of total effective demand is lagging behind. We find indications of declining rates of capacity utilization during the periods of expansion: 1955–57 and 1959–60.[7] Differences in developments among branches of industrial activity, expectational factors, and so forth, may imply a zone of indifference or hesitancy, making the exact timing of the turning point indeterminate within a certain interval.

The largest variations of investment demand occur in inventory investment. The "normal" GNP share of this item averages between 0.5 and 1 per cent, but may be slightly negative in a recession year and rise to some 1.5 to 2 per cent in the ensuing recovery year. This investment category represents a powerful contributor, or even generator, of recessions which lead to a substantial decline of the ratio of actual to potential GNP below the intersection of the longer-run ex ante savings and investment schedule in Figure 8.1. On the other hand, inventory investment tends to play a role of similar or even greater importance with regard to the reversal of the decline in economic activity. However, inventory investment as a share of GNP has tended to reach a maximum rather early during the

7. See, for instance, John R. Meyer and Robert R. Glauber, *Investment Decisions, Economic Forecasting and Public Policy* (Cambridge, Mass., 1965), table on p. 68, and Hickman, *Investment Demand,* Chap. 5.

expansion period, and has therefore not been active in carrying the economy further toward the potential output path during the following phases of expansion.

Residential construction, although accounting for a much larger average GNP share (of about 4 per cent) shows much smaller cyclical variations which, as already mentioned, to some extent tend to be stabilizing over the cycle; but just because of the latter characteristic they, too, cannot be expected to support an approach to the potential path in the later stages of expansion. This pattern is, however, not given as a part of a "pure" cycle mechanism; it is rather a function of the recurrent reactions of monetary policy.

Cyclical variations of the GNP share of gross business fixed investment, similar to the variations in the share of inventory investment, do contribute to recession and recovery, though generally to a smaller extent. From the point of view of our schematic model it is natural to ask why business fixed investment cannot continue expanding at a rate sufficient to match the residual of potential full-employment saving. In principle the issue is of the same type as when dealing with inventory investment. From the bottom of the recession, a capital stock adjustment process is started during which inventories are once again built up in response to the increase of the desired levels determined by rising output and turnover. A maximum rate of adjustment is likely to occur at a rather early stage of the expansion, when the volume of output and sales is rising rapidly and the gap between actual and desired stocks is largest. It is from this point of view natural to expect a lower rate of inventory investment at later stages of the expansion—if no new acceleration of demand occurs.

Let us say that after a year of recovery the economy would need another 2 per cent offset to the ex ante savings ratio in order to reach potential output. Then a corresponding increase of the GNP share of business fixed investment in excess of the longer-run ratio would imply that production capacity in the business economy would increase rather rapidly due to the low capital-output ratios in this sector. This might lead to a rapid decline of capacity utilization which under normal circumstances (with regard to savings and consumption propensities) could not be sustained. Finally, given the longer-run tendencies, it is also unlikely (except for accidental reasons) that a rapid approach to the path of potential output in the later stages of expansion occurs because of a rise in the GNP share of net exports. Thus the longer-run tendency to inadequate demand, once established, will tend to affirm itself also in the face of cyclical fluctuations.

It should be added—as a final remark in this connection—that the sensitivity of the public part of the total savings ratio to the ratio of actual to potential GNP might not only prevent potential GNP from being fully realized during the prosperous phases of the business cycle, but it will regularly also imply an alleviation of the impact of recessions. The saving-investment mechanism discussed would thus result not only in a premature braking of the expansion before full employment was reached but would act also as a built-in stabilizer during recession, when a rapid short-term decline in total ex ante saving and, correspondingly, in the ratio of saving to GNP, prevents cumulative processes from developing on account of consumption. The reductions in the federal government surplus and in undistributed corporate profits (after taxes) are so large in relation to the relative or absolute decline of GNP that personal income over the short periods of contraction is kept relatively stable. Any decline in disposable income to a point below its trend that does occur will furthermore be prevented from proportionately affecting consumption demand by a temporary decline of the savings ratio of households.

It is important to recognize that the marginal relations applied in the savings-investment model discussed above refer to the expansion periods that have dominated during the postwar period. Annual and even quarterly consumption in constant prices rose during all the postwar recessions except that there was a decline in the 1958 recession, and this decrease corresponded to only about one fifth of the reduction in GNP. This means that the marginal consumption-GNP relation during the recessions was much lower than would correspond to the consumption function implied in the model. This can probably only to a minor extent be explained by the shortness of the contractions (perhaps reducing the multiplier by some 10 to 20 per cent).[8] There is a ratchet effect implying a multiplier at the margin as low as 1.3 to 1.4.[9] The marginal propensity to consume associated with a decline in GNP is only about 25 per cent. This effect is partly determined by a radical marginal effect on retained gross corporate profits during contractions. The tendency for gross profits before taxes and dividends to decline relatively sharply during recessions is quite understandable because of rigidities in wages rates and fixed costs during short contractions, before cost adaptations have had time to come about. This stabilizing behavior—with regard to disposable personal income (including high stability in dividend payment) and consumption during contractions—is matched by a high marginal increase in corporate gross savings during the revival periods, when production and productivity rise rapidly while wage rates and fixed costs are relatively stable. During the postwar period no cumulative process has created such a gap between actual and desired fixed capital during the recession that an upturn called forth by other factors would not soon be supported by a revival of fixed business investment, as experience has clearly demonstrated. It is the more or less automatic revival of inventory investment and residential construction that under the conditions described accounts for the quick revival.

8. See Hickman, *Growth and Stability of the Postwar Economy.* (Washington, 1960), Chap. 9.

9. See James Duesenberry, Otto Eckstein, and Gary Fromm, "A Simulation of the United States Economy in Recession," *Econometrica* (October 1960), reprinted in *Readings in Business Cycles* (London, 1965).

THE ROLE OF POLICY

In the above sketch of a cyclical mechanism in the very simplest terms, presented in order to demonstrate the strategic equilibrating and disequilibrating forces at work, there are hidden presumptions of "given" policy parameters. A sort of neutrality of government policy is presumed that, however, is very difficult to define exactly. Are constant rates of interest or constant rates of increase in the volume of money the relevant assumptions of neutrality, or should we assume some flexible adjustments of interest rates and money supply to be included in the automatic reactions of credit markets during expansions and contractions? The same type of questions arises when we try to define neutral fiscal policy. It is easy to assume constant tax rates as given parameters, and we may also imagine some kind of cyclical conformity as to prices of government services. The difficulties are greater on the expenditure side. It is reasonable to imagine automatic responses with regard to payments of unemployment compensations (at given rates and policy standards). Should we include an easing of government loan policies for housebuilding following an "automatic" slack in general credit demand? Should a retardation of government expenditures during a boom because of backlogs be taken as automatic as well as the corresponding acceleration when resources become more easily available after the upper turning point? The answers should, according to our view, be affirmative, but the actual measurement of the relative importance of such automatic responses must be arbitrary within wide limits.

It can be argued that a certain trend movement of government expenditures (rather than constant expenditures) should be assumed as given when we discuss the actual instability of the economic system. In the United States this trend especially refers to the steady and rapid increase in state and local government expenditures. As argued in Chapter 3, the whole instability problem must be analyzed from the point of view of a growing economy, and this certainly implies in all developed countries a rather strong trend in government demand for goods and services. Parts of the deviations from such a rather arbitrary growth trend should then be regarded as discretionary policy actions or disturbances.

All this is necessarily rather inexact and arbitrary, and we must keep this vagueness in mind when discussing policy influences on the American cyclical experience. Take the problem of monetary policy effects as an illustration of the difficulty of isolating the relevant changes. It is customary to take the period 1946–51 as an example of passive monetary policy. The business cycle mechanism could operate undisturbed by active monetary policy changes, as the surplus liquidity inherited from the war time was combined with a policy aiming at interest rate stability. But we could nearly as well regard the inherited surplus liquidity as a policy of very active ease that was more or less preserved during this period. Policy measures had to be taken during the Korean inflation to preserve the high liquidity position and prevent interest rates from rising. Anyhow, it is interesting to observe, independently of more or less artificial definitions, that during this type of passive monetary policy both a recession of the postwar "normal" type (1948–49), especially characterized by a break of a strong inventory boom, as well as a severe inflation could occur. This experience allows us to observe that not all United States recessions have been preceded and aggravated by a period of monetary restriction. But we may also maintain that the absence of such restrictions gave room for inflation and full employment (in 1948 and 1951)—but of course under the very special conditions of war expenditure and large backlog demands.

The accord between the Treasury and Federal Reserve made the following cyclical experiences more interesting for an assessment of monetary policy. This is especially the case of the period 1955–61, when there were quite considerable parameter changes.

In an interesting study, Modigliani reached the conclusion that monetary policy during this period was relatively successful from a stabilization point of view.[10] He measured the degree of success by the changes in money supply in relation to changes in nominal GNP, and was able to demonstrate how this type of visible effect of policy was quite well timed during the period. But we do not get to know how strong and with what kind of time lags eventual effects came about. Therefore the results are quite inconclusive from our point of view. The reader should also be reminded that changes in money supply are unreliable indicators of changes in active policy.

Several attempts have been made to measure the impact of policy changes with regard also to the lag distribution. The results must be considered to be very inconclusive. If we take the results reached by Kareken and Solow as giving the correct order of size of the impact, then an increase of the interest-rate level by 1 per cent (as an indicator of credit restrictions) should have resulted in a substantially lower level of inventory investment within a year's time (than otherwise would have been the case); the effects on fixed business investment would via changes in new orders have been much slower (the maximum effect being reached after two to three years) but also quite considerable.[11]

Now the unfortunate situation is that econometric analysis of this type—using time-series data and distributed lag techniques—must give uncertain results within wide limits. The specifications of the models may vary widely—without reducing significantly the high correlation coefficients usually reached. The disturbing fact is that a number of highly regarded econometricians (like Tinbergen and Eisner) have attained good explana-

10. Franco Modigliani, "Monetary Policy in the United States, Some Empirical Tests of Monetary Management and of Rules versus Discretion," *Journal of Political Economy* (June 1964).

11. John Kareken and Robert M. Solow, "Lags in Monetary Policy," in *Stabilization Policies*, prepared for the Commission on Money and Credit (Englewood Cliffs, 1963).

tions of short-run investment variations without paying attention to interest rates and other monetary variables. One of the main difficulties in the interpretation of econometric research results, and therefore in choosing from among alternative model structures, arises from the high degree of collinearity among the variables given by the time series. This means that time series usually do not give sufficient evidence to make important structural distinctions.[12]

Another important reason why regression analysis of time-series data may give spurious results is the probable existence of nonlinearities or discontinuities in some of the strategic relations. In earlier chapters we have emphasized the possible or potential effects of restrictive monetary policy in specific business cycle situations, referring especially to the booms and the periods around the upper turning points, when a rising share of firms and sectors of industry become dependent on outside finance. A rise of interest rates, which act as proxy variables for credit availability, may during such periods have a considerable impact (with a time lag) on investment demand. Little or no influence of this sort may be apparent during the rest of the cycle; the inefficiency of monetary policy during contractions and depressions is a well-preserved and probably realistic Keynesian doctrine that dates back to the 1930s. We have also pointed out (see especially Chapter 6) that there might be a certain amount of nonlinearity in the relations: the

12. The following quotation from Meyer and Glauber, *Investment Decisions,* may be pertinent: "The historical experience of that period (1949–58) is just not sufficient to the task of decisively choosing from the large number of available possibilities" (p. 153). "Rather, a high degree of collinearity in the time-series data is a more likely explanation of the instability in the time-series estimates" (p. 159). "An important consequence of so much collinearity in time-series data is that time-series usually are just not of sufficient quality to permit the making of important structural distinctions" (p. 245). "Hypothesis testing with time-series data is at best hazardous; at times it can even be misleading or improper" (p. 139).

effects of small increases of interest rates may be insignificant, while relatively big ones (surpassing certain threshold values) may be quite effective (or too effective in vulnerable situations). There are limited possibilities of taking care of such discontinuities by breaking up time series and differentiating between the phases of the cycles. Meyer and Glauber have done this to a certain extent by applying alternatively "downswing and upswing models" to periods selected according to certain criteria.[13] In this way, and by looking closely into the behavior of the series in the various quarters, it was possible for them to ascertain that the interest rate variable was primarily effective in such years as 1953 and 1957, when the rates were relatively high and the cyclical positions were sensitive to monetary policy.

Such conclusions with regard to significant effects from monetary policy (as demonstrated by Kareken and Solow and by Meyer and Glauber) need not be in contradiction with Hickman's negative findings. As mentioned above, Hickman's research is concentrated on the interest rate effects on long-term equilibrium demand for capital stock, and he is able to show that this demand is quite insensitive to changes in the interest rate variable. However, this finding, as Hickman also points out,[14] does not exclude the possibility of short-term effects with regard to *the rate of adjustment over a period of time* of the actual stock of business capital toward the desired level.

However, we cannot be sure about the real significance of this distinction. The time-series data that cover a rather short period (1949–60) in Hickman's study must give very limited information especially as to the impact on equilibrium demand for capital of a variable like the long-term interest rate that has mainly shown an upward trend—together with the other variables (although some confirmation of the results is reached by

13. Ibid., pp. 159–70.
14. *Investment Demand*, pp. 19–21.

comparing the various branches of industry). We suspect that another set of time-series data that had offered a wider range of alternative interest rate levels might have given a greater weight to the interest rate variable. But it must even then be rather difficult to determine how this effect should be divided beween influence on the equilibrium demand for capital and the rate of response over a period of time. In any event, Hickman's analysis cannot show how the time shapes of investment response, with reference to the gaps between desired and actual stock of capital, have been influenced by the variables of monetary policy. Such effects, referring especially to periods of high sensitivity, will tend to be washed out by the technique of analysis applied for reaching the average profiles of investment response that are presented.

The econometric research referred to above does not and cannot give strong evidence about the effects of policy changes on the observed cyclical instability in the United States economy. The estimates are certainly helpful and stimulating in various respects—not least with regard to evidence given of the unimportance of certain variables. But there is apparently so much of contradictory evidence as well as built-in weakness in the methods that there will still be much room for qualitative judgments. Having this in mind, our tentative conclusion as to the effects of monetary policy would therefore be—as already suggested—that the periods of restrictive monetary policy to a large extent came in situations when—as in 1956–57 and 1960—the economy was relatively vulnerable to such disturbances because of declining demand pressure and lowered capacity utilization.

Even if it can be maintained that monetary policy has contributed to a dampening in the fluctuations of total investment in the private sector, this result at the same time should have been a factor in preventing the approach to full employment during the boom, contributing to some extent to the decreasing gap between desired and actual business capital, and possibly thereby also precipitating an earlier downturn than otherwise would have been the case. However, it is plausible that the main effect of the restrictive monetary policy from 1955 up to August 1957 (when the rediscount rate was raised just around the turn of the cycle) affected the time shape of the adjustment process, implying partly a postponement of expenditures to the 1958–59 revival. As mentioned above, the lags in monetary policy seem to be considerable and furthermore seem to vary with the conjuncture. From this the conclusion would follow that a passive monetary policy—with constant interest rates—and a greater increase of the money supply than actually came about would have meant a higher and more stable level of investment in 1957, probably more inflation, and, as a likely effect, a postponement of the turning point.[15] The same proposition can with greater confidence be made with regard to the 1959–60 expansion: the demand for business investment must have been dampened by the quick turn from easy to very restrictive credit policy during 1959. And this occurred in a more vulnerable situation than in 1956–57 with reference to a still smaller gap between desired and actual capital stock.

At last we come back to the old question of whether the stability of the United States economy would have been higher without the introduction of restrictive monetary policy during the upswings. Might not a prolongation of the expansion periods, propelled by rising private fixed investment, have resulted in destabilizing tendencies in the form of more rapid inflation, and complicated by balance of payments problems, to be followed eventually by a deeper recession?

15. However, it should be remembered that the conjuncture situation in 1956–57 was quite complicated, so that the above conclusion is not self-evident. Total demand (in real terms) was growing relatively slowly, but the slow growth was apparently partly an effect of severe bottlenecks in the capacities of the machinery and construction industries. One consequence of this was a ceiling on parts of investment expenditures, and considerable price increases that were diffused over the economy. The expansion was unbalanced relative to available capacity, but certainly these obstacles were aggravated by the restrictive policies.

The Western European experience, as well as the United States experience after 1962, shows that an assertion of this type is not necessarily well taken. Inflationary booms in Western Europe and Japan, with rapidly rising private investment, have usually been followed by very shallow and short recessions. The booms do not seem to have implied such an aggravation of disequilibriums, as to capital accumulation and its distribution or as to price-cost developments, so that the following recessions became deeper than the ones in the United States. The differences in the role of government budgets and fiscal policies in the various countries and at various times seem to have been strategic. We have already discussed the built-in flexibility of the United States federal budget system and its effects on expansion and contraction. This type of dampening effect as such has probably been as big or bigger in several of the Western European countries, if we consider the income side of the budget only. The crucial difference, however, refers to the more autonomous parts of government expenditures.[16]

The rapid rise of taxes and other government receipts during the expansion periods produced a public savings surplus and became a restriction on expansion in the United States economy, because government expenditures tended to rise relatively slowly.[17] Over the period 1953–63 total real government expenditures on goods and services expanded on average by only 1.1 per cent per year, implying a declining share in GNP. Between the peak years 1953 and 1957, federal government purchases of goods and services (at 1954 prices) fell by 7 per cent, and between the years 1957 and 1960 by 0.7 per cent. Compare this development with that of Sweden (Chapter 5) for

16. The high instability of federal expenditures in the United States has already been marked out. It is clearly reflected in the growth of total (federal, state, and local) government expenditures in Table A14 and in the international comparison of Table 3.2.

17. See, e.g. Chart 4 in the 1966 *Economic Report of the President*.

instance, where the government share in total expenditures rose from 20 to nearly 30 per cent over the period 1950–64. Also, the contraction of investment in stocks and fixed capital after the upper turning point is counterbalanced to a lesser degree by the expansion of government expenditures than in Western Europe. It may be maintained that a trend of federal governmment expenditures in the United States similar to the trend of central government expenditures in Sweden or Holland could have eliminated most of the deficit demand gap, have prolonged the expansion periods, and made the recessions more shallow. We may apply the simple technique presented above of comparing the behavior of investment and saving during an expansion period. A growth trend of government expenditures in relation to GNP as in these countries corresponding to some 1 to 2 per cent of GNP per year would (at given tax rates) have pushed the United States economy to a higher utilization of capacity in 1956–57 and 1960, raising the "capital stock adjustment gap" and stimulating fixed business investment—and therefore also implying less of a risk of disturbing effects of restrictive monetary policies.

It is conceivable that the period 1953–61, to which the discussion above has mainly referred, is an episode in United States economic history—just as the 1930s—and a bygone stage in the development of economic policy. We have often in this book referred to a learning process with regard to stabilization policy. It is quite likely that the frustrating experience of unfinished expansions and the domination of periods of deficit demand in relation to potential output, will, with a time lag, be followed by a new orientation of current economic policies. In any event, the American developments during 1961–65 look very different from the previous period. From the peak in 1960 to 1965, real GNP expanded by 4.5 per cent per year (compared to 2.3 per cent, 1953–60), and total unemployment finally approached 4 per cent by the end of 1965.

There is no reason to suspect a fundamental change in the "cycle mechanism" that should explain this exceptionally long and balanced expansion period from 1961. Against the background of the 1953–61 experience we must conclude that the main new element involves the successful avoidance of earlier policy mistakes and the introduction of a revised view. Attention has been directed during the period 1961–65 toward maintaining and supporting the expansion process, with less emphasis directed on the dangers of excessive developments. This has meant: the avoidance of such restrictive monetary policy as came about in the earlier expansions and, instead, the maintenance of rather stable interest rates up to 1965 and an expansive fiscal policy, partly in the form of expanding military expenditures but mainly in the form of the 1964 reduction of the tax rates for individuals as well as for corporations. The strong push on the economy from the multiplier effects of the reduced taxes apparently implied such an increase of total demand that the remaining deficiency with respect to the potential output path practically disappeared. Associated with these developments there was high and increasing utilization of industrial capacity which stimulated the demand for fixed business investment. The introduction of the investment tax credit in 1962 and a more favorable tax treatment of depreciation can also be expected to have promoted a more rapid rate of investment.

One very strategic aspect of the relatively successful policies of the 1960s refers to the change in attitude toward measures to protect the balance of payments by means other than the direct or indirect restriction of total demand. External equilibrium was no longer sought by restricting domestic expansion. Instead, the government measures were aimed *directly* at the capital and foreign aid items of the balance of payments by means, for example, of the interest equalization tax (passed in 1964), and a set of measures to secure voluntary restraints on the outflow of capital.

GENERAL SURVEY OF SOME SPECIFIC CANADIAN PROBLEMS

In the introduction to this chapter we pointed out the dominating similarities in the cyclical experiences of the United States and Canada. (Also see Figure 8.2.) The timing of the turning points is almost exactly the same, as is the general shape of expansions and recessions. There is also the same type of problem as to a slowing down of the growth rate from around 1956 and the appearance of a significant gap between actual and potential production, manifested by relatively high unemployment rates and below normal utilization of capacity. In both countries the return to a more normal growth rate during the period 1961–64 did not fully eliminate the problem of too-high unemployment and the existence of a production gap.

It is of course not at all surprising that economic developments in the two North American countries are quite parallel.

FIGURE 8.2
Quarterly Development of GNP at Constant Prices in the U.S. and Canada (ratio scale)

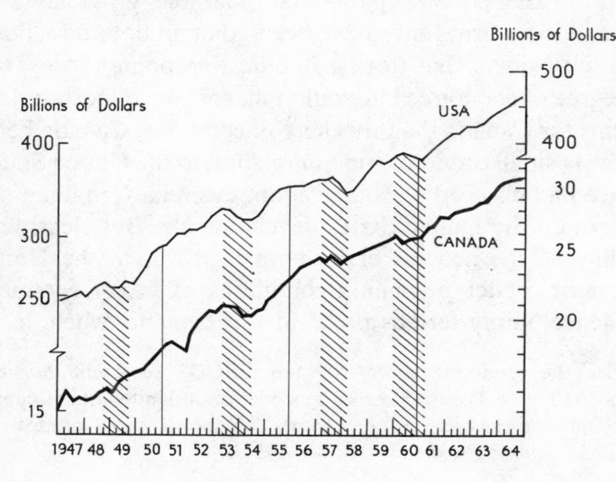

In fact the countries are from an economic point of view very closely integrated, much more so than practically any two European countries. Geography—4,000 miles of common frontier—is sufficient explanation, implying "nearly complete" mobility of labor and capital across the border. This mobility across the border tends to be much higher than the corresponding mobility between eastern and western markets inside Canada. The high degree of integration between these two economies is seen most directly in trade and capital movements: about 60 per cent of Canadian exports find markets in the United States, and a still greater share of Canadian imports consists of United States goods. United States capital plays a strategic role in Canadian business with regard both to financing and to direct investment. It is estimated that in 1959 about 60 per cent of Canadian manufacturing and mining and 75 per cent of the petroleum and natural gas industries were under United States control.[18] An important aspect of the integration issue—not least from the point of view of independent stabilization policies—is the fact that the financial and credit mechanisms of the two countries are very closely intertwined. Funds can move and do move freely between the countries, and during the postwar period considerable gross flows of short- and long-term funds have been going in both directions.

It is self-evident that from a stabilization point of view this high degree of economic integration means much more serious problems for Canada than for the United States, Canada being a relatively small economic unit in relation to the United States. We have had no need to bother about eventual Canadian disturbances on the United States developments. But clearly the instability of the process of economic growth in the United States must, under prevailing conditions of heavy economic dependence, imply serious problems for Canada, when, as an

18. See the economic survey by the OECD, *Economic Surveys: Canada*, 1963, p. 9. The problem of dependence on United States capital is thoroughly discussed in the reports of the Royal Commission, *Canada's Economic Prospects* (Ottawa, 1957).

autonomous nation, and not as one of the American states, it has ambitions to come close to its own targets of economic performance.

The case of Canada therefore gives us a new kind of instability issue. Fundamentally it is the problem of how and to what extent a relatively small economy, that is heavily dependent on and highly integrated with a dominating economy, has managed or can potentially manage to have some degree of independent development, especially from the cyclical point of view. This problem is clearly much bigger for Canada than for any of the other countries discussed in this volume. There are, however, also some other specific features, partly independent of the United States dependence problem, that are of great interest in this connection and must be kept in mind when analyzing the Canadian experience. These specific features refer to: (1) an unusually strong investment boom up to 1957–58 and consequent reactions to overcapacity situations, and (2) balance of payments disturbances under conditions of flexible exchange rates. The instability problems of the Canadian economy—as they have been mainly determined by the United States cycles—must be studied taking these specific features into account.

The postwar investment boom was longer and much more pronounced in Canada than in the United States and had some specific characteristics due to the structure of the Canadian economy. It is often said that Canada is a "dualistic" or even a "schizophrenic" economy. On the one hand, there has been since colonial times a strong orientation toward staple products (wheat, wood products, minerals, oil, gas), with a very high dependence on world markets, and on the other hand a strong tendency to develop secondary industries dependent on high mass consumption along the United States pattern. This latter development has been favored by a combination of high tariff walls and United States direct investments. During the early part of the postwar period—culminating with the Korean boom —the staple-oriented sectors of the Canadian economy were overstimulated at the same time that the secondary industries got their share in the buoyant economy. This resulted in an extraordinary investment boom partly financed by capital imports. During the period 1948–53, the development had the character of a rather general boom with excess demand arising from expanding exports, private and public investments, as well as consumption expenditures. But thereafter the dominant expansionary influence came from investment in resource development and related sectors. The relative importance of resource development as part of gross investment was in fact in this period nearly three times as great as investment in secondary manufacturing.[19] This development gave to Canada an unusually high gross investment ratio in 1957–58 (about as high as for Norway) and also implied a relatively high average and marginal capital-output ratio. When this boom in primary products ended around 1956–57, overcapacity had developed,[20] investments were reduced, and the future demand did not look so bright any longer. From the point of investment theory it is interesting to observe that the decline of business fixed investments from 1957 to 1962 (by some 20 per cent) occurred in spite of a substantial rise in the supply of gross business savings (by more than 25 per cent). Apparently the determining factor of the slowdown in business investment was the persistent excess capacity reached after the 1955–56 boom. In fact the unemployment rate remained consistently higher in Canada than in the United States during the period 1957–63.

A difficult adjustment problem arose when the future needs of the United States for Canadian minerals, oil, and wood products appeared to have been very much exaggerated.[21]

19. Resource development as a Canadian term includes mining, oil wells, forestry, electric power, railways, oil and gas pipelines, and manufacture of forest products, nonferrous metal products, and nonmetallic minerals.

20. See the *Report of the Royal Commission on Banking and Finance* (Ottawa, 1964), pp. 36–37.

21. See the Paley report of 1955.

The flow of new investments had to be shifted from the primary to the secondary sectors, at the same time as total investment—from a stabilization point of view—had to continue to expand in order to keep general demand growing rapidly enough. And this shift of resources involving both investment and employment had to occur under specific balance of payments restrictions.

The rapid economic growth up to 1957 was accompanied by an increasing deficit in the current account of the balance of payments. There were small surpluses in 1949 and 1952, but the tendency was clearly a successive rise in the deficit—from $300–500 million in 1950–51 to nearly $1,500 million in 1957; after that the deficit remained high (above $1,000 million) up to 1961. The rise in the deficit during the periods of rapid expansion can be partly attributed to the relatively slow increase of exports in relation to imports.

In fact import and export volumes tend to move at quite different rates both during the short and the long term. Gross investment seems to have a very high marginal import content, implying great variability in what seems to be a considerable part of total imports.[22] Under conditions close to full employment and rapidly rising gross investment, the total import volume tends to rise rapidly in relation to GNP. (That was the case during the boom years 1950–51 and again 1955–56.) The same tendencies may prevail in the longer run. There is no dependable pattern of behavior on the export side. There have been short and strong booms in Canadian mineral and wood-product exports, but the average growth rate during the 1950s is less than 3 per cent per year. Canadian exports seem to contain relatively few products with high "world income elasticity."

The rising and (since the middle of the 1950s) very large

22. See Rudolf R. Rhomberg, "Canada's Foreign Exchange Market," *International Monetary Fund Staff Papers* (April 1960). According to Rhomberg's econometric analysis: "The marginal propensity to import out of disposable income is 0.2, while the marginal propensity to import out of investment expenditure is 0.6" (p. 446).

current account deficits have been covered by short- and long-term capital imports, mainly consisting of United States direct investment and net sales of new issues of Canadian bonds on the New York market. The dependence of the Canadian economy on a high rate of capital imports seems in fact to be a very unstable factor. At its maximum in 1956 the net capital inflow (corresponding to a current account deficit of $1.5 billion amounted to 4½ per cent of GNP or about 20 per cent of gross investment. This meant that, to this significant extent, Canada supplemented the rate of internal saving mainly with United States resources and only thereby financed its very high gross investment ratio. This strong dependence on capital imports, which vary much over the business cycle, has implied a special kind of instability for the Canadian economy. During the 1962 crisis capital imports even tended toward a negative amount. The rate of domestic investment is probably more variable (and on average higher) because of foreign borrowing than it otherwise would be.

POLICY EXPERIMENTS IN CANADA

The policy issues that are of special interest follow from the account of the main instability experiences given above. The main problem can be said to have been to dampen the destabilizing impulses arising from the close interrelations with the United States economy. To what extent could a country with Canada's vulnerable position attain some degree of autonomy as to the working of its stabilization policy?

The specific and original trait of Canadian policy can be said to be the device of flexible or floating exchange rates during the period 1950–61, at least in theory implying scope for independent developments of prices, employment, and under certain conditions also of interest rates. We can visualize an ideal policy model such that, for instance, an inflationary boom in the United States is neutralized by a successive appreciation of the Canadian dollar. It is also possible to imagine a sufficient devaluation of the Canadian dollar, accompanying a recession in the United States so that exports are stimulated and import competition reduced to such an extent that depressive foreign trade reactions would be eliminated. Flexible spot and forward exchange rates might be developing in such a way that during short periods the Bank of Canada would have considerable room for an independent monetary policy with—compared to Federal Reserve policy—more restrictive parameter changes during booms and more expansive ones during recessions.[23] The same view should of course apply to fiscal policy.

In theory, if it were only a matter of smoothing short-term cyclical variations in prices and demand, there need not and should not occur any longer-term tendencies in the movement of the Canadian exchange rate. The whole conception of the creation of cyclical autonomy by means of flexible exchange rates is of course based on Canada's being such a small economic unit in relation to the United States (and the rest of the world) that such policies would not only be tolerated but also not made ineffective by countermeasures in other countries. In this way the disadvantage of being a relatively small dependent economy could be matched by the advantage of being allowed to apply unorthodox policy measures to attain a degree of independence in short-run developments.

Actual developments since 1950 do not give the impression of successful policy results along the lines of neutralizing the cyclical impulses from the United States economy. In fact, as already mentioned, the cycles of booms and recessions are very similar to those of the United States. The recessions in 1949, 1954, and 1958 were milder; however, the retardation of growth and the rise of unemployment in 1957–61 was more pronounced in Canada than in the United States.

It is therefore easy to say that Canadian economic policy has not been successful in shielding the economy from cyclical dis-

23. For this type of argument see Bent Hansen, *Foreign Trade Credits and Exchange Reserves, A Contribution to the Theory of International Capital Movements* (Amsterdam, 1961), esp. Chap. 9.

turbances arising in the United States. However, we have to consider the specific reaction patterns of the Canadian economy as well as other disturbances than those coming from the United States economy. The Korean boom created especially strong inflationary impulses because of the great importance of primary production in Canada's economy. The strong investment boom up to 1956–57 referred mainly, as mentioned above, to the rapidly expanding demand for minerals, wood products, natural gas, electricity, and so forth. Heavy immigration and development of new communities added a building boom on top of the primary production boom. It is not difficult to understand that restrictive government policy could not easily be made effective by itself in dampening excess demand even if serious efforts had been made. That has been the experience of most countries.

In fact monetary and fiscal policies as carried out in Canada give no appearance of having been significantly more ambitious than in the United States (up to 1963). No explicit account of fiscal policies seems to be necessary; very little of active policy changes were tried, also perhaps implying fewer disturbances than in the United States.[24] The working of the automatic budget stabilizers was of the same nature as in the United States, accounting for a part of the stagnationary tendencies during 1958–61.

As to monetary policy, we can observe a characteristically higher amplitude of interest rate fluctuations in Canada than in the United States, with higher rate differentials during booms than during recessions. Thus short-term rates on treasury bills rose from about 1 per cent in the beginning of 1955 (close to the New York level) to about 5 per cent in 1957, reaching 2

24. There seems to be relatively little room for active changes in federal expenditures. The federal government is directly responsible for only about 40 per cent of total expenditures for goods and services of the public sector. Tax-rate changes as part of stabilization policy hardly occurred. During this period there was a great political reluctance to engage in deficit financing.

per cent above the corresponding New York rate. This type of experience was repeated in 1958–59 and again during the exchange crisis in 1962. We may take these relatively wide fluctuations of short-term interest rates (and corresponding movements in other rates) as an indication of a certain degree of policy autonomy and discuss how and to what extent this autonomy was related to the system of flexible exchange rates.

However, we should first comment on the effectiveness of these changes in monetary policy on investment and saving. According to research carried out for the Royal Commission on Banking and Finance of 1964—in the form of survey studies as well as econometric analysis—there seems to have been a very low degree of efficiency.[25] Considerable time lags—both inside and outside lags—and low sensitivity with regard to business investment and consumers' expenditures on durable goods seem to have had very limited effects on the 1955–56 investment boom and probably still less of stimulation in the 1957–58 recession, when the economy suffered from surplus capacity problems in various fields. According to rough measurements, it is even likely that monetary policy largely had destabilizing effects.[26] As in the United States, specific arrangements as to the supply of mortgage credit meant relatively high sensitivity for the volume of house construction with regard to credit availability.

As argued above, the Canadian policy issue is more interesting than just a question of this direct effect (on investment expenditures) of monetary and fiscal policy changes. The interrelations with the changes of the floating exchange rates must be considered; it is a question both of indirect effects

25. The methods and results of this research are presented in Chap. 12 of Harry G. Johnson's book *The Canadian Quandary* (New York, 1963).

26. Monetary policy changes should according to Johnson have implied a "net contribution" to stability only one month out of twelve during the period 1958–61. The score was a little better during the period 1950–57.

of monetary policy via changes of the exchange rate and of the actual or potential scope for policy changes created by the flexibility of the exchange rate.

THE SUCCESS AND FAILURE OF FLEXIBLE EXCHANGE RATES

A policy of flexible exchange rates was introduced at the end of 1950, when, after the 1949 devaluation (by 10 per cent in relation to the United States dollar), the inflow of short-term United States dollars became a difficult problem to manage. The result of this new policy was that the Canadian dollar, after a period of rather continuous rise up to 1952, reached a premium of about 4 to 5 per cent in relation to the United States dollar. (See Figure 8.3.) Compared with a discount of 10 per cent in 1949–50, the appreciation of the Canadian dollar by 15 to 20 per cent certainly meant that the inflationary and expansionary impulses from abroad were less than they would have been at a fixed exchange rate (at the 1949–50 level). There is no doubt for instance that some of the Korean war inflation impulses were neutralized in a more effective way than in other countries which had devalued much more than Canada in 1949 and had kept the exchange rate constant since then. Our conclusion can only be that the inflationary tendencies in Canada would have been still stronger after 1950 if this appreciation of the Canadian dollar had not occurred.

The problem is, however, how much of stabilizing exchange policy there was after the decision in 1950 to introduce flexible rates. Why did the appreciation not become large enough to dampen the 1954–56 boom more effectively? And why did not a depreciation come about after 1956, when recession and relative stagnation were the main stability problems? Before 1961 the Exchange Fund did not in a significant way actively enter the market in order to change the rate, except for smoothing out short-term fluctuations. This meant that the development of the exchange rate during this period should be considered as more or less the automatic result of changing market conditions and not as the direct product of an active exchange policy. In fact the flexible exchange rate worked well by any appropriate technical test, as capital movements tended to stabilize the rate. The most interesting feature of the policy constellation was that stabilization policies could be carried out without the usual narrow restrictions of fixed exchange rates that might have implied disturbing fluctuations of exchange reserves.

In one respect the policy of flexible exchange rates became a complete success: Canadian official holding of gold and United States dollars were kept at a nearly perfectly stable level (of about 2 billion) over the whole period between the end of 1950 and the end of 1961, with only very insignificant fluctuations. (See Figure 8.3.) This result meant that the functioning of the free exchange market was such that the variations in the exchange rate effectively cleared the market. From this point of view, net changes of exchange reserves were eliminated as disturbances on the money supply. The figure shows that this

FIGURE 8.3
Canadian Exchange Rates and Reserves, 1947–63

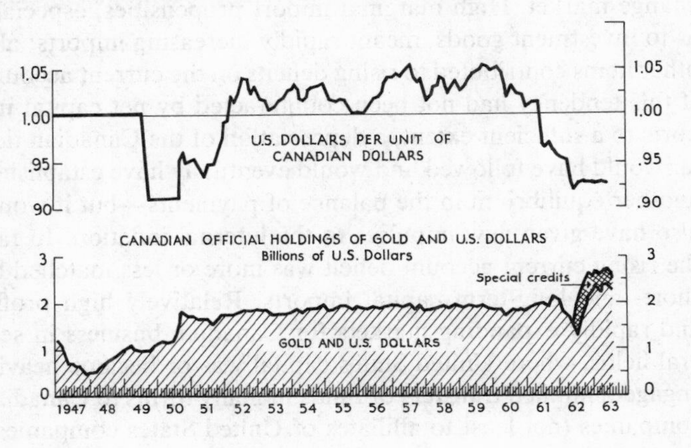

clearance of the market could be achieved by means of rather limited fluctuations of the exchange rate: after the initial appreciation from 0.90 cents to the United States dollar to a level above parity reached in 1952, the range of fluctuations kept within the limits of 1.00 and 1.06.

The narrow range of fluctuations of the exchange rate may be considered to be remarkable from the point of view of the big changes over the cycle in the Canadian current account balance. Apparently these changes were effectively counterbalanced by corresponding alterations on the capital account. These results may partly be due to the fact that shifts in the current and capital acounts both occur in response to changes in the level of domestic activity. In contrast to the conditions in the United Kingdom (see Chapter 4), it seems as if the relevant propensities and elasticities had such values that the ensuing adjustment of the balance of payments came about easily and smoothly. The demand and supply sides could therefore be kept in close equilibrium by means of these moderate changes in the exchange rate. Before discussing this question, let us give a short survey of the important phases of the development.

Looking first at the inflationary expansion developing from 1954, there were two countertendencies working on the exchange market. High marginal import propensities, especially as to investment goods, meant rapidly increasing imports; also other items contributed to rising deficits on the current account. If this tendency had not been counteracted by net capital imports to a sufficient extent, a depreciation of the Canadian dollar would have followed and would eventually have established another equilibrium in the balance of payments—but it would also have given new impulses to the internal inflation. In fact the rising current account deficit was more or less matched by short- and long-term capital imports. Relatively high profits and rapidly expanding markets for Canadian business in several fields, where United States capital was or became heavily engaged, implied transfers of funds in many forms to Canadian companies (not least to affiliates of United States companies).

There was a rather continuous and rapid rise of foreign direct investment in Canada from the beginning of the 1950s up to 1960 (with a minor interruption in 1957 and 1958).[27] On top of this development there were "effects" of changes in the relative level of interest rates in Canada, making financing in New York by corporations, provinces, and communes more remunerative in the boom than in the recession. A rising gap between the rates would tend to stimulate transfers of funds to Canada.[28]

One of the main policy issues refers to possible relations between the interest rate differential (in the above sense) and the movements of the exchange rate. There was a longer time lag in Canada than in the United States with regard to restrictive monetary policy during the 1955–56 boom. From the middle of 1954 to the spring of 1955, short-term interest rates were declining in Canada while at the same time they were rising in the United States. Thereafter up to the fall of 1955 they were rising more slowly in Canada. We can observe that the Canadian dollar depreciated slowly up to the end of 1955 (by about 3 per cent from the middle of 1954). However, during the following period of more rapidly rising interest rates in Canada (in relation to the United States) resulting in a differential of 0.5 to 1 per cent by 1957, the Canadian dollar appreciated by 5 per cent.

We can apparently regard the rise of the Canadian dollar

27. See the diagram in OECD, *Economic Surveys: Canada* (December 1963), p. 20.

28. There seems to be a high elasticity of both short- and long-term capital flows with regard to the interest rate differential. According to Rhomberg's econometric results, a rise of one percentage point in the Canadian long-term rate would attract 90 million dollars of long-term capital per quarter, thus, for instance, covering one third of the average yearly current account deficit during 1956–60. A differential of 1 per cent per year in favor of Canada for the short-term interest rate would, according to the same study, attract 30 million dollars in speculative funds per quarter. Rhomberg, "Canada's Foreign Exchange Market," p. 446.

from the end of 1955 as a rather weak and lagged amplifier of the restrictive monetary policy. According to the studies in the Report of the Royal Commission on Banking and Finance, the extra effect was, however, very limited.[29] Our conclusion is that the flexibility of the exchange rate in the Canadian policy setup hardly seemed to imply any visible degree of more effective stabilization policy than in the other countries surveyed, which did not enjoy this space for maneuver. A comparison with Sweden, for instance, rather gives the impression of a relatively weak stabilization policy in Canada during this period. But in any event the parameter changes worked in the right direction. This was hardly the case during the following recession and stagnation, when the policy reactions in fact worked in a still more ineffective, partly even perverted way.

THE DEFICIENCY OF SUPPORTING POLICIES IN CANADA

When after 1957 the investment boom broke down, overcapacities appeared, and export markets became sluggish, there did not appear much in the way of autonomous equilibrating processes to help the Canadian economy adjust itself to the new conditions. The import surplus and current deficit in the balance of payments remained very large (of nearly the same order of size as in 1956–57) during the following years up to the end of 1961, thus aggravating the total deficit de-

29. Some very crude estimates—based on a case study of the credit restraints in 1958–60—may be indicative also of the order of size of the 1955–57 effects. Econometric research, survey studies, and pure guesswork combined gave as a result an estimate of total direct and indirect effects corresponding to 0.5 to 1 per cent of GNP. If the plausible effects of the consequent appreciation of the Canadian dollar are added, there could be an additional effect of 0.25 to 1 per cent of GNP. The report clearly underlines the hazards in these estimates, but maintains that they give "a reliable indication of the orders of magnitude." *Report on Banking and Finance,* pp. 438–44.

mand situation of the stagnating Canadian economy. The Canadian dollar did not depreciate "automatically," as should have been expected from an equilibrating market mechanism, but stayed above par with the United States dollar up to 1960. This lack of reaction depended again on the continued large inflow of capital, and this in turn was apparently to a large extent determined by the relatively high interest rates on the Canadian money and capital markets. The rapid rise of interest rates in Canada during 1958 is accounted for by a number of factors: a big conversion loan,[30] fear of inflation, and lack of confidence, apparently partly related to the large budget deficit of 1958–59. The development was in this respect similar to that of the bond market in the United States (the "panic" of August 1958). This decline of bond prices and corresponding rise of interest rates during 1958–59 may be regarded as a sort of market response to the needs of financing the budget deficit, as the tendencies were not effectively counteracted by an expansive monetary policy.

This type of "market mechanism" implied a perverse reaction: high interest rates (an increased gap in relation to New York) stimulated large capital imports with consequent high demand for the Canadian dollar and a persistent premium, meaning continued stimulus to imports and obstacles to exports.

In this case of needed stimulation of the economy during and after the 1957–58 recession, it is relatively easy to imagine a more effective policy. The central bank could have controlled the development of interest rates, could for instance have prevented the rise by abstaining from the conversion loan and by creating more liquidity (for example by financing the budget deficit in the banks). A sufficient dose of monetary expansion would have created a favorable reaction on the exchange rates,

30. According to Johnson's estimate this conversion to longer-term government debt was equivalent to an 8 per cent reduction in the money supply. *The Canadian Quandary*, pp. 181–82.

a depreciation that would have had stimulating effects on the Canadian economy. In this case we know that this is not only a theoretical proposition: a policy of active depreciation was in fact carried out later (after about three years), when the bad effects of the actual policy efforts in 1958–60 had been clearly recognized. We may consider this belated reaction as implying a considerable time lag; it in fact involved a rather radical change in policy attitudes (and a change of governor in the Bank of Canada).

However, our account should also include some kind of understanding or explanation of the actual policy reactions. One part of the defense of the actual policy referred to "financial confidence." A lack of confidence in an expansionary monetary policy might have appeared from the side of Wall Street as well as in financial quarters in Montreal and Toronto. Such a lack of confidence might have resulted in a quick depreciation of the Canadian dollar. A combination of expansionary policy and depreciation could therefore already in 1958 have given rise to a double push on the economy by reducing or eliminating the import surplus and stimulating internal expenditures. Fears of a "runaway inflation" and too rapid depreciation apparently existed and blocked the way for such policy reactions. There was also another type of argument that we have met before in defense of passive attitudes to stabilization policies. It was argued—especially by the governor of the Bank of Canada—that the stagnation in the Canadian economy since 1957 and the high unemployment rate were not the effects of deficient demand but were caused by a structural maladjustment that could not be solved and should not be covered by "inflationary methods."

It is of interest to note that the shift in policy from the second half of 1961 was in fact followed by an exchange crisis. However, it can hardly be argued that the developments in 1961–62 confirm the fears of 1958–59. The Canadian experience rather shows how a policy change in a correct direction but coming too late can create short-run difficulties.

THE ENDING OF THE CANADIAN EXPERIMENT

In the 1961 budget, presented in June 1961, the government first publicily announced that it would facilitate the movement of the Canadian dollar to a significant discount. This took place in an orderly way during the second half of 1961 by means of intervention by the Exchange Fund and also by reducing the gap between Canadian and United States interest rates. But when the government at the end of the year announced that the 95-cent dollar rate reached at that time was about right and started to defend this position, then heavy speculative forces entered the market, resulting in a growing short-term capital outflow and a drying up of the long-term inflow. A pegged rate of 92.5 cents was announced in May 1962, but the result was an intense speculative pressure on the Canadian dollar and a crisis of confidence. The loss of exchange reserves accelerated, so that during 1962 up to the end of June, Canada had lost about one billion dollars, corresponding to nearly half of its exchange reserves existing at the end of 1961. Emergency measures were introduced at the end of June, including measures to stop the outflow of capital and create confidence with regard to the speculative forces as well as measures designed to reduce the trade deficit (by means of heavy surcharges on imports) and in this way also the need for capital imports. The central bank increased the discount rate to 6 per cent, the budget deficit was reduced (partly by cutting government expenditures), various external borrowing arrangements were made (from the International Monetary Fund, the Export-Import Bank, the Federal Reserve System, and the Bank of England to a total sum of 1.05 billion dollars) and the depreciation of the Canadian dollar to 92.5 cents was confirmed.

The emergency program of June 1962, implying a domestic austerity program and massive international support for the Canadian dollar, put an end to the exchange speculation. The deficit on current account fell quickly and significantly, at the same time as imports of long-term capital were resumed. The result was that the official gold and foreign exchange reserves had been restored to the precrisis level as early as the end of 1962. In a way this emergency policy was surprisingly successful; the effects of the high interest rates and the import surcharges came so quickly that no disturbances had time to occur with regard to the rapid expansion that had started in the spring of 1961. The rather drastic moves and the effective foreign exchange support restored confidence in the Canadian dollar nearly overnight, so that the restrictive measures could be abandoned before the end of the year. A lasting measure was the devaluation of the Canadian dollar by 10 per cent, implying a strengthening of Canada's competitive position and some loss in the terms of trade.

One could finish this survey of Canada's policy experiences with the conclusion that the experiment with floating exchange rates was not very successful. Canada's economy reached balance and came back to rapid growth first after a return to a fixed, depreciated rate. Such a statement would, however, be an oversimplified misinterpretation of the facts. First, the high growth rate in 1962–64 must partly be regarded as a reaction from the low level reached after the relative stagnation between 1957 and the 1961 recession. The development is again quite parallel to that of the United States. More important, the experiences with flexible exchange rates during the period 1950–61 tell us little more than nothing about the *potential* possibilities. As discussed above, the stabilization policies carried out—especially with regard to monetary policy—were badly adapted to the changing demands, and this judgment refers especially to the years after 1957. A more restrictive policy applied earlier during the boom that developed from 1954, and a consistent expansive policy during at least the years 1958–59, could have meant an interesting experiment in success or failure. Such policies would have tested the possibilities of attaining a more independent development in relation to the United States. On the basis of actual events, it does not seem possible to answer the strategic question to what extent first an appreciation and then a devaluation of the Canadian dollar would have created not only the needed scope for independent policy maneuvers, but in addition how the rate fluctuations would also have implied a strong support for the stabilization policy in question. But in fact as we have seen, Canadian and American policies and developments were in quite close conformity during this period.

We can to a certain extent theorize about these possibilities and give a persuasive scientific flavor to our assertions regarding the good prospects of such policies. The unfortunate fact is, however, that we cannot prove anything more definite by, for instance, applying the quantitative relations of Rhomberg's model with regard to the 1950–61 experiences. His results refer only to the relatively narrow movements in exchange rates and interest rate differentials that actually occurred during this period. We know nothing about what would happen with wider variations into a range in which Rhomberg's econometric equations might very well be inapplicable. This problem specifically refers to the stabilizing effects of short-term capital movements, being one of the most interesting results of Rhomberg's analysis. He shows how exchange rate fluctuations within narrow limits (1 to 2 per cent in a quarter) tend to induce stabilizing speculation, implying sufficient inflow or outflow of funds to cover the deficits or surpluses of the current plus long-term capital account. The sensitivity of capital flows with regard to exchange rate fluctuations seems to have been high enough—under given conditions as to interest rate differentials, and so forth—to prevent any tendency to cumulative appreciation and depreciation. The elasticity of expectations[31] underlying this result may be interpreted as based on some kind of "parity psychology," implying confidence that the fluctuations would not surpass certain limits and that the rate would return to a normal level. Ultimately this confidence must be considered as

31. Rhomberg makes the plausible argument that fluctuations in exchange rates will induce stabilizing speculation when the elasticity of exchange rate expectations is less than unity. See "Canada's Foreign Exchange Market," pp. 442–43.

founded on experience with actual developments, which were in fact governed by such close conformity between policies and developments in Canada and the United States that the exchange rate could keep within these narrow limits.

This type of circular reasoning does not lead us further than to the original statement that, if in Canada a policy deviating significantly from that in the United States had come about, then the exchange rate would have had to deviate so much from normal levels that there might eventually have been no stabilizing short-term capital flows. Under these conditions—after breaking through the "confidence wall"—it would have been easy to get a cumulative appreciation or depreciation of the Canadian dollar. Then the art of manipulating interest rates would have been a real test of skillful management, at the same time as effects of the changing exchange rates on trade and expenditures would have been felt. But this type of policy experiment was never tried. There was fear of inflation and budget deficits during the recessions, and acceptance of inflation as unavoidable and uncontrollable during the booms, which are not uncommon policy attitudes. The Canadian policy attitude also included a determined aversion to accept cumulative or wide changes in the exchange rate under the floating exchange system.[32]

32. This attitude is clearly written out in the *Report of the Royal Commission on Banking and Finance* (p. 488): "Indeed, it is unlikely that a flexible rate which had fluctuated over a wide range would have achieved the degree of international acceptability which was accorded the Canadian rate and is vital to the workability of any exchange rate system. Moreover, wide swings in a fluctuating rate might have been difficult to contain. If the policies followed in Canada had led to the view that there was no reasonable limit to the likely moves in the exchange rate, speculative capital movements might have become violently destabilizing."

APPENDIX

VARIATION AND VARIABILITY OF THE GROWTH OF GNP AND ITS EXPENDITURE COMPONENTS IN FOURTEEN COUNTRIES, 1950–64

Notations:

$\Delta y_t / y_{t\ 1}$ rate of growth of GNP at constant prices

y_t. GNP at constant prices in year t

c_t private consumption at constant prices

g_t public purchases of goods and services at constant prices

$i_{f,t}$ private fixed investment at constant prices

$i_{s,t}$ inventory investment at constant prices

x_t exports at constant prices

m_t imports at constant prices

p_t price of GNP (GNP-deflator)

M average rate of growth of GNP and its expenditure components in terms of percentages of GNP lagged one year

D average deviation of the annual percentage rates of growth of GNP and its expenditure components around their respective average rate of growth, M (This measure is referred to in the text as index of variation.)

D/M ratio of average deviation to the respective average rate of growth (index of variability)

Sources of underlying data: OEEC, *General Statistics* (Paris, various issues), for 1949–53; OECD, *Statistics of National Accounts 1950–61* (Paris, 1964), for 1953–55; OECD, *Statistics of National Accounts 1955–64* (Paris, 1966), for 1955–64; U.N. *Yearbook of National Accounts Statistics* (New York, various years), for Japan (completed with the help of some official Japanese sources); Eidgenössisches Volkswirtschaftsdepartement, *Die Volkswirtschaft* (Bern, September issue of 1964 and of 1966), for Switzerland; U.S. Department of Commerce, OBE, *Survey of Current Business,* for the United States. U.N., *Some Factors in Economic Growth in Europe During the 1950s* (Geneva, 1965), chap. 4, Table 7; and U.N., *Yearbook of National Accounts Statistics,* were used for splitting public and private investment, which are not separated in the above OEEC and OECD publications.

TABLE A1

AUSTRIA

	1950	1951	1952	1953	1954	1955	1956
$\Delta c_t / y_{t-1}$	4.8	2.2	1.5	4.8	4.3	7.0	3.9
$\Delta g_t / y_{t-1}$	(1.3)	1.3	—0.5	0.3	0.6	1.0	0.0
$\Delta i_{f,t} / y_{t-1}$	(3.5)	3.3	—0.1	—2.7	3.8	5.6	—0.7
$\Delta i_{s,t} / y_{t-1}$	—6.6	1.2	—5.2	—2.8	1.6	2.4	—1.7
$\Delta x_t / y_{t-1}$	5.9	0.9	0.7	4.8	4.3	0.7	4.7
$-\Delta m_t / y_{t-1}$	1.4	—2.0	3.8	—0.6	—6.0	—5.5	—1.1
$\Delta y_t / y_{t-1}$	10.4	6.9	0.3	3.9	8.6	11.1	5.1
$\Delta (y_t P_t) / y_{t-1} P_{t-1}$	23.1	33.1	15.9	2.9	12.4	15.4	9.7
$\Delta P_t / P_{t-1}$	11.5	24.5	15.6	—1.0	3.5	3.9	4.4

TABLE A2

BELGIUM

	1950	1951	1952	1953	1954	1955	1956
$\Delta c_t / y_{t-1}$	5.2	0.9	—0.2	1.0	2.6	4.4	1.3
$\Delta g_t / y_{t-1}$	(1.5)	(2.5)	0.6	0.5	0.2	—0.6	0.3
$\Delta i_{f,t} / y_{t-1}$	(0.8)	(—2.7)	0.4	0.9	1.4	0.6	1.5
$\Delta i_{s,t} / y_{t-1}$	—0.9	1.7	—0.5	—0.3	0.3	—0.8	0.9
$\Delta x_t / y_{t-1}$	2.7	3.7	—1.6	3.0	3.0	4.7	2.7
$-\Delta m_t / y_{t-1}$	—4.3	—0.4	0.4	—1.1	—3.8	—2.9	—3.7
$\Delta y_t / y_{t-1}$	5.0	5.7	—0.9	4.0	3.7	5.5	2.9
$\Delta (y_t P_t) / y_{t-1} P_{t-1}$	3.6	15.4	2.1	2.0	4.3	6.4	6.6
$\Delta P_t / P_{t-1}$	—1.3	9.2	3.0	—1.9	0.6	0.9	3.6

1959	1960	1961	1962	1963	1964	M	D	D/M
3.3	4.1	3.2	3.5	3.3	2.4	3.59	0.98	0.27
0.5	0.6	0.4	0.4	0.8	0.9	0.65	0.38	0.58
1.2	2.8	1.6	—0.4	0.4	1.8	1.47	1.69	1.15
—0.6	3.6	—1.2	—2.5	0.4	1.5	—0.62	1.92	3.10
2.2	2.8	1.9	2.1	2.5	2.3	2.56	1.33	0.52
—3.7	—5.6	—1.3	—1.5	—3.0	—3.0	—2.08	2.04	0.98
2.8	8.3	4.6	1.6	4.4	6.0	5.60	2.40	0.43
4.8	12.6	10.0	5.2	7.1	9.9	11.80	5.56	
1.9	4.0	5.2	3.5	2.6	3.7	5.89		

1959	1960	1961	1962	1963	1964	M	D	D/M
1.3	4.1	1.5	3.0	3.6	2.7	2.21	1.36	0.62
1.1	0.6	0.4	1.4	1.8	0.5	0.77	0.60	0.78
1.0	2.3	1.8	0.3	0.0	1.3	0.54	0.90	1.67
0.5	—0.6	0.5	—0.3	—0.1	0.4	0.01	0.64	64.00
2.4	3.4	3.0	3.6	2.8	5.2	2.63	1.09	0.41
—3.7	—4.1	—2.5	—2.9	—3.3	—4.9	—2.44	1.56	0.64
2.6	5.6	4.7	5.0	4.8	5.2	3.69	1.64	0.44
2.9	6.5	5.9	6.8	7.8	10.1	5.80	2.57	
0.3	0.9	1.1	1.7	2.9	4.7	2.04		

TABLE A3

CANADA

	1950	1951	1952	1953	1954	1955	1956
$\Delta c_t / y_{t-1}$	4.3	0.9	4.3	3.4	1.4	4.8	4.1
$\Delta g_t / y_{t-1}$	0.7	3.2	3.8	0.0	—0.5	0.7	0.6
$\Delta i_{f,t} / y_{t-1}$	1.6	1.3	1.1	2.1	—1.0	1.1	4.8
$\Delta i_{s,t} / y_{t-1}$	2.0	1.1	—1.0	0.1	—2.9	2.4	2.3
$\Delta x_t / y_{t-1}$	—0.1	2.0	2.3	—0.2	—0.8	1.6	1.5
$-\Delta m_t / y_{t-1}$	—2.0	—2.4	—0.9	—1.7	1.1	—3.2	—3.7
	0.4	0.0	—1.6	0.1	—0.1	1.2	—1.0
$\Delta y_t / y_{t-1}$	7.0	6.1	8.0	3.8	—2.9	8.6	8.7
$\Delta (y_t P_t) / y_{t-1} P_{t-1}$	10.1	17.6	13.4	4.3	—0.6	9.1	12.8
$\Delta P_t / P_{t-1}$	2.9	10.8	5.0	0.5	2.4	0.5	3.8

TABLE A4

DENMARK

	1950	1951	1952	1953	1954	1955	1956
$\Delta c_t / y_{t-1}$	4.7	—2.1	0.9	2.0	4.3	0.0	1.4
$\Delta g_t / y_{t-1}$	(1.8)	0.9	0.7	1.3	1.0	0.2	0.1
$\Delta i_{f,t} / y_{t-1}$	(0.2)	—0.6	0.9	1.2	0.9	—1.1	0.6
$\Delta i_{s,t} / y_{t-1}$	2.5	—3.8	—0.9	2.1	—0.3	—1.4	1.4
$\Delta x_t / y_{t-1}$	6.6	3.5	—0.6	3.0	2.3	2.4	0.8
$-\Delta m_t / y_{t-1}$	—7.0	1.8	0.5	—3.8	—5.4	0.0	—2.1
$\Delta y_t / y_{t-1}$	8.8	—0.2	1.6	5.8	2.8	0.1	2.1
$\Delta (y_t P_t) / y_{t-1} P_{t-1}$	15.0	7.4	6.7	7.2	4.7	4.4	7.1
$\Delta P_t / P_{t-1}$	5.7	7.6	5.0	1.3	1.8	4.3	4.9

1959	1960	1961	1962	1963	1964	M	D	D/M
3.1	2.1	2.1	3.1	2.8	3.8	0.91	0.45	0.49
0.2	0.4	0.5	0.7	0.0	0.8	1.07	0.94	0.88
—0.9	—0.9	—0.2	0.3	1.0	2.5	0.12	1.94	16.17
2.1	—0.1	—0.9	1.4	—0.2	—0.4	2.60	1.05	0.40
0.7	0.8	1.4	1.0	1.8	2.6	—2.82	2.53	0.90
—2.3	0.1	—0.5	—0.6	—0.6	—2.5	4.28	2.54	0.59
0.4	0.1	0.0	0.6	—0.1	—0.3	8.32	2.72	
3.3	2.5	2.5	6.7	4.6	6.5	3.87		
6.1	3.9	3.2	8.2	6.5	8.9	2.94	0.87	0.30
2.7	1.4	0.7	1.4	1.8	2.3	0.81	0.74	0.91

1959	1960	1961	1962	1963	1964	M	D	D/M
4.0	3.3	5.1	4.5	0.2	4.1	0.79	1.24	1.57
0.9	0.8	1.4	1.9	0.5	1.4	0.11	1.42	12.91
3.5	1.6	2.0	1.4	—0.4	3.7	0.98	0.85	0.87
3.0	1.6	—2.0	1.2	—2.7	2.8	—1.15	1.30	1.13
2.2	2.7	1.4	1.8	3.5	3.4	—0.01	0.43	
—6.4	—3.4	—1.6	—5.1	0.5	—7.6	4.53	2.66	0.59
7.2	6.6	6.4	5.7	1.7	7.8	7.40	3.77	
11.1	7.9	10.8	12.5	6.6	12.6	2.75		
3.6	1.2	4.1	6.4	4.8	4.5	2.39	1.86	0.78

TABLE A5
FRANCE

	1950	1951	1952	1953	1954	1955	1956
$\Delta c_t / y_{t-1}$	4.1	5.1	2.1	2.9	2.5	3.8	4.0
$\Delta g_t / y_{t-1}$	1.4	0.8	2.5	0.7	—1.2	0.1	2.1
$\Delta i_{f,t} / y_{t-1}$	0.2	0.9	—0.9	0.0	1.0	1.9	1.2
$\Delta i_{s,t} / y_{t-1}$	0.4	—0.9	0.0	—0.9	0.8	—0.4	1.2
$\Delta x_t / y_{t-1}$	2.6	2.0	—0.4	0.2	2.5	1.0	—1.2
$-\Delta m_t / y_{t-1}$	—1.0	—1.8	—0.7	0.1	—0.8	—0.7	—2.2
$\Delta y_t / y_{t-1}$	7.7	6.0	2.5	3.0	4.8	5.8	5.0
$\Delta (y_t P_t) / y_{t-1} P_{t-1}$	15.8	22.7	17.2	4.4	5.9	7.1	10.5
$\Delta P_t / P_{t-1}$	7.5	15.8	14.3	1.4	1.0	1.2	5.2

TABLE A6
GERMANY (Federal Republic)

	1950[a]	1951	1952	1953	1954	1955	1956
$\Delta c_t / y_{t-1}$		4.1	4.4	6.6	3.2	5.6	4.9
$\Delta g_t / y_{t-1}$		2.1	1.9	0.3	0.8	1.1	0.4
$\Delta i_{f,t} / y_{t-1}$		1.1	1.0	2.5	2.5	3.7	1.2
$\Delta i_{s,t} / y_{t-1}$		—0.4	1.4	—2.4	1.0	1.6	—0.9
$\Delta x_t / y_{t-1}$		4.3	2.3	2.8	4.0	3.5	3.2
$-\Delta m_t / y_{t-1}$		—0.7	—2.7	—2.3	—4.1	—3.9	—1.9
$\Delta y_t / y_{t-1}$	(14.3)	10.5	8.3	7.5	7.4	11:5	6.9
$\Delta (y_t P_t) / y_{t-1} P_{t-1}$	(13.0)	22.0	14.3	7.3	7.5	14.0	10.2
$\Delta P_t / P_{t-1}$	(—1.1)	10.4	5.5	—0.2	0.1	2.2	3.1

a. Details only partially available.

b. Impact on 1960 figures of the inclusion of the Saar and West Berlin from 1960 onward was discounted.

1959	1960	1961	1962	1963	1964	M	D	D/M
1.2	3.6	3.8	4.5	4.3	2.8	3.27	0.98	0.30
1.1	0.4	0.8	0.9	0.6	0.7	0.74	0.59	0.80
0.3	1.2	1.6	1.2	1.1	1.8	0.95	0.57	0.60
—1.4	1.8	—1.7	1.2	—0.7	0.9	0.04	0.84	21.00
1.6	2.5	0.9	0.5	1.3	1.2	1.05	0.84	0.80
0.2	—2.2	—1.0	—1.3	—1.9	—1.9	—1.03	0.68	0.66
3.0	7.4	4.4	7.1	4.7	5.5	5.03	1.37	0.27
9.3	10.8	7.9	11.4	11.0	9.2	11.35	3.47	
6.1	3.2	3.4	4.0	6.0	3.5	6.01		

1959	1960[b]	1961	1962	1963	1964	M	D	D/M
3.2	4.3	4.0	3.5	1.5	3.1	3.90	0.94	0.24
1.7	1.5	1.4	2.1	1.5	0.4	1.22	0.52	0.43
2.3	2.2	1.8	0.9	0.3	2.4	1.64	0.85	0.52
0.3	1.4	—1.0	—0.8	—0.4	0.8	0.03	0.92	30.66
2.9	3.6	0.8	0.8	1.9	2.2	2.62	0.96	0.37
—3.4	—4.3	—1.6	—2.3	—1.7	—2.4	—2.55	0.81	0.32
7.0	8.8	5.4	4.2	3.2	6.5	6.86 (7.36)[c]	1.86 (2.19)[c]	0.27 (0.30)[c]
8.4	12.0	9.9	8.7	6.3	9.7	10.44 (10.61)[c]	2.94 (2.97)[c]	
1.3	2.9	4.2	4.3	3.0	3.0	3.31 (3.02)[c]		

c. Includes respective figure for 1950.

TABLE A7
ITALY

	1950	1951	1952	1953	1954	1955	1956
$\Delta c_t / y_{t-1}$	3.5	3.4	2.8	5.4	1.5	2.6	2.6
$\Delta g_t / y_{t-1}$	0.5	1.6	2.4	0.6	1.1	0.4	0.6
$\Delta i_{f,t} / y_{t-1}$	1.8	1.4	1.4	1.0	1.6	2.0	1.8
$\Delta i_{s,t} / y_{t-1}$	0.7	0.8	—2.0	0.4	0.0	1.2	—0.6
$\Delta x_t / y_{t-1}$	2.0	1.2	—0.1	2.4	1.2	1.6	1.4
$-\Delta m_t / y_{t-1}$	—1.4	—0.7	—1.5	—2.2	—0.3	—1.1	—1.7
$\Delta y_t / y_{t-1}$	7.1	7.6	2.9	7.6	5.1	6.7	4.2
$\Delta (y_t P_t) / y_{t-1} P_{t-1}$	11.0	15.9	6.2	9.6	6.6	9.4	7.8
$\Delta P_t / P_{t-1}$	3.6	7.7	3.2	1.9	1.4	2.5	3.5

TABLE A8
JAPAN

	1950	1951	1952	1953	1954	1955	1956
$\Delta c_t / y_{t-1}$	5.5	5.6	10.3	5.5	2.1	4.3	3.7
$\Delta g_t / y_{t-1}$	0.0	1.2	3.8	2.9	0.7	0.3	0.0
$\Delta i_{f,t} / y_{t-1}$	1.4	0.6	2.2	1.3	0.3	0.2	5.0
$\Delta i_{s,t} / y_{t-1}$	0.7	4.3	—3.3	—0.6	—2.3	4.9	2.3
$\Delta x_t / y_{t-1}$	5.5	3.7	1.1	2.0	1.4	2.0	1.4
$-\Delta m_t / y_{t-1}$	—0.7	—3.1	—2.7	—4.5	1.1	—0.7	—3.8
$\Delta y_t / y_{t-1}$	11.7	13.6	10.9	6.7	3.3	11.2	8.7
$\Delta (y_t P_t) / y_{t-1} P_{t-1}$	16.9	37.9	12.4	15.8	5.4	10.7	10.1
$\Delta P_t / P_{t-1}$	4.7	21.4	1.4	8.5	2.0	—0.4	1.3

1959	1960	1961	1962	1963	1964	M	D	D/M
3.3	4.0	4.8	4.6	6.2	1.7	3.37	1.10	0.33
1.0	1.1	0.8	0.2	0.9	0.5	0.97	0.47	0.48
1.6	2.9	2.6	2.4	1.7	—2.5	1.42	0.79	0.56
0.4	0.9	—0.1	0.0	—0.4	—0.3	0.07	0.54	7.71
2.4	3.0	2.9	2.0	1.2	2.2	1.79	0.73	0.41
—1.3	—5.2	—2.8	—2.9	—4.4	1.4	—1.71	1.20	0.70
7.3	6.8	8.3	6.3	5.3	3.0	5.91	1.41	0.24
6.9	9.0	10.5	12.6	14.3	9.3	9.57	2.20	
—0.4	2.1	2.0	5.9	8.5	6.1	3.45		

1959	1960	1961	1962	1963	1964	M	D	D/M
4.5	4.7	4.6	4.0	4.4	4.0	4.68	1.91	0.41
2.6	1.3	3.8	3.6	3.3	2.2	1.89	1.20	0.63
4.4	8.7	5.7	—0.3	1.8	4.6	2.69	2.09	0.78
7.6	0.1	3.1	—4.4	4.1	—1.7	0.57	3.07	5.38
1.6	1.9	1.1	1.9	1.2	3.3	2.05	0.86	0.42
—3.1	—2.6	—3.0	0.1	—3.0	—1.3	—1.82	1.50	0.82
17.5	14.1	15.3	5.0	11.9	11.1	10.09	3.53	0.35
20.7	16.8	21.9	11.2	12.4	16.6	14.65	5.88	
2.7	2.4	5.7	5.9	0.4	5.0	4.09		

TABLE A9

NETHERLANDS

	1950	1951	1952	1953	1954	1955	1956
$\Delta c_t / y_{t-1}$	1.1	—1.6	0.3	3.4	4.2	4.3	4.7
$\Delta g_t / y_{t-1}$	—0.4	0.1	1.3	1.6	0.4	0.7	0.9
$\Delta i_{f,t} / y_{t-1}$	1.2	—0.7	—1.3	2.4	2.7	2.9	2.4
$\Delta i_{s,t} / y_{t-1}$	4.2	—1.5	—5.6	0.3	4.7	—1.3	0.2
$\Delta x_t / y_{t-1}$	9.0	3.9	4.0	6.1	5.7	4.5	1.6
$—\Delta m_t / y_{t-1}$	—11.4	2.6	3.5	—7.0	—10.2	—3.5	—6.4
$\Delta y_t / y_{t-1}$	3.7	3.0	2.0	8.5	7.3	7.7	3.4
$\Delta (y_t P_t) / y_{t-1} P_{t-1}$	10.9	14.5	4.8	6.7	11.5	12.0	7.6
$\Delta P_t / P_{t-1}$	6.9	11.2	2.7	—1.7	3.9	4.0	4.1

TABLE A10

NORWAY

	1950	1951	1952	1953	1954	1955	1956
$\Delta c_t / y_{t-1}$	2.4	—1.4	2.2	2.5	2.0	2.2	1.8
$\Delta g_t / y_{t-1}$	(0.4)[a]	1.4	1.3	1.9	0.8	—0.2	0.4
$\Delta i_{f,t} / y_{t-1}$	(—0.1)[a]	—0.7	1.4	2.8	1.1	1.5	0.2
$\Delta i_{s,t} / y_{t-1}$	—1.4	2.6	—1.4	—2.6	1.3	—0.7	2.0
$\Delta x_t / y_{t-1}$	6.5	3.7	—0.5	2.4	3.6	2.5	3.8
$—\Delta m_t / y_{t-1}$	—2.5	—2.6	1.1	—2.8	—4.5	—3.0	—3.2
$\Delta y_t / y_{t-1}$	5.3	3.0	4.1	4.2	4.3	2.3	5.1
$\Delta (y_t P_t) / y_{t-1} P_{t-1}$	10.4	23.9	10.4	1.1	7.8	6.2	12.9
$\Delta P_t / P_{t-1}$	4.8	20.3	6.1	—3.0	3.4	3.8	7.4

a. 1950 public consumption resp. total fixed investment.

1959	1960	1961	1962	1963	1964	M	D	D/M
2.7	3.7	3.3	3.8	3.9	3.5	2.51	1.66	0.66
0.4	1.2	1.0	1.0	0.7	0.8	0.75	0.57	0.76
2.1	2.5	1.2	0.8	0.4	3.5	1.14	1.41	1.24
0.5	3.0	—0.5	—1.1	—0.2	2.5	0.23	1.87	8.13
5.8	7.1	1.7	3.4	3.3	6.9	4.66	1.69	0.36
—6.3	—8.6	—3.1	—4.1	—5.2	—9.0	—4.55	3.70	0.81
5.2	8.9	3.5	3.8	3.1	8.2	4.76	2.30	0.48
7.0	11.2	6.0	7.1	7.9	16.2	8.91	3.05	
1.7	2.1	2.4	3.2	4.7	7.4	3.97		

1959	1960	1961	1962	1963	1964	M	D	D/M
2.3	3.6	3.6	1.6	2.1	2.3	1.91	0.81	0.42
1.1	0.5	0.9	1.4	1.4	1.3	0.92	0.45	0.49
—1.8	0.2	3.3	1.3	2.0	0.0	0.90	1.01	1.12
0.2	2.2	0.3	—0.9	—0.9	1.8	—0.05	1.43	28.60
3.9	4.0	3.3	2.7	5.2	5.8	3.30	1.35	0.41
—2.0	—5.0	—4.8	—3.1	—4.8	—4.2	—2.92	1.23	0.42
3.7	5.6	6.4	3.0	5.0	6.9	4.06	1.38	0.34
6.1	6.3	9.0	7.5	6.3	11.0	8.31	3.70	
2.3	0.7	2.4	4.4	1.2	3.8	4.09		

TABLE A11
SWEDEN

	1950	1951	1952	1953	1954	1955	1956
$\Delta c_t / y_{t-1}$	3.7	—1.3	2.1	2.1	2.8	2.5	2.1
$\Delta g_t / y_{t-1}$	1.6	0.8	1.4	2.0	1.0	0.6	0.9
$\Delta i_{f,t} / y_{t-1}$	1.5	—0.6	—0.1	1.9	1.9	—0.4	0.5
$\Delta i_{s,t} / y_{t-1}$	—1.8	3.6	—0.3	—4.2	1.8	2.1	—0.7
$\Delta x_t / y_{t-1}$	4.6	1.0	—1.6	2.2	2.6	1.4	2.4
$-\Delta m_t / y_{t-1}$	—4.3	—4.0	1.3	—0.5	—3.6	—2.6	—1.6
$\Delta y_t / y_{t-1}$	5.3	—0.4	2.8	3.6	6.5	3.6	3.4
$\Delta (y_t P_t) / y_{t-1} P_{t-1}$	6.8	22.6	9.6	2.2	6.4	7.9	8.3
$\Delta P_t / P_{t-1}$	1.4	23.1	6.6	—1.4	—0.1	4.2	4.7

TABLE A12
SWITZERLAND

	1950	1951	1952	1953	1954	1955	1956
$\Delta c_t / y_{t-1}$	3.2	0.6	0.6	1.9	2.9	2.7	3.2
$\Delta g_t / y_{t-1}$	1.7	0.8	1.0	—0.3	—0.1	0.2	0.3
$\Delta i_{f,t} / y_{t-1}$	1.5	2.7	0.4	1.8	1.9	1.8	2.5
$\Delta i_{s,t} / y_{t-1}$	3.3	2.8	—3.7	—1.7	2.0	1.8	0.9
$\Delta x_t / y_{t-1}$	3.3	2.9	0.7	3.3	1.8	2.4	2.9
$-\Delta m_t / y_{t-1}$	—5.9	—1.7	1.9	—0.5	—2.7	—3.6	—3.7
$\Delta y_t / y_{t-1}$	7.2	8.1	0.8	4.5	5.6	5.3	6.0
$\Delta (y_t P_t) / y_{t-1} P_{t-1}$	6.2	10.1	4.9	4.6	6.1	6.7	7.4
$\Delta P_t / P_{t-1}$	—0.9	1.9	4.1	0.1	0.5	1.3	1.3

1959	1960	1961	1962	1963	1964	M	D	D/M
2.3	1.0	3.2	2.2	3.1	3.1	2.13	0.78	0.37
1.5	—0.5	0.6	1.5	1.7	1.2	1.06	0.46	0.43
1.5	1.5	1.6	0.8	0.9	1.2	0.93	0.68	0.73
—0.2	2.8	—0.6	—1.0	—1.0	1.4	0.02	1.66	83.00
1.2	3.1	1.1	2.1	1.9	3.1	1.89	1.08	0.57
—0.8	—4.3	—0.3	—1.8	—1.6	—2.7	—2.01	1.33	0.66
5.5	3.6	5.6	3.7	5.0	7.2	4.00	1.48	0.37
6.4	8.6	9.0	8.4	8.6	10.4	8.47	2.18	
0.9	4.8	3.2	4.5	3.4	3.0	4.36		

1959	1960	1961	1962	1963	1964	M	D	D/M
3.3	3.2	4.7	4.2	3.3	3.1	2.63	1.04	0.40
—0.3	—0.2	1.4	1.0	0.9	0.5	0.57	0.52	0.91
3.2	3.0	4.0	2.7	1.7	2.4	1.92	0.94	0.49
1.7	2.4	1.2	—1.0	—1.1	0.1	0.32	1.81	5.66
3.7	2.2	2.4	2.0	1.7	2.3	2.20	0.75	0.34
—4.4	—4.7	—6.4	—3.8	—2.0	—3.4	—2.72	1.89	0.69
7.2	5.8	7.3	5.1	4.6	5.1	4.91	1.81	0.37
7.4	9.5	12.0	11.0	9.4	10.3	7.54	2.27	
0.2	3.5	4.4	5.6	4.6	4.9	2.53		

TABLE A13

UNITED KINGDOM

	1950	1951	1952	1953	1954	1955	1956
$\Delta c_t / y_{t-1}$	2.0	—1.1	—0.3	2.7	2.8	2.6	0.6
$\Delta g_t / y_{t-1}$	0.4	1.4	1.8	0.7	0.0	—0.3	0.1
$\Delta i_{f,t} / y_{t-1}$	0.4	—0.1	0.1	1.3	1.2	0.7	0.7
$\Delta i_{s,t} / y_{t-1}$	—1.4	4.8	—2.9	0.5	—0.5	1.3	—0.3
$\Delta x_t / y_{t-1}$	3.5	—1.2	—0.6	1.1	1.6	1.1	1.1
$-\Delta m_t / y_{t-1}$	—0.5	—1.8	1.7	—1.9	—1.0	—2.4	0.1
$\Delta y_t / y_{t-1}$	4.4	1.9	—0.3	4.3	4.1	3.0	2.2
$\Delta (y_t P_t) / y_{t-1} P_{t-1}$	5.5	10.7	7.8	6.9	5.7	7.0	8.6
$\Delta P_t / P_{t-1}$	1.1	8.6	8.1	2.5	1.5	3.9	6.3

TABLE A14

UNITED STATES

	1950	1951	1952	1953	1954	1955	1956
$\Delta c_t / y_{t-1}$	4.3	0.6	1.7	2.9	1.2	4.5	1.6
$\Delta g_t / y_{t-1}$	—0.2	6.4	4.4	1.9	—2.6	—0.9	0.0
$\Delta i_{f,t} / y_{t-1}$	2.8	—0.6	—0.5	0.8	0.3	1.9	0.1
$\Delta i_{s,t} / y_{t-1}$	3.8	0.7	—2.0	—0.6	—0.7	2.1	—0.4
$\Delta x_t / y_{t-1}$	—0.6	0.8	—0.3	—0.1	0.2	0.5	0.8
$-\Delta m_t / y_{t-1}$	—0.6	—0.1	—0.3	—0.4	0.2	—0.5	—0.3
$\Delta y_t / y_{t-1}$	9.6	7.9	3.1	4.5	—1.4	7.6	1.8
$\Delta (y_t P_t) / y_{t-1} P_{t-1}$	11.0	15.3	5.2	5.5	0.1	9.1	5.3
$\Delta P_t / P_{t-1}$	1.3	6.9	2.0	1.0	1.5	1.4	3.4

1959	1960	1961	1962	1963	1964	M	D	D/M
3.1	2.7	1.5	1.3	3.1	2.4	1.77	0.88	0.50
0.5	0.5	0.9	0.7	0.4	0.7	0.49	0.44	0.90
1.0	1.4	1.1	—0.4	0.4	2.3	0.72	0.53	0.74
0.3	1.7	—1.1	—0.9	0.4	1.1	0.16	1.20	7.50
0.6	1.1	0.7	0.6	1.2	0.7	0.83	0.66	0.82
—1.3	—2.6	0.3	—0.3	—0.8	—2.0	—0.89	0.91	1.02
4.3	4.7	3.4	1.1	4.6	5.2	3.04	1.42	0.47
5.3	5.9	6.7	4.9	6.3	7.7	6.61	1.18	
1.0	1.1	3.2	3.8	1.6	2.4	3.49		

1959	1960	1961	1962	1963	1964	M	D	D/M
3.8	1.9	1.3	3.2	2.6	3.6	2.34	1.14	0.49
0.1	0.0	1.2	1.4	0.4	0.2	0.95	1.42	1.49
1.4	0.0	—0.4	1.3	0.6	0.9	0.47	0.85	1.81
1.4	—0.3	—0.3	0.8	—0.1	—0.2	0.19	1.05	5.53
0.2	0.7	0.1	0.4	0.4	0.8	0.24	0.38	1.58
—0.6	0.1	0.0	—0.5	—0.2	—0.3	—0.26	0.19	0.73
6.4	2.5	1.9	6.6	3.8	5.0	3.97	2.64	0.66
8.1	4.2	3.2	7.7	5.2	6.7	6.21	2.75	
1.6	1.7	1.3	1.0	1.3	1.6	2.15		

LIST OF REFERENCES

This bibliography is an alphabetical list of books and articles specifically referred to in this study and is designed as an aid to the reader who may want a particular reference.

Allen, G. C., *Japan's Economic Recovery,* London, 1958.

Arndt, H. A., *The Economic Lessons of the Nineteen-Thirties,* London, 1944.

Arvidsson, Guy, "En enkät rörande verkningarna av investeringsavgiften, kreditåtstramningen och räntehöjningen på den svenska industrins investeringar 1955," *Ekonomisk Tidskrift,* Nr. 1, 1956.

Beld, C. A. van den, *Conjunctuurpolitiek in en om de jaren vijftig,* Central Planning Bureau, monograph No. 8, The Hague, 1963.

———, *Forecasts and Realization,* Central Planning Bureau, monograph No. 10, The Hague, 1965.

———, "Short-term Planning Experience in the Netherlands," in Bert G. Hickman, ed., *Quantitative Planning of Economic Policy,* Washington, D.C., The Brookings Institution, 1964.

Böhler, Eugen, "Die alten und die neuen Herren der Konjunktur," *Industrielle Organisation,* Nr. 6, 1963.

Bowen, W. G., *Wage Behavior in the Postwar Period: An Empirical Analysis,* Princeton, 1960.

———, and T. A. Finegan, "Labor Force Participation and Unemployment," in Arthur M. Ross, ed., *Employment Policy and the Labor Market,* Berkeley, 1965.

Bry, Gerhard, *Wages in Germany 1871–1950,* National Bureau of Economic Research (hereafter NBER), Princeton, 1960.

Burns, Arthur F., "Progress Towards Economic Stability," *American Economic Review,* March 1960.

Canada, Royal Commission on Banking and Finance, *Report,* Ottawa, 1964.

———, Royal Commission on Canada's Economic Prospects, *Report,* Ottawa, 1957.

Dean, Joel, "The Concept and Economic Significance of Regula-

rization of Business Investment," in *Regularization of Business Investment,* NBER Conference Volume, Princeton, 1954.
Denison, E. F., "A Note on Private Saving," *Review of Economics and Statistics,* August 1958.
———, *The Sources of Economic Growth in the United States and the Alternatives Before Us,* New York, 1962.
Denton, Frank T., and Sylvia Ostry, *An Analysis of Post-War Unemployment,* Staff Study No. 3, Economic Council of Canada, Ottawa, 1964.
Dicks-Mireaux, L. A., "The Interrelationship between Cost and Price Changes, 1946–1959," *Oxford Economic Papers,* October 1961.
Dow, J. C. R., *The Management of the British Economy 1945–60,* Cambridge, 1964.
Drabble, G. J., *Potential Output 1946 to 1970,* Staff Study No. 2, Economic Council of Canada, Ottawa, 1964.
Duesenberry, James, Otto Eckstein, and Gary Fromm, "A Simulation of the United States Economy in Recession," *Econometrica,* October 1960; reprinted in *Readings in Business Cycles,* London, 1965.
Economist, The, September 1, 1962.
Economic Planning Agency, *Economic Survey of Japan,* various issues, Tokyo, 1957–64.
Eliason, Gunnar, *Investment Funds in Operation,* Occasional Paper 2, Stockholm, Konjunkturinstitutet, 1965.
Forrester, J. W., *Industrial Dynamics,* New York, 1961.
Friedman, Milton, *A Theory of the Consumption Function,* NBER, Princeton, 1957.
———, and Anna Jacobson Schwartz, *A Monetary History of the United States, 1867–1960,* NBER, Princeton, 1963.
Galenson, Walter, and Arnold Zellner, "International Comparison of Unemployment Rates," in *The Measurement and Behavior of Unemployment,* NBER, Princeton, 1957.
Gehrig, G., *Eine ökonometrische Analyse des Konsums von 1925 bis 1938 und 1950 bis 1957,* Schriftenreihe des Instituts für Wirtschaftsforschung, Nr. 52, Berlin-München, 1963.
Gilbert, Milton, "The Postwar Business Cycle in Western Europe," *American Economic Review, Papers and Proceedings,* May 1962.
Gordon, R. A., *Business Fluctuations,* 2d ed. New York, 1961.
———, "Full Employment as a Policy Goal," in Arthur M. Ross, ed., *Employment Policy and the Labor Market,* Berkeley, 1965.

List of References

Grüning, Ferdinand, *Die makroökonomischen Determinanten des Wirtschaftspotentials,* herausgegeben von Klaus Dieter Arndt und Rolf Krengel, Deutsches Institut für Wirtschaftsforschung, Sonderhefte N. F. Nr. 52, Berlin, 1960.

Hall, Robert, "Reflections on the Practical Application of Economics," *Economic Journal,* December 1959.

Hancock, Keith, "Unemployment and the Economists in the 1920s," *Economica,* November 1960.

Hansen, Alvin H., "Was Fiscal Policy in the Thirties a Failure?" *Review of Economics and Statistics,* August 1963.

Hansen, Bent, *Foreign Trade Credits and Exchange Reserves, A Contribution to the Theory of International Capital Movements,* Amsterdam, 1961.

———, *A Study in the Theory of Inflation,* Uppsala, 1951.

Hastey, Millard, "The Cyclical Behavior of Investment," in *Regularization of Business Investment,* NBER Conference Volume, Princeton, 1954.

Hessel, Wilhelm, "Quantitative Planning of Economic Policy in the Netherlands," in Bert G. Hickman, ed., *Quantitative Planning of Economic Policy,* Washington, D.C., The Brookings Institution, 1964.

Hickman, Bert G., *Growth and Stability of the Postwar Economy,* Washington, D.C., The Brookings Institution, 1961.

———, *Investment Demand and U.S. Economic Growth,* Washington, D.C., The Brookings Institution, 1965.

Hildebrand, George H., *Growth and Structure in the Economy of Modern Italy,* Cambridge, Mass., 1965.

Jacoby, Neil H., and J. Fred Weston, "Financial Policies for Regularizing Business Investment," in *Regularization of Business Investment,* NBER Conference Volume, Princeton, 1954.

Järv, J., and E. Lundberg, "Business Investment and Corporate Savings," *Quarterly Review of Skandinaviska Banken,* No. 1, Stockholm, 1964.

Johnson, H. G., "Monetary Theory and Policy," in *Survey of Economic Theory, 1,* New York, 1965.

———, *The Canadian Quandary,* New York, 1963.

Jöhr, W. A., *Gegenwartsfragen der Konjunkturtheorie,* Sonderdruck aus *Jahrbücher für Nationalökonomie und Statistik,* Stuttgart, 1965.

———, *Die Konjunkturschwankungen: Theoretische Grundlagen der Wirtschaftspolitik,* Band 2, Zürich, 1952.

Kaldor, N., *Essays on Economic Policy, 1,* London, 1964.

Kareken, John, and Robert M. Solow, "Lags in Monetary Policy," in *Stabilization Policies,* prepared for the Commission on Money and Credit, Englewood Cliffs, 1963.

Keynes, J. M., *The General Theory of Employment, Interest and Money,* London, 1936.

Kirschen, E. S., and Associates, *Economic Policy in Our Time, 2* and *3,* Amsterdam, 1964.

Klein, L. R., and A. S. Goldberger, *An Econometric Model of the United States, 1929–1952,* Amsterdam, 1955.

Knowles, James W., "The Potential Economic Growth in the United States," Study Paper No. 20 of the *Study of Employment Growth and Price Levels,* U.S. Congress, Joint Economic Committee, Washington, D.C., 1960.

Kragh, Börje, *Finansiella Långtidsperspektiv,* Stockholm, 1967.

———, *Konjunkturbedömning,* Stockholm, 1964.

Lamfalussy, A., *The United Kingdom and the Six,* London, 1963.

Lary, Hal B., and Associates, *The United States in the World Economy,* Washington, D.C., 1943.

Levy, Michael E., *Fiscal Policy, Cycles and Growth,* Studies in Business Economics, No. 81, National Industrial Conference Board, New York, 1963.

Lewis, W. A., *Economic Survey 1919–1939,* Philadelphia, 1950.

Lindbeck, Assar, *A Study in Monetary Analysis,* Stockholm, 1963.

Lintner, John, "Distribution of Incomes of Corporations Among Dividends, Retained Earnings and Taxes," *American Economic Review, Papers and Proceedings,* May 1956.

Lipsey, R. G., "The Relation Between Unemployment and the Rate of Change of Money Wage Rates in the United Kingdom, 1862–1957: A Further Analysis," *Economica,* February 1960.

Lundberg, Erik, *Business Cycles and Economic Policy,* London, 1957.

———, *Studies in the Theory of Economic Expansion,* Stockholm, 1937.

Maddison, Angus, "Economic Growth in Western Europe 1870–1957," *Banca Nazionale del Lavoro Quarterly Review,* March 1959.

———, *Economic Growth in the West,* New York and London, 1964.

———, "The Postwar Business Cycle in Western Europe and the Role of Government Policy," *Banca Nazionale del Lavoro Quarterly Review,* June 1960.

Matthews, R. C. O., *The Trade Cycle,* Cambridge, Eng., 1959.

Meyer, John R., and Robert R. Glauber, *Investment Decisions, Economic Forecasting and Public Policy,* Cambridge, Mass., 1965.

Modigliani, Franco, "Monetary Policy in the United States, Some Empirical Tests of Monetary Management and of Rules versus Discretion," *Journal of Political Economy,* June 1964.

Morgenstern, Oscar, *International Financial Transactions and Business Cycles,* NBER, Princeton, 1959.

Morrissens, L., "Economic Policy in Belgium," in E. S. Kirschen, and Associates, *Economic Policy in Our Time, 3,* Amsterdam, 1964.

Myers, Robert J., "Unemployment in Western Europe and the United States," in Arthur M. Ross, ed., *Unemployment and the American Economy,* New York, 1964.

National Institute Economic Review, various issues.

Neal, A. C., "Pricing Aspects of Business Cycle History," in U.S. Chamber of Commerce, *Pricing Problems and the Stabilization of Prosperity,* Washington, D.C., 1947.

Nederlandsche Bank, *Report for the Year 1962,* and *1964,* Amsterdam, 1963 and 1965.

Neild, R. R., *Pricing and Employment in the Trade Cycle,* National Institute of Economic and Social Research, Cambridge, Eng., 1963.

Netherlands, Central Planning Bureau, *Central Economic Plan 1961,* The Hague, 1961. *See also* Beld.

Nurkse, Ragnar, *International Currency Experiences,* Geneva, League of Nations, 1944.

Okun, Arthur M., "Potential GNP: Its Measurement and Significance," in American Statistical Association, *Proceedings of the Business and Economic Statistics Section,* Washington, D.C., 1962.

Olsson, Ingvar, *On National Accounting,* Stockholm, 1953.

Organization for Economic Cooperation and Development, *Economic Surveys: Canada,* Paris, 1963.

———, *Economic Surveys: Japan,* Paris, 1965.

———, *Economic Surveys: United Kingdom,* Paris, 1965.

———, *Manpower Statistics 1950–62* and *1954–64,* Paris, 1963 and 1965.

———, *Techniques of Economic Forecasting,* Paris, 1965.

Organization for European Economic Cooperation, *The Problem of Rising Prices,* Paris, 1961.

Paish, F. W., *Studies in an Inflationary Economy,* London, 1962.

Patrick, Hugh T., "Cyclical Instability and Fiscal-Monetary Policy in Postwar Japan," mimeo., September 1963.
Phillips, A. W., "The Relation Between Unemployment and the Rate of Change of Money Wage Rates in the United Kingdom, 1861–1957," *Economica,* November 1958.
Rehn, Gösta, and Erik Lundberg, "Employment and Welfare: Some Swedish Issues, *Industrial Relations,* February 1963.
Rhomberg, Rudolf R., "Canada's Foreign Exchange Market," *International Monetary Fund Staff Papers,* April 1960.
Salter, W. E. G., *Productivity and Technical Change,* Cambridge, Eng., 1960.
Schiffer, Hubert F., *The Modern Japanese Banking System,* New York, 1962.
Schmidt, Carl T., *German Business Cycles 1924–33,* NBER, New York, 1934.
Schoenman, Jean-Claude, *An Analog of Short-Period Economic Change,* Stockholm, 1966.
Schumpeter, J. A., *Business Cycles, 2,* New York, 1939.
———, *Capitalism, Socialism, and Democracy,* 2d ed., London, 1943.
Shackle, G. L., "Recent Theories Concerning the Nature and Role of Interest Rates," in *Survey of Economic Theory, 1,* New York, 1965.
Shinohara, Miyohei, *Growth and Cycles in the Japanese Economy,* Tokyo, 1962.
Simons, Henry C., *A Positive Program for Laissez Faire: Some Proposals for a Liberal Economic Policy,* Chicago, 1934.
Stanback, Thomas, *Postwar Cycles in Manufacturers' Inventories,* NBER, Princeton, 1962.
Statistisches Reichsamt, *Statistisches Jahrbuch für das Deutsche Reich,* various issues, Berlin.
Svennilson, Ingvar, *Growth and Stagnation of the European Economy,* Geneva, United Nations Economic Commission for Europe, 1954.
Tella, Alfred, "The Relation of Labor Force to Employment," *Industrial and Labor Relations Review,* April 1964.
Theil, H., *Economic Forecasting and Policy,* Amsterdam, 1958.
Tinbergen, Jan, *Statistical Testing of Business Cycle Theories: Business Cycles in the United States of America 1919–1932,* Geneva, League of Nations, 1939.
Turner, H. A., "Wages, Productivity and the Level of Employment: More on the Wage Drift," *Manchester School,* January 1960.

List of References

United Kingdom, Committee on the Working of the Monetary System, *The Radcliffe Report,* Cmnd. 827, London, 1959.

United Nations Economic Commission for Europe, *Financing of Housing in Europe,* Geneva, 1958.

———, *Some Factors in Economic Growth in Europe During the 1950's,* Geneva, 1964.

United States, Bureau of the Census, Report for the Subcommittee on Antitrust and Monopoly, *Concentration Ratios in Manufacturing Industry 1958, Part 1,* Washington, D.C., 1962.

———, *Economic Report of the President,* Washington, D.C., various years.

———, President's Committee to Appraise Employment and Unemployment Statistics, *Measuring Employment and Unemployment,* Washington, D.C., 1962.

———, Senate Committee on Labor and Public Welfare, Subcommittee on Employment and Manpower, *Toward Full Employment: Proposals for a Comprehensive Employment and Manpower Policy in the United States,* Washington, D.C., 1964.

Worswick, G. D. N., and P. H. Ady, eds., *The British Economy in the 1950's,* Oxford, 1962.

Zarnowitz, Victor, "Unfilled Orders, Price Changes, and Business Fluctuations," *Review of Economics and Statistics,* November 1962.

INDEX

Page numbers in italics indicate references to tables or figures

Austria: growth and instability of GNP and components, *86, 118–21, A1;* postwar starting levels of production, *126*

Balance of payments: absence of problems, 206–08; and confidence crises, 163–64, 177, 392, 394–95, 396; constraint on policy, 133–35, 162–65, 174, 187–90, 234, 273–74, 323–24, 328–29, 334–35, 344; and exchange rates, 282–83, 386–96; and international capital movements, 35–36, 338 n., 378 n., 381, 382, 386–92, 393, 395–96; and inventory investment, 328–29; and liquidity, 139, 275, 289–90; and Marshall Plan, 35; and monetary policy, 139, 334–37, 338 n.; postwar shifts, 128; response to, rise in investment, *281,* tax reduction, *280,* wage increase, *282*

Belgium: full-employment gap and price change, *113;* growth and instability of GNP and components, *86, A2;* postwar industrial production, *89;* postwar and interwar instability, *29;* potential and actual GNP, *103, 110–11;* starting levels of production, *126;* unemployment, interwar and postwar, *32*

Budget balance: as built-in stabilizer, 237–41, 357, 365, 374; effects of automatic response of, 355–66; full-employment surplus of, 240–41, 356–57, 365, 374; and monetary policy, 168–72, 235–36

Business cycles. *See* Conjunctures; Instability

Canada: capital movements, 378 n., 381, 382, 386–92, 393, 395–96; confidence in dollar, 392, 393–94, 396; deficient demand vs. structural explanation, 392; dependence on U.S. economy, 377–79, 382–85; excess capacity, 380; foreign exchange, crisis, 392–94, policy of flexible rates, 382–83, 386–96, reserves, *387,* rate fluctuations, *387;* growth and instability of GNP and components, *86, A3;* interest rate differential to U.S., 384–85, 389, 391; investment, boom of *1950s,* 379–81, marginal import content of, 381 n.; main postwar instability features,

377–82; monetary policy, effectiveness of, 384–86, 388–92; potential and actual GNP, *104;* price change and full-employment gap, *113;* quarterly GNP compared with U.S., *377;* unemployment, interwar and postwar, *32*

Capacity index: and exports, 270–71; and investments, 274–76

Capital: international movements of, 35–36, 163–64, 338 n., 378 n., 381, 382, 386–92, 393, 395–96; -output ratio, 153–*54,* 323, 346, 361–62; saturation and overcapacity, 74–76, 130, 145, 151, 363, 380; scarcity, 80; stock adjustment process, 76, 358–59, 364–65, 371, 375; structural imbalance of, 346–47

Confidence: and the British pound, 163–64, 177; and the Canadian dollar, 392, 393–94, 396

Conjunctures: and concept of business cycles, 8; and corporate sector, 59–61; and employment structure, 56–58; flexible exchange rates and autonomy of, 383; the Great Depression, 74–80; interwar and postwar declines, *29;* interwar and postwar unemployment levels, *32;* and market structure, 63–71; and policy influence, 135–46; potential and actual GNP, 102–*13;* and price vs. order stock variations, 67–71; severe setbacks, 24, 26, *29, 73;* stability of behavior patterns, 42–54; synchronization of turning points, 73–74, 88–92, 210–11; transmission of impulses, 26–27, 141–42, 210, *377*–79. *See also* Instability

Consumption: average and cyclical share of, *120,* 315; and consumer credit control, 178–81; function, interwar vs. postwar, 51–53, cyclical shift of, 52–53, 365–66, and multiplier effect, 262, 365–66, permanent income hypothesis, 61, short-run, *198,* 277–78, 365–66; growth and instability of, *118*–19, 121, 146, *A1–14*

Credit: imbalance of market for, 248–49; importance of financing by, 332–33; rationing, effects of, 252–55, 335–40. *See also* Monetary policy

Demand (total): backlogs of, 126–27; deficiency of, 102, 109–10, 202, 349–52, 355–66; excess of, 13–14, 93–94, 112–13, 126–32, 174, 212–18; growth and pressure of, 349–52; underestimation of, 174

Denmark: balance of payments and growth, 133–34; full-employment gap and price change, *113;* growth and instability of GNP and components, *86, 118–21, A4;* interwar and postwar instability, *29;* interwar and postwar unemployment, *32;* potential and actual GNP, *104,* 110; starting levels of production, *126*

Econometric model of Dutch economy, 264, 267–79; critical questions on, 306–12; and data problems, 268–69, 306–07; forecasting performance, 297–306; as framework for policy, 264, 284; inequality coefficients,

297–300; interdependent character of, 307–08; pedagogic value of, 279, 296; and survey method forecasts, *303;* turning point errors, 300–01; underestimation bias, 299–301
Employment, changes in structure of, 56–58. *See* Full employment
Exports: average and cyclical GNP share of, *120, 315;* effects of home demand and foreign recession on, 326–28; estimated equation for, 270–74, 308; and growth of, 272–73; growth and instability of, *118–21, A1–14;* interwar declines of, *73;* and relative wage level, 272–73; response of, to increase in investment, *281,* to reduction of taxation, *280,* to rise of wages, *281,* to world trade, 271; share in world trade and prices of, 160–62

Fiscal policy: and budget deficits, 220–21; built-in effects of, 237–41, 355–66; direct effects of, 175, 284–87; effects on investment, 175, 181–84; effects of tax reduction, 280–82; in the *1930s,* 83; inadequate timing of, 287; initial allowances, 167 n.; investment allowances, 167 n., 228–32; investment funds, 226–32, 244–47; investment tax, 225–26; and public pension fund, 249–52; public works, 221–23. *See also* Budget balance; Policy
Forecasting: comparison of some Dutch and Swedish results, 305–06; conditional and unconditional, 302; errors, 213–14, 297–306; methods, 212–19, 276–306; of price and wage changes, 217–18. *See also* Econometric model of Dutch economy
Foreign exchange conditions and policy: crisis, 163–64, 392–94; destabilizing capital movements, 35–36, 163, 381–82; devaluations of *1930s,* 81–82, 83–84; during interwar and postwar period, 34–35, 81–82, 83–84; flexible exchange rates, 382, 386–96; Marshall plan and offshore purchases, 35; revaluation, 282, 283. *See* also Balance of payments
France: capital-output ratio compared, *154;* export prices and share in world trade, *161;* foreign exchange policy and growth, 134; full-employment gap and price change, *113;* growth and instability of GNP and components, *86, A5;* interwar and postwar instability compared, *29;* interwar setbacks, *73;* policy of *1930s,* 81–82; postwar industrial production, *89;* potential and actual GNP, *104;* starting levels of production, *113*
Full employment: alternative norms of, 92–93, 96–99; budget surplus, 356; ceiling, 189, 204–05; output 96, 101–12, *113, 360;* output gap and price changes, 112–14; saving and investment ex ante, *360*

Germany: capital-output ratio compared, *154;* consumption behavior, interwar, 53; downturn in late *1920s,* 80; expansionary policy of *1930s,* 81; export prices and share in world trade, *161;* growth and instability of GNP and components, *86, A6;* interwar and postwar instability, *29;* postwar industrial production, *89;* potential and actual GNP, *105,* 110; price change and full-employment output gap, *113;* starting levels of production, *126;* unemployment, interwar and postwar, *32*

Government expenditures: growth and instability of, *118–21, A1–14;* and instability of the U.S. economy, 374–75; relative scale of, 37. *See also* Fiscal policy

Gross national product (GNP): of Canada and the U.S., quarterly, *377;* declines of, interwar and postwar, *29;* full-employment gap of, and change of price level, 112–14; gross and net variation of growth, *121*–22; instability of growth rate, *86;* potential and actual, 96, 101–12, 360; share of expenditure components in the growth of, *120, 315,* 374–75; variation index and variability ratio of, 115–16, *118;* variation of and instability of components, 114–20, *A1–14*

Growth: and backlogs of demand, 126–27; and balance of payments constraint, 133–35, 162–65, 174, 187–90, 234, 273–74, 323–24, 328–29, 334–35, 344; balanced, 10–11; catching up effect on, 24, 33–34, 125–*26, 320;* deviations of actual from potential, 96–114, *360;* and expectations, 131–32; export-propelled, 153–58, 160–63; interrelations with instability, 123–32, 149–53; interwar and postwar, *24;* and policy restrictions, 133–40; potential and actual, 96–114, 355–66

Imports: growth and instability of, *118, 120, 121, A1–14;* and industrial production, *316;* interwar and postwar growth in relation to GNP, *54;* marginal ratio of, 54, 262, 263, 277, 324–25, 381 n.; and multiplier effects, 262; offsetting variations of, 122, 262

Industrial production: branch cycles, 91–92, 210–11; and imports, *316;* interwar declines of, *73;* maximum interwar and postwar declines, *29;* postwar deviations from trend, *89;* relative starting levels after world wars, *126*

Inflation: and full-employment output gap, *113;* inflationary gap, 127, 212–18; postwar annual rates of, *A1–14;* tendencies, 142–43. *See also* Prices, level of

Instability: alternative measurements of, 92–123; and autonomous factors, 128–32; and balance of payments disturbances, 133–34; as deviations from balanced growth, 10–11; as deviations from full-employment growth, 101–14; and external shocks, 95, 141–42, 173; gross and net variation of GNE components, *121*–22; of growth of GNE components, 117–23, *315,* 352–55, *A1–14;* of imports and

industrial production, *316;* as inflation, 142–43; interrelations between growth and, 123–32, 149–52; and policy changes, 132–40, 140–43; of postwar industrial production, *89;* potential, 8; types of, 1–13, 20–21, 24–26. *See also* Conjunctures
Interest rates: and capital movements, 382, 384–85, 389, 391; changes of, 158, 170–71, 234; and investment, 369–73; and investment tax, 225
International trade, interwar and postwar growth, 27, 53–54. *See also* Exports; Imports
Inventory investment: and balance of payments, 164, 276–77, 328–29, 336–37; effects of monetary restriction on, 182–83, 328–29, 336–37; growth and instability of, *118–21, 315, A1–14;* as generator of recession, 363–64, interwar and postwar pattern of, 48–49; overinvestment in inventories, 69; and private fixed investment, quarterly, *317;* reactions during expansion, 143–45
Investment, fixed: acceleration effects of, 341–43; break of boom in, 342–45, 379–81; and capacity, 276; and capital budgeting, 61–62; declining ratio to GNP, 358–61; financing of, 329–34; functions, 46–47, 274–76, 308–09; in the Great Depression, 74–78; growth and instability of, *118–21, 315, A1–14;* and liquidity situation, 275; and profits, 47, 275–76; quarterly development of, *317;* and saving ex ante at potential GNP, 355–66; surveys of plans, 213, 242–43, 245–46, 303. *See also* Policy; Residential construction
Italy, balance of payments disturbance of growth, 134–35; capital-output ratio compared, *154;* growth of GNP and instability of components, *86, 118–21, A7;* instability, interwar and postwar, *29,* of postwar industrial production, *89;* potential and actual GNP, *105,* 110; price change and full-employment gap, *113;* unemployment, interwar and postwar, *32,* structural, 111

Japan:
balance of payments: constraint on growth, 323–24, 328–29, 334–35, 344; and inventory investment, 328–29; and monetary policy, 334–37, 338 n.
capital-output ratio, 323, 346
devaluation of yen in *1931,* 83–84
export prices and share in world trade, *161,* 325
exports, effect of home demand and U.S. recessions, 326–28
GNP: change between turning points, *314;* composition of cyclical change, *315*–18; percentage composition, 315; potential and actual, *106*
growth: and balance of payments, 322–27; instability of, *86,* 313–18, *A8;* international space for, 320, 338 n., 340–41, 344; process of "catching up," *320;* and profits, 330;

and structural change, 318–21
imbalance of capital structure, 346–47
imports, marginal ratio of, 324–25
instability of imports and industrial production, *316*
investment: acceleration, 341–43; break of boom, 342–45; financing of, 329–34; fluctuations of, *317;* and instability risks, 321–32
monetary policy: and balance of payments, 334–37, 338 n.; and capital imports, 338 n.; effectiveness of, 335, 340; and exchange reserves, 334–35; instruments, 338–39; lags in, 335–37; role of bank credit, 333–34
profits and investment, 330–33
saving ratio of households, 331
undervaluation of yen, 83–84, 325–26
wage(s): flexibility and bonus system, 321 n.; and labor productivity changes, 321

Labor: excess demand for, 151, 257–58; market policy, 257–60; mobility, 151, 159, 257–60; potential employment of, 100–01; productivity, 112, 160, 184–85, 189, 209–10, 257, 321; productivity and wage changes, 160, 186–87, 209, 321; union attitude, 199–202. *See also* Unemployment

Monetary policy: "American" vs. "Swedish" approach, 253–55; and balance of payments, 139, 289–90, 328–29, 334–37, 338 n.; before and after downturn of *1929* in the U.S., 76, 78; control of bank advances, 235–36, 335–36; control of consumer credit, 178–81; control of credit supply, 234–36, 252–56; control of money supply, 232–34, 288–90; debate in the U.K., 176–87; effectiveness of, 176–87, 255–56, 289–90, 335–40, 368–73, 384–86, 388–92; effects on fixed investment, 181–84, 241–43, 275, 370–73; effects on inventory investment, 182–83, 336–37, 369–70; effects on residential construction, 50, 223–24, 385; and flexible exchange rates, 388–92, 396; interaction with fiscal policy, 168–72; passive, 234, 268, 373; Radcliffe Report, 178, 181–83; time lags in, 236, 247, 255, 335–37, 369–73; vulnerability of wholesalers and importers to, 336
Money supply: and balance of payments, 139, 275, 289–*90,* 387; changes in, 232–34, 255–56, 287–*90;* discretionary vs. automatic changes in, 288–*90;* and quantity theory, 288
Multiplier, 262, 365–66

National budget approach, 216–19; educative value of, 218–19
Netherlands:
automatic vs. discretionary liquidity changes, 288–*90*
balance of payments: constraint on and response to policy, 234, 263–67, 273–74; effects of revaluation, 282–83; and money supply, 275, 289–90; response to rise in investment,

281; response to tax reduction, 280; response to wage increase, 281–82; variations of current account, 273–74
capacity effects: on export growth, 270–71; on investment growth, 274–76
capital-output ratio compared, *154*
consumption equation, 277–78
econometric model of CPB, 264, 267–79; critical questions on, 306–12; and data problems, 268–69, 306–07; forecasting performance, 297–306; as framework for policy, 264, 284; inequality coefficients, 297–300; interdependent character of, 307–08; pedagogic value of, 279, 296; and survey method forecasts, *303;* turning point errors, 300–01; underestimation bias, 299–301
export equation, 270–74
forecasts and realization, 297–306; for predetermined variables, 298, 301–03; for target variables, 298
GNP, actual and potential, *107*
import growth, stabilizing variation of, 262
imports, marginal ratio of, 54, 262, 263, 275, 277
instability: interwar and postwar setbacks, *29;* of postwar industrial production, *86;* sources of, 261–62, 265–66, 278
investment: equation, 274–76; in inventories, 276–77; and liquidity situation, 275; and profit squeeze, 275–76
monetary conditions, 288–90
multiplier, 262
policy: effects of forecasting errors on, 304–05; first-year and second-year effects, 280–81; fiscal, 284–87; instruments, 264–65; and learning process, 287; quantitative appraisal of effects, 279–95
price stability as target, 266–67
tax reduction, estimated effects, 280, 282
unemployment: average interwar and postwar levels, *32;* and vacancy rates, *292;* and wage changes, 293–94
wage(s): and cost of living, 292–93; equation, 293–95; low level of, 272, 273, 289, 291 n.; policy, 265, 291–95; and unemployment, 293–94
Norway: capital-output ratio compared, *154;* degree of instability, 116; growth and instability of GNP and components, *86, 118–21, A10;* interwar and postwar declines compared, *29;* potential and actual GNP, *107;* price change and full-employment gap, *113*

Order stocks, stabilizing influence of, 67–71
Overcapacity problems: interwar period, 32–34; postwar, 34, 130, 145, 151, 363

Policy: autonomy, 383–84; balance of payments constraint on, 133–35, 162–65, 174, 187–90, 206–08, 234, 273–74, 323–24, 328–29, 334–35, 344, 392–96; as causal factor, 135–40, 165,

173, 236–47; change in attitudes toward, 39–40; climate, 193–97, 295–96; conflict between stabilization and growth, 344; cycles, 165, 166–72, 190, 203–04; differentiated vs. general types of, 258; difficulty in isolating influence of, 18–19, 143; direct effects of, 173, 175–76, 284–90; effects on time pattern of investment, 241–47; "go-stop" pattern of, 166–68, 190; instability induced by, 135–36, 172; instruments, 219–36, 264–65; interaction between fiscal and monetary policy, 168–72; lags, 173–75, 236, 247, 255, 335–37, 369–75; learning process in, 190–91, 193, 229–30, 287, 375–76; and national budgets, 216–19; neutrality of, 367–68; of the *1930s,* 81–84; preferences, 139–40; quantitative model for, 284; strategies, 172, 189–91, 212; targets, 37–42, 97, 266–67; timing of measures, 173–74, 221, 287, 330, 335. *See also* Monetary policy; Fiscal policy

Potential output: definition of, 96; gap and ex ante saving and investment, *360;* gaps and price changes, 112–14; measurements, 101–12, *113;* Okun's law, 360 n.

Prices, level of: deflation, 27–28, 30; and demand pressure, 112–14, 184–87; flexibility of, 66–70; and full-employment gap, *113;* inflation, 27–28, 142–43; and market structure, 66–67; postwar annual changes of, *A1–14;* price-wage mechanism, 56, 184–87, 307; stability of, vs. unemployment, 97

Productivity. *See* Labor, productivity

Profits: countercyclical variation of distributed share, 59–61; cyclical variation of, 59–60, 330, 365–66; and growth, 330–31; and investment, 47, 275–76

Residential construction: conjunctural sensitivity of, 130; control of, 145, 181, 222–24, 364, 385; cyclical experiences of, 49–51, 74–75, 79–80, 223–24, 353–54, 364, 385; overinvestment, 74–75

Saving: excess ex ante saving over investment at potential GNP, 355–66; financial saving, 250–51; and full-employment budget surplus 356; and public pension fund, 249–52; ratio of households, 331; sectoral distribution of, 248–52

Sweden:
- balance of payments, absence of problems, 206–08
- built-in fiscal stabilization, 237–41
- capital-output ratio compared, *154*
- export prices and share in world trade compared, *161*
- fiscal policy, 220–32; automatic vs. discretionary changes in expenditures, 237, 238–40; emergency public works, 221–23
- forecasting: deficiency for exports, 213–*14;* deficiency for inventory investment, 215; methods, 212–19

full-employment ceiling, 204–05, 257
full-employment budget balance, compared with United States, 240–41
GNP, actual and potential, *108*
instability: general postwar features of, 197–212; interwar, *73,* 79; interwar and postwar compared, *29;* interwar and postwar unemployment, *32;* offsetting of, between specific branches, 210–11; of postwar industrial production, *89*
investment: funds, 226–32, 243–47; plan surveys, 212–13, 242–43, 244, 245, 246, 303; and saving, 248–52; tax 224–26
labor market policy, 257–60
learning process in policy, 193, 219, 229–30
model sequence of instability pattern, 203–12
monetary policy: "American" vs. "Swedish" approach, 253–55; bank lending and bank liquidity, 232–36; control of bank advances, 235–36; control of liquidity ratios, *233–36;* credit rationing, 252–56; effects on investment, 242–44; lags in effects, 236, 247, 255; money supply and bank lending changes, 232–34
physical controls, 219–20, 248
policy: climate, 193–97; cycle, 203–04, 247; general vs. differentiated, 258; instruments, 219–36; and national budget, 216–19; of *1930s,* 81, 220
productivity growth, *209*–10, 257
Public Pension Fund, 249–52
synchronization of conjuncture with European cycle, 210
unemployment: gross vs. net figures, 222–23; interwar and postwar, *32*
wage: "drift," 202; increases and job vacancies, *200;* labor union attitude in collective bargaining, 199–202, 258–59; multiplier, 200–01; policy, -price explosion, 199
wages, prices and productivity, *209*
Switzerland: growth and instability of GNP and components, *86, 118–21, A12;* interwar and postwar instability, *29;* interwar and postwar unemployment, *32;* overvaluation in *1930s,* 81; potential output, calculation problems, 111 n.

Turning points: covariance of, 73–74, 88–92, 210–11; errors of forecasting, 300–01; and interwar policy, 143

Unemployment: comparison of interwar and postwar rates, 30–*32,* 99–100; cyclical variability of, 32; feasible vs. desired minimum level of, 97–99; frictional, 96–97; gross and net figures of, 222–23; international comparability of data on, 30–32, 98–100; rates and labor market policy, 222–23; structural, 96–97
United Kingdom:
balance of payments constraints, 133, 162–65, 174, 187–90

Index

capital-output ratio compared, 153–*54*
confidence and the pound, 163–64, 177
consumer credit control, 178–81
export: and output, 153, 155–63; prices and share in world trade compared, *161*
GNP, actual and potential, *108*
growth: lack of international space, 133, 162–65, 174
initial and investment allowances, 167 n.
instability: interrelations with growth, 149–65; interwar, *73;* interwar and postwar setbacks compared, *29;* of postwar industrial production, *89*
interest rate changes, 171
model sequence of instability pattern 157–66, 188–91
monetary policy: debate, 176–87; effects on investment, 181–84
policy: cycles, 165, 166–72; direct effects of, 173, 175–76; interaction between fiscal and monetary, 168–72; lags in response and effects, 173–75; strategies, 172, 189–91
productivity, price and wage changes, 159–60, 185–89
Radcliffe report, 178, 181–83
unemployment, interwar and postwar, *32*
wage-price mechanism, 184–87
United States:
budget, effects of automatic response, 355–66
capital: saturation, during *1920s,* 74–76; stock adjustment model, 358–59, 364–65, 371
capital-output ratio: secular decline of, 361–62; compared, *154*
consumption function: interwar and postwar, 51–53; stabilizing shift during *1930s,* 52–53, 365–66
demand pressure and growth, 109, 349–52
ex ante saving and investment, 355–66, and full employment gap, *360*
export prices and share in world trade, *161*
full-employment budget surplus, 356–57, 360 n., 374–75
GNP, potential and actual, *109*
government expenditure, role of, 374–75
Great Depression, causes of, 74–78
growth, interwar and postwar compared with Europe, *25*
instability: comparison with Europe, 348–55; interwar, *73;* interwar and postwar, *29;* offsetting among GNP components, 354–55, *121*–22; of GNP components, 352–55; persistence of full-employment gap, *109,* 349–50; of postwar industrial production, *89;* postwar pattern, 362–66; of quarterly GNP, *377*
investment: declining ratio to GNP, 358–59, 360, 361; in inventories, 353, 363–64; and interest rate changes, 369–73
monetary policy: before *1929, 76;* effectiveness, 368–73
multiplier, 365–66
policy: and learning process,

375–76; "neutrality," 367–68; of *1930s,* 82–84, 79; uncertainty of distributed lag effects, 369–70
profits, and disposable income, 365–66
residential construction: cyclical variation, 354, 364; overinvestment during *1920s,* 74–75, 79 n.
unemployment: feasible minimum rate, 98–99; interwar and postwar, *32*
U.S. economy as engine of international cycle, 26–27, 74, 78–80

Wage(s): cyclical reactions of, 28–30, 293–95; drift, 202; equation, 293–95; flexibility, 65, 83–84, 321 n.; multiplier, 199–202; Phillips curve analysis of, 293–94; policy, 199–202, 258–59, 291–95; and price interaction, 65–66, 181–87, 199; and productivity, 160, 186–87, 209, 321; rate reductions, 28, 30; and trade unions, 65–66, 199–202